Cambridge, 1978

METHUEN'S HISTORY OF THE GREEK AND ROMAN WORLD

General Editor: M. Cary, M.A., D.Litt.

# V

# A HISTORY OF THE ROMAN WORLD FROM 146 TO 30 B.C.

## METHUEN'S HISTORY OF THE GREEK AND ROMAN WORLD

GENERAL EDITOR: M. CARY, M.A., D.LITT.
Professor Emeritus of Ancient History in the University of London

DEMY 8VO

I. *A HISTORY OF THE GREEK WORLD FROM 776 TO 479 B.C.* by H. T. WADE-GERY. *In preparation.*

II. *A HISTORY OF THE GREEK WORLD FROM 479 TO 323 B.C.* by M. L. W. LAISTNER. With four maps.

III. *A HISTORY OF THE GREEK WORLD FROM 323 TO 146 B.C.* by M. CARY. With three maps.

IV. *A HISTORY OF THE ROMAN WORLD FROM 753 TO 146 B.C.* by H. H. SCULLARD. With four maps.

V. *A HISTORY OF THE ROMAN WORLD FROM 146 TO 30 B.C.* by F. B. MARSH. Revised by H. H. SCULLARD. With five maps.

VI. *A HISTORY OF THE ROMAN WORLD FROM 30 B.C. TO A.D. 138* by E. T. SALMON. With five maps.

VII. *A HISTORY OF THE ROMAN WORLD FROM A.D. 138 TO 337* by H. M. D. PARKER. With four maps.

# A HISTORY OF THE ROMAN WORLD

## FROM 146 TO 30 B.C.

BY

FRANK BURR MARSH

Ph.D., F.R.Hist.S.

*Revised with additional Notes by*

H. H. SCULLARD, M.A.Ph.D.

READER IN ANCIENT HISTORY IN THE UNIVERSITY OF LONDON

WITH FIVE MAPS

METHUEN & CO., LTD. LONDON

36 *Essex Street, Strand, W.C.2*

*First Published January 10th, 1935*
*Second Edition, revised 1953*

2.1
CATALOGUE NO. 4367/U

PRINTED IN GREAT BRITAIN

# PREFACE

THE present volume will, I trust, require no introductory explanation to make its purpose clear to the reader, but there are one or two points to which I wish to call attention. In my notes I have been somewhat sparing of my citations of authorities. The sources for the earlier part of the period have been collected by Greenidge and Clay in their *Sources for Roman History*, in which the basis for any statement may readily be found under the proper year. I have, therefore, given references only when the passage on which I relied is either omitted or not easy to find. After 70 B.C. the ninth volume of the Cambridge Ancient History will in most cases furnish an adequate guide to the sources, so that references seemed to me unnecessary except on special points. In the selected bibliography I have included comparatively few works in foreign languages, except those referred to in the notes, because my aim was simply to furnish a guide to the books and articles most likely to be of interest to the general reader.

I wish to take this opportunity to acknowledge my indebtedness to Professor W. J. Battle and Professor H. J. Leon of the Classical Department of the University of Texas for their assistance on many points, and to Professor P. M. Batchelder for his help in preparing the manuscript for the press.

F. B. M.

AUSTIN, TEXAS,
*Feb.* 28, 1934

# PREFACE TO SECOND EDITION

WHEN I was honoured by an invitation to undertake the responsibility of seeing a second edition of the late Professor F. B. Marsh's volume through the press, the obvious course appeared to be to reprint the text as it stands. Professor Marsh was a man of independent thought and judgement, and this book is written from an independent and personal point of view: in consequence it would not, I think, have been proper to have made any alterations to the text itself (apart from a few trivial matters). I have therefore appended a body of notes (pp. 403–441). In these attention is drawn to the chief modern literature that has appeared since the first edition, and to the new evidence (little enough, chiefly epigraphical) that has accrued; at the same time I have on occasion expanded a point or two where Professor Marsh's treatment may seem to some to have been a little abrupt. These notes are not intended to be independent summaries, but to be read in close connexion with the text. They all appear at the end of the book, and a star is placed in the margin of every relevant page by the side of the line in question.

H. H. SCULLARD

KING'S COLLEGE,
LONDON.
*June* 1952

# CONTENTS

## CHAPTER I



## CHAPTER II



## CHAPTER III



## CHAPTER IV

## CHAPTER X



## CHAPTER XI



## CHAPTER XII



## CHAPTER XIII



## CHAPTER XIV

## CHAPTER XV



## CHAPTER XVI



## CHAPTER XVII



## CHAPTER XVIII



## CHAPTER XIX

## CHAPTER XX



## APPENDICES

## MAPS

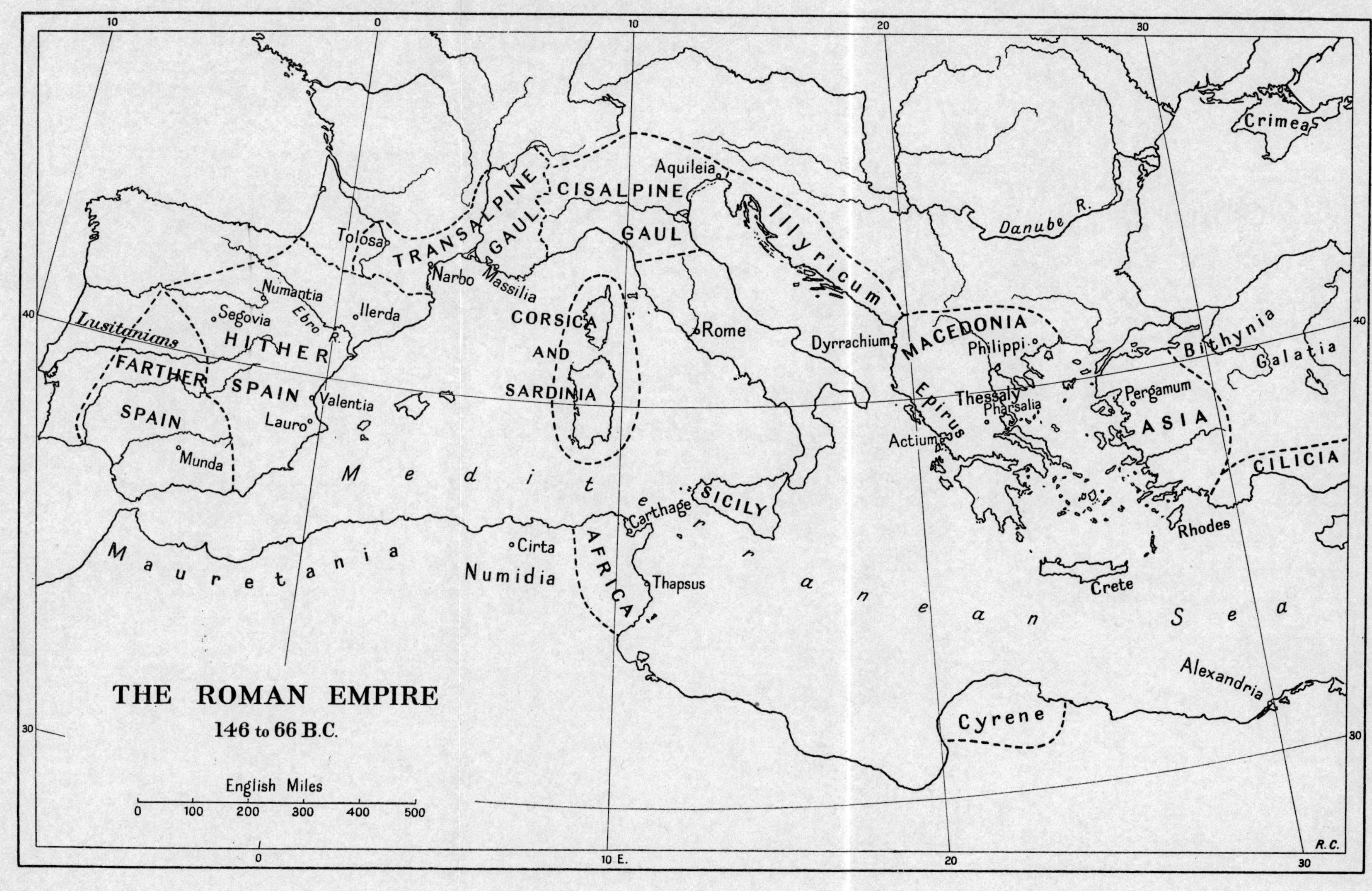
THE ROMAN EMPIRE
146 to 66 B.C.
English Miles
0 100 200 300 400 500
Crimea
Aquileia
CISALPINE
GAUL
TRANSALPINE
GAUL
Illyricum
Danube R.
Tolosa
Narbo
Massilia
Numantia
Segovia
Ebro R.
Ilerda
Lusitanians
HITHER
FARTHER
SPAIN
SPAIN
Valentia
Lauro
Munda
CORSICA
AND
SARDINIA
Rome
Dyrrachium
MACEDONIA
Philippi
Bithynia
Galatia
Epirus
Thessaly
Pharsalia
Pergamum
ASIA
Actium
CILICIA
SICILY
Carthage
Rhodes
Crete
Mauretania
Cirta
Numidia
AFRICA
Thapsus
Mediterranean Sea
Alexandria
Cyrene
R.C.

# CHAPTER I

# THE PENALTIES OF EMPIRE

## § 1. THE POSITION OF ROME IN 146 B.C.

UNTIL the beginning of her long struggle with Carthage Rome had been a purely Italian state with few interests outside the peninsula. As a result of that struggle and of the wars in which it involved her she found herself the mistress of the Mediterranean world. A considerable part of that world she annexed and governed directly. From 146 B.C. to the time of the Gracchi she had six provinces, namely, Sicily, Sardinia and Corsica, Hither Spain, Farther Spain, Macedonia, and Africa. The valley of the Po, known as Cisalpine Gaul, does not seem to have been regarded as one of the regular provinces, and a governor was sent there only when necessary, though such occasions seem to have been the rule rather than the exception. The power of Rome, however, was by no means confined to these provinces. The governor of Macedonia exercised a general supervision over Greece, and there were a number of allied states which were more or less under Roman influence and control, especially the kingdoms of Numidia in Africa, and of Pergamum and Bithynia in Asia Minor. Her splendid position was, nevertheless, accompanied by dangers, but these were internal and not external, the price which Rome like all other nations had ultimately to pay for glory and conquest. Her ascendancy abroad was purchased at the cost of economic disorganization in Italy, which finally culminated in a revolution whose various stages it is the purpose of the present volume to trace. At the beginning it is necessary to see clearly in what ways the acquisition of provinces outside Italy affected the Roman people and the actual working of the Roman government.

## § 2. THE SPOILS OF CONQUEST

In contrast with the conditions of the modern world, war in ancient times frequently yielded a large profit, and the successful campaigns of Rome from 200 to 167 B.C. had poured vast sums into the treasury. It has been computed[1] that the Roman generals brought back in the shape of booty during this period about 31,000 lbs. of gold and 669,000 lbs. of silver, and that Rome received in addition in the shape of indemnities something like £5,000,000. Expansion also added to the regular revenue of the state, and, while the wars entailed a heavy expenditure, there undoubtedly remained a large surplus. Since most of the precious metal thus obtained was used for coinage, the amount of money in circulation must have increased rapidly. With this influx of wealth all direct taxes in Italy were discontinued in 167 B.C., and henceforth the expenses of the state were met by the tribute of the provinces, by indirect levies, and by the proceeds of various public properties both in Italy and in the provinces.

While the state was thus becoming rich as a result of victory, the commanding generals and their staffs did not fail to secure their share. Many of the governing class accumulated large fortunes, often by means which were quite legitimate in Roman eyes, although there were doubtless some who did not stop with these. At any rate, it is clear that the wars brought with them a new standard of wealth and that a luxury hitherto unknown began to become more or less common among the upper classes.

Another change accompanying Rome's career of conquest was the spread of slavery. The captives taken in war were freely sold into bondage, and as a result the market was glutted and prices declined. Slave households on a scale hitherto undreamt of became common among wealthy Romans, and slave labour became more general than ever before. The slaves, moreover, were no longer of the old type ; many were in culture the superiors of their masters. The ruder types were put to work upon the estates of their owners, while the households of the nobles swarmed with Greeks, bringing with them the more refined tastes and accomplishments of an older and higher civilization. Under these circumstances Hellenism began to

[1] By Tenney Frank, *The Public Finances of Rome* 200–157 *B.C.*, pp. 3–4.

spread among the Romans of the upper class, and, though the masses of the people were little affected, some knowledge of Greek literature and thought became one of the common characteristics of a Roman gentleman. There were, it is true, sturdy puritans of the old Roman type who stood out stubbornly against the prevailing fashion, but their protests in favour of the old ways were unavailing. A change both for good and for evil was coming over the governing class. If contact with the art and literature of Greece was a refining influence, the rising standards of living and the new luxuries which went with it were far from elevating. To live the simple life of the older generation was more and more difficult, and to live in the fashion of the day was more and more expensive. Thus those members of the governing class who had not directly profited by the conquests of the legions must fill their purses as best they could and take full advantage of such opportunities as might come their way. An official career was no longer, if it ever had been, one of simple honour and service to the state; it was the path from poverty to affluence, and the Roman nobles competed fiercely for its prizes.

## § 3. THE RISE OF THE KNIGHTS *

While the governing class sought to acquire wealth from office, another class was seeking riches in the opportunities made possible by the empire of the Mediterranean world. This class was known to the Romans under the curious appellation of "knights." They were, in fact, the business men of Rome, and her conquests rapidly converted them into a powerful capitalist group. The transformation had begun long before, but the triumphs of the legions abroad greatly accelerated and completed it. From early times there had been men in Rome who made a business of government contracts. It was the old practice of the Republic to construct all public works, buildings, roads, etc., by bargains with those who could command the capital and the labour. No doubt the public contracts were often lucrative, and no doubt the influence of the knights, or equestrian class, was sometimes brought to bear to make them so. But when Rome began to acquire and rule territories outside the Italian peninsula the opportunities of the knights grew apace.

In some of her provinces Rome merely exacted from her subjects the tribute which they had paid their former rulers, and, having at hand no machinery for its collection, she resorted to the simple and pernicious system of farming the taxes. In Sicily, for instance, where the people had been long accustomed to pay their Carthaginian and Greek masters one-tenth of the crop, the right to collect this tithe in a given district was sold to the highest bidder. It was then the business of the successful competitor to send his agents to the district and collect his tenth. Out of the proceeds he was required to pay to the Roman treasury the amount stipulated in his bid and the rest he could keep for himself. Had the tax-farmer bid upon a single crop such a procedure would have been pure gambling, but the contracts were let for five years at a time and thus the bidding could be put upon a reasonably safe basis; a poor crop in one year would be balanced by a good crop in another so that the average for five years could be estimated with reasonable certainty. Though in Sicily the bidding was open to all and the tithe was often purchased by the various municipalities or by wealthy individuals, the Roman knights were quick to take advantage of the opportunity. They commonly joined together to form syndicates, substantially the same as our stock companies, which made a business of farming the taxes. Although the Roman state turned over to private individuals or corporations the collection of the tithe, it realized the necessity of keeping them under strict control; the Roman governor was bound to assist the tax-farmer by compelling the provincials to pay the tithe, but it was no less his duty to see that the tax-farmer or his agents took no more than the law allowed. Such a system looked fair on paper, but it could not possibly work fairly in practice; the more the tax-farmer could collect the greater his profits, and, when the contract was let to a syndicate of Roman knights, they possessed votes and influence in Rome with which they could put pressure on the governor. If the governor had further political ambitions he was not slow to realize that too much zeal in the protection of the provincials would injure his chances. He, therefore, found it expedient to be somewhat lax in the performance of his duty, where laxity was to the advantage of the knights, and to allow much to happen which he was bound in theory to prevent. As a result the Sicilians paid considerably more than was required by law, and the profits of the equestrian syndicates were highly satisfactory.

The system of farming the taxes was not applied in all the provinces. In Spain, for example, each of the communities which made up the two Roman provinces was assessed a definite amount. This the local government raised in any way it pleased and paid over to the governor, who accounted for it to Rome. But in all the provinces, whatever the method of collecting the tribute, the Roman business man could be sure of special protection in trade, so that commerce, to which the acquisition of an empire must have given a great impetus, tended to fall largely into Roman hands and to enrich many of the knights.

The conquest of the Mediterranean world had, moreover, brought about a concentration of capital in Rome. The plunder that had poured into her treasury had poured out again into the pockets of the more fortunately situated of her citizens. The inevitable result was that the Roman knights began to assume the functions of international bankers. If a town in Sicily or Spain wished to construct a new temple or public bath and needed to borrow money for the purpose, it often found itself obliged to deal with Roman knights or equestrian syndicates, since they were the only class who possessed the necessary funds, and it was the duty of the Roman governor to see that such loans were duly paid, a duty which he could not venture to neglect unless he was prepared to brave the enmity of the business men of Rome.

Thus, although at first the profits of conquest went to the state and its governing class, in the end the knights reaped an abundant harvest. Year by year they grew more wealthy and more powerful and the victories of the legions abroad exalted the capitalists at home.

## § 4. THE ECONOMIC CRISIS

While the fruits of empire were highly agreeable to the upper classes, the masses of the Roman people soon began to pay the penalties. The acquisition of provinces by the Republic profoundly affected the economic life of Italy, and ultimately produced an agricultural crisis which had far-reaching results.

The long war against Hannibal had been fought chiefly within the peninsula and had entailed widespread devastation. This was especially true in the South, where the struggle between the Romans and the invader had been most prolonged and intense. Hannibal had ravaged the lands of those communities which adhered to Rome, and the Roman armies in revenge laid waste those parts which had joined the Carthaginians. When Hannibal at length withdrew there was in the South little left to destroy outside the walled towns, and the small farmers who survived were faced with the problem of re-establishing themselves on the land from which they had been forced to flee in the heat of the struggle.[1] Having lost all—tools, houses, and domestic animals—they were forced to make a new beginning. Some gave up in despair and remained in the towns which had furnished them a refuge, selling their property for whatever it would bring; others attempted to resume their former occupation, but this they could only do by mortgaging their farms. Some of the land thus passed almost immediately into the hands of those with ready money to invest in land and slaves, while such of the former peasantry as returned to the land were forced to struggle not only to extract a livelihood from the soil, but also to pay the debts with which they had been obliged to encumber it.

Under favourable conditions they might have been successful and the effects of the war on Italy might have proved transitory, but new burdens were immediately laid upon them. The Second Punic War was only the prelude to others which, while they established Rome as the supreme power in the Mediterranean world, made unprecedented demands upon her citizens for military service, and that under conditions which made it more onerous than it had ever been before. Up to this time the Romans had done little fighting outside the peninsula, except in Sicily, which might be considered as really a part of it. While Rome's wars were confined to Italy the term of service was short and consequently did not permanently disturb the life of the small landowner, whose pay would compensate him for his comparatively brief absence from his farm. After Hannibal had been expelled from Italy,

[1] The heavy loss of life in the war must have left many farms without owners able to make any serious attempt to resume their cultivation.

however, the wars which followed each other with scarcely a breathing space between were carried on at such distances that the term of service was inevitably lengthened, with serious results. Moreover, each new province required a garrison, so that the forces which the Republic now kept under arms in time of peace were larger than had formerly been required in time of war. In earlier times the Republic had seldom put into the field more than four legions at once, but after 200 B.C. the number seems to have averaged eight each year, and this number was on occasion increased to ten or twelve.[1] As the Roman armies at this period were conscripted chiefly, if not exclusively, from the class of small landowners, it is easy to see that the expansion of Rome's empire was accompanied by heavy demands upon this class, even allowing for the fact that the government sought to spare them by drawing an increasing proportion of the recruits from the Italian allies. Nor was the burden lightened by an increase in the population. The census statistics given us by Livy show clearly that the total number of known citizens had diminished rather than increased during this period, a phenomenon which is not difficult to understand if we take into account the heavy losses sustained by the Romans in their long struggle with Hannibal.[2] In addition to the increase in the number of recruits annually demanded by the state, we must also take into account the lengthened term of service resulting from the greater distance at which the wars were fought or the garrisons in the provinces stationed. Those who were sent to Spain were now taken from their farms and families for six years, and the others must have been held in the ranks for from two to four. This would make an enormous difference to the small farmer, since it was now by no means certain that his pay would furnish an adequate compensation for his long absence from home. There was, of course, a share in the plunder when the campaign had been successful, but in spite of Rome's victorious career she experienced frequent disasters, so that the common soldier often received little or nothing from the spoils. In many cases he must have returned to find that his family had lost the farm or been unable to keep it up and that

[1] Frank, *idem.*, pp. 10–11.

[2] For a discussion of the census statistics in Livy which seems to me in the main sound, see Frank, *Roman Census Statistics*.

he did not possess the means of repairing the damage. When, in addition, account is taken of the many who never did return, it is obvious that the military service must have been a very serious burden to the small farmer, especially in regions where the devastations of the Second Punic War had left him already handicapped with debt.

In another way the expansion of Rome's power wrought havoc with the small landowner, since, after the annexation of Sicily, he was obliged to compete with the cheap grain of the provinces. This competition would have been serious enough if it had been of a purely economic character, for grain could be grown in some of the provinces more cheaply than in Italy, but the policy of the Roman state had much more to do with the matter than the cost of production. The tribute of Sicily was paid in grain to the tax-farmers, and they in turn largely discharged their obligations to the government by turning over a part of the grain to the state. The grain so received was used to feed the armies, and, when there was more than enough for this purpose, the surplus was thrown on the market and sold for what it would bring. Moreover, since it was then regarded as a duty of the state to keep down the cost of living, whenever the price in Rome rose appreciably the government intervened to buy grain and sell it at a loss so as to bring down the price in the city. Thus while the price tended to fall in time of peace it was not permitted to rise in time of war. The tax-farmers in their operations made matters even worse. They collected large quantities of grain in Sicily which cost them nothing more than what they had to expend on its collection. The easiest method of disposing of this grain was to ship it to Italy and sell it in the coast cities. Water transportation was cheap, and they could thus afford to dispose of their grain at a price below that at which the Italian farmer could afford to raise it. Thus at the very time when the devastations of Hannibal had plunged many of the farmers into debt, their principal crop was becoming comparatively worthless. Small wonder then that in parts of the peninsula the poorer farmers were ruined and forced to take refuge in the cities as though from a new invader.

It must be borne in mind, however, that the effects of the cheap grain were very unevenly felt. If transportation by water was cheap in ancient times, transportation by land was expensive. It was impossible for the provincial grain to go far even over the best Roman roads without losing much of its cheapness. Hence, while in those districts which depended for their market on some coast town the farmer who relied on grain was ruined, there were many regions where grain still yielded a profit and others which were entirely unaffected. In the vicinity of Rome the small farmer had to turn to the cultivation of other crops or lose his farm, but in Picenum, Umbria, Samnium, and the Po valley he was confronted with no such dilemma. Here and in many other places which were sufficiently remote from the coast cities his only difficulties were those occasioned by the devastations of war and the military demands of the newly acquired empire.

There was, then, a combination of forces resulting from the conquests of the Republic which pressed hard upon the small farmer. In some regions all forces were at work at once, while in others one or more of them was very little felt. There were districts where the small farmer almost completely disappeared, others where he maintained a precarious existence, but there were many where he remained fairly prosperous and could still live in the traditional fashion except for the increasing burden of military service. Nevertheless, the crisis was widely enough felt to bring about serious economic, social, and political changes.

### § 5. THE SOCIAL AND ECONOMIC RESULTS OF THE CRISIS

As a direct or indirect result of the Republic's foreign wars and conquests the small farmers were declining steadily in numbers and their holdings were being thrown together into great estates. A few of the Roman people were growing rich, while many were sinking into abject poverty. The men possessed of ready capital were steadily acquiring the lands of their poorer neighbours and establishing themselves as great proprietors. The reasons for this change are fairly obvious. While slaves could be bought cheaply it was possible to operate a great estate at a profit where the small farmer could no longer survive, for the farmer had a family to provide for and some standard of living, while the slave had only himself and must accept any conditions which his master imposed. Moreover, the great landowner was not limited to the cultivation of grain; he possessed the capital necessary to set out olive orchards and vineyards, and could employ new and improved methods of agriculture. In the slave market he could find not merely brute strength in the Spaniard or the Gaul, but also eastern slaves from regions where scientific agriculture had been more highly developed than in any other part of the ancient world. Here were men who could be purchased for a trifle and who were familiar with the best methods for the cultivation of many crops which had hitherto been comparatively unimportant in Italy and for which there was an extensive demand not only in the peninsula but in the provinces of Rome beyond the seas. The average Italian farmer had always relied chiefly on grain, and, even if he realized the hopelessness of continuing to grow it, he was often without the special knowledge or the capital to make a change. To set out a vineyard, even if he knew how to manage one, required time before the vines became productive, and during part of this time nothing else could be grown on the land. To make the change the farmer must have the means to live after he had ceased to grow grain until he could begin gathering grapes, and it seems clear that many of them did not have the means to tide them over this period. The natural consequence was that in some parts of Italy the great plantation worked by slave labour became common. This development was most marked in Etruria, while in Southern Italy the change proceeded upon somewhat different lines. Here as in the North the small farmer disappeared, if indeed he ever reappeared after the Second Punic War, but his place was taken by ranches rather than by plantations. The nature of the country readily lent itself to pasturage, and large districts were occupied by herds of sheep and cattle tended by a few slave herdsmen. The rancher had no competition to fear, since the ships of ancient times could carry economically only such products as would keep well without refrigeration, chiefly grain, olive oil, wine, and manufactured goods. Thus over extensive regions of the South as well as of the North the old type of agriculture ceased to be profitable and the sturdy peasantry who had once peopled these regions gave place to the great landowner and his slaves.

But the small farmer did not die when he was crowded from the land. In ever-increasing numbers he drifted to the cities and especially to Rome. Here he soon spent whatever money he had brought with him from the country and was forced to seek his livelihood side by side with the proletariat of the city. As the political life of Italy centred in Rome, it was only there that the growth of the urban rabble could seriously affect the course of history, affect it at least in ways which it is possible for us with our meagre and defective sources to trace. If Rome had been a great industrial centre the influx of the country folk resulting from the crisis in agriculture might have been absorbed by industries whose growth had been stimulated by the acquisition of an empire, though even in these circumstances there would have been the formidable obstacle of slave labour to be overcome. But Rome was not a great industrial city at any time, and, although we cannot doubt that her industries grew with her power, their growth was not sufficient to take care of the rapidly increasing number of her poor. Her eastern conquests had glutted the slave markets with the skilled artisans of lands which were far superior to Italy in the technique of most industries. It was hopeless for the rude Italian farmer to attempt to compete with the trained Greek and Oriental craftsmen, and in industry as in agriculture the slave and the freedman began to crowd out the free-born Roman citizen. There were no doubt many jobs and many kinds of work still open to the unskilled freeman, but with the steady increase in the number of the proletariat the chances of earning an honest livelihood must have become more and more precarious and the competition for such employment as was to be secured more and more fierce. It requires no profound acquaintance with economics to infer that the growing mass of poor Romans living in the city was sinking deeper and deeper into poverty, and no prophetic insight to foresee that such conditions were bound to result in serious trouble for the state. Rome was paying for her conquests by being obliged to face difficult and complicated, yet vital, problems upon every hand. She had mastered the Mediterranean world to enrich a handful of nobles and capitalists, to ruin large numbers of the small farmers to whose dogged courage she owed her victory, and to increase the number, the poverty, and the political importance of the city rabble.

# CHAPTER II

# THE IMPERIAL REPUBLIC

## § 1. THE FRAMEWORK OF THE GOVERNMENT

THE development of Roman political institutions up to this time has been dealt with in the preceding volume, but a brief sketch of the organization of the government in 146 B.C. seems a necessary preliminary to any discussion of the political consequences of the economic crisis. The general theory of the constitution had undergone little change as a result of Rome's expansion, but there had been many modifications of detail. The Republic was still governed by the annual magistrates, the senate, and the assembly, and each of these must be examined in turn.

As the territory subject to Rome's authority expanded, the number of the magistrates was increased from time to time. In 146 there were 2 consuls, 6 prætors, 10 tribunes, 4 ædiles (2 curule and 2 plebeian), and 12 quæstors. The law now required that these offices should be held in a regular sequence, the quæstorship preceding the prætorship and the prætorship the consulship. To hold the quæstorship a man must be at least twenty-eight years of age, and two years must elapse between the holding of successive offices.[1] Neither the ædileship nor the tribuneship was a necessary part of the *cursus honorum*, but one or the other was usually held between the quæstorship and the prætorship, since both gave opportunities for acquiring popularity. At intervals of about five years two censors were chosen from the ex-consuls. Among their duties was the taking of the census, and, as this was a complicated matter, they were allowed to hold office for eighteen months.

[1] The interval is often spoken of as three years, since he could hold the next office in the third year after the first. If a man held the prætorship in 146 he could hold the consulship in 143.

In the earlier period, when the Republic was faced with a serious crisis, a dictator had been appointed, but this office had now fallen into disuse.

Not only were the magistrates numerous but they possessed extraordinary facilities for hindering each other's action and for obstructing public business. Each consul could veto (forbid) any act of his colleague, while any one of the tribunes could veto any act of any of the other magistrates or tribunes and of the senate and assembly as well, nor could all the other tribunes combined override the veto of a single one of the ten. The tribunician veto was, however, limited to Rome, since the tribune was forbidden to go beyond the immediate neighbourhood of the city during his year of office. Such abundant opportunities for obstruction might have been expected to render the constitution well-nigh unworkable, but the predominant influence which the senate gradually acquired was for a long time sufficient to enable the government to function with a fair degree of efficiency.

Originally the senate had been simply a council whose advice the magistrates might ask if and when they chose to do so, but in the course of time the conscript fathers, as the senators were styled, gained almost complete control of the government. In theory the magistrates always retained a large measure of independence; in most matters they were not legally obliged to consult the senate at all, and, if they did so, they were not bound to follow its advice. Nevertheless the senate ultimately succeeded in establishing an unwritten rule that it *must* be consulted on all matters of importance and that its advice when given in the form of a decree *must* be accepted and obeyed by the magistrates. This rule, however, never acquired the force of law and there was always the possibility that some exceptionally determined or obstinate consul or tribune might disregard the senate's authority and persist in his own policy regardless of its opposition. Such cases were rare, however, and usually the senate was able to enforce its wishes without serious difficulty, so that the magistrates became little more than the ministers through whom it carried on the administration.

The senate no doubt owed something of its power and influence to its composition. Its number was fixed in theory at three hundred, though it must have varied somewhat in practice, and, whenever a census was taken, it was one of the duties of the censors to revise the list of its members. If the censors agreed, they could deprive a senator of his seat by striking his name off the list, but otherwise he held his position for life. The vacancies in the body the censors filled from the ranks of the ex-magistrates, beginning with the quæstors, and only when all ex-magistrates had been provided for could men of any other class be chosen. The censors would thus exercise little choice in the filling of vacancies since the number of the lower magistrates would now supply enough names for the purpose. The senate was, therefore, a body of ex-magistrates, and this meant that it included within itself practically all the official experience in Rome, and the opinions of such a body could not fail to have great weight with those who were at the moment in charge of the government but who would soon lay down their offices and take their places among those who were now advising them.

In its parliamentary procedure the senate followed rules peculiar to itself. It met only when summoned by a magistrate and it could vote only on motions put by a magistrate. If either of the consuls was in Rome he usually convened the senate and presided; if both were absent, the urban prætor took their place, and in rare cases a meeting was convened by one of the tribunes. The presiding magistrate formally announced the subject to be considered and then asked each senator in turn to give his opinion. The order in which the senators were called upon to speak was based upon the offices held, beginning with the ex-censors and ex-consuls and closing with the ex-quæstors. When the debate was finished the presiding magistrate put the question to a vote, which was taken by division. It is to be noted that no senator could make a motion and compel a vote upon it. When a senator had the floor, he could speak on any subject he pleased and suggest any motion which he wished to have considered, but his suggestion might be ignored even if a majority expressed themselves in sympathy, for the presiding magistrate had complete control of what questions should be put to a vote and also of the form in which they should be voted on. Such powers were theoretically great, but the senators would certainly have resented any abuse and few magistrates desired or dared to face their resentment. Moreover, when the presiding magistrate had finished the business for which he had convened the senate any of the other magistrates had the right to take charge of the meeting and to submit such further matters as he chose. Thus if the majority wished to vote on a certain motion which the consul refused to put, as soon as he had finished his business one of the tribunes could put it. Finally a tribune could veto any decree of the senate and such a veto deprived it of all legal force, although the senate had the right to vote on the question and record the result, that is to say, the right to put its opinion on record. In matters where the decree of the senate was purely advisory in character the tribunician veto was probably of little importance, for the recorded opinion of the senate might have as much weight as its formal decree, but there were matters where a formal decree was necessary and the passing of such a decree could be prevented by any one of the tribunes.

The supreme power in the Republic was vested in the popular assembly. This assembly was a mass meeting held in Rome which every Roman citizen had the right to attend. Of course, not all the citizens were able to exercise their right but those who were present acted in the name of all and the absent were ignored; just as we to-day ignore voters who do not take the trouble to vote. There is, however, one important difference; to-day every qualified voter can vote if he chooses, but in ancient Rome a large part of the citizens lived so far from the city that it was practically impossible for them to cast their ballots there. To this fact the Romans paid no attention, and they regarded those citizens who appeared at any given meeting as the Roman People.

The assembly was the basis of the entire government. It elected the magistrates, thus indirectly choosing the senators, and it alone was competent to enact laws. All laws were absolutely binding on the state and no distinction was made between ordinary statutes and constitutional amendments. The senate might advise the magistrates as to the interpretation of a law or as to their action in some matter which was not covered by any statute, but the conscript fathers were powerless to alter a law which had been formally enacted by the people. In only one way could they set it aside, and that was by declaring that a given bill had never been legally passed by the assembly. The rules governing the action of the assembly were so complicated and the means of obstruction so numerous that some defect in the procedure of legislation was not infrequent, and, when this was the case, the senate could set aside the law as null and void because of this defect. The conscript fathers seem to have felt no obligation to decide such questions in a judicial spirit. If they considered a law good they were ready to ignore some irregularities; if they disapproved of it, they looked with care for any technical flaws in its enactment. This did not mean that they could permanently thwart the will of the people; all they could do was to insist that the people should express their will in a regular and legal fashion. Such a power was clearly necessary, for without such a safeguard the whole constitution might be subverted at any moment by a packed crowd of voters, and the legal requirement that due notice must be given of the provisions of a bill before a vote was taken on it in the assembly was useless, unless there was somebody competent to decide whether or not such notice had been given in fact.

A constitution in which the supreme power is vested in the people might seem to deserve the name of a democracy, at least as democracy was understood in ancient times, when representation was not used and all votes had to be cast in the chief city of the state. Nevertheless, the Roman government was never really democratic, since, whatever the outward forms, Rome was actually governed by a small ring of families known as the nobility, and it is essential to examine briefly who these nobles were and by what means they were able to dominate the Republic.

## § 2. THE ROMAN NOBILITY

In their nobility the Romans possessed a unique form of aristocracy in that a family attained this rank as a result of the direct action of the sovereign people, for a noble was simply a man one of whose ancestors had been elected by the assembly to a curule office (consulship, prætorship, or curule ædileship). The first member of a family to attain such an office was known as a new man (*novus homo*) because none of his ancestors had ever held such office, but his son was a noble as were all his later descendants. In theory any Roman could become the founder of a noble family and we might have expected that such families would be very numerous, but the reverse was true. From very early times the families already ennobled began to draw together into a narrow and exclusive circle. They came to feel that they possessed a right to hold in turn the offices which the people had conferred upon their ancestors, to resent the intrusion of new men, and to unite to keep out such intruders. This policy met with a greater and greater measure of success, so that the number of noble families was restricted to a comparatively small group which became the governing class of Rome.

The combination of the noble families into an exclusive and cohesive group did not of course result simply from pride of birth or a contempt of their inferiors. Both sentiments were strongly felt, but the chief power that bound them together was the substantial unity of their economic, and hence of their political, interests. The earlier Romans had been essentially an agricultural and pastoral people among whom wealth consisted chiefly of land or cattle and sheep. The rich man in early days was a farmer on a larger scale than his neighbours. Since the state paid no salaries to the magistrates and senators, it was necessary to choose them from those who were rich enough to serve their country without remuneration, and this class in such a community was that of the wealthy farmers. Very early it became apparent to these landowners that they could use their control of the government for their own advantage. As Rome conquered Italy she forced the vanquished communities to cede a portion of their territory to her, and this public land was so managed by the state that a large part of it passed in one fashion or another into the hands of the governing class. When other sources of income and new forms of lucrative investment began to develop the law stepped in and closed many kinds of business to members of the senate and hence practically to the nobility. Whatever the motives behind such legislation, the effect was to keep the aristocracy a body of great landowners. The noble families had thus in their common economic interests at once a powerful bond of union and a compass by which to steer the ship of state. It was with them not only a matter of sentiment to keep the offices within their own circle, but it was to their material advantage to prevent any other class with divergent economic interests from obtaining any political power or leverage by means of which it could exert an influence on public policy.

## § 3. THE ORGANIZATION OF THE ASSEMBLY

Since the popular assembly was the supreme power in the Republic, the success of the ring of noble families in their attempt to dominate the state ultimately depended upon their ability to control this body, and its organization was such as to render this comparatively easy, since the vote of the people was taken not by individuals but by groups, and group voting always makes it possible for the will of a minority to prevail. To see this it is only necessary to examine briefly the nature of the groups into which the people were divided and by which the action of the assembly was determined.

In the later Republic there were two principal assemblies whose only important difference lay in the group which was used for the purpose of voting. They were known as the assembly of centuries (*comitia centuriata*) and the assembly of tribes (*comitia tributa*).[1] As the names indicate, the first voted by centuries and the other by tribes, and, since the centuries had come to be based upon the tribes, it is the latter which must first be considered.

The tribe was originally a territorial division. The earliest ones were very small in size, somewhat like the wards and parishes or townships of a modern state, and occupied the primitive territory of Rome, which was very limited in extent. As the Roman state expanded it settled numbers of its citizens upon the conquered territory and organized new tribes of larger size and situated farther and farther from the city. This went on until there were thirty-five tribes, of which four were wards of the city itself and sixteen lay in the immediate vicinity, covering the original territory of the Republic, while the remaining fifteen had been created as a result of subsequent expansion. Whatever the area of a tribe or its geographical situation, its members were the Roman citizens who resided within its boundaries. When the assembly voted

[1] I have ignored the *comitia curiata*, because it had become a purely formal body, and I have also ignored the distinction between the *comitia tributa* and the *concilium plebis*, because there was no longer any serious difference between the two, since the number of the patrician families had become so small that their exclusion from the latter can have had little practical importance.

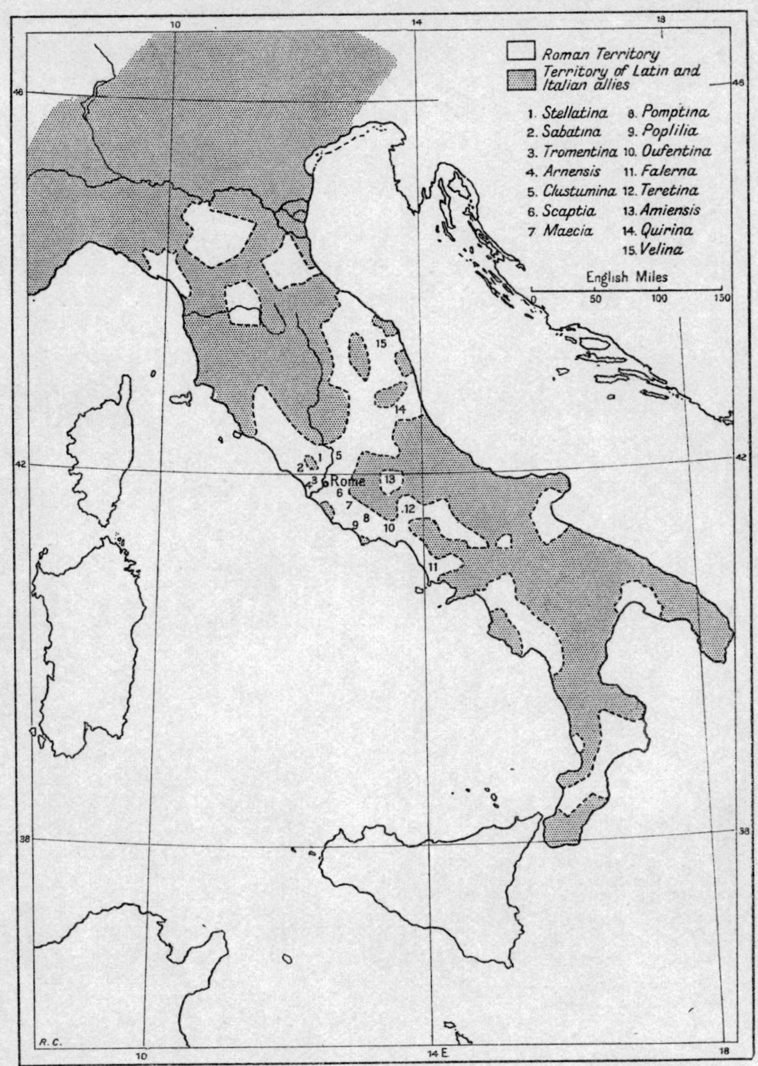


ITALY, SHOWING THE TERRITORY OF THE ALLIES AND THE LOCATION OF THE LATER RURAL TRIBES

by tribes each tribe had one vote, and how that vote should be cast was determined by the members of the tribe who were present in the assembly at the meeting in question. The process of voting was simple enough in its broad outlines, though some of the details are shrouded in complete obscurity. The assembly met in a large open space as a single body, and the magistrate who had summoned the meeting (a consul, prætor or tribune) presided over it. The question before the assembly was first announced and the people were then directed to separate into their tribes. Around the open space where the crowd had gathered were thirty-five enclosures, each with a single entrance, one for each tribe. The citizens from a tribe who were present now entered their proper enclosure, and, when they were all within, they passed out again through the entrance, on each side of which a teller was stationed to whom they gave their votes, at first orally but later by ballot. When the tellers had ascertained how the majority had voted, they informed the magistrate that the tribe in question had voted for or against a bill, or for certain candidates if the business of the meeting was an election. The vote of the tribe was recorded by the magistrate and the result announced to the people.[1] In the tribal assembly no distinction was made between rich and poor, old and young, but every citizen was placed upon an equal footing except in so far as the unequal numbers attending the meeting from the different tribes gave more or less weight in the final decision to the voice or ballot of the individual voters. This last consideration is of great importance, for it is obvious that, if only one hundred farmers had come in from a rural tribe while a thousand members of one of the city tribes were present, then each farmer had as much influence on the final result as ten artisans. Since there were only four city tribes as compared with thirty-one rural, it is clear that, although the urban populace might greatly outnumber the country folk, they were politically negligible unless they could attract support from the citizens outside the city. Such a system may seem unfair to us, but in early times it secured to the Romans some of the advantages of a representative government. As long as the great majority

[1] In elections the tribes voted simultaneously, but in legislation they seem to have voted successively and the vote of each tribe was announced as it was cast.

of the Roman people were engaged in agriculture it compensated the farmer for the inevitable disadvantages of his occupation. It was less easy for him to attend the assembly and it must often have happened that large numbers of the farmers could not leave their work. The taking of the vote by tribes prevented the citizens who resided in the city from carrying measures contrary to the wishes or interests of those living in the country, that is, upon the assumption that those farmers who went to Rome to vote held substantially the same views as those who stayed at home.

In the division of the citizens into centuries age and wealth were considered as well as residence. The voters of each tribe were divided into five classes on the basis of their property, the richest forming the first class and the poorest the fifth. Then in each tribe each of the five classes was divided into two centuries on the basis of age, the older men forming one and the younger the other. This made 350 centuries, ten from each tribe, and to these there were added 18 from the richest men, known as the centuries of knights, though many nobles were included in them,[1] and 5 centuries from the poorest citizens, making a total of 373 centuries.[2] The procedure in this assembly was practically the same as in the tribal assembly except that the groups were more numerous and contained fewer voters.

The two assemblies were composed of the same people, and the chief difference between them was whether the vote was taken by centuries or by tribes. The centuriate assembly did little except elect the censors, consuls, and prætors, while the lesser magistrates were elected and legislation enacted by the vote of the tribes. It should be noted that the rural element nominally predominated as strongly in the one as in the other.

[1] At first the senators voted in these centuries, but by the time of Cicero they had been excluded. The young nobles, however, continued to be enrolled in them and remained there until they entered the senate. See Willems, *Le sénat.*, I, 195–96. It seems clear that the nobles cannot have been sufficiently numerous at any period to fill the eighteen centuries, which must have included a considerable number of wealthy men not connected with the nobility.

[2] There has been much discussion of the organization of the centuriate assembly after the so-called Servian Constitution was discarded, apparently not long after 241 B.C., when the last two of the thirty-five tribes were organized. I have followed the theory most generally accepted, but none of the other theories would materially affect the discussion which follows. See Botsford, *The Roman Assemblies*, pp. 211–27.

## § 4. THE ARISTOCRATIC MACHINE

Such being the general structure of the Roman government, it is clear that the ring of noble families could only control it if they could find some means of dominating the assembly, and the method of group voting furnished them the opportunity of accomplishing this. Since the rural tribes numbered 31 out of 35 and their centuries 310 out of 373, they were evidently the key to the situation. If the nobles could secure enough votes to carry a majority of these tribes and their centuries they would be masters of the assembly. This was after all not a very difficult undertaking, since under ordinary circumstances the attendance from these tribes must have been small, so that it would usually be possible for the result to be determined by a comparative handful of voters if only they were properly distributed. The residents of the city must long since have come to be a large majority of those present at the meetings of the assembly, but, as they were confined to four tribes, their number was of no practical importance. Of the rural tribes, some were situated in the immediate neighbourhood of Rome, while many lay at a considerable distance. With the means of travel then available to the poor it seems a safe assumption that few of the small farmers would, except on special occasions, be able or willing to make a long journey in order to vote, and their unwillingness would be rendered all the greater by the uncertainty of whether, if they did go, they would have a chance to vote, for the assembly might always be adjourned owing to unfavourable omens[1] or to the obstruction of some magistrate. We may, therefore, conclude that the number of voters present on any occasion from the nearest of the rural tribes was much smaller than from the city tribes and that from many of the rural tribes there were very few voters.

A landowner had long enjoyed the privilege of being registered in any tribe where he owned land, regardless of his place of residence. The nobles, who were almost all landowners, would naturally take advantage of this privilege to enrol themselves in the rural tribes, where their votes would count

[1] The centuriate assembly was always subject to dissolution on the report of unfavourable omens (*obnuntiatio*), and all forms of the tribal assembly were made subject to this method of obstruction by the *lex Ælia Fufia* in 156 B.C. Probably it had already been applied to some forms of this assembly. *

for much more than in those of the city. Yet by themselves they were not numerous enough even then to control the assembly, and to strengthen themselves still further they made use of their retainers. From the earliest times the important families had surrounded themselves with clients and freedmen. A client was a freeman who had put himself under the protection of some powerful neighbour, while the freedman was a slave whose master had set him free, though still retaining some control over him. The legal status of both classes underwent modifications in the course of time with which it is unnecessary to deal. In the later Republic the actual condition of the clients and the freedmen was often much the same. If the client was a citizen when he became a dependent he remained one afterward, while the slave received a partial citizenship, including the right to vote, along with his freedom. A noble seems generally to have controlled the votes of both classes of dependents, and it was thus possible for him to form a band of retainers on whose support he could rely. Obviously such dependents would be most valuable politically if they voted in the rural tribes, and the nobles succeeded in registering many of their freedmen in these tribes while the clients, being already registered, were probably recruited chiefly from the country districts. At first no doubt the great families could require their dependents to come to Rome and vote on occasion, but later many of these dependents who moved to the city kept their registration in the rural tribes. Such retainers were always at hand to attend the assembly, and by their help the nobles were able to obtain control of the thinly attended tribes and finally of the tribal assembly under ordinary circumstances. When the centuries came to be based upon the tribes the same thing was true of the assembly of centuries.[1]

The control of the assembly by the nobles was always somewhat precarious, since it was based on the assumption that a comparatively small minority of the Roman people could outvote the majority, owing to the small attendance in many of the rural tribes. If at any time and for any reason an unusually large number of farmers belonging to those tribes should appear in the assembly the nobility might suddenly find itself powerless. In such a case the nobles must either suffer a defeat or by a resort to obstruction postpone a vote

[1] For a fuller discussion, see Appendix 2.

until conditions seemed more favourable to them. But an occasional defeat, however unpleasant, was not generally very serious; a particular bill might be passed, but, if its effect could not be neutralized in some way, it could be endured, while a magistrate whom they disliked would only hold office for a year and could often be prevented from accomplishing much in so short a time.

The nobles were thus able gradually to build up a political machine by means of which they were able to dominate the government. The assembly passed all legislation and elected the magistrates while the ex-magistrates formed the senate. Necessarily the senate included all of the principal leaders of the machine and members of a majority of the families which composed the governing class. It was wholly natural that the machine should choose to act through the senate and should seek in every way to augment the power of that body. It seemed to them the proper thing that the magistrates should be chosen by the machine and from their own exclusive circle; once chosen they ought of course to obey the orders of the machine, and these orders could most conveniently be given through the senate. When the expansion of Rome's power brought new problems to the fore, the nobles preferred to have them dealt with by the senate without a consultation of the assembly. Indeed, such a consultation under the circumstances would have savoured of the ridiculous, for it would have been in actual fact rather like asking the senate to consult itself.

## § 5. THE SUPREMACY OF THE SENATE

It is a commonplace to say that the authority of the senate grew steadily with time, that it successfully assumed one power after another, until it became the real governing body of the Republic, but the reasons for this have seldom been clearly seen by historians. Generally they attribute it to the high moral qualities of the Roman nobles, and some of them have expressed surprise that the assembly acquiesced so tamely in this development and have credited the Roman people with extraordinary self-control and keen political insight in recognizing the superior fitness of the senate to direct the government. Yet the real explanation seems at once more simple and more human. The rule of the senate was often short-sighted and selfish, more than once it committed disastrous blunders in policy, but its shortcomings could not shake its power, which rested on a well-organized political machine; the Roman people offered no serious opposition because under the circumstances they were helpless. Not even agitation was possible, for the Roman law permitted public meetings only when called by a magistrate and gave to him complete control over all proceedings. Thus private citizens could not meet or speak in public except with the consent of some magistrate, and when all of these were the tools of the machine the people were not only helpless to act but gagged as well. Backed by so efficient a machine it is not remarkable that the senate was able to make itself supreme and to retain this supremacy for a considerable period. In spite of many manifest shortcomings, the nobles might justly claim the credit for some great achievements. It was under the direction of the senate that Rome broke Carthage and conquered the Mediterranean world, and we may well doubt whether any other class would have done better or even as well.

After the machine had acquired control of the assembly, political strife in Rome almost ceased except for factional and personal disputes among the nobles themselves, and the senate made its authority felt in every department of the government. The magistrates, practically selected by the machine, were naturally subservient to it and the senate directed their policy without serious difficulty. Not only did they consult it on all important questions of administration, but they almost invariably submitted all bills for its approval before taking them to the assembly for formal ratification. The advice of the conscript fathers when given was treated as a command, and it was seldom that a magistrate refused to obey a decree of the senate or ventured to refer a bill to the sovereign people without the preliminary sanction of the conscript fathers. Even if a magistrate occasionally attempted to pursue a policy of his own, he could generally be promptly checked. Any administrative act in Rome itself, and by consequence the passage of any bill by the assembly, could be stopped at once by the veto of a tribune, and the machine could almost always find at least one among the ten ready to defend its interests. Outside the city the tribune's veto could not be employed, but here the senate had other means at its disposal. The chief place where independent action was possible was in the provinces, and, since Rome's expansion outside Italy did not begin until the power of the nobility was fairly well consolidated, the senate successfully assumed a large authority in this field. Originally the government of the provinces had been intrusted to the prætors, and the number of these magistrates had been increased with each new annexation, but, when the number had been raised to six, the nobles called a halt, probably in large part because a further increase would have required an extension of their circle by the promotion of new men.[1] However, the senate could not avoid new annexations, and, to meet the need for more magistrates with the *imperium*, it made greater and greater use of the promagistracy. Originally the promagistrate had been an exceptional official. Under special circumstances the *imperium* of one of the consuls or prætors had been prolonged for a second year, and he had, after the expiration of his term of office, been styled a proconsul or propraetor. At first the *imperium* had been extended just as it had been conferred by a vote of the people, but the senate soon assumed the power of granting the extension, although it never claimed to confer the *imperium*, doubtless because the right of the people in this respect was too firmly established in constitutional law. In any case this prerogative was of little importance while the nobles controlled the elections. With the steady growth of the empire and the steady increase in the judicial business at Rome the senate made a larger and larger use of proconsuls and propraetors in the provinces, until after 146 it is probable that most of them were ordinarily governed by promagistrates. Every year the senate named two consular and six prætorian provinces, and the consuls and prætors drew lots to determine which one should obtain each province. Every year the senate voted to prolong the *imperium* of such of the provincial governors as it chose to leave in office for another year and of those magistrates who, having remained in Italy during their year of office, were to be sent out as provincial governors. This power of the senate to extend the *imperium* gave it a strong hold upon the provincial administration. A governor now knew that his chance of enjoying a second year in his

[1] For a further discussion of this point I must refer the reader to the first chapter of my book, *The Founding of the Roman Empire*.

province depended upon the will of the conscript fathers, and he was, therefore, little disposed to quarrel with them. Control of the provincial governors carried with it to a large degree the control of foreign affairs, for Rome's relations with other states were likely to depend mainly on the conduct and attitude of the governor of the nearest province. What more was needed to give the senate the direction of Rome's foreign policy was quietly assumed. It received ambassadors, sanctioned or cancelled treaties, and declared war with scarcely any attempt at interference from the people.

The power of the conscript fathers went still further, for, if a governor was accused of maladministration in his province, he could be prosecuted before a special court in Rome, where a prætor decided the legal questions involved but a jury composed exclusively of senators decided on the facts. Every governor, therefore, knew that he might ultimately have to defend himself before a jury of nobles, and that, while they might condone some kinds of misconduct, they were not likely to look leniently on a servant who had refused to carry out their orders.

Last, but perhaps most important of all, the senate took upon itself to fix the armed forces of the state and to make all appropriations from the treasury. The Roman people probably acquiesced the more readily in letting the conscript fathers assume this last prerogative because the expenditures of the state had ceased to be a matter which affected them directly. The English-speaking world has always resisted taxation without the consent of the people, but the Roman people had ceased to pay any direct taxes to the state and the revenues which the senate undertook to manage were chiefly derived from the provinces. Since it never occurred to the Romans that they should consult their conquered subjects as to what tribute they should pay, there was no reason to demand economy nor any cause to fear that extravagance would affect their own interests. The senate was, therefore, able to acquire new powers of the highest importance. The governor received no salary, but the senate allowed him a certain sum for the necessary expenses of his office. If, when his term came to an end, there was any of this money remaining unspent he was under no obligation to return it to the treasury, but could dispose of it as he pleased. It was thus materially profitable to be on good terms with the senate, as the provincial governors cannot have been slow to discover. Over the prætors and proprætors the senate had not only these checks, but another as well. If they had any ambition for the consulship, it was extremely dangerous to incur the wrath of the machine which practically controlled the elections. Opposition to the senate was thus not only likely to prove futile, because of the varied means of obstruction at its disposal, but might destroy all hope of further advancement. Under such conditions there was little to tempt any magistrate to independent action and many weighty considerations to keep him loyal to the senatorial machine, which had put him in office. The only difficulties which the conscript fathers encountered for many years were such as arose from quarrels and rivalries among themselves and from the incompetence of magistrates chosen because of their family connections without reference to their ability. An aristocracy can hardly be expected to ignore the claims of birth, and no doubt the Roman nobles often preferred a stupid man belonging to a consular family to an able man whose ancestors had never risen above the prætorship, to say nothing of a new man. Moreover, in addition to such prejudices the assignment of the provinces by lot was obviously inefficient and must frequently have put the wrong man in the wrong place; excellent lawyers and judges without military training or capacity might find themselves charged with the conduct of a war, while experienced soldiers were sent to govern tranquil provinces. Such a system could not fail to result in occasional disasters, but it had one advantage which more than compensated for its defects, namely, that it enabled the nobles to govern with a minimum of friction among themselves. If the senate had undertaken to designate the governors of the provinces specifically the noble families would certainly have quarrelled over the distribution of the spoils. Under the system of lot each family in the governing ring had its chance, and if it drew a blank it was luck and not the intrigues of some rival family that was to blame. It is difficult to imagine any more effective method of preventing the machine from being shattered on the rocks of internal dissension. Yet, although aristocratic prejudices and aristocratic methods were responsible for many failures and disasters, the senate had the judgment and patriotism when matters became serious to take the necessary measures, however distasteful, to save the situation. There was a theoretical justification for the senate's authority in that it was only under the control of a powerful governing class that the clumsy and complicated constitution of Rome could work with any degree of efficiency. Such a view may have gone far to induce many thoughtful Romans to accept the supremacy of the senate as a necessity, although we may incline to think that it was this very supremacy that prevented any serious attempts at constitutional reform by making it possible for the ill-constructed government to carry on the business of the state in a tolerable fashion without them.

### § 6. THE POLITICAL RESULTS OF THE ECONOMIC CRISIS

The power of the senate had been well established before Rome began the acquisition of her empire, and that empire, as we have already seen in the previous chapter, was the cause of a grave economic crisis in Italy. Such a crisis could not fail to have important political consequences. The immediate effects would undoubtedly be all to the advantage of the nobles and would strengthen their machine. The successful wars not only poured a vast amount of booty into the treasury, but coming as this did immediately after the devastation of Southern Italy in the Second Punic War, and when the effects of the cheap grain from Sicily had had time to make themselves felt, the nobles were able to increase their estates at small expense. The ruin of the small farmer offered the opportunity for those who possessed some capital to become great proprietors, for many peasants were forced to sell their holdings for whatever they could get, and the possession of capital made possible, not only the purchase of these holdings to form large estates, but also the introduction of new types of cultivation much more profitable than the old. With land to be had for a trifle and slaves cheap because the markets were glutted with prisoners of war, a great estate could not only be obtained at small cost, but could be made to pay handsomely. Since the nobles and the knights were the two wealthy classes among the Romans, it was they who chiefly profited by the new conditions. The knights, however, being business men, directed their activities mainly to taking advantage of the opportunities offered in the provinces, so that the nobles encountered little serious competition in turning to their profit the situation within the peninsula itself.

The first result, therefore, of Rome's victories abroad was to enrich the nobles and to turn them into landholders on a large scale. Their new wealth was also of political value since, combined with the low price of slaves, it enabled them to multiply their freedmen and clients beyond all former limits. Not only was this politically advantageous, but it might also be financially profitable as well. Among the slaves who filled the market were many skilled artisans whose labour would be more or less wasted if employed on a rural estate. The best way to exploit such slaves was to set them free, furnish them the means to open a small shop in Rome, and exact a portion of their earnings, for we can hardly doubt that they would work more industriously and intelligently if they had a direct personal interest in the proceeds than otherwise. The same considerations would of course apply to the poor freeman, only there was in his case no initial expense for his purchase.

Under such conditions we can hardly wonder that at first the machine rapidly increased and consolidated its power, since the incentives for the nobility to seek complete control of the state were as great as the opportunity. If the classes whom the economic developments were pushing to the wall should gain political supremacy, they might seek to save themselves by measures which, whether ultimately successful or not, would certainly be most obnoxious to the nobles. To mention only such measures as were familiar to the Romans of that day, the nobles would naturally view with dismay laws cancelling or reducing debts, or a law requiring them to employ a certain number of free labourers on their estates. Moreover, there was much public land in Southern Italy which, if a complacent government would only look the other way, they could seize to augment their estates without cost to themselves. Under the spur of such fears and of such hopes we should expect them to work eagerly to strengthen their machine, the more so as the easiest methods of so doing were calculated to increase their income.

While the first results of Roman expansion were thus to the

advantage of the nobles and the senate which they controlled, some of the after-effects were the reverse. When a peasant lost his land he generally drifted to the cities, especially to Rome. While a farmer he had been a citizen and a voter, although he might never actually have cast a vote; in Rome he remained a voter, but now he was so situated that he could vote at every election and on every bill brought before the assembly. Moreover, the censors amid the multitudinous duties of their office, all of which must be completed within eighteen months, could find no time to make inquiries into the actual place of residence of the poorer citizens, even if such inquiries had ever been expected of them, and in consequence they left the small farmer who had moved to Rome still registered in the country tribe within whose boundaries was situated the farm which he had lost or sold. Thus the ruined peasant became politically more powerful than he had been when prosperous. There had doubtless always been some members of the Roman populace who voted in the rural tribes, but in early times the number must have been small. With the economic changes after the Second Punic War this class must have increased rapidly and have begun to assume considerable proportions. At first, no doubt, the nobles were able to multiply their freedmen and clients fast enough to avert any danger from this development, but, as the influx continued, the task became more difficult, since neither freedmen nor clients could be indefinitely created and still remain a source of profit to their patrons.

Another danger to the control of the machine developed in the course of time. The nobles had no monopoly upon the methods by which they had been able to dominate the assembly; it was perfectly possible for the wealthy knight to buy a country estate, have himself registered in a rural tribe, and form a band of retainers of whose votes he could dispose. This they at length began to do, since they also found that political power could be used to further their business interests. These interests were by no means always identical with those of the nobility, since their activities were turned in a different direction. They were contractors, tax-farmers, bankers, or engaged in commerce, hence their views on the issues which came before the state might differ sharply from those of the great landowners of Italy. They had no desire to hold the offices, but they did desire to exercise an influence on the policy of the government. They were quite content to leave the magistracies and the senate to the nobles and were interested chiefly in finding some means of putting such pressure on the government as to compel it to adopt the course which promised to yield the largest profits to themselves. To secure this object they began to build up a machine of their own by securing a considerable number of retainers voting in the rural tribes. Of course on many questions where the conflict lay between rich and poor the capitalist would join hands with the great landowner to defend the rights and privileges of property. Thus in some ways the growth of the political power of the knights strengthened the aristocratic machine, while in other directions it undermined the authority of the senate.

To maintain the senate's supremacy it was necessary that the nobles should act together, and that they and their retainers should outnumber all the other voters present in 18 of the 31 rural tribes. As the agricultural crisis developed, the grip of the nobility on the assembly was ultimately weakened, until by the time of the Gracchi it had become feeble and precarious. Within the rural tribes there seem to have been only three considerable groups, the nobles and their retainers, the knights and their retainers, and the members of the city populace registered in the rural tribes, but not clients. It is clear that by 146 B.C. the knights had come to hold the balance of power; with their support the aristocratic machine was usually irresistible, but, if they chose to join hands with the city populace, the nobles were powerless. The course of Roman history during the last century of the Republic will continually reveal this fact, and, if the senate remained in control during the greater part of this time, it was solely because the knights had few interests in common with the Roman mob and merely used the votes of the rabble from time to time in order to score off the nobles. It is necessary to emphasize this situation because historians have so frequently overlooked or forgotten it. It should be kept constantly in mind that, owing to the system of group voting, the city mob was *never* able to dominate the Republic, and that the wealthy minority was *always* able to outvote the poor in the assembly if that minority was united.

# CHAPTER III

## TIBERIUS GRACCHUS AND THE AGRARIAN PROBLEM

### § 1. THE PROBLEM

ALTHOUGH the Romans had no very clear perception of economic problems, the changes which were taking place in Italy as the empire expanded outside the peninsula had some consequences to which no one could be blind. Generals found that the recruiting of the army became more and more difficult as the class to which the conscription was applied diminished in number, and politicians could not ignore the increase in the city rabble which was revealed by the steadily growing number of voters in the rural tribes. Moreover, the misery of the rabble grew constantly greater, since the creation of freedmen to consolidate the control of the machine inevitably contracted the field of employment open to the free labourer or artisan. In the course of time the manumission of slaves became a less and less effective expedient, and the wealthy classes began to rely to a considerable extent on dependents recruited from such of the proletariat as were registered in the rural tribes. The actual condition of such dependents was often very similar to that of freedmen, but to assist a poor freeman to open a small shop not only saved the initial cost of a slave, but turned a potential opponent of the machine into a supporter.

Since they could not ignore the problem, it was natural that the more far-sighted of Roman statesmen should make some attempts to solve it, and equally natural that, until it became acute, the attempts should have been half-hearted and have failed in the face of the bitter opposition of those whose immediate interests were threatened. The most prominent figure in Rome in the days before the appearance of the Gracchi was Scipio Æmilianus, and he and his friends were responsible for some slight reforms, but they were either too wise or too timid to accomplish anything of real importance. It was left, therefore, to Tiberius Gracchus to make the first serious and determined effort to deal with the evils which were patent to the eyes of all.

The reformer was by birth a member of one of the most distinguished families of the Roman nobility. His father had attained the censorship (in 169) and had twice held the consulship (177 and 163). The son married into the great Claudian house and began his political career by serving as a quæstor in Spain. We are told that on his way to Spain he was deeply impressed by the spectacle of Etruria, where the plantation system was flourishing and the free peasantry had been largely replaced by agricultural slaves working under oppressive conditions. Perhaps the repudiation by the senate of a treaty with the rebellious Spaniards to which he had pledged his honour[1] may have contributed to alienate him from the machine and its methods, but there is no need to seek for personal reasons to explain his course. He had seen with his own eyes the conditions in Etruria, and an object lesson in the danger of such a development met him on his return from Spain. In Sicily a servile revolt broke out in 135, and was only put down after strenuous efforts in 132 ; it thus began before he became tribune and continued throughout his term of office, and it may have had much to do with his determination to carry his reform.

The agrarian problem as it presented itself to him seems to have worn a comparatively simple aspect, and there is no evidence that he perceived the economic causes which produced it. He held the traditional Roman view that the small farmer was the backbone of the state, and he saw clearly that this class was disappearing while the number of slaves steadily increased. If more was needed, he had the events in Sicily to convince him that something must be done and done at once. From this point of view the obvious remedy was to increase the numbers of the class whose disappearance appeared to threaten the safety of the state, in other words, to meet the danger arising from there being too few small farmers by the simple expedient of making more. There were plenty of men at hand for this purpose, so that nothing but

[1] See the preceding volume.

the land with which to furnish them with farms was needed. The whole problem in his eyes seems to have presented only one difficulty, namely, that of finding the land, and with the help of two eminent jurists (Crassus Mucianus and P. Mucius * Scævola) he discovered a way to overcome it.

## § 2. THE AGRARIAN BILL

When, therefore, in 134 Tiberius stood as a candidate for the office of tribune he had his scheme already in mind, and perhaps completely elaborated. How far it was made public in advance we cannot determine; neither can we discover whether the senatorial machine made any serious effort to defeat him. If any such effort was made, it was unsuccessful, and we may assume that, if seriously opposed, he owed his election to the same elements which afterward enabled him to pass his bill. In any case, he became one of the ten tribunes for 133, and was able to bring his project before the assembly.

The bill which Tiberius laid before the people was somewhat complicated and some of its details are uncertain. In general, however, its provisions are clear enough. He proposed that the state should take possession of all public land illegally held by private individuals and should distribute it in small allotments to the poor. To appreciate the significance of this a word or two is necessary in regard to the Roman public land.

During the conquest of Italy it had been the regular practice of the Republic to take from each of the conquered communities a portion of its territory and to declare it the property of the Roman people. This land might be allotted to Roman citizens, sold, leased, or rented as the government saw fit to determine. Another course was, however, possible, and was frequently taken. This was to do nothing at all with the land beyond declaring it the property of the state. In this case anyone who pleased was permitted to cultivate the land and pay a small rent for its use. Roman citizens frequently took advantage of this permission, but it also sometimes happened that the original holders were not disturbed, so that the Italians actually retained the land which they had nominally ceded to Rome. Those who occupied public land in this way were styled possessors, as distinguished from owners, and the state retained the right to eject them whenever it thought proper to make some other disposition of the land. Since the great landowners ordinarily controlled the government, they early discovered that it was to their advantage to leave much of the public land open to occupation and to take possession of it themselves. Attempts were made from time to time to prevent this, either by forcing allotment of the public domain or by imposing restrictions on the amount of it that any one person could occupy. As the power of the nobles grew they were able to put a stop to the allotment of the land, and, while they controlled the government, they were able to disregard all restrictive laws with impunity. Thus it happened that a large part of the land which nominally belonged to the Roman people had passed into the possession of great landowners who not only could show no legal title to it, but who held it in defiance of the law.

What Tiberius proposed was to enforce the old laws limiting the amount of public land which could be held by one person, to evict the possessors from what they had illegally acquired, and to resume the practice of distributing the public land among the poor citizens on an unprecedented scale. To the possessors he was willing to make some concessions. The law allowed an individual to occupy 500 *jugera* of the public domain, and so much Tiberius was not only ready to permit him to keep, but he proposed to give him a clear title to it and even further to allow 250 *jugera* for each of two sons if the possessor had a family, but 1000 *jugera* was to be the maximum retained.

The value of such a scheme from any point of view must be pronounced doubtful. On the face of it, it would certainly increase considerably the number of small farmers, but how long they were likely to survive would depend on economic conditions which we cannot estimate in our ignorance of the location of the public domain, and it is doubtful whether Tiberius took any interest in this phase of the matter or had much better information than we have on the subject. Neither do we know how he intended to select those to whom the land was to be allotted, although much would obviously depend on whether he expected to make small farmers out of the idle riff-raff of the city streets or had some scheme for selecting men with a knowledge of farming. Certainly we cannot assume that *all* the small farmers whom his bill would create were bound to fail merely because grain growing in certain parts of Italy no longer paid, for there were many other parts of the peninsula where it still yielded a fair return, and grain was not the sole crop which could be cultivated by the small farmer. In our ignorance of details it is impossible to judge the scheme with any certainty, but it may well be doubted whether there was a reasonable prospect of success on a large enough scale to alter materially the existing situation, still less to arrest the agricultural revolution which was taking place, since nothing was done to make the large estates unprofitable or to make the peasant proprietor better able to resist the competition of his richer neighbour. Much of its effect would be purely temporary, breaking up one great estate that another might shortly take its place,[1] and, even if, as is highly probable, much would be accomplished that would be permanent, it is still extremely doubtful whether the final results could be worth the disturbance which the bill was bound to cause.

That the bill was justified from a technical legal standpoint there can be no question, but there was another side to the matter. The possessors who were to be evicted from the public lands were practically never the ones who had occupied it illegally.[2] In many cases it had been held by the same family for several generations, and public land thus held had long been regarded by everyone as practically the same as private property; it had been bought and sold, mortgaged, and disposed of by will until the present possessor had often little or no connection with the original violator of the law. The state had failed to assert or enforce its rights until they had been forgotten. Even the small rent originally imposed for the use of the land had ceased to be collected, and there had been nothing to remind the holder of any difference between the land which he legally owned and that of which he was merely in possession. Under such circumstances the possessors might claim to have a case in equity if not in law,

[1] The agrarian law made the allotments inalienable, but this restriction was later repealed. Gracchus probably inserted the provision to prevent speculation.

[2] The occupation of the public lands in Southern Italy must have occurred after 200 B.C. In Etruria and Central Italy it probably took place earlier.

and they were certain to feel that their essential rights were being violated under cover of a legal technicality.

Tiberius Gracchus seems to have been a well-developed type of the doctrinaire reformer. He saw a great evil, he thought he saw the remedy, and he was determined to carry through his bill. All that we know of him goes to show that he was constitutionally incapable of seeing both sides of a question, or even of seeing that there were two sides. Supremely confident of his own rectitude, utterly convinced that his policy was right, he was unable to conceive of such a thing as honest difference of opinion and could only account for the opposition which he met by assuming that his opponents were rogues whenever he did not put them down as fools. With such a man there was no hope of compromise or intimidation, and the nobles could only prepare for a fight to the last ditch. That they would tamely submit to an act which seemed to them nothing short of the confiscation of a considerable part of their property no one but Tiberius Gracchus could imagine, and if he was able to achieve this flight of fancy he had a prompt and rude awakening. *

## § 3. THE BATTLE FOR THE BILL

As soon as the proposals of Tiberius were known, the nobles, who were nearly all possessors, began a bitter resistance, in which they were supported by a large number of the knights. Even when the knights held none of the land themselves they were sometimes directly interested as creditors, and, in any case, they were as a class deeply concerned in the security of all property rights. In his haste to secure action Tiberius shortened the customary procedure by taking his bill directly to the assembly without a consultation of the senate. At first glance it might seem that he would have small prospect of success, since the retainers of the rich were almost solidly arrayed in opposition. But this proved to be one of the rare occasions when the grip of the machine, even reinforced by the knights, was greatly weakened. The city rabble, having many votes in the rural tribes, were caught by his programme, some because newly come from the country they were anxious to return to their old mode of life, some because, although they had themselves no wish for an allotment of land, they hoped the bill would reduce the number competing for such employment as the city had to offer, some from mere envy of the rich, and some because they were carried away by the eloquence of Tiberius or the high moral and patriotic grounds on which he appears to have defended his measure. If this had been all it is not unlikely that the machine could have defeated him, but the news had been passed about in the country districts and country folk had flocked to Rome to vote. Hence the assembly was crowded with out-voters who had rarely or never attended its meetings. We may well imagine that the small farmer on the verge of ruin made an extraordinary exertion to come, hoping to gain a fresh start as a result of the bill, and that the free farm labourer, of whom there were still many, would make great sacrifices to secure a farm of his own. No doubt opponents of the bill likewise came in, but they were few in comparison with its supporters. The nobles realized that it would be impossible to defeat it under the circumstances of the moment, so they fell back upon their second line of defence.

When the day arrived for taking the vote in the assembly they were confident, since they had finally found one of the other tribunes, M. Octavius by name, who was prepared to fight the battle of the machine by using to the utmost his legal power of obstruction. It must be remembered that each tribune possessed a veto over every act of any or all his colleagues, and was thus able to block legislation by preventing some necessary step in the enactment of a law. When the assembly met Tiberius delivered a speech dwelling especially upon the state's need of men for the army. Rome, he declared, had grown great by conquest, and it was now a question whether she would not lose what she had gained, instead of acquiring the rest of the world, as a result of her diminishing man power. He drew a contrast between the value to the state of the freeman liable to military service and the slave, declaring that, if necessary, the rich ought to be willing to give the land freely to the poor so that they might rear families. He contended, however, that no gift was called for, and assured the possessors that they were given ample compensation in receiving a clear title to 500 *jugera* of the public land and 250 more for each of two sons.[1]

[1] I have followed Appian (*b.c.* i, ch.11), though not literally, in my account of this speech, and, indeed, I have relied upon him for my entire account of Tiberius. See Appendix 3.

Having finished what was doubtless a powerful harangue, Tiberius proceeded to the first legally necessary step for bringing the bill to a vote by directing the clerk to read it to the people. At this point Octavius arose and forbade the clerk to do so, thus interposing his veto and putting a stop to all further proceedings. Tiberius reproached him bitterly and adjourned the meeting till the following day. The object of the adjournment was to attempt to reach an understanding with Octavius, since his veto held good for that particular occasion only, and, if he could be induced to absent himself from the next meeting, the bill could be enacted, if no new obstacle presented itself. Whatever negotiations took place, Octavius refused to abandon his opposition and on the next day repeated his veto. This was followed by disputes among the tribunes and some disorder in the crowd gathered to vote upon the law. Some leading citizens urged the tribunes to submit their differences to the senate, and Tiberius, with a sublime confidence in the obvious rightness of his measure, accepted the suggestion.

In the senate what any man capable of seeing things as they were would have anticipated happened. Instead of putting pressure on Octavius to induce him to withdraw his opposition, the conscript fathers turned on Tiberius with bitter reproaches. The reformer, however, was not the man to be deterred from saving his country, and opposition stiffened rather than intimidated him. Righteousness must prevail and a way out of his difficulties must be found. To an ordinary man those difficulties would have appeared insurmountable, but Tiberius, like many of his type, was somewhat of a casuist. As it was plainly impossible to persuade Octavius to be quiet or to override his veto, Tiberius resolved to remove him from office, and seems to have succeeded in persuading himself that such a step was legal. A tribune, he reasoned, was a representative of the commons, and, when he thwarted their will, the sovereign people might justly deprive him of his powers by removing him from office. Had such a procedure been applied to the consuls it would have been an innovation in constitutional procedure, but the action, however novel, would have been legal, since the consuls possessed no veto on the actions of the tribunes and could not, therefore, have prevented a valid and binding vote of the people. But the whole difficulty with Octavius had arisen from the fact that, being a colleague of Tiberius in the tribunate, he possessed a veto on every act of his fellow-tribune. It was, therefore, just as impossible to depose Octavius legally, if he were present at the meeting, as it was to pass the bill under the same conditions, for, if he could prevent a legal vote upon the bill, he could equally prevent a legal vote on the question of removing him from office.

Tiberius, however, had become so desperate that he was ready to grasp at any sophistry. The constitutional course for him to take was to drop the bill for that year and to seek to secure the election of ten tribunes for the next who were all pledged to pass the measure. This course was closed to him, however, by the nature of the majority on which he was forced to rely to overcome the aristocratic machine. At the moment he was confident of carrying the rural tribes because of the exceptional number of country voters who had come to Rome on purpose to support the bill. These voters must have been mostly poor and they could not afford to idle about the city indefinitely. Neither, if they once went home, was it certain that they would be able to make the journey to the city again. Tiberius was probably more or less clearly aware after what had passed that his great reform must be carried promptly if it was to be carried at all. In such a situation it is not surprising that a man like Tiberius was able to blind himself to the patent illegality of the device to which he resorted.

Accordingly, after his curiously naïve appeal to the senate Tiberius turned back to the assembly, and despite the protests of Octavius proceeded to take a vote on the deposition from office of his resolute opponent. A majority was easily secured and Octavius, probably fearing violence from the supporters of his rival, left the meeting. Tiberius immediately had the vacant tribuneship filled by the election of one of his friends, and then the bill was put to a vote and formally proclaimed a law.

One might expect that the senate would at once declare it null and void because of the illegal act which had preceded its passage. The conscript fathers did not, however, venture to take this course, perhaps because they felt that they had no clear justification for it. Although the deposition of Octavius was illegal, the fact that he had left the assembly and had made no attempt to interpose his veto when the bill was finally put to a vote might suffice to make the passage of the bill legal. The senate may also have hesitated to annul the law because such direct and open action might arouse bitter resentment among the country voters who had left the city as soon as the law was carried and bring them back again in support of their champion. It might, therefore, seem wiser to let the law stand and to seek by indirect means to prevent its enforcement and so deprive it of all practical effect.

## § 4. THE PERGAMENE TREASURE

To carry out the law Tiberius had provided for the appointment by the people of an Agrarian Commission of three members, himself, his younger brother, and his father-in-law, Appius Claudius. This commission was given the power to decide what land was public and what private, to resume possession of such public land as was not exempt under the law itself, and to allot the expropriated land to the new settlers. Such a task was bound to be expensive and the senate had control of the treasury, so that the work of the commission could be greatly hampered by the refusal of adequate funds. After what had passed Tiberius could hardly expect generous support from the conscript fathers, and he seized eagerly upon an unexpected opportunity to finance his reform.

This opportunity was furnished by the death of Attalus III, king of Pergamum.[1] This monarch, the last legitimate representative of his house, left a will bequeathing his kingdom to the Roman people. By the traditions of the Roman constitution all action on such a matter should have been left to the senate, but Tiberius at once proposed a bill appropriating the treasures of the king to the use of his commission for distribution among the new settlers, so that they might have the means of erecting houses, purchasing tools, stock, etc. He also gave notice of another bill which he meant to propose and in which he would define the status of the cities of the former kingdom. For the moment he seemed to have

[1] See Appendix 3.

completely beaten the senatorial machine, but it remained to be seen if he would be able to escape its vengeance.

## § 5. TIBERIUS' CAMPAIGN FOR RE-ELECTION

When the country voters left the city after the passage of the Agrarian Law, Tiberius soon perceived that his position was one of serious danger, for it was obvious that his enemies were preparing to attack him. While he remained tribune they could do nothing, but they threatened that, as soon as he laid down his office, they would institute a prosecution against him for the violation of the sanctity of the tribunate of which he had been guilty in deposing Octavius. From the early days of the Republic the tribune's person had been sacred, and all who hindered him in the exercise of his functions were liable to severe punishment. To remove a tribune from office in order to prevent his using his legal and constitutional right of veto might certainly be considered as a crime, and it was a charge which Tiberius was in no position to meet. Whatever arguments he might advance in defence of his act, he could not hope that they would make any impression on his enemies, who would control the court before which he would have to plead his cause. A prosecution of this sort would come before the popular assembly, and the vote would be by centuries or by tribes according to the punishment demanded by the prosecution; the centuries alone could sanction the death penalty, but fines of any amount could be imposed by the tribes. In the centuriate assembly the possessors and their allies would be able to control a majority of the centuries, and they could probably control a majority of the tribes, for, now that the country voters had gone home, the rural tribes would probably be dominated by the retainers of the nobles and the knights. Accordingly Tiberius, although he might be convinced that his course was justified, could have no hope of convincing those who would be the real masters of the assembly. So clearly did he realize the peril of his position that he determined to avoid a prosecution at any cost, and the only way open to him was by seeking re-election as tribune.

At first glance it might seem that his chances of re-election were no better than those of acquittal, but in reality there were some points in his favour. Since the assembly was a mass meeting of citizens its actual composition varied greatly from time to time. The presence or absence of a considerable number of the country voters would depend on how busy they were upon their farms and hence on the time of the meeting. The election of the tribunes would normally take place in July, but it might be adjourned until later in the season. On the other hand, the date of a trial could be largely determined by the prosecution. Another and probably a much more important factor was that as a candidate Tiberius would have an opportunity to put forth a programme which might enable him to gain some support even from the ranks of his present opponents, to win over waverers, and to arouse fresh enthusiasm among his followers.

A programme such as the occasion required was not easy to improvise in haste, but Tiberius attempted it. Perhaps his proposals in regard to the legacy of King Attalus were dictated not only by the need of the Agrarian Commission for funds, but also by electioneering considerations. The distribution of the royal treasure among the new settlers may have been intended to draw the country voters back to Rome, and his announcement that he would deal with the cities of the kingdom in the assembly may have been a bid for equestrian support; the traditions of the senate were opposed to expansion, but many of the knights were eager for more provinces to exploit. This section of the equestrian class would probably be ready to support both proposals, perceiving that the seizure of the royal treasure could hardly fail to result in hostilities with Aristonicus, an illegitimate claimant to the throne of Pergamum, and that such hostilities once begun were likely to end in the annexation of the kingdom. If Tiberius succeeded in carrying his proposal in regard to the treasure, as seems probable, his success may have been due largely to equestrian support. His announced intention of dealing with the cities through the assembly looks very much like a bid for such support, and he seems to have made a further bid by proposing to give places to the knights in the juries of the standing courts, the chief of which had been created to try governors charged with extortion in the provinces. This would give the knights a position in the government which they were anxious to secure, as will be seen more fully in the next chapter. In addition to the knights Tiberius sought to gain support from other classes of voters, and his programme included some further proposals which are very imperfectly known. He promised to extend the right of appeal from the courts to the people,[1] and to reduce the term of military service,[2] but details are entirely lacking.

## § 6. THE DEATH OF TIBERIUS GRACCHUS

This hastily improvised programme may have produced a considerable effect, but not enough to discourage the senatorial opposition. The nobles continued to exert their influence to the utmost to bring about his defeat and destruction. Some of the other tribunes who had played a passive part during the battle over the Agrarian Law seem to have deserted him, and the election was held in the summer, when the country voters were busy with the harvest. His fate, therefore, depended upon his success in dividing the ranks of his enemies. When the day came and the voting began the first two tribes recorded their suffrages in his favour. The objection was at once raised that votes for him should not be counted, since the re-election of a tribune was illegal. The tribune Rubrius, who had been chosen by lot to preside, hesitated and agreed to transfer the presidency to Mummius, the tribune who had replaced Octavius. The other tribunes, however, protested that, if Rubrius retired, his successor must be selected by lot. As a result of the dispute the assembly was adjourned till the next day.

As to the question at issue the opponents of Tiberius seem to have had a strong case. Whether the immediate re-election of a tribune was actually forbidden by law is uncertain, but it was contrary to the general spirit of the constitution, and to custom so well established as to have something of the force of law. Such arguments, however were far from conclusive, since the Roman people, being sovereign, could elect Tiberius in spite of law or custom. This they could do by formally exempting him from the law or by simply disregarding any disqualification. The latter course might be held to

[1] Plutarch, *Ti. Gracchus*, ch. 16.
[2] Plutarch, *idem*: Dio, fragments of bk. xxiv, 83.

grant the exemption by implication, but it was necessary that the tribune who presided over the election should receive and count the votes cast for him, since it was the right of the presiding magistrate to decide on the legality of any person's candidacy for office. If a tribune unfriendly to Tiberius should be chosen to preside, his re-election would become impossible, and, since it was evident that there were a number of his colleagues upon whose support he could no longer depend, such an event was not unlikely.

Tiberius saw the net closing around him and gave way to counsels of despair. He attired himself in black and went about the forum leading his son, for whom he implored the protection of the voters, as though he himself were a man already under the shadow of death. Not trusting wholly to such appeals, he assembled his partisans before daybreak and occupied the place on the Capitoline hill where the assembly was to meet. What his purpose was cannot be determined. Possibly he merely meant to protect himself from the violence of his enemies, or perhaps he hoped to overawe them by an organized demonstration. When the assembly convened he tried to have his eligibility decided by a vote, and, when some of his colleagues prevented it, he gave a signal to his followers. He may have intended merely a demonstration, for his supporters began shouting, but the signal let loose a riot. Fighting broke out in the crowd and the other tribunes fled in haste, leaving the Gracchans in possession of the field.

His triumph was but for the moment. The senate met while wild rumours flew about the city, and the conscript fathers, in their hatred of the reformer, were ready for anything. The presiding consul, however, resolutely refused to take any violent or illegal action, and his attitude so enraged the majority that finally Scipio Nasica left the meeting calling on all who wished to save the state to follow him. A large number of the senators responded eagerly and were joined by many of the wealthy class and their retainers. Led by Nasica the excited mob, for it was nothing else, rushed to the assembly, where they found Tiberius still surrounded by his followers. The Gracchans, whose excitement had, perhaps, already spent itself and who may have been frightened to find that events had gone far beyond their expectations, made no serious stand but broke almost immediately,[1] and the senatorial forces beat down and killed many who were unable to flee quickly enough. Among those slain was Tiberius himself; he was caught near the temple of Jupiter Capitolinus and struck down at its closed door.

## § 7. THE RESULTS OF HIS CAREER

The reformer was dead, but the manner of his death was hardly likely to be a source of much satisfaction to the nobles. On this occasion mob violence had turned out to their advantage, but a dangerous example had been set. Perhaps in the hope of throwing some semblance of legality over what had happened, perhaps simply to intimidate those among the people who cherished resentment, the senate created a special court under P. Popillius Lænas, one of the consuls for 132, which proceeded to try and execute a number of Tiberius' supporters. The opposition seemed for the moment to be completely cowed and the senatorial machine to have regained its old supremacy. Nevertheless, beneath the surface the conscript fathers realized that their position had been weakened and that some concessions were necessary. Nasica, the special object of popular animosity, was sent off on a special mission, and a breach with the knights was avoided by accepting the legacy of King Attalus. Tiberius had merely seized the royal treasure, and it was, perhaps, in connection with this that Nasica was sent to Asia, but to get possession of it involved the senate in a war with the pretender Aristonicus, which lasted for four years (133 to 129) and led to the annexation of the kingdom of Pergamum and its organization as the province of Asia. *

Neither did the senate deem it wise to attempt any direct interference with the Agrarian Commission. P. Licinius Crassus Mucianus was elected to succeed Tiberius and under his direction the commission began its work. Although Crassus had been a friend of the reformer and had assisted him in

[1] Appian (*b.c.* i, ch. 16) attributes their failure to make a serious stand to the awe which they felt for Nasica and the senators. This may have been a factor, but I think it would hardly have been enough without the other causes mentioned above. If the Gracchans were already frightened at the turn of events the sight of the senators might turn the scale.

the preparation of his Agrarian Law, recent events seem to have moderated his zeal, and he was willing to come to an understanding with the nobles. The operations of the commission were commenced in regions where they would involve as little loss as possible to the senators,[1] and the machine permitted the election of Crassus as consul for 131. In the following year, however, when C. Gracchus, the brother of Tiberius, succeeded Crassus as the active head of the commission, no such moderation was to be expected, and the resumption and distribution of the public land was energetically pushed without regard to the interests of the nobles. This strenuous activity produced immediate confusion and was fruitful of difficulties. In many places it was no easy matter to distinguish public land from that privately owned, for the early records were imperfectly preserved and many landmarks had been swept away. The possessors stubbornly disputed every step of the commission, which soon found itself wellnigh overwhelmed with legal proceedings of all sorts. The Agrarian Law had, however, given the commission full judicial powers, and under C. Gracchus these powers seem to have been resolutely used.

During the next year (130) Appius Claudius Pulcher replaced Gracchus, and there was probably a relaxation in the activity of the commission, for Appius died in the last half of the year. His death and that of Crassus[2] led to the election of two new members,[3] both of whom were men from whom little moderation was to be expected. The prospects of the future, therefore, were far from reassuring to the possessors, and their agitation against the commission steadily increased. They were joined in their protests by many of the Latin and Italian allies who held portions of the public land, and moderate men like Scipio Æmilianus became convinced that it was time to call a halt. A direct attack upon the Agrarian Law or the commission was not necessary; it was enough to pass *

[1] Carcopino, *Autour des Gracques*, pp. 239–42. I have accepted his conclusions as to the operations of the commission. His view is that each member of the commission in regular rotation had the active direction of its work. *

[2] Crassus was killed in Asia, where he was in charge of the war against Aristonicus.

[3] M. Fulvius Flaccus and C. Papirius Carbo. Flaccus, who succeeded Crassus, was a strong partisan of Tiberius and would be head of the commission in 129.

a measure depriving the commissioners of their judicial powers and transferring the duty of deciding disputed cases to the consuls. In favour of such a bill it could be argued that the commissioners were bound to be partial, and that the * new arrangement would secure justice for all parties. The bill was passed in 129,[1] and produced the result which its supporters had secretly intended; every case was now disputed and the consuls did nothing to decide them. In consequence the resumption of the public land ceased and all that the commission was able to do was to distribute that which had already been seized. It is quite probable that there was a considerable amount of such land, and, when in this year the royal treasures of Attalus finally reached Rome,[2] it would be possible, if the commission received it, to allot some land which required considerable improvements to fit it for distribution. The commission was not formally abolished but its importance would rapidly diminish until its existence became little more than nominal.

Thus the senate succeeded finally in getting rid of the Agrarian Law as well as of its author. The nobles had, however, been forced to allow the commission a brief period of activity, and in this time it had undoubtedly accomplished something, though how much it is impossible to say. That many small landowners had been created there can be no doubt, but the number cannot be determined.[3] Neither can it be discovered how many of the new farmers were successful and how many soon abandoned their allotments. After all, the mere numbers are comparatively unimportant beside the significant fact that the policy of Tiberius unquestionably failed to solve the agrarian problem or to bring about any permanent improvement in the condition of the city

[1] H. Last (*Camb. Anc. Hist.*, IX, pp. 42–44) suggests that no such law was passed, but that Scipio secured a decree of the senate warning the commission not to touch public land held by the allies on the ground that this would raise international issues with which it was the senate's business to deal. In theory the allies were independent states bound to Rome by treaty.

[2] Justin, xxxvi, ch. 4. How large the treasure was at first and how much ever got to Rome is entirely unknown.

[3] The census returns for 130, according to which there were some 318,000 Roman citizens, as compared with those of 125 giving some 394,000, have been taken to show the number of the new farmers. Although this interpretation of the figures is doubtful, the number thus arrived at is neither impossible nor improbable.

proletariat. When, in 123, his brother Gaius came forward as a reformer he attempted to deal with the situation by new methods even while still professing to continue Tiberius' work. This change is in itself sufficient to show that, even if it had been loyally carried out, the Agrarian Law was no adequate remedy, and that it was the work of an idealist rather than of a clear-sighted and practical statesman.

## CHAPTER IV

# GAIUS GRACCHUS AND THE DEMOCRATIC PARTY

### § 1. THE BEGINNINGS OF A NEW STRUGGLE

IN spite of the death of Tiberius Gracchus the opposition to the senate continued to grow. The knights were becoming a more and more important factor in politics, and the rabble had been thoroughly alienated from the nobility. The fate of the reformer and the punishment of his supporters had naturally left an aftermath of bitterness. This might in time have passed away but for the fact that the poor had learned how little they could hope for from the senate. The feelings of the rabble would not have mattered much, for the aristocratic machine was safely in control as long as the retainers of the knights supported it in the country tribes, but there were many occasions when at least a section of the capitalist class was out of harmony with the nobles, and, even without a great leader to rally and unite all the elements of the opposition, occasional measures were carried against the wishes of the senate. In 131 B.C. a tribune, C. Papirius Carbo, succeeded in passing a law extending the vote by ballot, already in use for elections, to legislation. He also tried to give formal legal sanction to the re-election of tribunes, but the attempt failed for the moment, although some measure of the kind may have been carried within the next few years. Perhaps both his proposals received the support of many of the knights who felt that secret voting would weaken the nobles more than themselves and that they had no reason to fear serious difficulty with the tribunes; they might indeed desire the re-election of a tribune who was serving their interests, and they could always eliminate a mere demagogue by combining with the senatorial machine. It is quite possible that the ballot law met little opposition, since in elections it does not appear to have materially weakened the hold of the higher classes on their retainers, so that in 131 the senate may have thought it wise to accept an apparently popular reform which was really harmless.

In the same year that the Agrarian Commission was practically deprived of its powers (129 B.C.) the most influential man in Rome, Scipio Æmilianus, died suddenly.[1] He had always shown himself a moderate in politics, and his death removed a check upon the popular leaders. The Italians, who had been much alarmed by the proceedings of the Agrarian Commission, continued restless. Many of them held public land, and, though the commission was now powerless, its activity might be revived at any time by some new reformer. If such a reformer appeared they were in a much worse situation than the Roman possessors because they could not make their opposition felt in the assembly. A cautious agitator might, therefore, see in them precisely those whom it would be easiest and safest to attack. Their danger in the past and their fears for the future both pointed to the franchise as the best weapon of defence, and it is probably for this reason that they now began to seek citizenship. They had, of course, many other causes of discontent, since the Roman government had long been forcing them to furnish a larger and larger proportion of the recruits for the army and in many other ways was showing a disposition to treat them unjustly. Nevertheless, it seems reasonable to conclude that it was the agrarian agitation that brought their growing dissatisfaction with their position to a head.

In 126 Manius Aquilius, who since 129 had been busy stamping out the embers of the war with Aristonicus and organising the new province of Asia, returned to Rome and celebrated a triumph. His settlement, however, met with opposition, and he was prosecuted for extortion on the ground that he had accepted bribes in connection with his eastern arrangements. The senatorial jury acquitted him, although the verdict gave rise to considerable scandal, and the senate

[1] Some Romans believed that he was poisoned, which means that they did not understand the cause of his death. In the state of medical science at the time this is not surprising and their suspicions need not be taken too seriously. *

found it expedient to repudiate some parts of his settlement.[1] Probably the knights were chiefly responsible for the agitation, and it may have been owing to their discontent that M. Fulvius Flaccus, who was a member of the Agrarian Commission, was elected consul for 125. At any rate his election seems to show that the opposition to the senate was gaining strength from some quarter.

Flaccus attempted to placate the Italians by proposing a bill to grant them Roman citizenship. Probably his motive was to quiet their opposition to the Agrarian Commission and so pave the way for some measure which would enable it to resume its work. If Appian is to be trusted, they were willing to give up the public land in their possession in return for citizenship, but the bill met with little favour and Flaccus was induced by the senate to abandon it and then despatched to Gaul to take charge of military operations there. Nevertheless the issue had been raised, and, when the hopes excited by the bill were seen to be vain, Fregellæ, a Latin colony, revolted. There was as yet little unity among the allies, whom it had been the policy of Rome to isolate as much as possible from each other, so that prompt and concerted action on their part was impossible. Rome was, therefore, able to stamp out the revolt before it spread further ; Fregellæ was duly punished, but the discontent continued to smoulder.

## § 2. THE ELECTION OF C. GRACCHUS

The events so far mentioned were merely the preliminary skirmishes in a new struggle against the control of the senatorial machine. This struggle began in earnest with the election as tribune for 123 B.C. of Gaius Gracchus, the younger brother of Tiberius. He had been too young to take a prominent part in politics during the reformer's life, but he had been gradually coming to the front. He had served as a member of the Agrarian Commission, having been put upon it in spite of his youth by Tiberius, and in 126 he had acquired some reputation in Sardinia, where he had gone as quæstor. When his and his superior's term was twice prolonged by the senate,

[1] Especially in regard to Phrygia, which Aquilius had given to the king of Pontus. Greenidge (*Hist. of Rome*, I, p. 185) suggests that the knights wished it annexed. See also Frank, *Econ. Hist. of Rome*, pp. 141–50.

he returned to Rome in defiance of the second extension and in 124 became a candidate for the tribuneship.

How he came to be elected along with nine colleagues, none of whom offered any serious opposition to his policy, we can only conjecture. Perhaps the land question had become acute and there was an influx of country voters. In this connection it should be borne in mind that, although the Agrarian Commission had been unable to take the public land from the possessors since 129, it could continue the work of allotting what it had already seized, and it may have been two or three years before this side of its activities altogether ceased. Thus those who were genuinely anxious to secure a new chance as farmers would only gradually abandon all hope, and there would be nothing very surprising in a revival of interest in the question on the part of the country voters about this time. There is, however, another possible explanation of the defeat of the aristocratic machine, and it must have been defeated, since it is impossible to believe it would have permitted the election of Gaius and of nine timid, subservient, or like-minded colleagues either voluntarily or through carelessness. Once in power Gaius passed several laws which were highly advantageous to the knights. Unfortunately we do not know how much of his programme was made public when he first became a candidate, but it is not impossible that he had some sort of understanding with the knights from the first and that in 124 they threw the support of their retainers to him and his friends to an extent sufficient to outvote the retainers of the nobles in the rural tribes. It is not unlikely that there is some truth in both hypotheses, and that both knights and country voters contributed to the result.

In any case in 123 Gaius found himself in office without an Octavius to hamper him in carrying out his programme. Whether that programme was already fully formulated or not, it seems highly probable that during the ten years that had elapsed since his brother's death he had arrived at a clear conception of its broad outlines. It can hardly be doubted that he had been deeply embittered against the nobles by what had passed and that he was a determined enemy of the senatorial machine.[1] It is very likely, therefore, that when he

[1] H. Last (*Camb. Anc. Hist.*, IX, pp. 53 ff.) contends that at first Gaius took a conciliatory attitude toward the senate and sought "to effect necessary

stood for office it was with the fixed intention of breaking the power of the nobles and that he had long meditated on the subject. The only method of achieving such a purpose was to destroy the grip of the machine upon the rural tribes in the popular assembly. His brother's career must have made it clear that the country voters could not be relied upon; they might flock to Rome occasionally to vote for a particular bill or a particular candidate, but they could not be expected to remain there indefinitely, and, as soon as they had returned to their homes, the machine slipped back into power. The only hope of enduring success for the opposition lay in the creation of an anti-senatorial majority among the voters who resided in the city and were, therefore, always on hand in the assembly. Such a majority would be secured if the retainers of the knights could be united with that element among the city rabble which voted in the rural tribes but which was not included among the dependents of the nobles. After he became tribune Gaius undoubtedly tried to bring about such a combination, and we may safely assume that the design had been clearly conceived before his election.

reforms with the smallest amount of friction. For a time he succeeded: but at length his opponents declared open war through the mouth of Livius Drusus, and from that moment Gracchus was driven to the less pleasing methods of a party politician" (p. 55). This view is based chiefly on the contradictions in our sources in regard to some of his bills. Last would reconcile their differences by assuming two proposals, the first comparatively mild, the second much more radical. For my part I can see no reason to suppose that Gaius was ever on good terms with the senate. Among his first bills were the one legalizing the deposition of tribunes and the one banishing Popillius, both of which were direct attacks on the senate and its tools, and, if the conscript fathers did not immediately oppose him, it was because they could do nothing until they found a tribune ready to fight their battle and a point of attack which offered a reasonable chance of success. I think it very probable that Gaius sometimes modified his original proposals, either because he found that he had gone too far or not far enough. Thus his jury law, as described by the epitomator of Livy, seems to me much more drastic than the one he actually carried. According to the epitomator he proposed to add 600 knights to the senate (Plutarch says 300) and have the juries chosen from the enlarged senate. I do not see how Last (p. 70) can regard such a measure as moderate, since it would deprive the old senators not only of the control of the juries but of the senate as well. If Gaius made such a proposal, and I am inclined to think that he did, he finally compromised and contented himself with removing the senators from the juries.

## § 3. THE ATTEMPT TO CREATE A DEMOCRATIC PARTY

Gaius Gracchus held the tribuneship for two consecutive terms (123–122), and in these two years he succeeded in passing a number of laws. It is impossible to determine their chronological order or even to distribute them between his two terms of office. It is, therefore, not only permissible but necessary to group them logically, placing together those which seem to have had a common purpose, however diverse in subject.[1] It will be desirable to begin with those measures which were intended, at least in part, to build up a democratic party so powerful and well organized that it could overthrow the supremacy of the senatorial machine. The success of this undertaking would in no respect have freed Rome from the grip of *a* machine, for it would merely have substituted a new machine for the old one, but it would have meant that the old governing class would be replaced in the control of the state by other classes with different interests and hence with more or less different views of public policy. In this part of his programme Gaius had little room for choice. If he meant to remain in public life and wished to be re-elected tribune when his first year of office was over he must seek the support of a majority in the assembly. Since, even if he desired it, he could not hope to win the favour of the nobility, he was obliged to look elsewhere. The majority he needed could under existing conditions only be found in a coalition between the knights and the proletariat, and such a coalition could only be brought about if he was prepared to pay the price. It was imperative for him to devise a programme which would attract both these classes without alienating either. Such a programme he contrived to frame with a truly remarkable political insight.

He, of course, revived his brother's Agrarian Commission by restoring to it the judicial powers of which it had been deprived. Such a measure no doubt appealed to the country voters, whom he could not afford to ignore, although he could not depend on them for steady support. For the genuinely urban element in the rabble who had no desire to return to the

[1] Several laws of minor importance have been omitted.

land he had something else to offer in the shape of a corn law. This provided that any Roman citizen could buy grain from the government at a fixed rate considerably below the normal market price.[1] This proposal was enthusiastically welcomed by the city poor, since it very obviously reduced the cost of living, and it would not materially affect the country voters, since Rome had long ceased to be a market where Italian grain could be sold at a profit. Neither would the Corn Law disturb the interests of the knights, although the farmers of the Sicilian taxes probably disposed of much of their grain in the city, for the Roman state would now be obliged to purchase their grain and there was no reason why they should lower the price. The only sufferers on any considerable scale would be the treasury and the nobles who in one way or another were enriching themselves from it. We might expect that any new activity on the part of the Agrarian Commission would alarm both the knights and the Italians, but there is no record that they offered serious opposition. Perhaps Gaius was able to placate the Italians sufficiently by promising to revive the project of Fulvius Flaccus for an extension of citizenship, and the knights may have been willing to make some sacrifices in return for the compensation offered them by his other measures. It seems unlikely that many of the wealthy business men in Rome had invested more than a small part of their capital in land, and they may well have thought that they would gain far more than they lost from his programme as a whole.

His principal benefactions to the knights were two. By one law he introduced into the province of Asia the tithe system with its attendant farming of the taxes, and provided not only that the bidding should take place in Rome but that the right to collect the tithe of the whole province should be sold to a single bidder. These last provisions practically excluded local competition, since the capital necessary for transactions on so large a scale could only be raised by a syndicate of Roman knights, who were thus given a chance to exploit Asia to the best advantage.

His second measure was ostensibly intended to purify

[1] How great a reduction was made it is impossible to determine with certainty, but the popularity of the law and the difficulties of the treasury as a result of it seem to indicate a considerable lowering of the price.

the courts. The chief standing court[1] at that time was the one which tried provincial governors charged with extortion, and, as has already been pointed out, the jury which decided on the guilt or innocence of the accused was composed exclusively of senators. There had recently occurred some instances in which these juries had acquitted men generally believed to be guilty and the scandal so occasioned gave Gaius a pretext for proposing a change. He carried a law by which the juries were henceforth to be selected entirely from the knights. It is possible that he believed the law would make some improvement; if so he must have been imperfectly acquainted with the capitalists of Rome. The knights wanted to secure the juries for a perfectly simple and intelligible reason, which was to gain a means of putting pressure on the governors, on whose attitude their profits depended in no small degree. If a syndicate was collecting the tithe in any district in Sicily (and henceforth, of course, in the whole province of Asia), it naturally wished the governor to shut his eyes to the extortions of their agents. If a Roman knight or syndicate had loaned money to a provincial community, it was obviously financially desirable that Rome's representative should be prepared to go all lengths to compel the payment of the debt. In this connection the governor's powers were very wide, as was also his discretion; he might go so far as to imprison the local senate, composed of the wealthiest and most prominent citizens of the community, until they provided the necessary funds either by levying fresh taxes or by the sacrifice of their own property. Moreover, questions constantly arose over the validity of loans. It might be claimed that the annual magistrates of a town had no right to borrow money without the previous sanction of the local senate or assembly and that this sanction had never been given. Sometimes the loan was a wholly fraudulent transaction which would not bear investigation, sometimes the Roman bankers might have acted in ignorance of the local constitution, but in either case the court of the provincial governor would have to adjudicate the matter. Even if the validity of the loan was not disputed, the rate of interest specified in the bond might be attacked. Provincial governors

[1] There may have been one or two others, but their existence is doubtful and they had little political importance.

often undertook to fix the legal rate of interest by an edict, and their successors might either enforce such edicts strictly or might admit of exceptions under certain circumstances. It will be obvious from these illustrations that the governor's attitude would very materially affect the profits of the knights doing business in his province, but the full extent of his power will only be appreciated when it is realized that he not only presided over the highest court in the province, but that he practically controlled its decisions. In theory his procedure was the same as that of a prætor in Rome; he decided the legal questions involved in a case and submitted the hearing of the evidence and the decision on the facts to a jury. There was, however, one immense difference between the prætor and the governor; the prætor had little option in the selection of the jury,[1] but the governor was practically unhampered and could appoint such persons as he chose. He could thus always arrange that in one way or another the knights should win their cases, and this affected all Romans of any class doing business in the province. If every governor knew that on his return to Rome he might be called upon to face a jury of knights, the latter could reasonably expect that in self-defence he would go far rather than risk a quarrel with them.

Inevitably the effects of the judicial law of Gaius were pernicious. The complaint against the senatorial juries was that they allowed governors who had practised extortion in the provinces to escape unpunished; the new equestrian juries soon made it clear that they would punish any governor who did not permit them to plunder and exploit the provincials without hindrance. Under the old system bad governors sometimes escaped, under the new good government was deliberately penalized. It is, of course, easy to be wise after the event and Gaius probably failed to anticipate the worst consequences of his law, but it is not so easy to believe that he sincerely thought that his measure would improve the courts, since it is difficult to imagine any reason why the knights should desire to serve on the juries except that such service would enable them to intimidate the

[1] He had none at all in the standing courts, and in the ordinary courts he was checked by precedent and custom if not by positive law. Moreover, in cases involving serious penalties an appeal could be made from the ordinary courts to the assembly.

governors, and it is equally difficult to see why they should wish to gain such a power except to increase their opportunities for plundering the provincials. The conclusion can hardly be avoided that Gaius to some extent deliberately sacrificed the provincials in order to secure the support of the knights for his democratic party. His best excuse would seem to be that it was necessary to pay the price, that the heaviest blame should fall on those who determined the conditions of the bargain, and that he hoped by it to gain power which he meant to use for the lasting benefit of Italy. Few Romans of that day would have hesitated, or thought that there was room for hesitation, if they were confronted by a conflict between the interests of provincials and those of Romans and Italians, and, if Gaius had been among those few, he would probably have left no mark upon the history of his time. *

By the measures so far mentioned Gaius expected to secure in the tribal assembly a steady and reliable majority of which he would be the unquestioned leader, and for a time he seemed to have been completely successful in creating a democratic machine capable of governing the Republic. His brother's career, however, was a sufficient warning of some of the dangers in his path. Although at the moment his colleagues were in harmony with him, or too timid to offer any opposition, there was always the possibility that an Octavius would some day appear. To deal with such a situation the simplest method was undoubtedly to depose the troublesome tribune from office, but the legality of this course was extremely doubtful at best. A law legalizing it would amount to a public confession that Tiberius had violated the constitution; Gaius was naturally unwilling to admit this and wished to amend the constitution without condemning his brother. The only way of doing so was to enact some law which assumed the validity of Tiberius' action, and was based upon that assumption. Gaius, therefore, proposed a bill providing that any person who had been deposed from office by the Roman people should be ineligible to hold office again. Although drawn in general terms, everyone knew that the bill affected only one man. Since his deposition by Tiberius, Octavius had, apparently, taken no part in politics, and most Romans, failing to see the real motive of the measure, which, of course, Gaius could not openly avow, regarded it as a vindictive attempt to put a stigma on a harmless private citizen. This appearance caused so much dissatisfaction that Gaius dropped the bill, professedly because of his mother's entreaties.

In another direction he felt the need of safeguarding his position as leader of the people. After his brother's death the senate appointed a special commission under the consul, P. Popillius, which executed a number of his brother's partisans. If the conscript fathers could at their pleasure create a court from whose judgment there was no appeal, and could authorize it to punish any conduct which they chose to consider dangerous to the state, those who opposed the senate obviously did so at the peril of their lives. To meet this danger Gaius proposed and carried a law banishing any magistrate who had put Roman citizens to death without permitting an appeal to the people. This law clearly applied to Popillius, who retired into exile, a result which no doubt gave Gaius much pleasure. Nevertheless, his chief purpose was to deprive the senate of the formidable power which it had assumed, and he was so far successful that the senate abandoned the practice of creating special courts and devised a new weapon with which to deal with emergencies, a weapon whose efficiency was first tested against Gaius himself.

## § 4. THE PROGRAMME OF REFORM

The success of Gaius in constructing a new governing machine seemed for a time to be complete; the coalition of the knights and the rabble was an accomplished fact, and the assembly met merely to ratify his will. How long such a coalition would last was another matter, which was rendered all the more uncertain by his own character. If he had been merely a self-seeking politician his career would doubtless have been longer, but to his own undoing he was also a statesman and a patriot. He had not created his machine simply to re-elect him to the tribunate year after year; he intended to use it to solve the pressing problems of the day and to carry through reforms of permanent benefit to his country. If he was ready to sacrifice the interests of the provincials, he aimed steadily to secure the welfare of Rome and Italy, and it was these nobler aims which destroyed him.

Historians have generally regarded the corn law as merely

a bribe to secure the support of the rabble, but there is another side to the matter which we are bound to consider because it must have had its influence on the tribune. The problem which the Romans had to face has become familiar to the world since the World War, for it was simply the problem of unemployment. In Rome there had been steadily accumulating a mass of men for whom there was no work. The agricultural crisis and the cheapness of slave labour were the basic causes of this condition, and the situation became steadily worse. If the government did nothing to help the poor, the rabble must soon reach such a depth of misery that desperation would result. Then what had happened in Greece would begin at Rome; the poor would rise against the rich, massacre and counter-massacre would follow, and, if one of these domestic convulsions coincided with a foreign crisis, the whole fabric of the empire might collapse. Under such circumstances prevention was wiser than repression, and action by the state to relieve the growing poverty of the mob of Rome was a far-sighted insurance against future calamity. The obvious remedy, perhaps the only one possible, was some form of unemployment dole, and this is precisely what the corn law was. By it the state came to the rescue of the citizens who could not obtain enough work for their support and assisted them by stabilizing and reducing the cost of living. The grain was not yet given gratuitously to the needy, because they were able to earn something by their own exertions. Later, as conditions grew worse, the state went further,[1] but Gaius was not responsible for that, for he exerted himself to the utmost to prevent the growth of poverty.

The corn law was only a part of his programme for dealing with the unemployment problem; he had two plans which would tend to prevent the growth of the rabble and even to diminish its numbers. Through the Agrarian Commission something might still be done, but to keep the farmer on the land was obviously far more important than anything the commission could accomplish. Partly for this purpose Gaius

[1] The explanation which attributes to mere demagogism the extension of state aid to the rabble by reducing the price of grain until it was given gratuitously seems to me too simple a solution: the economic conditions must surely have had much to do with it.

carried a law providing for an extensive scheme of road building. Incidentally this would provide work for many, although the rough labour would be done by slaves, but that was probably a minor consideration. The Romans had already constructed an extensive system of roads in Italy, but they had been designed primarily for military purposes. The new roads were intended rather for commerical use and would, therefore, link up with the old in such a way that the farmer would be able to get his grain or other crops to market more easily and cheaply.

In addition to this help to agriculture Gaius planned to draw off a portion of the surplus population by founding colonies on a considerable scale. Here he was probably thinking chiefly of relieving the congestion of Rome and other cities, since the colonies he proposed were of a commercial and urban, rather than an agricultural, character. In Italy itself two once important towns had been strangled by the policy of Rome, namely, Capua and Tarentum. If the restrictions on them were removed and new settlers sent in, they might regain something of their old prosperity. The same thing applied to Carthage, which the Romans had completely destroyed, with the difference that here the colonists would be settled outside the peninsula. This was a drawback, although a purely sentimental one, which did not deter Gaius from proposing to build a new city on the old site. Such a colonization programme was entirely feasible and would do something to reduce the number of the unemployed who required the assistance of the state. If Gaius had had a longer lease of power he would doubtless have developed this side of his policy, but it is quite improbable that he could have gone far enough to render the corn law unnecessary. Neither is it likely that he wished to do so, for such a success might be suicidal by weakening his control of the assembly. In any case it should be observed that Roman statesmanship never discovered better methods of dealing with the problem of unemployment, which, largely as a result of slavery, proved to be permanent, than those of Gaius ; even Cæsar at the height of his power only prescribed the Gracchan remedies of colonization and public works, leaving the residue of the populace to be kept quiet by the corn dole.

Another problem which Gaius attempted to solve was the

increasing discontent of the Latin and Italian allies. He proposed to extend full citizenship to the Latins and to give the Latin rights to the Italians.[1] Here again he showed real statesmanship by seeking to deal with the question before it had become acute. His failure and that of his successors to secure concessions to the allies by peaceful means was the direct cause of the Social War, which brought Rome to the verge of ruin.

## § 5. THE OPPOSITION

The programme of Gaius, if carried out, would in many respects have been highly beneficial to Rome, but as soon as he attempted genuine reforms his newly constructed machine began to break to pieces. His policy and success had already filled the nobles with fury, and their bitterness was not in any degree lessened by the fact that for the moment they were helpless. From their point of view his methods were worse than his measures. To execute his laws he regularly appointed special commissions, either named in the bill or appointed by the assembly after its passage. He himself was a member of some of these commissions, for the combination of such special offices with one of the regular magistracies was perfectly legal, and he was thus drawing into his own hands a steadily increasing part of the administration. If he continued to pursue this course for any length of time the senate and the magistrates might be reduced to shadows and most of their duties might pass to the leading tribune and a variety of special commissions practically appointed by him.[2] It is not surprising, therefore, that the nobles and the senate grew desperate and resolved to remove the great tribune by any means that offered. When Gaius ceased to propose bills which were in effect bribes to one or another element in the assembly, and, confident of having secured a solid and dependable majority in that body, undertook real reforms, the senate's opportunity came and was seized upon with eagerness.

Gaius was not entirely wrong in his reliance on his majority;

[1] Appian (*b.c.* i, ch. 23) is not very clear, but his language has generally been interpreted in this sense.

[2] Probably this was part of a deliberate policy and he hoped to hold in Rome a position similar to that of Pericles at Athens, but his course may have been due merely to distrust of the senate and the magistrates. In any case the result was the same.

he was still too strong for a direct attack, but he was greatly weakened by the fact that many who had hitherto supported him disliked one or another of the measures which he was now advocating. The Roman assembly was, as has been shown, a delicately adjusted mechanism where the introduction of a comparatively small number of new voters might have far-reaching consequences. All social classes which possessed any political influence were likely, therefore, to view changes in its composition with some apprehension. If Gaius enfranchised the Latin allies it would create a large body of potential voters. No one could say in advance how many of them would ever vote, but it was quite possible that enough might avail themselves of the privilege to upset the balance of power, since a handful of voters might decide the vote in some of the rural tribes. Those members of the rabble who were registered in the rural tribes might see their importance seriously diminished, and the influence of the knights was largely due to their bands of retainers who voted in these tribes.[1] The capitalists may have been friendly to Gaius, but in politics gratitude has been well defined as a lively sense of favours to come; having gained everything which they particularly desired at the moment, they had no wish to see Gaius emancipate himself from their control. The new citizens, owing their privileges to him, might outnumber their retainers sufficiently to render their support unnecessary, and a reformer who could not be kept within bounds was not at all to their liking. Certainly the introduction of new voters in the rural tribes, where most of the Latins would be registered,[2] would not benefit the knights and might be dangerous to them. It was not inconceivable that the Latins might combine with the nobles to kill the Agrarian Commission and might then assist the rabble to carry measures more or less harmful to the big business interests in Rome. Moreover, it was obvious that, if they became citizens, the poorer Latins could take advantage of the corn law; if the treasury could not stand the increased cost, the law would have to be restricted in some way or additional revenues

[1] The same consideration would apply to the nobles, but since they were against Gaius anyway I have omitted them here.

[2] They might be organized into new tribes, but the same considerations would apply, since the more tribes there were the more it was necessary to control to have a majority in the assembly.

found, perhaps at the expense direct or indirect of the rich. In short, the extension of the franchise was an experiment by which no class could be certain of profiting and from which every class must run some risk of loss. Naturally enough no class cared to try such an experiment, and nothing but the personal ascendency of Gaius gave it a chance of success.

The nobles were not slow to see that here was his vulnerable point, and on it they concentrated their attack. Among the tribunes for 122 there was one, M. Livius Drusus, who was prepared to play their game, whether from sincere conviction or for other reasons. He had been elected as a member of the popular party, and he did not openly desert it. To the extension of the franchise he declared himself unalterably opposed, but he offered some minor concessions to the allies. He also attacked the colonial policy of Gaius on two grounds; he objected to sending Romans across the sea to Africa, and he declared that much more might and should be done for them in Italy. In place of two colonies in the peninsula he advocated twelve and the senate eagerly gave its approval to his proposals.

### § 6. THE FALL AND DEATH OF GAIUS GRACCHUS

Drusus was thus in the position of outbidding Gaius for the leadership of the people, and Gaius made the mistake of underestimating the danger. He knew himself to be immensely popular and thought that he could easily dispose of his unexpected rival. Only thus can we account for his venturing to leave Rome for an inspection of his projected colony in Africa. In his absence his enemies worked feverishly and when he returned he found that his machine was seriously shaken. Fulvius Flaccus, whom he had left in charge, had proved unequal to the task of holding it together, so that in the elections for the tribunes for 121 Gaius was defeated, and in December of 122 he became a private citizen.

The senate seemed triumphant but it was well aware that, unless it could go further, its victory would prove an empty one. It is unlikely that there was enough land available for the colonies which Drusus had promised,[1] and, as soon

[1] At any rate they were never established.

as this fact became manifest, Gaius was likely to return to power, and practically certain to do so if he could regain the support of the knights. He was far too able a man to be despised and the senate had no illusions on this point. The exact details of what followed are obscure, but the policy of the nobles is clear enough, although they may have been only partially conscious of it themselves and have owed their success rather to good fortune than to their own astuteness. Their purpose, whether clearly conceived or not, was to provoke disorder and in suppressing this to eliminate Gaius forever. The means came to hand in connection with the proposed colony in Africa.

When Rome destroyed Carthage the ground on which her hated rival stood was elaborately cursed. Sinister omens were now reported from Africa, which were interpreted as an indication of the wrath of the gods at the disregard of these curses. The conscript fathers made haste to recommend that the law for the establishment of the colony should be repealed. Gaius, although now a private citizen, resolved to oppose this measure. He came to the assembly with a large body of his followers, many of whom were armed though he himself was not. In the intense excitement which prevailed only a spark was needed to kindle the flame. A supposed insult to Gaius was avenged by the dagger of one of his supporters, and the riot was on. The assembly broke up and the consul, L. Opimius, who was a bitter enemy of Gaius, hastily summoned the senate and called upon the senators and knights to bring armed slaves to defend the constitution. The senate promptly instructed Opimius to defend the commonwealth.[1] Meanwhile Gaius had lost control of the situation, and Fulvius Flaccus, a headstrong and violent man, armed a large number of the rabble and seized the Aventine, where Gaius reluctantly joined him and vainly attempted to negotiate with the senate. The conscript fathers demanded unconditional surrender, to which Gaius would not agree, for many of the democrats had violated the law and Gaius would not desert his followers however much he disapproved of their course.

[1] Such a formula afterwards acquired the name of the *senatus consultum ultimum,* " the last decree " of the senate. Its significance and development will be discussed in the first section of the next chapter.

Nothing remained but to fight. The result was never doubtful, for Opimius, with the help of experienced generals, easily captured the Aventine; to avoid future unpleasantness he took pains that the democratic leaders should perish in the struggle by offering a reward for their heads. Gaius attempted to escape, but finding himself surrounded he committed suicide by falling on the sword of one of his slaves, the slave afterwards killing himself upon his master's body.

In his stormy career Gaius had accomplished much and little. Most of the measures which he probably regarded as means to an end had been carried, but he had failed to achieve the end. The revived Agrarian Commission accomplished nothing of great importance; his colonies and his plans for the Italians failed; he had sacrificed the provincials to the knights, but the knights deserted him as soon as they had got their pound of flesh. To counterbalance the sufferings of the provincials, there remained only his roads and the corn law. By the one he had undoubtedly benefited the rural population to some extent, and by the other he had prevented the rabble of the city from becoming a serious danger to the wealthy. But the power of the senate had not been broken and the aristocratic machine resumed control of the government, dispelling the hope which Gaius had cherished of deposing it from power by the creation of a democratic party sufficiently strong and united to dominate the Republic.

# CHAPTER V

# THE RISE OF MARIUS

## § 1. THE POLITICAL SITUATION AFTER THE GRACCHI

THE political agitation of which the Gracchi had been the leaders seemed to subside without having produced any essential change in the situation. Before Tiberius appeared upon the scene the senate had been the governing body of the Republic, and such it remained after the death of Gaius. Its power, however, rested on the support of the aristocratic machine, and the control of this machine over the assembly had already been undermined by the social and economic changes of the last half-century. The Gracchi exposed the senate's actual weakness and aroused to conscious life the latent antagonism which the rule of the nobility had provoked not only in the slums of Rome but among her wealthy business men as well. The knights had learned how much they could accomplish by an alliance with the mob, and they were likely to resort to such an alliance whenever their interests were ignored or flouted by the conscript fathers. The rabble also had learned that their poverty could be relieved by the state, but that it was hopeless to look for help to the senate, and they were henceforth ready at all times to support an attack upon the nobles by any leader who chose to place himself at their head. It was only at intervals, however, that a leader was found, for without the help of the knights he could accomplish nothing. When a leader was lacking, discontent, even if widespread and bitter, had no outlet for expression, since the Roman law tolerated no public meetings except such as were summoned by a magistrate and permitted no one to address a meeting without the consent of the magistrate who had called it, so that as long as the knights and nobles acted together, the rabble was not only powerless but inarticulate. After the death of C. Gracchus the knights, having gained what they wanted at the moment, were willing to leave the government in the hands of the nobles until some new cause of antagonism arose.

Although the senate apparently recovered its dominant position, it had been greatly weakened by the loss of its control of the courts, and it had been taught by bitter experience the danger of a coalition between the knights and the populace. Accordingly no immediate attack was made on the equestrian juries or the corn law,[1] and the senate contented itself with defending the new weapon which it had employed so successfully against Gaius. When Opimius laid down the consulship he was prosecuted before the people by one of the tribunes, but the trial ended in an acquittal, and the verdict is not difficult to explain. The senators no doubt exerted all their influence, and the knights, who had a strong interest in the maintenance of order, probably supported them, fearing that a condemnation would leave the government with no effective means of dealing with the mob, whose violent tendencies seem to have been first revealed in the recent agitations.[2] The result was of far-reaching importance, for by this verdict the Roman people practically admitted that a decree of the senate could confer extraordinary powers on the magistrates. On the authority of the senate's instructions to defend the state, Opimius had raised an armed force and restored order with a high hand. In doing so he had clearly overstepped the law; he had treated Roman citizens as outlaws by offering a reward for the heads of the leaders of the sedition, and he had imprisoned others without the sanction of a court.[3] By acquitting him the people conceded that under the vaguely worded decree of the senate these acts were legitimate. On the face of it the senate

[1] The corn law seems to have been modified by a M. Octavius (not the opponent of Ti. Gracchus) in the interest of the treasury. (Cicero, *Brutus*, ch. 62, 222; *de off.*, ii, ch. 21, 72.) We do not know what the new arrangements were nor when they were introduced, but a date three or four years after the death of Gaius seems probable. The equestrian juries were not attacked till 106 B.C.

[2] So far as is known the peace of the city had not been seriously disturbed within the memory of men then living.

[3] The epitomator of Livy (lxi) makes this last the formal charge against Opimius, but Cicero (*de orat.*, ii, ch. 30, 132 and elsewhere) implies that the death of Gracchus was involved in the case

had merely advised the consul that a critical emergency had arisen and urged him to use his powers to the utmost to protect the commonwealth. It was obviously the duty of the magistrates to suppress open sedition, by force if necessary, but Opimius had evidently assumed that the decree extended his legal powers, and the people acquiesced in this assumption.

The senate was naturally encouraged by its initial victory to advance more and more sweeping claims. In later times the last decree, that is, the formula that the magistrates should see that the Republic suffered no harm, was often accompanied by others declaring certain persons public enemies and suspending from office any magistrates who were suspected of sympathizing with them. According to the senatorial theory the last decree amounted to a proclamation of martial law, and while it remained in force the magistrates whom it directed to save the state were clothed with all the powers of the old dictators, who had been exempt from the veto of the tribunes and had possessed the power of life and death over all citizens. Most of these claims seem to have been accepted without dispute. It was never denied that the magistrates could raise an armed force and bring it into the city, or that they could arrest and imprison citizens who were considered dangerous; the suspension of magistrates suspected of seditious tendencies and of the tribunician veto seem also to have gone unchallenged, nor was any question raised as to those citizens who were killed in the fighting by which a riot was put down. The only serious attack was on the right of the magistrates to put to death, without a legal trial and an appeal to the people, citizens who had been arrested before they had actually taken up arms or who, having been captured during the struggle, were in custody after order had been practically restored.[1]

The agitation of the Gracchi had left a number of other questions which the senate disposed of in the next few years. Not only were the colonies of Drusus quietly dropped, but the colonies projected by Gaius were also abandoned, although those who had already received assignments in them were not disturbed. The Agrarian Commission was soon abolished,

[1] The Catilinarian conspirators were executed, although they had never actually taken up arms. Cæsar admitted that they might be imprisoned, but denied that they could legally be put to death.

and in 111 B.C. the question of the public land was settled by a law which practically made such land the private property of those who then held it. This turned over to the possessors whatever the Agrarian Commission had not seized, and at the same time recognized the titles of those to whom the commission had actually given allotments. *

A further step in the development of the empire was taken in the year of C. Gracchus' death (121 B.C.). Rome had become involved in a war with two powerful Gallic tribes, the Allobroges and the Arverni, and had defeated both. Advantage was taken of the victory to construct a road across Southern Gaul to Spain, and a settlement of Roman veterans was established at Aquæ Sextiæ to protect it. This led to the formation of a new province. A proposal to found a colony at Narbo followed ; the senate, reluctant to assume additional military burdens, opposed the measure unsuccessfully. Probably the failure of the conscript fathers was due to the attitude of the knights, who saw in Narbo a centre for profitable dealings with the Southern Gauls.[1] *

## § 2. JUGURTHA AND THE NUMIDIAN PROBLEM

The senate had, however, only regained power with the acquiescence of the knights, and it was not long before a fresh break occurred between the two orders in connexion with a war in Africa. Since the war itself was of little serious consequence, its details are of importance only on account of their political effects and will be dismissed as briefly as possible.

After the destruction of Carthage Rome had been content with annexing the immediate territory of her rival as the province of Africa. To the west of this province lay the protected kingdom of Numidia, whose king, Massinissa, had aided Rome in the struggle. His son, Micipsa, succeeded him upon the throne, and at his death in 118 left the kingdom to three heirs, his two sons, Hiempsal and Adherbal, and his nephew, Jugurtha. The three quarrelled and Hiempsal was murdered by Jugurtha, who then went to war with Adherbal and ignominiously defeated him. Adherbal fled to Rome and appealed to the senate, which thus found itself obliged to arbitrate between the two princes. Probably the conscript

[1] Heitland, *The Roman Republic*, II, p. 336.

fathers cared little about the matter and the majority were inclined to favour Jugurtha, partly perhaps because, having in his youth fought in Spain with the Numidian auxiliaries in the Roman army, he had there contrived to gain the friendship of a number of the Roman nobles, partly, no doubt, because he was the king in possession and to support him appeared the course least likely to require serious exertion.[1] Adherbal, however, found a champion in M. Æmilius Scaurus, one of the most eminent and influential of the senators, and it was finally decided to divide the kingdom, for which purpose a commission was despatched to Africa (116 B.C.)

The commission, which was headed by the ex-consul, L. Opimius, awarded the eastern part of Numidia, including the capital, Cirta, together with the principal towns, to Adherbal, leaving the western portion of the kingdom to Jugurtha. This division had an appearance of unfairness since Jugurtha, although having the weaker dynastic claim, received the larger share, but it may have been dictated solely by Roman interests. Adherbal, who was an unambitious and easy-going man, might well appear a safer neighbour to the Roman province than his more energetic rival, while Jugurtha was obviously more competent to keep in order the turbulent tribes who occupied the greater part of the country. In any case, the division was accepted by both princes and for a few years the senate was able to forget Numidia.

This happy state of things was of short duration, for Jugurtha was determined to secure the whole kingdom, and he soon resorted to war to accomplish his purpose. Adherbal naturally appealed again to Rome and the senate despatched a new commission to adjust the trouble, consisting of comparatively young senators, probably because the conscript fathers did not think that a quarrel between two petty African princes was a matter of much importance. By the time the commission arrived Jugurtha had driven Adherbal into Cirta and was besieging the city. He treated the commissioners with courtesy and respect, but he refused to let them enter the beleaguered town or to suspend his operations, so that the commission returned to Rome without accomplishing any-

[1] Sallust (ch. 13) attributes the result to wholesale bribery. Presents were doubtless given, but it seems quite unnecessary to suppose that they had much influence.

thing. The senate, doubtless irritated by this treatment of its representatives, sent out a third commission made up of older and more prominent men with Scaurus at the head, but they were unable to do more than their predecessors.

While Jugurtha was discussing matters with the Romans and evading their demands, he was pressing the siege of Cirta, which was finally forced to surrender. Jugurtha seems to have felt confident that, once he was in full possession of Numidia, the senate would accept the accomplished fact, and in this he was probably correct. The capture of Cirta, however, proved to be his ruin. When the city fell he put Adherbal and his principal supporters to death, but he either caused or failed to prevent the massacre of a number of Italian merchants who were settled in the place and had aided Adherbal in its defence. Perhaps Jugurtha, a barbarian with a thin veneer of civilization, was so enraged by the prolonged resistance that he was for the moment reckless of consequences; more probably he lost control of his troops, who were half-savage tribesmen, and in the hour of triumph they plundered and butchered indiscriminately. At any rate, a considerable number of Italian traders lost their lives, and this event produced an explosion of wrath in Rome.

The senate was still reluctant to go to war, but it was unable to face the storm; the knights were furious at the fate of the traders, and the populace was more than ready to join them in attacking the nobles. Moreover the opposition found a leader in C. Memmius, one of the tribunes elect. Making a virtue of necessity, the senate named Numidia and Italy as the consular provinces for the next year (111), and Numidia fell to L. Calpurnius Bestia. He raised an army and set out for Africa, taking with him on his staff a number of the leading senators, including Scaurus. The conscript fathers still hoped to avoid any serious entanglement in Africa and wished to end the war with as little fighting as possible.[1] Jugurtha and Bestia seem to have understood each other, for the Numidian allowed the Romans to gain some successes and then humbly sued for peace. A treaty was promptly concluded by which, in return for a formal submission accompanied by a few concessions, he was allowed to keep the entire kingdom.

[1] This seems clear from the fact that they rejected the offer of alliance made by Bocchus, king of Mauretania, about this time. (Sallust, ch. 80.)

Bestia now returned to Rome to hold the elections, thinking perhaps that his mission had been successfully accomplished.

In Rome he was met by a storm of indignation. There was much to be said for the treaty, and the senate might under other circumstances have been glad to ratify it. The conscript fathers did not desire the annexation of Numidia, yet it must somehow be kept quiet and governed. Jugurtha, whatever his misdeeds in the past, was obviously the most competent person at hand to occupy the throne. The alternative to his recognition was a long and difficult war from which no real advantage was to be gained for Rome except the gratification of avenging her insulted majesty. To many senators it may well have seemed better to accept a peace with little honour than to plunge into an adventure in Africa at a time when all available soldiers might soon be needed nearer home. In Thrace barbarians were menacing Macedonia,[1] after having inflicted a serious defeat on the Romans in 114, and in 113 the Cimbri had appeared upon the borders of Illyricum and routed a consular army, afterwards moving west into Gaul, where they were now threatening Rome's newly acquired province. The senate's reluctance to engage in a serious war with Jugurtha is thus entirely intelligible, but public opinion, probably very ill-informed in regard to the situation on the frontiers, could see no explanation of the senate's attitude except wholesale corruption. Knights and populace alike were furious at the thought that Jugurtha, after defying Rome and butchering her citizens, should be let off with a merely nominal punishment. Memmius, now in office as tribune, took advantage of the opportunity to demand an investigation into the whole matter of the treaty. In the hope of getting evidence against those who had taken the king's bribes, he had Jugurtha summoned to Rome under a safe-conduct and brought before the assembly. His purpose was, however, thwarted by the action of another tribune, who forbade the Numidian to answer the questions of Memmius. This only increased the prevailing suspicion, and the folly of Jugurtha brought about a crisis.

There was then living in Rome another member of the

[1] Minucius Rufus, the colleague of Albinus in 110, was carrying on a campaign in Thrace as proconsul in 109.

Numidian royal house, Massiva by name, and some of the senators, frightened by the violence of popular and equestrian feeling, began to consider substituting him for Jugurtha. This development frightened the king so much that he had his potential rival murdered. The murderer, however, was caught and confessed that he had been instigated by one of Jugurtha's retinue who stood high in the king's confidence. After this confession no one could pretend to believe in the innocence of Jugurtha, especially when he hastily smuggled the accused officer out of Italy.

The peace party realized that nothing more could be done, so the senate cancelled the treaty, sent Jugurtha home, and prepared for war. The command fell to one of the consuls for 110, Spurius Postumius Albinus. When he reached Africa he found the army so demoralized that he was able to accomplish nothing and spent his time in trying to restore discipline until he was obliged to return to Rome for the purpose of holding the elections. He left his army in charge of his brother Aulus, who, eager for glory or for gold, took the offensive and attempted to capture a town where a large part of Jugurtha's treasure was kept. The attempt failed disastrously and Aulus was not only defeated but forced to surrender. (Early in 109.)

At the news of this fresh disgrace the rage in Rome flared up again. One of the tribunes carried a law creating a special court to try generals and senators suspected of corruption. Apparently the court was to be under the direction of three commissioners elected by the people, while the decisions were to be rendered by equestrian juries. Scaurus, who had been concerned in the recent treaty, managed to have himself elected as one of the commissioners and so avoided a trial, but Bestia and Albinus, along with a few others, including L. Opimius, were condemned. Probably the number of those who were put on trial was not very great, although the names that have reached us can hardly be a complete list. No real investigation seems to have been attempted, and the condemnations were based not on evidence but on rumour and popular passion,[1] so that the guilt of the sufferers is entirely uncertain. The most important result was to give the senate

[1] Sallust (ch. 40, 5) says that the investigation was conducted *aspere violenterque ex rumore et lubidine plebis.*

a warning which it could not disregard against any further negotiations with Jugurtha.

The command in Africa was assigned to Q. Cæcilius Metellus, one of the consuls for 109 B.C., a partisan of the senate whose personal integrity was generally considered as above suspicion. With the support of the senate and amid popular enthusiasm he set about recruiting an army for a serious war, choosing for his staff competent soldiers such as C. Marius rather than prominent senators or diplomats, and when he sailed from Italy the hopes of all parties ran high.

Metellus did not reach Africa till late in the year, and the forces which he found there were so demoralized that he felt it necessary to postpone active operations until discipline could be thoroughly restored. The senate, however, prolonged his *imperium* and was evidently ready to leave him in charge as proconsul as long as might be necessary to end the war. Jugurtha on his side was likewise engaged in organizing his forces and in vain attempts to open negotiations with Metellus. At length the Roman general invaded Numidia and Jugurtha retreated before him, hoping to draw him into the interior and there to surround and destroy his army. Metellus pushed on until the king suddenly attacked him on the Muthul river. Here a battle was fought in which the forces of Jugurtha were repulsed and dispersed. Metellus could report to Rome that he had won a victory, but in reality he had gained very little, for the Numidian people were still loyal to Jugurtha, so that he could gather a new army at will. Nothing but the capture of the king would end the war, but Jugurtha constantly eluded pursuit and baffled the intrigues which Metellus set on foot with the aim of securing his person through the treachery of some of his trusted friends. Although Metellus pressed his operations he was unable to achieve any decisive success, and the war seemed likely to drag on indefinitely.

## § 3. THE RISE OF MARIUS

In Rome the appointment of Metellus to the command had allayed the popular discontent, but his failure to end the war disappointed the public expectations and provoked ugly suspicions. It was difficult to believe that Metellus had been bought as his predecessors were supposed to have been, but men began to suspect that he was either incompetent or that he was letting the war drag on in order to retain his command. Such suspicions might have produced no result if there had not been malcontents in the camp of Metellus, who by his somewhat arrogant bearing offended Marius. Moved by resentment and ambition, the latter began to court popularity with the soldiers and also with the Roman traders in Africa. He succeeded in impressing them with the belief that he and not Metellus was the man to end the war, and letters from the traders soon began to spread this view in Rome. There the public readily seized upon a suggestion so much in harmony with the dominant mood. The knights and people alike were disgusted with the continued failures of the aristocratic generals, and were ready to try what a new man who had fought his way to the front by sheer ability could accomplish. Marius had learned or guessed enough of the drift of sentiment in Rome to realize that there was a chance for him to gain the consulship, and he at length succeeded in extorting from Metellus a furlough so that he could return to Italy to canvass for the office. He was enthusiastically received and triumphantly elected in spite of the efforts of the nobility.

The new consul was not merely a new man but one who had risen from humble origins, his father being a farmer in the neighbourhood of Arpinum. The conscription, which fed the Roman armies from the countryside, sent the young man to Spain to serve under Scipio Æmilianus, then engaged in the war against Numantia. By courage and efficiency Marius attracted the attention and won the commendation of his general, and he returned to Rome resolved on a political career, through which alone it was possible to reach a high position in the army. With the support of the great house of the Metelli he succeeded in securing the quæstorship and the tribuneship. As tribune he showed himself independent and fearless, not hesitating to defy the senate and his own patron, Metellus. Probably because of the offence thus given he was defeated when he offered himself as a candidate for the ædileship, but soon afterwards he was elected prætor, though only with difficulty. After his year of office in Rome he was sent as proprætor to Farther Spain, where he found himself for the first time with an independent military command. By holding the prætorship

Marius had forced his way into the ranks of the nobility, for, though he himself would always remain a new man, his descendants would be nobles. Higher than the prætorship he could not hope to rise under normal circumstances, since the nobles guarded the consulship with the utmost jealousy. For a time, therefore, he took no further part in public life, but he was able to marry into the family of the Cæsars, his wife being an aunt of the great Julius. Marius had early abandoned agriculture for business and had invested money with profit in equestrian syndicates. Such speculations may have led the knights to regard him as more or less one of themselves in spite of his senatorial rank. When he was appointed to the staff of Metellus a new phase of his career opened, and the dexterity or good fortune which led him to seize the opportune moment enabled him to break through the barriers of aristocratic pride and exclusiveness and to secure the consulship.

There was still, however, an obstacle in his path. By a law of C. Gracchus the senate was obliged to designate the consular provinces before the election, and it had prolonged the *imperium* of Metellus in Africa,[1] assigning other tasks to the new consuls. It seemed, therefore, that Marius, although elected by the people to take charge of the Jugurthine war, would have nothing to do with it, but the people were not in a mood to see their will thwarted by the action, intentional or unintentional,[2] of the senate, so a tribune introduced and carried a law conferring the command in Africa upon the popular general. The conscript fathers were obliged to submit and to grant Marius whatever he demanded in the way of soldiers and equipment for fear that what they refused would be immediately given by the people.

In the interval between his election and the time when he could take over the command, Marius set about the task of recruiting his army. He made no attempt to apply the unpopular conscription; instead he called for volunteers and accepted all who were fit for the service without regard to other qualifications. In taking this step Marius was almost certainly blind to its importance, for he was destitute of

[1] Sallust, ch. 73, 7.

[2] It is not certain whether or not the senate foresaw the election of Marius when it made the provincial arrangements.

political insight or statesmanship. As a practical soldier he had learned by experience the poor military quality of small farmers torn from their homes and forced to fight for a cause in which they felt no interest, and he preferred to fill his ranks with veterans out of work and men who freely offered themselves to a trusted leader in the hope of profiting by his success in the field. With a force so gathered he sailed for Africa in 107.

On his arrival he found himself faced by the same difficulties which had confronted Metellus, and he was soon forced to adopt the same plan of campaign, namely, to defeat Jugurtha in the field whenever he could be induced to fight, and to seize and garrison as many of his strongholds as possible in the hope that his influence would finally be so weakened that his subjects and allies would abandon him. Success by such means was likely to be slow, but unless Jugurtha could be killed or captured there was no other way of conducting the war, since the economic and political life of the country was too primitive for any victory in the field or the occupation of any town to be decisive. Marius acted with energy and pressed far into Numidia, but the country with its mountains and deserts was well adapted to guerrilla warfare; the king, eluding the Romans, contrived to retain sufficient prestige to raise new armies and to find allies. When Marius' term as consul expired he had apparently accomplished little, but the senate, perhaps glad to be freed from all responsibility for the war, continued him in command as proconsul.

It is impossible to say how long the war might have continued if Marius had not been fortunate in having as his quæstor L. Cornelius Sulla. This young man, a noble of extraordinary ability, succeeded by his coolness and daring in accomplishing what his superior had failed to achieve. Marius had pressed Jugurtha so closely that the king had taken refuge with Bocchus, king of Mauretania, with whom he was then allied. Sulla, staking his life on his success, went on a diplomatic mission to Bocchus and persuaded him to betray his ally. No doubt the energy of Marius had done much to convince Bocchus of the Roman power, yet it seems unlikely that this impression would have sufficed without the cleverness and audacity of Sulla. At any rate, the war ended with the capture of Jugurtha, and Marius, for the time being at least,

* received the credit in Rome. As to Numidia, the western part was given to Bocchus, while the eastern part remained a client kingdom under Gauda, a prince of the old royal house.

### § 4. THE CIMBRI AND TEUTONES

The Numidian war had ended none too soon, for Rome had need of Marius and his army to defend Italy. A danger, long threatening from the north, had suddenly become critical in consequence of a great military disaster. Some years before two German peoples, known to the Romans as the Cimbri and Teutones, had abandoned their homes near the Baltic and pushed southward in search of new lands. They seem to have made their way along the valley of the Elbe to Bohemia and thence to the valley of the Danube near Belgrade. Here they were defeated by the warlike natives and retreated up the Drave into Pannonia. The Romans had never made any attempt to conquer this region, but they had entered into alliances with some of its tribes. When the Germans menaced her allies, Rome sent Cn. Carbo, consul for the year 113 B.C., with an army to protect them. He might have secured his object without fighting, but in his desire for glory he provoked a battle near Noreia with the result that he was badly beaten and Italy left open to invasion. The Cimbri and Teutones, however, retreated, and making their way slowly around the Alps, entered Gaul, where they were reinforced by other Germans and by a number of Celts. Rome despatched M. Junius Silanus, consul for 109, to Transalpine Gaul,[1] but he also was defeated. The German horde now broke up, some pushing into the interior of Gaul while others remained near the Roman province, where a revolt broke out in Tolosa (Toulouse) and the vicinity, probably because of Rome's failure to protect the people from the Cimbri. In 107 B.C. Marius' colleague in the consulship appeared upon the scene and won some initial success, but his campaign ended in a disaster in which he lost his life and most of his army.

So far neither the knights nor the populace had interfered with the senate in its conduct of affairs in the North. Probably the knights were not greatly concerned about disasters which did not touch their interests, but in 106 the nobles

[1] This province had been organized after the colonization of Narbo.

committed the blunder of alienating them. One of the consuls for that year, Q. Servilius Cæpio, introduced a bill depriving the knights of their control of the juries; the measure seems to have been carried, only to be repealed two years later.[1] Its political effects may perhaps be seen in the election of a new man, Cn. Mallius Maximus, to the consulship for 105.

After the passage of his bill Cæpio took over the command of Gaul, but he accomplished nothing beyond the suppression of a revolt in Tolosa. The suppression of this revolt yielded a large amount of treasure, which was seized by robbers on the way to Rome. Suspicion followed before long and many believed that Cæpio was in league with the bandits, but the senate, disregarding such suspicions, if they had yet arisen, prolonged his *imperium*, and he continued in command of his army as proconsul. In view of the seriousness of the situation Mallius was despatched with a second army. Cæpio should have acted as a subordinate of the consul, but the haughty noble refused to take orders from a new man and the two commanders quarrelled constantly. The senate remonstrated with them and at length the two armies were united at Arausio (the modern Orange), but the disputes between the commanders continued unabated, and they could agree upon no plan of action. Finally, after Mallius had agreed to negotiate with the Cimbri, Cæpio ordered his men to attack them. The result was that the Roman armies blundered into a battle in which they were defeated in detail (Oct. 6, 105). The disaster was the greatest which had befallen Rome since Cannæ; if we may believe the reports, 80,000 Romans were slain. The passes of the Alps now lay open to the Germans, but again they missed their opportunity and preferred the pillaging of Gaul to the invasion of Italy. This gave the Romans a respite in which to reorganize their army, but, as such good fortune was beyond anticipation, the news of the disaster at Arausio produced a panic. Marius and his army were still in Africa and he was legally ineligible for a second consulship, but the law was ignored in view of the public

[1] There is some doubt as to whether the bill was passed, but in this connection the question is of little importance, since the proposal would itself be enough to alienate the knights. For a discussion of the subject with references see Holmes, *The Roman Republic*, I, p. 354, and Last, *Camb. Anc. Hist.*, IX, pp. 162–63.

*

danger,[1] and he was elected in his absence with another new man as his colleague. Cæpio was deprived of his proconsular *imperium* by a vote of the people, and later both he and Mallius were driven into exile.

While the people were taking vengeance for past disasters, Marius was busy with preparations to avoid new ones in the future. Re-elected to a third consulship in 103 B.C., he made use of the time given him by the Cimbri and Teutones to remodel the Roman army. He recruited his forces, at least in part, by the volunteer method, which he had found effective in his African campaign, improved their organization, imposed a rigid discipline, and adopted a new system of drill, based on that employed in the schools for training gladiators, a system which had already been to some extent introduced into the camp by Rutilius Rufus, the colleague of Mallius in the consulship.

By the time of the elections for 102 B.C. (sometime in 103) the nobles had recovered something of their confidence. The condemnation of Mallius and Cæpio had no doubt allayed popular anger, and Rome again possessed efficient armies as a result of Marius' strenuous exertions. The aristocracy determined that they would no longer submit to the humiliation of the continued re-election of a new man to the highest office and ventured to put forward candidates of their own. The death of his colleague forced Marius to come to Rome to preside over the election, and he soon found that he would encounter vigorous opposition. To secure a fourth consulship he allied himself with the most influential of the tribunes, L. Appuleius Saturninus. The combination was successful in electing Marius, but one of the candidates of the nobility, Q. Lutatius Catulus, was chosen as his colleague. It was fortunate for Rome that Marius remained in office, for it was in 102 B.C. that the long-dreaded invasion finally came.

The failure of the Cimbri and Teutones to follow up their victory at Arausio by attacking Italy is probably to be explained by the fact that at the time they had no designs upon that country. What they were seeking was a place in

[1] In this period there was no regular time for the consular elections, and I have assumed that they took place after the defeat at Arausio was known. If they were held earlier, the result may have been due in part to the irritation of the knights over Cæpio's law.

which they could settle permanently, and they still hoped to find it in Gaul. This hope they were finally forced to abandon; it was comparatively easy for such a horde to invade and plunder an ill-organized and ill-defended country, forcing the inhabitants to take refuge in the walled towns. These towns, however, proved to be an insurmountable obstacle, for until they were captured a permanent occupation of the land was impossible, and the invaders were unable to capture them. The barbarians had neither the organization, the discipline, nor adequate supplies to make prolonged sieges practicable, and they lacked the technical and engineering skill to capture fortified places by assault. The plunder of the country would support them for a time, but their presence in any district by making agriculture difficult soon forced them to move on. They could not cultivate the soil themselves, because to do so they would be forced to scatter over the land and expose themselves to sallies from the towns. Thus they moved from one district to another, finding no place where they could settle down. By the end of 103 the exhaustion of Gaul was probably so great that they were forced to turn elsewhere. The Cimbri had already made an unsuccessful attempt to invade Spain while the Teutones remained in Gaul, and now both peoples resolved to cross the Alps into Italy.

The new movement was more or less carefully planned; since their number was too great to make it easy to live off the country they traversed if they moved as a single mass, it was agreed that the Teutones should proceed through the Transalpine province, while the Cimbri should circle around the Alps and enter Italy through the Brenner pass, of whose existence they had learned in their wanderings.[1]

In the summer of 102 the Teutones, having crossed the Rhone, began their march toward Italy along the Roman military road. Marius was at hand with his army, but he preferred to take no chances and contented himself with watching them closely. Finally, at Aquæ Sextiæ, he hazarded a battle. By posting a body of men, partly camp followers, in a position where they could remain invisible till the proper time and then appear in the semblance of a fresh force in the

[1] I have omitted the movements of the Tigurini, a Celtic tribe akin to the Helvetii, who had joined the Germans, because after the defeat of the latter they returned to their homes without reaching Italy.

rear of the Germans, he threw the Teutones into a panic and annihilated them as a fighting force.

The invasion of the Cimbri was somewhat delayed because of the longer route which they had taken, but all Italy knew that they were coming. Marius received a fifth consulship (for 101 B.C.), and hastened with his army from Transalpine to Cisalpine Gaul, where the Cimbri had already appeared while he was busy with the Teutones. Catulus, Marius' colleague as consul, had sought to check them, but his troops proved unreliable and he was forced to retreat. For his success in extricating his army he claimed much credit, and, as he was a thorough-going aristocrat, the senate was ready to prolong his *imperium*. In 101 Marius joined him with his army, but this time the noble and the new man co-operated and together they destroyed the invading host in the battle of the Raudine plain, a level district in the Po valley near Vercellæ.

Italy breathed freely at last and was ready to greet her hero. Marius shared his triumph with Catulus, but in the eyes of all save a few jealous nobles it was he who had saved Rome. This was the hour of his glory; if he had retired to private life at the end of his fifth consulship, it would have been well for him, for his reputation, and for Rome. But even if he wished to do so, and there is no reason to suppose that he did, he was bound by his military reforms to continue active in politics. To understand this necessity, as well as much in the subsequent history of Rome, it is desirable to examine those reforms in more detail.

## § 5. THE MILITARY REFORMS OF MARIUS

Before Marius the Roman army was based upon conscription, which was applied theoretically to all citizens who owned a certain amount of property, though in practice the burden fell chiefly on the landowners and especially on the poorer members of this class. The bulk of the Roman citizens serving in the ranks were thus small farmers forced by the state to exchange the plough for the sword and often doing so with extreme reluctance. Marius abandoned this system and called for volunteers, and from this time on the new mode of recruiting prevailed. It will be seen at once that it essentially altered the character of the army. The reluctant farmer disappeared, and his place was taken by men with nothing to lose who saw in service under a successful general their only prospect of escape from poverty. Of course there were some who enlisted in the hope of adventure rather than of gain, but the economic motive was the dominant one, and with the adoption of the volunteer system began the development of a professional army. Other changes naturally followed. As long as the soldiers were taken from the propertied class and were expected to furnish their own equipment there were inevitably distinctions in the service based on wealth. These had been losing their original justification as in the course of time the property qualification was lowered[1] and the state provided part of the equipment. With the new type of recruits all such distinctions were abolished and nothing was expected of the men except themselves. They were now armed and taught the use of their weapons after they had volunteered, and the new training, borrowed from the gladiatorial schools, while it produced more skilful swordsmen, required a longer time to turn the raw recruit into an efficient soldier.

Marius also carried to completion a reorganization of the legion which had already been begun, by which maniples lost their old importance and the cohort became the principal unit. The legion, whose nominal strength was 6000 men, was divided into 60 centuries each under a centurion, and these centuries were grouped into ten cohorts commanded by legates of the general. The staff officers were still supplied by the military tribunes, but since these were mostly young men of the wealthier classes they were less and less trusted with important military duties. In the new army the distinction between the higher and the lower officers was increased, and the common soldier had less and less chance of promotion beyond the rank of centurion.

These changes undoubtedly increased the efficiency of the army, but their main significance lay in the substitution of the volunteer for the landowner. This had consequences of the most far-reaching character, whether for good or evil. It freed the small farmer from a heavy burden which was fast becoming unbearable, and opened a new source from which

[1] The property qualification for the fifth class was lowered, in fact, by the decline in the value of money, though it does not seem to have been otherwise changed.

an abundant supply of recruits could readily be obtained without inflicting serious hardship upon any class, but at the same time it created a proletarian army over which the state could exercise only a very imperfect control.

That after the reforms of Marius the Roman armies were proletarian in composition has long been recognized by historians, but too often they have neglected to look further. There were in the Roman world two distinct kinds of proletariat. In the first place there was the urban rabble in Rome and other cities of Italy, without adequate employment and relying on the government for help to enable them to live. In the country districts there existed another proletariat made up of agricultural labourers, who in spite of slavery were still numerous in parts of the peninsula, and small farmers so burdened by debt that they were on the verge of ruin. The aspirations of the new armies make it clear that the urban rabble, apart from those who had recently drifted in from the country, furnished few recruits, and that most of the volunteers came from the rural proletariat. The agricultural labourer naturally wanted a farm of his own, and the small proprietor about to lose his land looked anxiously for an opportunity to make a fresh start free from debt. Both classes henceforth saw in the army the best means of securing what they ardently desired, but they were not disposed to rely entirely upon their pay and their share of the booty, and the general in search of recruits found it necessary to offer other inducements, the most effective being the promise that, when the army was disbanded, the soldiers should be further rewarded by an allotment of land. Such a promise was enough to bring the rural proletariat flocking to the standards if they believed that the man who made it was likely to lead them to victory, and that he could be trusted to fulfil his promises. Since the average noble, even though elected to high office by the aristocratic machine, seldom possessed these qualifications, when the state came to rely on volunteer armies, it found itself more and more driven to seek the help of the men who could secure the recruits.

The new type of army, therefore, gave great importance to the few men who had somehow won the confidence of the rural proletariat. They might be nobles or new men, supporters or opponents of the senate, for the country folk cared little for politics in comparison with land, but in an emergency these men were indispensable. If there was time enough to organize a regular recruiting campaign it might be possible for the average noble to get soldiers, perhaps with a little help from the conscription, which was never formally abolished, but since the Republic had no considerable standing army and raised the forces necessary for a serious campaign only when the need arose, disbanding them as soon as possible when the need was over, it generally delayed its preparations until prompt action was essential and thus found itself obliged to turn to one of the generals with established reputations whose names would bring recruits promptly.

The new system had other consequences as well. Henceforth the army belonged to the commander to a degree unknown in the past. The soldiers had enlisted to fight under a particular general, and they would not patiently permit him to be superseded by another, who might not hold himself bound by his predecessor's engagements.[1] Nor were the soldiers willing to trust the senate, since here they were dealing with a corporate body which could easily find pretexts for evading the fulfilment of its pledges. The allotments for the soldiers would require legislation, and the senators could raise objections on matters of detail to any bill proposed or defeat it in the assembly through the power of their machine if they dared not oppose the measure in the senate itself. In either case it would be impossible to hold anyone in particular responsible. The soldiers, therefore, stood by their general, and, once he had been commissioned by the state to raise an army, it was impossible except in very unusual circumstances to take it from him, nor would his army hesitate to support him against the government if he could find a decent pretext for attacking it. This last qualification is one whose importance is uncertain but was probably considerable, for although the armies were proletarian in character they were made up of Romans, and even the poorest Romans had some respect for the constitution; hence we may reasonably

[1] H. Last (*Camb. Anc. Hist.*, IX, p. 135) holds that the soldiers were anxious to remain in the army as long as possible. I believe, on the contrary, that they desired to get their farms as soon as they could. The veterans of Lucullus who re-enlisted under Pompey probably did so to improve their chances of getting land, feeling that neither Lucullus nor the senate would reward them.

doubt whether they would have followed a general bent openly on his own aggrandizement, however ready to champion his cause if he should seem illegally attacked by enemies in power.

If the army fell more than ever under the control of its general, the general in turn became a servant of his army. It was impossible for him to retire from public life when he had won the victory and disbanded his soldiers, for he had still to redeem the promises by which he had gathered his recruits. He must, therefore, continue to take an active part in public life until the necessary measures had been passed. Marius, like Pompey afterwards, could not escape his obligations to his men, but was forced by his military success to attempt to play a leading part in politics.

# CHAPTER VI

# POLITICAL DISSENSIONS AND THE SOCIAL WAR

## § 1. MARIUS AND THE DEMOCRATS

WHEN Marius became a candidate for a sixth consulship he found the aristocracy united against him, and so was forced to rely on the democrats, whose leaders at the moment were Saturninus and Glaucia. A combination was arranged by which Marius was to be consul, Glaucia prætor, and Saturninus tribune. Moreover, since Marius had little ability as an orator, the carrying out of his programme was to be undertaken by his partners, in which task the most important role fell to Saturninus. C. Servilius Glaucia seems to have been a coarse but witty and effective mob orator. Of his previous career we know very little, except that he had been tribune and had carried a law in regard to extortion in the provinces which restored the juries to the knights.[1] L. Appuleius Saturninus seems to have been an abler man ; he was an eloquent speaker and seems to have taken up the role of a popular leader because of a personal grievance against the senate. During his quæstorship (105 or 104 B.C.) he had been in charge of the corn supply, but on account of a rise in the price the senate superseded him by transferring this charge to its leading member, Scaurus, and this contemptuous treatment turned Saturninus into an enemy of that body. Having been elected tribune for 103 B.C., he proposed a bill reducing the price at which grain was distributed to the rabble,[2] in spite of the protests of one of the quæstors in charge of the treasury that it was impossible to defray the expense and a resolution of the senate condemning

[1] It did so if Cæpio's bill was passed ; if not, Glaucia's law must have contained other provisions favourable to the knights (Cicero, *Brutus*, ch. 62, 224).

[2] See H. Last in *Camb. Anc. Hist.*, IX, pp. 165–66.

the measure. Whether the bill was ultimately passed or not, it no doubt served its purpose by securing the favour of the mob for its proposer. Saturninus also brought forward a bill for distributing land in Africa to the veterans of Marius, which he carried by driving from the assembly a tribune who attempted to interpose a veto. In addition to his laws[1] Saturninus in this same year assisted Marius to secure election to his fourth consulship. Saturninus was thus allied with Marius as early as 103 B.C., and he had shown himself ready to resort to violence to gain his ends. In the next year Metellus, who had preceded Marius in the command against Jugurtha and who had assumed the surname of Numidicus, was censor, and he attempted to expel both Saturninus and Glaucia from the senate, but his colleague thwarted the attempt. In 101 B.C. both men supported Marius against the nobility, and he on his side availed himself of their services. Neither party to the bargain indeed had much choice, for although Saturninus and Glaucia had retained their seats in the senate, they probably needed the protection of office against further attacks and could hardly hope to obtain it without the help of Marius, while he needed their assistance to redeem his promises to his soldiers.

The elections for 100 B.C. (in 101) were bitterly contested. Marius had disbanded his army after his triumph and the city was full of his veterans, but, even so, it was necessary to resort to bribery. Marius was returned as consul with a subservient colleague, and Glaucia secured the prætorship. Saturninus, however, encountered greater difficulty, and when it seemed likely that he would be defeated by another candidate, the soldiers set upon and killed his competitor, and Saturninus was declared elected. He was naturally credited with having instigated the murder, and the event, whether he was innocent or guilty, was a sinister omen for the future. Why the democrats were more successful in the assembly of centuries than in the tribal assembly we can only conjecture, but it is probable that the knights supported Marius and Glaucia with greater unanimity than Saturninus, and that Marius was popular with the country gentry, who could probably control a number of the centuries of the higher

[1] Saturninus also passed a law concerning treason, the *lex Appuleia de maiestate*, but its date (103 or 100 B.C.) and its provisions are very uncertain.

classes in the rural tribes but were unable to control some of these tribes when they voted as tribes. Moreover, many of the soldiers were Latins or Italians, and it is not unlikely that most of the citizens among them came from a few of the outlying rural tribes where farm labourers and small landowners were still numerous, so that their influence in the assembly was not as great as might have been expected.

## § 2. THE FAILURE OF THE COALITION

Once in office Marius and his partners attempted to carry out their programme. They seem to have aimed simply at satisfying the veterans, and Saturninus brought forward an agrarian bill which provided for the assignment of lands in Transalpine Gaul and for the founding of colonies outside Italy; the Italian allies were to share in the distribution, and in each colony Marius was authorized to bestow full Roman citizenship on three of them. The bill included a clause by which all senators were required to take an oath to observe it on pain of banishment. This clause was obviously intended to prevent the cancellation of the law by the senate, since its proposer must have foreseen that it could only be carried by violence, as was actually the case.

The conscript fathers were thus placed in a dilemma, and the question of the moment was whether or not to take the oath. All eyes were fixed on Marius and he bungled the matter. Possibly, as some ancient writers believed, he was overcome by a desire to ruin Metellus in return for his scornful attitude in former years; perhaps, however, he trusted to assurances that his men should have the lands if he would extricate the senate from its difficulties; or perhaps the plain, blunt soldier under pressure from both sides attempted to evade the issue and to please everybody. At first, either influenced by the senators or with a malevolent eye on Metellus, he declared that he would not take the oath; then after Metellus had publicly said the same, Marius changed his mind and at the last moment swore to observe the law "as far as it was legal." Metellus scornfully refused to break his word and went into exile, but the rest of the senators readily followed the example of Marius, for by his qualification he had made the oath at once inoffensive and worthless. No senator had any objection to swearing to observe a law, for this he was constitutionally bound to do, and the addition of those few words left him quite free to inquire at any time into the legal validity of the law so that the purpose of the clause was defeated in its observance.

By his course Marius had practically broken with his partners, and they were left in a very precarious position. Since they did not dare to retire into private life and face the prosecution which would inevitably be brought against them, they were prepared to go to any lengths to remain in office. In the elections for 99 B.C. Marius was not a candidate, perhaps believing that with the agrarian law passed he had achieved his purpose,[1] or perhaps foreseeing defeat. Saturninus and Glaucia were thus left to their own devices. The former was elected tribune for the third time, and Glaucia stood for the consulship illegally, since he was actually prætor and the law required an interval of two years between different magistracies. Nevertheless, his candidacy was accepted, but this proved insufficient, since his opponent Memmius seemed almost certain to be successful. In desperation he had Memmius assassinated and so precipitated his own doom. Probably the knights were already sick of the mob leader, and the murder of Memmius threw the game into the senate's hands. Saturninus and Glaucia seized the Capitol and prepared for a struggle, while the conscript fathers passed the last decree instructing Marius to restore order by suppressing his former friends. After a brief hesitation Marius obeyed the senate's instructions ; by cutting off the supply of water, he compelled Saturninus and Glaucia to surrender, promising that their lives should be spared. The general had tried to make the best of a bad business, but he failed to protect his prisoners, who were murdered by a mob of knights and nobles.

Marius was of course politically ruined, for his vacillation and blundering had alienated all parties. Soon after he laid down his sixth consulship he left Rome for a prolonged trip in the East. On his return he found himself a nonentity, and he would probably never have emerged from obscurity if events had not suddenly taken a new turn.

[1] Either in this year or the next Marius established a colony in Corsica, showing that he began at least to carry out the agrarian law.

## § 3. THE REVIVAL OF THE SENATORIAL MACHINE

With the overthrow of Saturninus and Glaucia the control slipped back into the hands of the senate, for the knights, probably alarmed by the violent methods of the popular party, had rallied to the support of the aristocratic machine. For the moment the world was moderately peaceful, for a second slave war in Sicily, which had broken out in 103 B.C., was finally suppressed (in 99), and a revolt in Spain (97–93 B.C.) was successfully handled. In the East the senate in 96 accepted the legacy of Cyrene, which was controlled (or left uncontrolled) from Utica, and this forward step was doubtless gratifying to the knights. Altogether the capitalists of Rome seem to have thought that the nobles were doing well enough and that attacks upon their government were unnecessary.

Once more securely in power, the senate made short work of the laws of Saturninus, which were promptly cancelled. * The Marian veterans, as well as the class from which they came, must have lost any illusions they may have cherished in regard to the senate's attitude. Real statesmanship would have seized the opportunity to convince them that they could trust to the gratitude of the senate and not solely to their general for a reward for their services to the state, but the nobles were too short-sighted to rise to the occasion and the opportunity was missed.

Once rid of the laws of Saturninus, the machine took a turn at legislation in its own interests. In 98 B.C. the Cæcilian-Didian law was passed, requiring the publication of a bill at least seventeen days before a vote was taken on it in the assembly and making it illegal to legislate on more than one subject in a single bill. The law was entirely justified, but it was probably intended as a check on future agitators like Saturninus rather than as a safeguard for the people. It would prevent a tribune from taking the machine by surprise, and from carrying an unpopular measure by combining it with one which met with greater favour from the rabble or the knights. In 95 B.C. the Licinian-Mucian law strengthened the precautions against non-citizens voting in the assembly and so increasing the votes which were likely to be cast against the machine in the rural tribes. Probably neither of * these laws was opposed by the rabble or the knights.

The conduct of the government may have been agreeable enough to the knights, but the use made of the juries by the latter was becoming intolerable to the senate. The knights had long been abusing their power in the courts to put pressure upon the governors of the provinces, who were, of course, invariably prominent and influential senators. In the eyes of the nobles the cup of equestrian iniquity was filled to overflowing in 92 B.C. when one of their juries condemned Rutilius Rufus, whose sturdy integrity had interfered with their profits in Asia. In revenge they charged him with extortion and drove him into exile. In ironic answer to the verdict of the jury he retired to the very province which he had been convicted of plundering and passed the remainder of his life amid the respect and affection of his alleged victims. This scandalous verdict aroused such resentment that a powerful section of the nobility was ready to venture an attack upon equestrian privileges.

## § 4. THE TRIBUNATE OF DRUSUS

The leader of the new movement was M. Livius Drusus, the son of the man who had done so much to ruin C. Gracchus. He now came forward in the role of a Tory-Democrat, was elected tribune for 91 B.C., and with the support of a majority in the senate put forward an extensive programme of reform. Whatever may have been the character of the father, the younger Drusus was undoubtedly honest and well-intentioned, but with a very exalted opinion of his own virtue and wisdom. As a reformer he seems to have had two main objects in view, to strengthen the senate and to extend Roman citizenship to the Italian allies.

To achieve the first object he proposed to double the size of the senate by including in it some 300 knights and to take the juries henceforth from the new senate and the knights.[1] On the surface the measure seemed to be intended chiefly to reorganize the courts, but its purpose was probably deeper than this. The nobles had learned by bitter experience that the senatorial machine could not control the assembly without the help of the knights and their retainers in the rural

[1] As to the provisions of the bill I have accepted the view of P. A. Seymour, *The Policy of Livius Drusus the Younger*, p. 422.

tribes, and that such help must be paid for by subservience in all matters seriously affecting the interests of the class which held the balance of power. To some of the senators this state of affairs had come to seem unendurable and the scheme of Drusus was a well-considered plan to remedy it. If 300 knights were transferred from the equestrian order to the senate, they would be compelled to modify their investments in conformity with the law, and henceforth they could engage in no business enterprises except such as were open to the senators. Since their economic interests would thus become identical with those of the nobility, they could hardly help falling into line with the older senators. In this way the aristocratic machine, strengthened by their support and that of their retainers, might regain a firm control of the assembly. Thus at one stroke the senate would be freed from the need of conciliating the knights and from the fear of their vengeance through the courts.

The extension of the franchise to the allies may have presented itself to Drusus and his supporters as an independent and separate measure, or it may have had in part the same purpose as the bill concerning the juries. If the Latins and Italians were given the right to vote, it was obvious that very few of them would be able to make use of it. The few who did would under normal circumstances come from the propertied class, and, although there were doubtless many business men among the allies likely to side with the knights, the majority might belong to the landed gentry, who could reasonably be expected to ally themselves with the nobles. At any rate, some of the senators seem to have become convinced that in the existing condition of affairs the chance was worth taking. Moreover, since it would be necessary either to distribute the new citizens among the existing tribes and centuries or to form them into new ones, it might be possible to carry out their registration in a way advantageous to the senate.

Such considerations will account for the fact that at first Drusus found a majority of the conscript fathers prepared to give some of his proposals a half-hearted support. That a strong minority should be bitterly opposed to them was only to be expected, for to increase the size of the senate was to outrage the aristocratic exclusiveness of a large section of the nobility, and to bestow a vote on the allies would seem to many a veritable "leap in the dark." There were fears that the new senators might form a party by themselves, and there was a certainty that the reforms, whatever their ultimate effect, would provoke an immediate storm. Moreover, it was very doubtful if the measures could be carried, and many of the more cautious nobles were little inclined to face the wrath of the knights and the rabble uselessly. The knights as a class were sure to fight against the jury bill to the last ditch, for, while some of them might hope to secure seats in the senate, the great majority could only lose by it. Moreover, it may be doubted whether most of the richest members of the class had any wish to change their status; hitherto they had preferred business to politics and they were now invited to abandon business and to accept the burdens of public life with few of the rewards. The nobles were not likely to support the new senators as candidates for office, and mere membership in the senate without a chance of office was not a particularly attractive bait. In spite, therefore, of its apparent concession to the knights, the jury bill was sure to encounter their united resistance, and the rabble, whose interests were not affected, would probably join them against the nobles. As to the extension of citizenship to the allies, both the knights and the populace were likely to be of one mind.

The chances that Drusus could carry his reforms were, therefore, slight, and he recognized that he must somehow contrive to break up the opposition. Any bid to the knights was useless, but it was not impossible that the rabble might be won by adequate bribes. Accordingly he put forward several other measures intended to gain popularity for himself, including a bill for founding colonies in Italy and Sicily, perhaps a revival of his father's plan, and an extension of the corn law; probably to get money for this extension he proposed to debase the currency. The colonial proposal aroused considerable apprehension among the allies, who still retained some of the Roman public land in their possession,[1] and they were only kept quiet by his promises of citizenship. This addition to his programme did not make his task easier, for each new bill brought new enemies into the field against him. As the year wore on

[1] The settlement of 111 B.C. may not have applied to public land held by the allies, or they may have feared that it would be violated to establish the colonies.

it became clear that if his measures were voted on one by one, even if he could so far overcome the systematic obstruction of his opponents as to bring them to a vote at all, they were certain to be defeated. His only hope of success was to ignore the recently enacted Cæcilian-Didian law and combine several of his measures in a single bill. By this means and by violence he secured a majority for some of his bills, but his success was of brief duration, for in the senate his opponents won over enough members to cancel his laws.

Although one part of his reform programme had failed, he refused to abandon the second part, probably because he had committed himself too deeply to the Italians to draw back, and he prepared to bring a bill granting citizenship to the allies before the assembly. He had already entered into close relations with the leading men in some of the Latin and Italian communities; these relations were viewed with great suspicion by his opponents, who published an oath supposed to have been taken by Drusus and his Italian friends. Treason was openly charged, and it seems clear that, whether the oath was genuine or not, Drusus was being driven steadily in the direction of leading the Italians in an insurrection against Rome if his law in favour of the allies should be defeated.[1] He was saved from a situation from which he could not extricate himself with honour by the hand of an assassin; one evening as he was dismissing a crowd of visitors he was stabbed by someone in the crowd and died in a short time, asking those about him if the Republic would ever have such a citizen again.[2]

No attempt was made to discover the murderer, whose crime put an end to the hopes of the Italians that they could obtain citizenship by peaceful agitation. Moreover, many of their leaders felt that they were compromised by their relations with the dead tribune and that their own safety now called for resolute action. The death of Drusus was, therefore, the signal for a revolt on the part of the allies.

[1] We hear of an army of 10,000 Italians which started to march on Rome in the lifetime of Drusus, but was persuaded to turn back by representations that the senate was friendly to their claims. (Diodorus, xxxvii, ch. 13.)

[2] Velleius, ii, ch. 14, 2.

## § 5. THE SOCIAL WAR

The revolt of the Italian allies began at Asculum in Picenum * and quickly spread through Central Italy and Samnium. The rebels established their headquarters at Corfinium, which they re-named Italia, and here they set up a government * modelled more or less closely on that of Rome. From the scanty information at our disposal it is impossible to reconstruct the details of the war which followed and which is known as the Social War;[1] only the broad outlines emerge clearly. The rebels had no lack of trained soldiers who had fought in the Roman armies, but, since the higher officers of these armies had always been Romans, they were lacking in experienced generals. Nevertheless, they found leaders capable of directing their forces with success; the first year of the war seemed to give them a good prospect of victory, and in the end Rome was only able to suppress the insurrection by concessions.

The winter (91–90 B.C.) was spent by both sides in preparations. At Rome the party which had opposed Drusus was sufficiently strong to pass a law proposed by Q. Varius, one of the tribunes, bringing the friends of the reformer to trial on the charge of treason, and a number of the senators and nobles who had supported Drusus were banished. The overtures of the allies for a peaceful settlement were rejected, and in the spring one consul took the field in the North with Marius as one of his legates, while the other, among whose legates was Sulla, was given charge of the forces operating in the South against the Samnites. In the North the Romans, in spite of some reverses, were so far successful as to be able to besiege Asculum, but in the South the rebels won Apulia and Lucania to their cause and invaded Campania. On the whole, therefore, the Romans had decidedly lost ground, and with winter came a revolt in Etruria and Umbria, which had hitherto been loyal. The situation thus became so menacing that Roman pride gave way, and toward the close of the year (90) a law[2] was passed granting full citizenship to such allied communities as had not revolted or should at once return to their allegiance. This concession checked the spread of the

[1] The war is called the Social War because it was between Rome and her * allies (*socii*).

[2] The *lex Julia*.

ITALY
English Miles
0 50 100 150 200
Vercellae
Mantua
CISALPINE
GAUL
Mutina
Po R.
Luca
Faesulae
Arno R.
Arretium
ETRURIA
Perusia
UMBRIA
PICENUM
Ariminum
Ancona
Asculum
Adriatic Sea
ILLYRICUM
CORSICA
Cosa
Tiber R.
Corfinium
Rome
Praeneste
Marsi
Arpinum
Fregellae
Samnites
Minturnae
Capua
Nola
CAMPANIA
Misenum
Naples
SARDINIA
Tyrrhenian
Sea
LUCANIA
Brundisium
Tarentum
BRUTTIUM
Naulochus
Messana
Lilybaeum
SICILY
AFRICA
R.C.
10
14
18
46
42
38
14 E.

insurrection and largely restored Roman authority in Etruria and Umbria, but in Central Italy the war continued.

In 89 both consuls were in the North, and Sulla, as the legate of one of them, was given the chief command in the South. The tide now turned in Rome's favour; in the North the rebellion was broken, while Sulla gained several important victories in the South. These successes in the field were, however, accompanied by new concessions to the allies. In the course of the year two tribunes carried a law[1] which provided that all Italians should receive citizenship who made application for it within sixty days. This measure in combination with the successes of the Roman generals decided the contest, although the Samnites still held out.

The protracted struggle at home had disastrous results abroad; before order could be restored in Italy, Rome was forced to make preparations for a campaign in the East, where Mithridates, king of Pontus, had taken advantage of the troubles in Italy to extend his power. In the elections for 88 Sulla was chosen consul, and the command in the East was assigned to him. Marius, however, did not approve of this arrangement, and he found a tribune who was ready to set it aside.

## § 6. MARIUS AND SULLA

The Social War had brought Marius again into public notice. In the hour of danger he had been entrusted with the command of an army, and he had rendered efficient service, but he had been discarded as soon as possible[2] and felt that he had not yet blotted out the memory of his sixth consulship. Seeing in the impending war against Mithridates an opportunity of regaining his old popularity, he was determined to obtain the command.

If the Social War had done something for Marius, it had also brought Sulla to the front. His career had been retarded by his poverty, and he had only secured the prætorship with difficulty. It seems likely that in normal times he would never have risen higher, but in the crisis of the struggle

[1] The *lex Plautia-Papiria*. *

[2] Plutarch (*Marius*, ch. 33, 3) says that he resigned on the ground of bodily infirmity, but in view of his eagerness to secure the command in the East we may safely assume that the resignation was involuntary.

between Rome and her allies military talent was all-important and Sulla rose rapidly. In purely political matters he had, so far as is known, taken no part, but he seems to have been regarded with favour by the aristocracy. The consulship was the reward for his victories against the rebels, although Sulla is said to have valued it chiefly because of the eastern command which went with it.[1] This is probable enough, and Sulla was not the man to let anyone deprive him of a coveted prize without a struggle.

At this time (88 B.C.) Roman politics were in a highly confused condition as a result of the war. At its outbreak the party hostile to Drusus had, as has already been mentioned, driven a number of the reformer's friends among the senators into exile on the charge of treason, and it seems fairly certain that this party was dominated by the knights. Before the first year of the war (90) had ended a reaction occurred and concessions were granted to the allies. In the next year the reaction went still further; not only were the concessions extended, but the knights were deprived of their monopoly of the juries.[2] This would seem a clear indication that the senatorial machine had regained control, and the knights were doubtless in a very bad humour. The concessions so far made, however, had not settled the Italian question; the allies had acquired citizenship, but in order to vote it was necessary that they should be registered in the tribes and centuries. How this registration should be carried out now became a burning issue. There was a strong party desirous of restricting them to a limited number of tribes, so as to leave the old citizens in control of the assembly, while another party wished to distribute them among all the tribes.[3] The senate seems to have favoured the policy of restriction, while the Italians were strongly opposed to it.

The leading tribune for the year was P. Sulpicius Rufus, who had been a friend of Drusus and was ready to come forward as the champion of the Italian claims. To do this with any chance of success he needed the support of the knights and perhaps of Marius as well. His enemies, of course, charged him with selling himself, asserting that Marius had paid his debts in return for the eastern command. In any case

* [1] Plutarch, *Sulla*, ch. 7, 1. [2] The *lex Plautia judicaria*.

[3] See Appendix 4.

Sulpicius brought forward several laws, one of which recalled the exiles, most of whom, if not all, were former friends of Drusus, and another provided for the registration of the Italians and the freedmen in all the tribes. The inclusion of the freedmen, who had long been restricted to one of the city tribes,[1] was probably a concession to the knights and a bid for their support. The bills of course encountered bitter opposition, and the political struggle soon became disorderly. The consuls, Sulla and Pompeius Rufus, seized the opportunity to proclaim a suspension of all public business, so that no meeting of the assembly could be held, probably hoping that delay would increase the senate's chances of defeating the bills. Sulpicius certainly acted as though he believed that this would be the result, for he met the proclamation by rioting, and did not hesitate to attack the consuls themselves; Pompeius Rufus narrowly escaped from the mob, while Sulla was compelled to seek shelter in the house of Marius. Finally the proclamation was cancelled, and Sulla left the city to join his army, which was then besieging Nola. Sulpicius promptly passed his bills, together with a further law transferring the command of the eastern war from Sulla to Marius. Such an act was without precedent, for Marius was then a private citizen, but it was not illegal if all forms were properly observed. The real objection to it was that Sulla was very unlikely to submit and that the violent means which Sulpicius had employed furnished an excellent pretext for resistance.

Sulla at Nola showed no hesitation in deciding on his course. His motives are open to various interpretations, and some historians have persuaded themselves that patriotism and the conviction that he was the fittest man for the task were among the chief. It is possible, however, to construe his conduct in a way less favourable to his character. All his life Sulla, a man who loved luxury and pleasure, had struggled with poverty. Since the general who defeated Mithridates would have an opportunity to amass a fortune, Sulla may have had no nobler desire than to acquire wealth which he could use for his own gratification. Certain it is that he paid no attention to the conduct of Sulpicius until his own prospects

[1] Unless a law passed by Æmilius Scaurus of whose provisions we are ignorant had made some change.

were threatened, and that he then became acutely aware of its riotous illegality. He believed that he could count upon his troops, since the men were devoted to him personally, and were as eager for the plunder of the East as he himself. Accordingly he assembled his soldiers and informed them of the transfer of the command, doubtless alluding to the recent disorder in Rome. Although he did not directly appeal to them to march on Rome under his banner, he said enough to elicit an expression of their feelings. Their response was all he could have wished, for, in addition to their devotion to him, they were afraid that Marius would take other troops to the East and leave them to complete the pacification of Italy. Sure now of his army, Sulla marched straight upon the city, and was joined on the way by his colleague, Pompeius Rufus. They probably justified their action by the assumption that Sulpicius was at the head of a mob which was coercing both senate and people to such a degree as rendered it necessary for the consuls to intervene and restore constitutional government by armed force. If the senate had not formally passed the last decree, it could be plausibly alleged that this was only because the conscript fathers did not dare to act.

Whatever pretexts were found or needed, Sulla was easily successful, and occupied Rome in spite of the attempts at resistance on the part of Sulpicius and his followers. With Sulla in control there could be no doubt of the sentiments of the senate; the Sulpician laws were at once annulled, and twelve leading opponents, among them Marius and Sulpicius, were proclaimed public enemies. The tribune was unlucky enough to be caught, but unfortunately for Rome and for himself, Marius succeeded in escaping from his pursuers. For the moment Sulla was undisputed master of the situation, and he used his opportunity to strengthen the senate by a law providing that no bill could be brought before the assembly without the senate's approval, and by some other changes concerning which we are left in much uncertainty.[1] In any case, he accomplished nothing that endured, and when

* [1] For some of them see Appendix 4. The statement of Appian (*b.c.* i, ch. 59) that Sulla added 300 new members to the senate at this time as well as during his dictatorship seems clearly a duplication of the same event, since the reason given for both additions is the same, namely, that the senate was greatly reduced in size. This reason was good in 81 B.C. but not in 88.

he held the elections he was unable to prevent the return of one consul, L. Cornelius Cinna, whom he regarded as untrustworthy. In spite of this defeat he probably considered the position of the senate safe enough, since it could count upon the other consul, Octavius, and the support of at least two armies still in the field against such Italians as were holding out stubbornly. He himself was anxious to set about his task in the East, and his soldiers were probably equally eager. Here again there is no need to invoke any lofty motives to explain the fact that Sulla, after hurriedly settling affairs in Rome, sailed for Greece at the head of his army.

## § 7. CINNA AND THE DEMOCRATIC REACTION

Sulla was not mistaken in his suspicions of Cinna. Our information concerning him is very unsatisfactory, being both scanty and partisan, but it seems clear that he was a man with more ambition than principle, although he may have been abler and less unscrupulous than his enemies were willing to admit. At the very least he was a convenient figurehead, if only because of his office, around whom all those whom Sulla's victory had exasperated could rally. The question of the moment was that of the registration of the new citizens, which the annulment of the Sulpician laws had again thrown open. Cinna took the side of the Italians, demanding that they be distributed among all the existing tribes, while his colleague Octavius advocated their restriction to a limited number. The struggle on this point became violent, but after serious rioting Octavius won the day and drove Cinna from the city. The senate hastened to depose him from the consulship and to declare him and his associates public enemies. This proved a blunder, for the step was unprecedented and enabled Cinna to appeal to the Italians as a martyr in their cause, perhaps also to many moderate men who were disgusted by the violence in Rome of which he seemed to be the victim. The result was that when he presented himself to the army in Campania the soldiers went over to him, and he was further reinforced by many of the new citizens. Others who were at odds with the senatorial government, whether because of sincere democratic leanings or because of recent events, joined his standard, among them

Marius, who emerged from hiding and whose name still had a considerable value.

Having secured an army Cinna, accompanied by Marius, followed the example of Sulla and marched on Rome. The senate tried to defend itself by calling Pompeius Strabo, consul for 89 B.C. and father of the great Pompey, from the North with the army which he commanded as proconsul. He came, but proved wholly unreliable, apparently playing simply for his own hand and supporting neither party. He did, it is true, beat off an attack by Marius, but he allowed Cinna and his supporters to invest the city. What his intentions were we are unable to guess, because in the midst of his dubious course he died (or was murdered) and his men joined Cinna. Another general, Metellus, engaged in completing the restoration of order in Samnium, was summoned to the city, but he likewise rendered no real assistance.

The cause of the senate was now clearly lost; after futile attempts at negotiation, it was forced to recognize Cinna as consul and surrender unconditionally, the victor promising that there should be no bloodshed. Marius remained outside the city till the decree of outlawry against him had been annulled, then he entered at the head of a body of armed slaves and took his revenge, regardless of Cinna's promises. All who had ever offended the old soldier were marked out for destruction, including some of the leading senators. The butchery continued until finally Cinna by surrounding and massacring the slaves restored some semblance of order. Nevertheless, it was amid terror and confusion that Marius was declared consul for the seventh time with Cinna as his colleague; but the old man's course was nearly run, and he had hardly taken up his new consulship when he died (86 B.C.). The blind fury and blood-lust which he displayed in the last days of his life, and which are quite out of harmony with his character as it had hitherto appeared, suggest that the hardships which he suffered while hiding from the pursuit of Sulla's myrmidons had unbalanced his mind, and that the Marius who returned from exile was no longer wholly sane.

The vacant consulship was given to L. Valerius Flaccus, and the new government which Cinna had set up prepared to grapple with the questions pressing on every side for solution. First of all the financial situation was acute, for the Social

War and the occupation of the province of Asia by Mithridates had precipitated a panic, which the reign of terror had done nothing to allay. Flaccus now carried a bill reducing all debts by three-fourths. Next in order came the Italian question, and this was settled as might have been expected by registering the new citizens in all the tribes, a measure which was carried out by the censors who were appointed for 86. The distribution of the Italian and Latin allies among the rural tribes made a decided change in their character; hitherto each rural tribe had been a more or less compact district, but, when each of the communities inhabited by the new citizens was put in one or another of the tribes, a tribe was composed of a number of detached pieces of territory scattered here and there over the peninsula and entirely isolated from each other.

Another and more difficult problem for the government was presented by Sulla, who was in the East at the head of his army fighting Mithridates. It was natural, obvious, and easy to remove him from his command and to appoint a successor in the person of Flaccus, but these measures had not the slightest effect on Sulla's army, and could be enforced only if he could be conquered in the field. The victory of Cinna in Italy made a civil war inevitable, though the preoccupation of Sulla with Mithridates served to postpone it for three years.

# CHAPTER VII

## SULLA'S WARS WITH MITHRIDATES AND THE DEMOCRATS

### § 1. CONDITIONS IN ASIA MINOR

TO understand the Mithridatic wars it is essential to bear in mind the general conditions in the East. When Rome annexed the old kingdom of Pergamum and organized it as the province of Asia (129 B.C.) she acquired a general supremacy over the whole of Asia Minor, for the Seleucid empire, which might have checked her influence to some extent, was then in the last stages of dissolution. The Parthians, a nomadic tribe living east of the Caspian Sea, had availed themselves of the weakness of the successors of Alexander the Great so successfully that by 100 B.C. they were in possession of most of Persia and Mesopotamia, while Syria and such other territories as the Seleucids still retained were in a state of chronic anarchy from the struggles between two rival branches of the dynasty. The Parthians were as yet too far away to give effective support to the princes and states of various kinds into which Asia Minor was divided, so that these had little choice but to obey the will of Rome. The difficulties of the Romans were due chiefly to the disorder in the remaining dominions of the Seleucids, where the weakness of the rulers led to a resumption of piracy on the part of some of the coast tribes. To check this Rome in 103 B.C. occupied some portions of Cilicia, and thus laid the foundations of a new province. The measures taken proved inadequate, however, and the Romans were too busy elsewhere to make any serious advance. The Republic had thus acquired two footholds in Asia Minor, the rich and important province of Asia and a poor and turbulent district in Cilicia. The northern part of the peninsula, bordering on the Black

Sea, was divided among the kingdoms of Bithynia, Paphlagonia, and Pontus. South of these lay the district of Galatia, which had been overrun by an invading body of Gauls, and was now divided into a number of petty states without any national unity. South-east of Galatia and north-east of Cilicia was the considerable kingdom of Cappadocia, while farther east and outside Rome's sphere of influence altogether were the growing empire of the Parthians and a new kingdom of Armenia, which had become powerful under a king named Tigranes.

## § 2. MITHRIDATES OF PONTUS

Pontus was a mountainous district on the Black Sea, where in the confusion which followed the death of Alexander a Persian by the name of Mithridates, who claimed descent from the old royal house of Persia, succeeded in establishing himself as king. The new state was of little importance until its rulers succeeded in extending their power over the Greek colonies on the coast. From this time on the kings of Pontus relied largely upon the Greek element in their kingdom and posed as the champions and protectors of Greek civilization, though they seem to have done little to spread it in the interior of their realm, which remained Oriental in character. The Greek cities were almost the only ones in the kingdom; the native peoples, who are said to have spoken twenty-two languages, dwelt in rural villages under the control of the king, the great nobles, or the priests of some rich temple.

About 120 B.C. the crown of Pontus descended to a young prince known as Mithridates Eupator and later styled Mithridates the Great. The early years of his reign were filled with danger from his mother and brother, and he was forced to hide among the mountains for a time. Finally returning to his capital, he recovered the throne and henceforth bent his energies to the consolidation and extension of his power. Although he had received a Greek education, he remained a good deal of an Oriental at heart, and possessed qualities which appealed strongly to Orientals. He was a bold hunter and a wild reveller, master of many languages, and at home among all classes of his subjects. We know him only as he is pictured by his adversaries, and it can hardly be doubted that they have drawn his portrait in unduly sombre colours. He seems to have been a man of vast ambition and of some capacity, but there is little reason for attributing to him any extraordinary ability; as a statesman he was lacking in real insight, as a general he won no glory, and as a ruler he displayed no unusual talent for organization or administration. When dealing with Orientals he made a good showing, but his successes against the Romans were ephemeral and were made possible only by the circumstances of the moment.

Once firmly seated on his throne he set about enlarging his kingdom, at first confining his efforts to regions where there was no danger of a conflict with Rome. He secured additional Greek towns near his frontier, in Colchis, and in the Crimea, constructing a strong fleet as a means of holding his scattered territories together. His army included large but ill-disciplined levies from his barbarian subjects, but its real strength lay in his mercenaries, who were trained and commanded by Greeks. The Greek cities not only furnished him with officers for his army and government, but also with the greater part of his revenue, so that he naturally wished to increase as much as possible the number of his subjects belonging to so serviceable a race.

He could further strengthen the Greek element in his kingdom only by an advance to the west and south, for which an opportunity soon presented itself. Paphlagonia had fallen into a state of anarchy, and Mithridates formed an alliance with Nicomedes II of Bithynia to divide that country and to establish their supremacy over Galatia as well. Rome protested, but for the moment she could safely be ignored, since the Republic was then fully occupied with the Cimbri and Teutones. At first Mithridates and Nicomedes were successful, but such an alliance between two ambitious and unscrupulous monarchs could not last long. Nicomedes by a sudden attack seized Cappadocia and expelled the king, whom Mithridates soon restored. The unfortunate prince, however, had too much spirit to be a pliant tool, so Mithridates had him murdered and then set up a government which was completely subservient. The Cappadocians revolted and proclaimed a new king, but Mithridates had regained possession of the country when in 92 B.C. Sulla arrived in Cilicia as proprætor. The new governor had very few Roman soldiers at

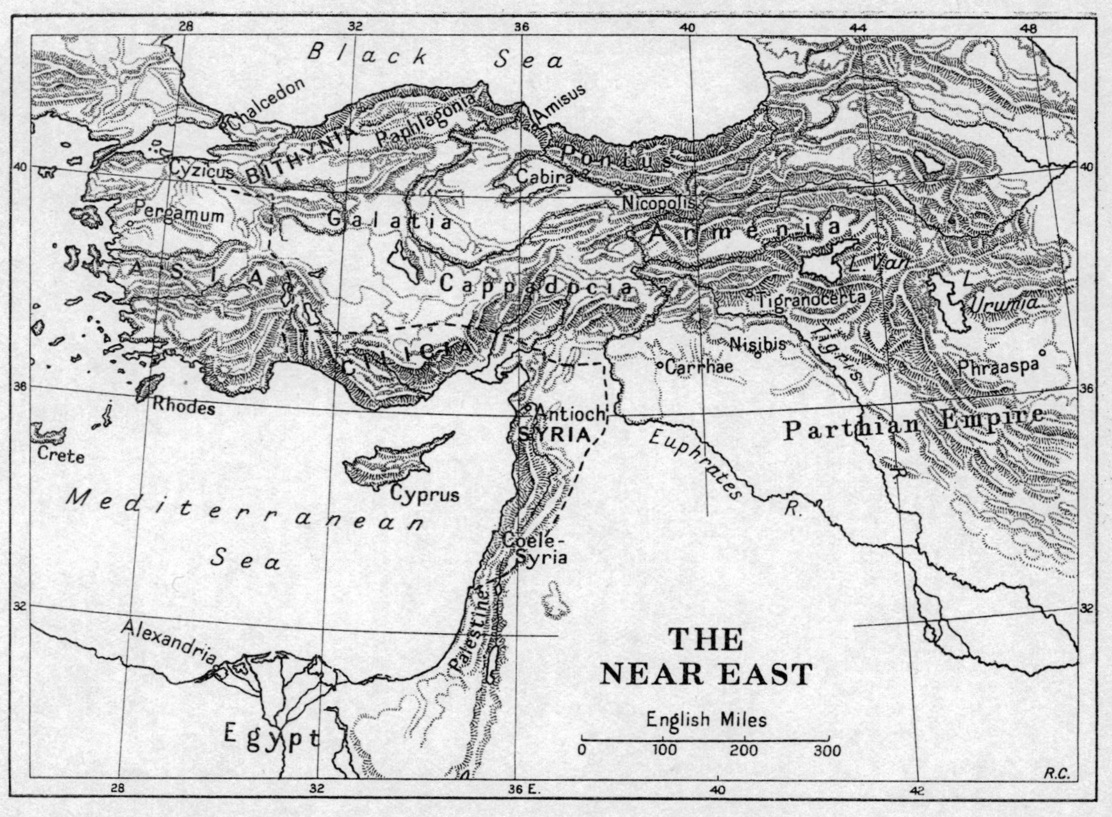
THE NEAR EAST
English Miles
0 100 200 300
Black Sea
Mediterranean Sea
Chalcedon
Cyzicus
BITHYNIA
Paphlagonia
Amisus
Pontus
Cabira
Nicopolis
Pergamum
Galatia
Armenia
L. Van
ASIA
Cappadocia
Tigranocerta
Urumia
Cilicia
Nisibis
Tigris
Carrhae
Phraaspa
Rhodes
Crete
Antioch
SYRIA
Parthian Empire
Euphrates R.
R.
Cyprus
Coele-Syria
Alexandria
Palestine
Egypt
28
32
36
40
44
48
36 E.
42
R.C.

his disposal, but he had audacity and the majesty of Rome on his side. Intervening promptly in Cappadocia with a handful of troops and a body of native auxiliaries, he overthrew the Pontic government there. Mithridates was so far overawed that he not only abandoned Cappadocia but agreed to give up the part of Paphlagonia which he had seized.

The success of Sulla was only temporary, for in 91 B.C. the Social War broke out and Rome was in no condition to compel Mithridates to keep his promises. Moreover, the death of Nicomedes led to a civil war in Bithynia in which Mithridates intervened in support of a pretender against the rightful heir. The victory of the Pontic army brought Bithynia under the complete control of Mithridates, for the pretender was king in name only. The defeated prince, of course, appealed to Rome, and the senate despatched Manius Aquilius, who had been consul in 101 B.C., as a special envoy to settle the matter. Mithridates, more timid than might have been expected, agreed to withdraw his troops from Bithynia and to abandon the pretender. Aquilius installed the rightful heir, Nicomedes III, and encouraged him to demand that Mithridates should withdraw from Paphlagonia as he had promised. Either Aquilius was bent on war or he overrated the extent to which Mithridates would go in the way of concessions, for not content with these demands he induced Nicomedes to attack districts which had long been held by Pontus, so that Mithridates was forced to take the field.

### § 3. THE FIRST PHASE OF THE MITHRIDATIC WAR

Mithridates had evidently not desired a war with Rome, but since it could not be avoided he determined to strike hard. All the conditions were in his favour ; there were few regular Roman troops in Asia Minor, so that he would have to fight chiefly Asiatics or Greeks, the exactions of the knights as tax farmers and money-lenders had made Rome unpopular in the province of Asia, and the Pontic army was more numerous, better disciplined, and better led than the opposing forces. As a natural result the Roman power collapsed at the first blow ; the Bithynian army was easily disposed of and the province of Asia invaded. The governor succeeded in escaping to Rhodes, but Aquilius was captured and paid for his rashness with his life. Throughout the province the towns eagerly welcomed the Pontic king as a deliverer, and at his order butchered all Romans who could be found.[1] The motive of the king in instigating this massacre is said to have been the hope that the crime would bind the cities to him by the consciousness of inexpiable guilt.

Mithridates, now supreme in Asia Minor, saw no reason to stop: the time for moderation had passed, and the more territory he could seize the stronger his position would be when the hour of reckoning came. The Hellespont was still in Roman hands, but the Pontic fleet was able to land an army in Greece, where Eubœa was easily occupied and Athens accepted an agent of the king, a certain Aristion, as her ruler. There may have been fickleness on the part of the mob of the city and they may have been over-credulous, but after all Athens had really little choice, for Aristion was at hand, backed by an army while his master's fleet commanded the sea, and no help could be expected from Rome in the immediate future. Most of Greece was in much the same position and therefore joined Mithridates. The triumph of the king seemed complete, but it rested on no firm foundation, for the Greeks accepted him at least as much from necessity as choice, and were ready to desert him as soon as the tide turned in Rome's favour. In the spring of 87 B.C., however, Mithridates was in possession of nearly all Asia Minor and Greece, together with Thrace and part of Macedon, while the Euxine and the Aegean were dominated by his fleet.

### § 4. SULLA AND MITHRIDATES

The struggle with Marius delayed Sulla's arrival in Greece, so that it was not until 87 B.C. that he landed in Epirus, with an army probably of about 30,000 men, but without the support of a fleet. His resources, even with such help as he could expect from the senate which he had left in power in Rome, were meagre indeed for the task before him, but he set about it with energy and decision. The presence of a Roman

[1] Plutarch (*Sulla*, ch. 24, 4) says that 150,000 were slain, but Valerius Maximus (ix, ch. 2, Ext. 3) puts the number at 80,000. Even the lower figure seems to me greatly exaggerated, but we may feel confident that the number was large. The victims were probably mostly agents of the tax-farmers and bankers, together with traders and lesser business men.

army made an immediate impression on the Greeks, who hastened to change sides.

From Epirus Sulla advanced rapidly into Bœotia, where he won a victory over Aristion and Archelaus, the general of Mithridates, and where he was joined by Greek auxiliaries. His initial success was promptly followed by the invasion of Attica and the siege of Athens, whither his adversaries had retreated, Aristion holding the city while Archelaus occupied the Piræus. Although the Greeks were now anxious to atone for their conduct and furnished Sulla with money and supplies as well as men, it was no easy matter to capture Athens while the enemy was master of the sea, so Sulla despatched one of his officers, L. Licinius Lucullus, to obtain ships wherever possible. In the meantime the siege of the city was closely pressed, and Sulla beat off an army sent to relieve it. After much fighting he was at length successful in cutting Athens off from the Piræus, and early in 86 he captured the city. The entry of the Romans was accompanied by looting and slaughter, and the leaders of the Pontic party were naturally killed, but Sulla saved Athens from destruction and treated her with leniency, partly perhaps because he wished to encourage other rebellious states to surrender by showing them that they could still hope for mercy, partly, no doubt, because of the respect for her great past which was felt by most cultivated Romans. The Piræus still held out, but Sulla directed such furious assaults upon it that, although he could not entirely dislodge Archelaus, the place was rendered useless as a base of operations. This accomplished, Sulla turned with the major part of his army to meet the enemy elsewhere.

In the North the Roman cause had fared badly, so that a large Pontic army had been able to invade Bœotia. Most of it was composed of ill-disciplined barbarians, and its real strength lay in a contingent of troops well-drilled in the Greek fashion. Confident in the superior quality of his men, Sulla marched against it, and at Chæronea he forced a battle on ground much more favourable to the Roman legions than to the Greek phalanx. Sulla was a skilful tactician who knew how to make the most of every advantage, and after a sharp fight he not only defeated but practically destroyed the Pontic host. Once again the trust of the Asiatic in mere numbers had proved vain, and the helplessness of the Greek phalanx, once it was thrown into disorder, was demonstrated. The remnant of the beaten army found a refuge in Chalcis in Eubœa, where Sulla's lack of a fleet made pursuit impossible.

While these events were taking place in Greece, Cinna had seized power in Rome and deposed Sulla from his command. This measure could obviously be made effective only by force, so Valerius Flaccus, who had succeeded Marius as consul in 87 B.C., was sent to Greece at the head of an army. By the time of Sulla's victory at Chæronea (March, 86) he had advanced into Thessaly, and Sulla promptly pushed north to meet him. Flaccus, realizing that he had little hold upon his men and fearing that his army would desert to Sulla if it were given a chance, decided that Mithridates was the safer person to encounter, and accordingly marched to the Hellespont, ostensibly to cut the communications of the Pontic king at that point and attack him in the rear, but really, perhaps, to get as far away as possible from the man he had come to supersede. Sulla made no attempt to follow him, since by this move Flaccus ceased to be a danger; in fact, by diverting the attention of Mithridates he might even render valuable assistance.

Sulla was now master of Greece, since the Piræus had been abandoned by Archelaus, who had joined his forces to the Pontic army which was destroyed at Chæronea. He had, however, plenty of work before him in reorganizing that country and in building ships to supplement the few that Lucullus had been able to collect. In the spring of the next year (85 B.C.) Mithridates hurled a new army against Greece by sea, for the fleet of Sulla was as yet too weak to accomplish much. The invaders landed in Bœotia, where Sulla met them at Orchomenus. Here a desperate battle was fought in which Sulla's troops wavered for a moment. Seeing the imminent danger he rushed to the front, seized the standard, and bade his men tell their friends how they left their general at Orchomenus. Spurred on by his example, his soldiers rallied, and another Pontic army was destroyed.

Driven from Europe in ignominious defeat, the hold of Mithridates on Asia was enormously weakened. The inhabitants of that unhappy region, who had hailed him as a deliverer from the tyranny of Rome, were discovering that an Oriental despot could be a worse oppressor than the Roman knights. As their discontent increased, the king became suspicious of their loyalty, and suspicion bred new freaks of tyranny, while defeat in Greece naturally enough resulted in heavier exactions in Asia. The power of Mithridates was fast crumbling when the Romans appeared upon the scene. Flaccus finally succeeded in crossing the Bosporus, but soon after perished in a mutiny instigated by his legate, C. Flavius Fimbria, whom the troops chose as his successor in command. The new general, who was something of a soldier, succeeded in capturing Pergamum, which Mithridates had made his capital when he conquered Asia. The king escaped, but he was now ready for peace, especially since Sulla was approaching. The fleet of Lucullus had at length won enough success to enable Sulla to advance to the Hellespont, and he was in a position to cross the straits at any time. Mithridates, with a true appreciation of realities, opened negotiations with him rather than with Fimbria. Sulla on his side was anxious to free himself from the eastern war in order that he might have an opportunity to deal with Cinna and his party in Rome.

Under these circumstances a treaty was finally concluded (85 B.C.) on terms honourable to Rome, although Mithridates fared much better than he had any right to expect after the provocation he had given. The king was left in undisturbed possession of his original kingdom, but was forced to abandon all his recent acquisitions, including the part of Paphlagonia from which he had promised Sulla years before to withdraw, and to surrender all prisoners and deserters. Sulla also demanded and received eighty ships of war and an indemnity in money, these last concessions being greatly to his advantage and strengthening his position against his own country.

The task of restoring order in Asia still remained before Sulla could turn his attention to Italy. The army of Fimbria was easily disposed of, for when Sulla marched against it the soldiers deserted to his standard and their commander killed himself. Sulla lost little time in settling affairs now that no one was left who could offer resistance to his decisions. He made no attempt at novelty, contenting himself with reorganizing the Roman province and restoring the vassal princes who had been driven out by Mithridates. Some of the most serious offenders were executed, but Sulla was more concerned with money than with vengeance. On the various communities he imposed heavy fines, collecting what he could immediately and leaving the rest to be paid in the future. He then appointed a governor and placed the former soldiers of Fimbria under his command to serve as a garrison for the province. Sulla's work in the East being successfully finished, he addressed a formal letter to the senate. In this he gave an account of his services to the state, especially in the war just ended, and informed the conscript fathers that he had received and assisted those whom Cinna had driven from Italy, among them his own wife and children, who had escaped with difficulty from the Marian reign of terror. For receiving the fugitives Sulla alleged that he had been declared a public enemy by his foes, but announced that he was about to return to punish those guilty of crimes against himself, the people, and the senate alike. The innocent and the new citizens, he concluded, had no reason to fear.

## § 5. THE CIVIL WAR

Sulla's letter caused general consternation in Rome. The senate attempted to open negotiations for peace, but the consuls, Cinna and Carbo, ignoring the senate, energetically set about preparing for war. Since Cinna had gained control of Rome in 87 B.C. the Republic had been governed, in fact, by a small group of politicians, styling themselves democrats but actually relying on force and showing as little respect for the rights of the assembly as for the authority of the senate. They seem to have secured the support, or at least the tolerance, of the new citizens and of the majority of the knights and to have paid little attention to constitutional forms. Sulla, if only for his own safety, must drive this gang from power, and to them the loss of power meant utter ruin. They had, therefore, no choice but to fight, and they determined to meet Sulla in Greece rather than to wait for him in Italy. Having gathered large numbers of recruits, Cinna undertook to transport them across the Adriatic. The soldiers, however, had little enthusiasm for the cause, and when Cinna tried to force them to embark he was killed in a mutiny.

The death of Cinna left Carbo the chief leader of the democrats. Abandoning all thought of leaving Italy, he concentrated his efforts on the organization of defence. He avoided holding an election to fill Cinna's place for the rest of the year, but he did not venture to retain office himself, so two other democrats took his place in 83 B.C. Italy seemed for a time to rally around the democratic government; the senate, after the failure of the futile attempts at negotiation, supported the group in power, and the people at large feared Sulla in spite of his apparent moderation and were awed by Carbo's army. What chances the democrats had of victory were thrown away by their own folly. The new consuls, Norbanus and Scipio Asiaticus, were worthless as soldiers, and the one military genius on their side, Sertorius, was sent off to Spain, leaving Carbo and the son of Marius the strongest men of the party in Italy.

At last in 83 B.C. Sulla landed at Brundisium, whose citizens yielded to him without a struggle. His army, including Greek auxiliaries, numbered from 30,000 to 40,000,[1] but he gathered reinforcements rapidly; in no long time Metellus Pius joined him with a body of troops, and others soon followed. The unity of Italy behind the democratic regime was more apparent than real, and discontent with the rule of Cinna and his successors was widespread. The son of Pompeius Strabo, who had played so ambiguous a part when Cinna was blockading Rome, raised a considerable force in Picenum, where his father had been popular, and came to the support of Sulla. Another young man of consular family who joined him was M. Licinius Crassus. His father and elder brother had perished in the Marian terror, from which he himself had found refuge in Spain, where his father had been governor and had made many friends. On the news of Cinna's death he had emerged from hiding, and with a body of recruits he finally succeeded in reaching Sulla's camp. Both Pompey and Crassus were able soldiers who soon won the confidence of their leader in spite of their youth, and who rendered services of great value in the war.

While Carbo was busy in Cisalpine Gaul raising additional troops, the consuls hastened to meet Sulla, who was advancing along the Appian Way. They did not unite their armies, however, and Sulla, when he reached Campania, defeated

[1] Velleius (ii, ch. 24) says not more than 30,000, while Appian (*b.c.* i, ch. 79) says about 40,000.

Norbanus, who fell back on Capua, and then advanced to meet Scipio. The defeat of Norbanus had discouraged both Scipio and his army, so that when Sulla sent envoys to negotiate, Scipio eagerly embraced the opportunity. The negotiations came to nothing, but while they were in progress Scipio's army was persuaded to join Sulla. Yet the greater part of Italy still adhered to the democrats. Carbo hastened to Rome, where he compelled the senate to declare Sulla and all who had joined him public enemies. This, of course, had no effect, but Sulla apparently thought his enemies too strong for an immediate attack, and spent the rest of the year (83) in minor operations and in sending agents to all parts of Italy to raise troops and to seek to conciliate the Italians and to win them to his side.

As consuls for 82 B.C. the democrats selected their strongest leaders, Carbo and the young Marius. They exerted themselves to the utmost in gathering recruits and were especially successful in Etruria, Cisalpine Gaul, and Samnium. The war, therefore, began to take on a new aspect, and to appear as a struggle between the Etruscans, Gauls, and Samnites against the Romans and the more thoroughly Romanized elements in Italy. The two consuls divided their responsibilities, Carbo taking command in the North and leaving Marius to defend Rome. Sulla on his side sent Metellus and Pompey to deal with Carbo, while he marched upon the city. Marius attempted to check Sulla's advance, but he was routed at the battle of Sacriportus and driven into the fortress of Præneste, where he was at once besieged.

After the battle of Sacriportus the democratic leaders saw clearly that they could not hold Rome, but before they fled they murdered four of the most prominent senators who still remained in the city, among them the *pontifex maximus*.[1] Although Sulla occupied Rome without resistance, he could not afford to remain there and almost immediately pushed on into Etruria. In the North Metellus and Pompey had been fairly successful in Umbria and Picenum, but Carbo was leading a large army southward from Cisalpine Gaul. Sulla met him near Clusium in central Etruria ; although the battle

[1] Livy (Ep. lxxxvi) speaks of a general massacre of the nobility who were in Rome, but Appian (*b.c.* i, ch. 88) and Velleius (ch. 26) mention four victims without any suggestion that there were more.

was indecisive, Carbo was checked, and the morale of the democrats was so weakened that desertions became frequent. Metellus now invaded Cisalpine Gaul, while Pompey and Crassus won a victory in Umbria. Under these blows the democratic leaders began to abandon all hope of success; some tried to make peace with Sulla by betraying their friends, while others, like Carbo, sought safety in flight.

It seemed for a time as though the war was over, but it flared up again in a final blaze. While an army from Etruria was seeking to raise the siege of Præneste, it was joined by large numbers of Samnites and Lucanians. Sulla hastened to the spot and defeated the attempt. The leaders of the relieving army, unable to break his lines, resolved to try a march on Rome as a last chance, hoping perhaps that by this means they would force him to loosen his grip on Præneste, and that the possession of Rome would give them sufficient prestige to enable them to prolong the struggle. They advanced so suddenly and swiftly that they nearly succeeded, but Sulla managed to reach the city just before them and the final battle of the war was fought before it. Although his troops were weary from forced marches, Sulla ordered an attack. The Battle of the Colline Gate began late in the afternoon (November 1, 82) and lasted into the night. The Samnites fought with stubborn fury, and for a time Sulla believed himself beaten, since the wing which he commanded was shattered and crushed against the walls of Rome. In the night, however, he learned that the other wing of his army, under Crassus, had routed the enemy and that the battle was won. In fact the next day brought a massacre instead of a renewal of the contest, the Samnites being ruthlessly butchered. The fall of Præneste, where Marius committed suicide when he saw that escape was impossible, soon followed, leaving Sulla master of Italy.

## § 6. THE PROSCRIPTION

The battle of the Colline Gate had ended the Civil War as far as Italy was concerned; there were still some scattered bands of democrats to be destroyed, but there was no serious or organized opposition in the peninsula. It remained to secure the acceptance of the result throughout the provinces,

9

in most of which the governors were members of the fallen party. Sicily and Africa were of the most pressing importance, because from them Rome drew the greater part of her grain supply, so Pompey was at once despatched to bring them to obedience. The democrats abandoned Sicily on Pompey's approach, and he at once passed over to Africa, where a single battle was enough to place that province and the client kingdom of Numidia at his feet (81). The other provinces offered little resistance with the exception of Spain, and Sulla's authority was soon supreme over almost all the Roman world.

Everyone must have expected that stern punishment would be meted out to the leaders of the vanquished party and to all those who were responsible for the crimes which had disgraced the democratic regime, but the vengeance of Sulla filled Italy with horror and dismay. He issued formal lists of the proscribed, and all whose names were included in these lists were declared outlaws and a price was set upon their heads; rewards were offered to informers, and all who sheltered the proscribed were threatened with punishment. Appian estimates that Sulla destroyed 90 senators, 15 consulars and 2600 knights, including those who were banished.[1] Since the very number of the victims makes it obvious that Sulla's purpose was not simply to punish past offences, he has been credited with the intention of destroying the democratic party by removing all possible future leaders. No doubt the list contained the names of all politicians who seemed capable of becoming troublesome, but Sulla must have been too familiar with the history of the last fifty years not to be well aware that the popular leaders of the future were likely to be found in the ranks of the aristocracy itself. Moreover, Sulla included in his proscription many wealthy Italians,[2] whom he can hardly have regarded as politically dangerous, so that it would seem that his real motives must be sought elsewhere.

To understand Sulla's purpose in this ruthless butchery both his position and character must be taken into account. He came of an old patrician house which had fallen into

[1] Appian, *b.c.* i, ch. 103. Probably he has included some who were captured and put to death in the course of the war, as at the fall of Præneste (ch. 94).

[2] Appian, *b.c.* i, ch. 96. Valerius Maximus (ix, ch. 2, 1) gives the total number on the proscription lists as 4700. This' is a probable figure, since Appian includes no Romans below the rank of knights and no Italians.

poverty and insignificance ; no member of it had risen above the prætorship for several generations, and Sulla's father had spent his life in complete obscurity. It may be doubted whether Sulla himself in his early life had had any relations with the more important and influential families of the aristocracy. He was rescued from a modest apartment in the poorer part of the city by two legacies, one from his stepmother and the other from a lady of no social standing but of some property who had become his mistress. He began his political career somewhat later than usual, but he was elected quæstor for 106 B.C. and sent to Africa with Marius. When Marius took command of the war against the Cimbri and Teutones he made Sulla one of his lieutenants. For two years Sulla served with distinction under Marius, but in 102, finding that Marius was not disposed to give him further opportunities to win a reputation, he succeeded in getting himself transferred to the staff of Catulus, a noble who was Marius' colleague in the consulship for that year. Thus, apparently, for the first time he became connected with one of the senatorial leaders, for his long association with Marius would suggest that his affiliations were with the democrats rather than with the senate. After the battle of Vercellæ we hear nothing of him for some years, but in 95 B.C. he stood for the prætorship only to be defeated. The next year, however, he was successful, and in 92 he was sent as proprætor to Cilicia. He returned to Rome in time to play a brilliant part in the Social War, and in 89 he came forward as a candidate for the consulship. This office he desired chiefly as a stepping-stone to the command in the East, to secure which he felt the need of senatorial support. Perhaps chiefly, if not entirely, for this purpose he contrived to marry into the family of the Metelli, then the most powerful and influential of the great houses, and thereby definitely ranged himself on the side of the nobles. Yet he still manifested little zeal in their cause until the democrats, under the leadership of Sulpicius Rufus, attempted to deprive him of the coveted command ; this attempt spurred him to prompt and energetic action in behalf of the senate. In his previous career there is nothing to show that he was an earnest and convinced partisan of the aristocracy or that he had any strong political preferences ; he appears rather as a man prepared to act with either party in order to advance his own fortunes. In 89 B.C. self-interest led him to ally himself closely with the nobles, and the course of events kept him true to them. Whatever his convictions, he was forced to become the champion of the aristocracy. When the close of the Civil War left him absolute master of Rome and Italy, two courses were open to him ; he might attempt to establish some form of monarchy, anticipating Cæsar and Augustus, or he might restore constitutional government and retire to private life. There seems no reason to think that he hesitated in his choice.[1] Always fond of ease and luxury, he was now in a position to indulge his tastes, thanks to the fortune which he had acquired in the East. His chief desire seems to have been to escape from politics, in which he had never shown any interest except as a means to an end, and to enjoy his riches in security. Before all else, however, he was clear-headed and practical. He owed his success chiefly to his ability to see beyond the outward appearances of things and to grasp the inner realities. He had boldly attacked Pontic armies vastly larger than his own, because he had formed a just estimate of their real military value, and in politics his vision was as clear as in war ; he had as few illusions in the one as in the other. To lay down power was simple, but he had no wish to have his luxurious retirement disturbed by anxieties and danger. As he had realized that the armies of Mithridates were far weaker than they seemed, so now he perceived that the democrats were far from being permanently crushed. Although the party was broken for the moment, its real strength was practically untouched, for that strength lay in the permanent antagonism between the city rabble and the senate and in the intermittent antagonism between the nobles and the knights. As long as these two factors in the situation remained unchanged, it was only a question of time, and possibly of a very short time, before the opposition to the senate would again raise its head and would find leaders to direct it. Such a revival was the easier because

[1] Carcopino (*Sylla*) has attempted to prove that Sulla intended to establish a monarchy, but was forced to abandon his design by a combination of Pompey and the nobles. His arguments seem to me unconvincing, and I have adhered to the commonly accepted view that Sulla had no desire to retain power longer than necessary. Nevertheless, I think that Carcopino is right in emphasizing the fact that before he stood for the consulship Sulla had no very definite party connections.

for many years the grip of the aristocratic machine on the assembly had been growing steadily weaker, and the nobility had suffered heavily in the last few stormy years. If before the Social War the senate could neither rule without the support of the knights nor keep on good terms with them, there was still less chance that, if the surviving senators were entrusted with power, they could long retain it. There is no reason to believe that Sulla had paid much, if any, attention to equestrian interests in his reorganization of the East, and in the Civil War the knights seem to have leaned to his opponents; with the rabble he can hardly have been popular, and the new citizens had furnished the main strength of the democratic armies, so that he could have no illusions as to their attitude. He had, of course, many friends, but aside from a comparatively small group of the nobility, there was no important class on which he could count in case he were attacked, and the number of his personal enemies made such an attack, if there were the least chance of success, a certainty. It was true that his veterans could be counted on to rally around him in the hour of danger, but he had no wish to trust to their protection, because to invoke it would mean new wars. Sulla meant to retire, but he was resolved to safeguard himself so well that he would have no need to draw the sword again. There was only one condition on which this was possible: he must find some way to entrench the aristocratic machine in power so firmly that it could remain in control of the government for a considerable period. This task Sulla undertook, and the proscription had a definite part to play in clearing the way for his reorganization by destroying the political power of the knights, who were the chief sufferers.

There was another motive which in part explains the extent of the proscription. Sulla had promised much to his men, and the time had now come when he must redeem his promises. Like all the Roman armies after Marius, their essential demand was for allotments of land. Although Sulla had brought back a large booty from the East, he had been obliged to spend freely in the Civil War, and did not have at hand sufficient funds to buy land to distribute among his troops. The proscription offered a way out of his difficulties: by confiscating the property of the proscribed and by including in the list a sufficient number of large landowners and rich men he could obtain the means of satisfying his troops and of filling the treasury as well. It was not necessary deliberately to include the innocent, for there were enough against whom something could plausibly be alleged. Extensive as it was, the proscription of individuals was not enough, so Sulla punished whole communities by confiscating their lands, which he assigned to colonies of his soldiers. No doubt it was chiefly the Italians who suffered by these wholesale measures, but with an army of twenty-three legions to provide for Sulla could hardly help making them pay a heavy price for their support of the democrats, even if he had felt any inclination to spare them.

It was probably because of this financial motive behind the proscription that Sulla showed such cynical carelessness about the drawing up of the lists. It mattered little who were included so long as there were enough for his purpose. He permitted his friends to add names at their pleasure, and some of his own partisans were thus murdered, though probably without his knowledge. At any rate the lists included many who were utter strangers to Sulla and who owed their inclusion to the ill-will of some enemy who happened to enjoy his favour.

Perhaps it was this cool indifference more than anything else that made the proscription seem so horrible to the Romans. In the murders of Marius there was something human and in a way excusable, at least intelligible. The great soldier, sneered at by the polished gentlemen of the aristocracy, hunted into exile and then brought back to power, giving way to his resentments and striking down his personal enemies, seemed far less repulsive than the nonchalant and careless aristocrat, cynically slaying thousands against whom he felt no animosity and of many of whom he had never even heard, simply as a matter of financial and political expediency. Rome ended by forgiving Marius, but she never forgave Sulla.

# CHAPTER VIII

## SULLA'S CONSTITUTION

### § 1. THE REVIVAL OF THE DICTATORSHIP

IN undertaking to reorganize the Roman government Sulla had no desire to be hampered by the prejudices or scruples of his partisans. He decided, therefore, to revive in a new form the obsolete office of dictator, and informed the remnant of the senate of his wishes by letter. Since opposition to his will was impossible, his suggestion was immediately accepted, and a law was passed by the assembly naming him dictator for the purpose of regulating the Republic (*reipublicæ constituendæ*). The new dictatorship had little in common with the old. In former times a dictator was appointed to meet an emergency, he was expected to resign as soon as the emergency was over, and in no case could he retain his power for more than six months. The office now (82 B.C.) conferred on Sulla was of indefinite duration and could be terminated only by his death or abdication. While it lasted he was free from all customary and legal checks, such as the veto or the right of appeal, which limited the authority of the ordinary magistrates. He held the power of life and death, and in him was vested an *imperium* which was supreme over all other magistrates or promagistrates. All his past acts were duly ratified, and his authority was so sweeping and complete that it would be difficult for him to do anything illegal in the future. The proscription, which had been begun before his appointment, thus received legal sanction, and it was not until June 1, 81, that the lists were finally closed.

The problem which confronted Sulla has already been briefly touched upon. His aim was not only to restore the aristocratic machine to power, but to strengthen it so that the senate, to which the direction of the machine would necessarily fall, could govern without extrinsic aid and could defy even a combination of the rabble and the knights. The influence of the knights had been shattered by the proscription, but Sulla must have been too clear-sighted not to perceive that they would soon recover. Capitalism naturally breeds capitalists, and as new men acquired wealth by the old methods, their wealth could be used to build up political power in the same way as before. The individuals and families who composed the equestrian order might be changed, but a capitalist class could not be destroyed or prevented from seeking to force their wishes on the government except by changes in the whole economic and political system so drastic that they probably never occurred to the dictator. The most that could be hoped for was to fortify the machine so thoroughly that for a long time to come it could successfully defend itself against the knights.

## § 2. THE NEW CITIZENS IN THE ASSEMBLY

The enfranchisement of the Latin and Italian allies created a new factor in the assembly which Sulla could not safely ignore. In mere numbers, if mere numbers had counted, the new citizens were not yet very important. The assembly voted by tribes or centuries, so unless a citizen was registered in a tribe and century he was unable to cast his ballot. After Cinna had seized power in Rome a law had been passed directing that the Latins and Italians should be registered in all the tribes, and censors had been appointed to carry this provision into effect. At the time we may reasonably guess that there were at least 400,000 of the old citizens,[1] and, if the figures for the census of 85 B.C. as they have come down to us are correct, about 60,000 new citizens were added to the number. If we accept these statistics, it is obvious that few of the new citizens were actually registered, a fact which is not in itself difficult to explain. The census was taken in Rome, and, although the censors sometimes sent agents to the provinces to enroll the Romans serving in the legions stationed there, they appear never to have tried to make matters easier for those in Italy. To be registered, therefore, required a journey

[1] Frank, *Roman Census Statistics*, p. 332.

to Rome, which a very large proportion of the Latins and Italians were doubtless unable to make. Moreover, since the Civil War was already in prospect, many who were able may have thought it well to let the opportunity slip, for conscription and taxation might be resorted to, and in that event the chances of evading both might be improved if their names and the amount of their property were not recorded.

Under the circumstances the failure of most of the new citizens to seek registration can be accounted for, but the importance of those who were registered is not to be estimated by their number. The law no doubt dealt with the Latins and Italians as communities and directed that they should be distributed among all the rural tribes.[1] This destroyed whatever remained of the original character of the tribes as territorial units somewhat like townships, parishes, or counties. At first a tribe had been a compact district, and when in the course of the conquest of Italy colonies were founded composed of Roman citizens a new tribe was formed to include all the Romans within the district. When the formation of new tribes ceased after 241 B.C., the settlers in new colonies may have been assigned to one of the existing tribes, and so a break made in their early unity and compactness. To distribute the Latin and Italian communities among the thirty-one rural tribes completely destroyed this unity, for these tribes would now consist of communities which might be, and usually were, widely scattered over the peninsula.

Our knowledge of the new arrangements is far from complete, but a few points emerge clearly, and an example or two will suffice. The original sixteen rural tribes were all close to Rome, and there is evidence to show that henceforth they included towns in various parts of Italy in addition to their primitive territory. Thus Spoletium in Umbria and Venusia in Southern Italy, both Latin colonies, were assigned to the tribe of Horatia; Samnium, including the Sabine country, was distributed among at least ten of the thirty-one rural tribes, five of which were among the original sixteen, while Umbria was divided among at least eleven, of which eight were primitive.[2] It will thus be seen that all the rural tribes

[1] We have no evidence that any communities in Italy were ever put in the four urban tribes.

[2] Kubitschek, *Imperium Romanorum tributim Discriptum.*

now embraced a number of communities, some near to Rome and others remote.

It has already been pointed out that the control of the rural tribes by the aristocratic machine was made possible by the fact that under normal circumstances few of their members attended the assembly, so that the votes of these tribes were usually cast by the retainers of the nobles. Later the knights formed similar groups of retainers, and the drift of the ruined farmers to Rome created a section of the city rabble which remained registered in the rural tribes. The political history of Rome since the Gracchi shows that the knights had gained the balance of power, so that whenever their retainers joined the rabble the combination could easily carry a majority of the tribes. The sudden introduction of even a small number of possible voters might have far-reaching results if it so chanced that they upset the balance in some of the rural tribes. To explain the control of the machine it must be assumed that there were few genuine country voters left in some of the original rural tribes, so that if districts in Central Italy were now added to these tribes, the effect might be important out of all proportion to the total number of the new voters.

It will be evident then that some 60,000 new voters might be a factor to be reckoned with in the assembly. Most of them would probably never appear there, but since they must all have been able to come to Rome to secure their registration, most of them could come to vote if they chose; if even a thousand of them actually did so, they might elect a candidate or defeat a bill. So far only the tribes have been considered, but the conditions in the centuries were broadly the same, since the centuries were based upon the tribes. The centuries of the propertied classes formed from the members of the rural tribes were a large majority of the whole, and under normal circumstances they were probably controlled by men living in Rome who owned country estates. The country gentlemen probably seldom took the trouble to appear, and it seems evident that the Roman knights and nobles had a better grip on the centuriate than on the tribal assembly. If now a number of wealthy Latins and Italians were added to these centuries, a comparative handful of them could exert an enormous influence. Moreover, since the new citizens were enrolled in the tribes by communities rather than as individuals, it is possible that the 60,000 were all men of property who registered to secure a vote in the centuries of the higher classes, while those who would find a place in the centuries of the fourth or fifth class did not take the trouble, since the votes of these centuries would count for little and they could, perhaps, vote in one of the tribes as members of a community. Who were likely to attend and how they were likely to vote was thus a matter which Sulla was obliged to consider.

The matter may not have been as complicated as it seems at first sight. The antagonism between the knights and the nobles had its roots in the conflict between the interests of the capitalists and those of the great landowners. It may have been comparatively easy to see to which side such of the Latins and Italians as came to Rome to vote were likely to incline. Judging by what happened later, it would appear that they leaned in the main to the side of the nobility, probably because they had little part in the tax farming and banking enterprises which concerned the knights so deeply. Yet although the Italians seem to have had no hostility to the aristocracy, they did not by any means share all its prejudices, and at times gave their confidence and support to men who were distasteful to the nobles; for example, the popularity of Pompey and Cicero seems to have been greater in Italy as a whole than in the city of Rome. Sulla may very well have discerned the aristocratic tendencies of the new voters, for he made no attempt to interfere with them, but on the other hand he seems to have had no desire to increase their number; it was not until 69 B.C. that they became a large proportion of the Roman citizens.[1]

Another difficulty which Sulla had to face was a result of his own policy. By his proscription he broke for the time being the power of the knights, but in doing so he ran the risk of making the assembly of tribes less manageable, for the retainers of his victims were likely to swell that element of the rabble which voted in the rural tribes.[2] It was, perhaps,

[1] Censors were appointed in 70 B.C., and the result of the census was to increase the number of citizens to 900,000.

[2] Unless he put them in the city tribes. We have, however, no record that Sulla exercised censorial powers during his dictatorship.

to neutralize this result that he liberated 10,000 slaves whom he selected from those belonging to the proscribed. He himself assumed the role of patron to these new freedmen, who took the name of Cornelius, and he may have enrolled them in the tribes where he thought their votes were most needed. He also repealed the corn law, perhaps hoping to drive a considerable part of the rabble out of the city.

The main device by which the dictator hoped to strengthen the machine was by a reconstruction of the senate. That body must have been much reduced in number by the democratic massacres, followed by the proscription and by the added loss of life in the Civil War, in which a number of its members had perished. It is a reasonable guess that there were only about 150 senators when Sulla began his constructive work. Many noble houses still survived in the sons of former senators, and the natural instinct of the nobility would certainly have been to fill up the senate to its traditional 300 from this class as far as possible and to admit as few new men as might be. Sulla, however, reverted to the plan of Drusus, and forthwith proceeded to appoint 300 new senators from the equestrian class.[1] This was double the number required to fill the vacancies and increased the size of the senate to about 450. He also raised the numbers of the quæstors from 12 to 20 and provided that each quæstor should enter the senate automatically by virtue of having held that office. This obviously meant that he intended the increase in the number of the conscript fathers to be permanent, and did not view it as a temporary expedient.

Sulla's motives in this reorganization of the senate, which he intended to make supreme, must remain a matter of conjecture. It is obvious at the start that by proscribing all

[1] H. Hill (*Sulla's New Senators*) contends that the new senators were taken chiefly, if not entirely, from the 18 equestrian centuries, in which many of the younger members of the noble families were enrolled. It seems to me highly probable that a considerable number of the 300 new senators were so taken and that Sulla did not give a majority in his enlarged senate to genuine knights. I think, however, that the equestrian centuries must have contained many persons who were not connected with the nobility and whose interests were identical with those of the knights. In the time of Cicero the young knights certainly controlled these centuries (Cicero, *de. pet. cons.*, ch. 8). To accomplish his purpose Sulla must have enrolled in the senate a considerable number of men who had previously been allied with the knights, whatever their family connections may have been.

his enemies in the senate and swamping the remnant with his appointees he created a body which his friends would dominate for a long time to come, so that he could lay down his power with the certainty that no attack on him would ever be countenanced by the conscript fathers ; there might be some turncoats and renegades among them, but the Sullan majority was too great to be affected.

There is, however, another and more important point to consider. The old machine was badly broken and required strengthening. The addition of a large number of knights to the surviving noble families would greatly increase their power. That the new senators would soon forget their equestrian origin and join with the machine was rendered probable by the fact that, as has been pointed out in connection with Drusus' project, their economic interests would become identical with those of the old nobles, so that their retainers would in general be at the disposal of the machine. The assimilation would be aided by the social prestige of the nobles and by the corporate feeling which naturally develops in all bodies whose membership is more or less permanent. The new senate would thus be stronger than the old, because its members would possess a larger proportion of the aggregate wealth of Rome and could afford to maintain a larger number of retainers to vote in the rural tribes. Sulla, by approximately doubling the size of the senate,[1] increased its influence on the assembly, for every knight to whom he gave a seat carried his retainers with him from the side of a potential opposition to the support of the machine. The equestrian order was thus dealt a second blow ; while some of its leading members were won over to the government, the power of the remainder was effectively diminished. Sulla might believe, and perhaps rightly, that for some time at least the senatorial machine, strengthened by his new senators, would be able to control the assembly without extraneous assistance.

[1] The size of the senate would obviously depend on the average life of the quæstors. Their number was not quite doubled, but before Sulla the censors had some voice. Under the new system the senate, in fact, seems to have numbered about 600.

## § 3. CONSTITUTIONAL REFORMS

The measures so far discussed, while enlarging the senate, did not otherwise modify its position or alter the constitution. In the past the authority of the conscript fathers had been based to a large extent upon custom and had, therefore, always been open to challenge. This condition Sulla determined to remedy by turning custom into positive law and so making any interference with the government of the conscript fathers unquestionably illegal. This was a necessary safeguard for the future, since it would leave the capitalists when they recovered from their temporary weakness without any opening for a successful attack upon the senate's policy. Since past experience seemed to show that any alliance between the rabble and the knights was likely to be short-lived, Sulla determined to reshape the constitution so that such an alliance could only hope to accomplish anything by years of steady and concerted action.

The assembly retained its old electoral rights in full, and there was nothing to prevent the choice of magistrates belonging to the opposition. The task of Sulla was to make such arrangements as would render it impossible for them to alter the policy of the government until, with the lapse of years, such elections should have affected the views of a majority of the new senate. Since the method by which the opposition had hitherto been able to interfere successfully was by legislation, Sulla naturally revived his earlier law which forbade the submission of any bill to the assembly until it had received the sanction and approval of the senate.[1] This deprived the tribunes of all power of initiative, but, since Sulla knew that they had generally been the leaders of anti-senatorial combinations, he felt it necessary to hamper and restrict them still further. Even without the right to propose legislation to which the senate objected, they could still hinder its action and intimidate it by the use of their veto and by holding

[1] The renewal of this limitation has been questioned, but I do not think that there are serious grounds for doubting it. It is possible that Sulla deprived the tribunes of all power to initiate bills, but I cannot believe that he would leave the consuls and prætors free to propose laws without the senate's sanction.

public meetings. Accordingly Sulla further enacted that no man who held this office should ever be eligible to any other. This, with the loss of their initiative, would render the office unimportant in itself and prevent any ambitious man from accepting it, especially since Sulla also prohibited immediate re-election. The prizes of official life now lay in the provinces, and the way to them was through the prætorship and consulship. The tribunes under Sulla's arrangements would always be insignificant persons who knew they had no chance of reaching the higher offices and were perforce content with such increase in their importance as the tribunate would bring. But even the most insignificant man might seek a little popularity and notoriety by using his brief emergence from obscurity to annoy the machine and perhaps extort concessions from it. A tribune still possessed a veto on all magisterial acts performed within the limits of the city and might thus thwart the senate's policy for a time, even if he could do little to enforce any other. Sulla had no wish to deprive the tribunes of their veto, which the senate might find useful to check independent consuls. He must have realized that a man who had been submissive to the machine in the lower offices might assert himself when he had reached the highest place, since subservience could then no longer be rewarded by promotion. In such a case the tribune's veto would be an effective weapon, and Sulla contented himself with placing some restrictions on it without abolishing it altogether. Any violation of these restrictions was made punishable by a fine which might be so heavy as to amount to the confiscation of the offender's property, and the decision was left to a jury composed exclusively of senators. With such a penalty hanging over their heads it was not likely that the tribunes in the future would dare to use any powers which they retained in a fashion displeasing to the conscript fathers. Thus restricted and hampered, the tribunes might occasionally be of real service to the senate and could hardly become obstructive or dangerous. Their chief function would henceforth be their original one of protecting individuals.

Sulla naturally re-enacted the *lex Villia annalis*, which prescribed a regular order in which the offices must be held: first the quæstorship, then the prætorship, and finally the consulship, with an interval of at least two years between each.[1] He took advantage of the opportunity to make some changes, however, permitting re-election to any office only after an interval of ten years, and raising the age of eligibility for each. Henceforth a man had to be thirty years old to be elected quæstor and forty to be elected prætor, so that he could not hold the consulship till he was forty-three.

It was, of course, inevitable that Sulla should deprive the knights of their privileges as jurors in the standing courts. These he thoroughly reorganized by a series of statutes, increasing the number and constituting the juries of senators. A minor reason for enlarging the senate may have been to provide an adequate supply of jurors for these courts, since the old senate of 300 members could not furnish a sufficient number. This can hardly have been the main reason, however, for several of the juries had little political importance and could have been left to the knights without serious danger. In remodelling the standing courts Sulla, by the Cornelian law concerning each, defined the cases over which it had jurisdiction, and prescribed the penalties as well as the composition of the jury. In this way he clarified and re-cast the criminal law of Rome, at least for all serious offences, and greatly limited the activities of the older prætorian courts, acting under the common law. This part of his work was of a permanent character, and it is not too much to say that he, more than any other one man, laid the foundations of the
* Roman criminal law.

### § 4. THE PROVINCIAL ADMINISTRATION AND THE ARMY

Before Sulla's time the senate had been gradually substituting promagistrates for magistrates as governors of the provinces. This change Sulla accepted and completed; henceforth the consuls and prætors regularly remained in Italy during their year of office, and were sent out to govern the provinces as proconsuls and proprætors during the following year. Normally the proprætors would then return to Rome as private citizens for at least a year before they were eligible to stand for the consulship. During this year of private life they were open to prosecution, impossible while

[1] The interval was three years if the time between candidacies is counted, two years between the time when a man laid down one office and the time when he could enter on the next.

they held the *imperium*, for any illegal acts which they might have committed as prætors or proprætors; moreover, if a charge was pending against them at the time of the election, they were barred as candidates. Under exceptional circumstances the senate could extend the *imperium* for a second year, but Sulla probably thought that this would only occasionally be necessary, since it would tend to render the proprætors, at least, less easy to call to account and destroy the main object of the two-year interval which he insisted upon.

If the senate was to govern through the promagistrates without resorting to an extension of their *imperium* with any frequency, it was necessary that they should have at their disposal a sufficient staff of governors. Surveying the empire, Sulla concluded that there were only ten regions where a governor with the *imperium* was likely to be regularly needed. He thus recognized the existence of ten provinces (the two Spains, Sicily, Sardinia and Corsica, Africa, Macedon, Asia, Cilicia, and the two Gauls), and to provide enough governors he increased the number of prætors from six to eight, so that with the two consuls there would be enough promagistrates in normal times. The command of the army was entrusted as before to the provincial governors, and the number of soldiers stationed in each province, together with the amount of money allowed the governor for the pay of his troops and the expenses of administration, was determined by the senate. In the assignment of provinces likewise Sulla made no change; every year the senate decided which provinces should be consular and which prætorian, and they were then distributed by lot among the magistrates.[1] In continuing the old system in spite of its manifest inefficiency Sulla's motives were probably the same as those which had led the oligarchy to devise and maintain it, namely, that it was the best means available of preventing factional strife within the senate and the aristocracy.

It has often been said that Sulla failed to appreciate the danger to his constitution which might arise from an ambitious

[1] The senate could, but rarely did, assign a particular province to a prætor. In the case of the consuls it could only advise them to settle the matter in a certain way by agreement instead of by drawing lots, but either could refuse and insist on the lot.

proconsul. It should be remembered, however, that the ordinary provincial governor was not likely to give trouble. The army which he commanded was usually small, too small at least for a successful march on Rome, and the real danger lay in the man whom the necessities of the time forced the senate to place in charge of an important war. This was unfortunate, but there was no help for it. Under existing conditions a large army could only be raised quickly by calling for volunteers, who would not come forward promptly unless the general possessed the confidence of some section of the rural proletariat. Once the army was raised it belonged, as Sulla had himself demonstrated, to the general and not to the state from which he received his command. What such a general might do was obvious, but there was probably nothing in the nature of a safeguard that Sulla could devise.

The only way in which the Republic could be protected from its armies was to secure their allegiance to the senate rather than to their general. To do this it would have been necessary to establish a permanent standing army large enough to cope with any situation likely to arise, and to provide some way in which the senate would be responsible for providing land for the veterans when their term of service expired. It is not likely that Sulla had sufficient originality of mind to think of such a plan ; even if he did, the difficulties in the way may have been insurmountable. It is very doubtful whether the treasury could have borne the strain,[1] and probably no class in Rome would have accepted a standing army at that time. If Sulla's system was to stand even for his lifetime, it must have some defenders and be able to count upon the support of some important classes of society. Sulla's new senate would probably have viewed with great disfavour the expenditure of large sums of money on an army for which there was no immediate need, and, even if he possessed profounder insight than his generation, he may well have perceived that to go too far in advance of his contemporaries was to court certain failure for the sake of guarding against perils which might not arise for a long time to come. While

[1] Even with the greatly increased revenue at his disposal, Augustus found serious difficulty in providing for his soldiers when their term of service expired. In Sulla's time such provision may have been beyond the resources of the treasury.

he lived he could maintain his constitution, and it is possible that he cared little what might happen after he was gone. For the present the senate had a bodyguard in his veterans, to whom he had assigned lands and who to defend their titles would be forced to support his system.

### § 5. THE ABDICATION AND DEATH OF SULLA

When he had completed his reconstruction of the aristocratic machine and his reorganization of the government, Sulla was ready to retire to private life. In 80 B.C. he assumed the consulship for the second time with Metellus Pius as his colleague, and took care to have his laws formally ratified by the assembly. In 79, after declining a third consulship, he appeared before the people, laid down his dictatorship, dismissed his lictors and bodyguard, and returned to his home a private citizen. He soon quitted Rome altogether and withdrew to his country estate in Campania, where he spent the remainder of his life, occupying his leisure with the writing of his autobiography, which unfortunately has perished, with rural pursuits, and with other less innocent pleasures. He had attained at last one of his ambitions, a life of ease with every luxury which he desired and which money could buy.

He was not destined to enjoy his retirement long, for in the next year (78) he died suddenly at the age of sixty. His enemies found what consolation they could in picturing him enduring the long agonies of an imaginary disease,[1] but the fact is certain that his death was sudden and that he was able to transact business almost to the last. His funeral was the most splendid which Rome had ever witnessed. His body was borne in state to the city under the escort of his former soldiers, and the fear of these men was such that all Rome seemed to mourn. Contrary to the custom of the Cornelian *gens*, who had always buried their dead, the body of Sulla the Fortunate, as he had styled himself, was burned with great ceremony in the Campus Martius. A tablet erected to his memory bore an inscription, written by himself, which declared that no man had ever done him so much good or evil that he had not repaid it in full.

[1] Phthiriasis, where the flesh turns to worms.

As to the character of Sulla everyone must form his own opinion. It is certainly possible to interpret his whole career as that of a poor aristocrat seeking wealth for the sake of the pleasures and luxuries which wealth will buy, without strong convictions and prepared to join or forsake any party to secure his own advancement. The easiest path to wealth lay through the magistracies to a province or to a profitable war. Sulla pursued this path without scruple, hesitation, or remorse. He arrived at supreme power and wealth at the same time, and he used his power to reorganize the constitution and the aristocratic machine in such a way that he could fling aside the power, which had been a means to an end in so far as it was not thrust upon him by events, in order that he might enjoy the wealth which had been the true object of his ambition. Such a reading of his character seems too simple to be wholly true, for men are rarely without complexities and contradictions. On the surface Sulla had them, for, while he was a gay, cultivated, pleasure-loving man of the world, he was also a gallant soldier, a great general, and a clear-sighted statesman whom nothing could turn from his purpose. Did the contradictions go deeper and did he have sincere convictions and higher aspirations than mere wealth? It seems probable that he had something, perhaps much, of genuine Roman pride and patriotism, that he rejoiced to fight Mithridates not only for gain but to avenge his country's wrongs. His constant pose as a favourite of the gods and his assumption of the surname of Felix may have been intended to impress his superstitious soldiers, or they may have been partly the form taken by his consciousness of his own abilities. In reorganizing the state he had little choice, but in strengthening the senate he may have acted on a real political conviction; it is clear that in his reorganization he went beyond his purely personal interests and aimed to give Rome a stable and efficient government of the kind he may have honestly believed was best suited to her needs. With all its shortcomings the rule of the senate might well appear better than that of the rabble and the capitalists, and if Sulla in his cool ironic cynicism had few illusions about the merits of the nobles, he might still prefer them to the only alternative. Some patriotism and political conviction should doubtless be added to the character of the noble in search of a fortune, but in precisely what proportions it is impossible for us, and would perhaps have been impossible for him, to say.

The greatness of Sulla cannot for a moment be denied. He was one of the strongest and ablest men whom Rome produced. Whatever object he aimed at he pursued with a courage, resolution, and ability which must command our admiration in spite of any disapproval of some of the means employed. That he rendered real services to his country must be admitted, though it is possible to exaggerate their extent. He captured Jugurtha, but the Numidian was a nuisance rather than a danger ; he gained glory in the Social War, but the war was really won by concessions and not by the sword ; he conquered Mithridates, but there were others who were equal to the task and could have done it quite as well. Sulla is entitled to great credit for his victories, because he fought his enemy under such adverse conditions, but these conditions were largely the result of the violent means by which he had retained his command. There is no reason to doubt that had Sulpicius Rufus been allowed to settle the Italian question, and had Marius been permitted to undertake the conduct of the war even with the half-hearted support of the government at Rome, he would have beaten Mithridates, and beaten him, perhaps, sooner and more thoroughly. Able as Sulla undoubtedly was, little of his work was destined to prove lasting. The reaction in Italy which his violence produced not only left him to fight Mithridates under heavy handicaps, but obliged him to leave that monarch in possession of his kingdom, and thus to make another war possible ; while his new constitution survived him but eight years and was destroyed by two of his own lieutenants.

For this speedy failure of his work Sulla was not responsible. Had there been no democratic reaction in Italy, he would probably have disposed of Mithridates permanently ; had he been able to find better materials for an oligarchy, he would no doubt have used them. That his senate was incapable of holding the power he had given it was due to one essential weakness which he was powerless to remedy. It could maintain itself only if he left behind him enough popular and loyal generals to enable it to deal with all difficulties which might arise with their assistance. In fact, so far as we can judge, Sulla left but four competent generals, Metellus, Lucullus,

Pompey, and Crassus. The rebellion of Sertorius in Spain forced Sulla to send Metellus to deal with him and the remnants of the democratic party which had found a refuge in his camp. Of the other three, Lucullus seems to have been loyal to the senate but to have lacked popularity, while Crassus and Pompey were popular but untrustworthy, a fact that Sulla himself recognized. Nevertheless they were the only men on whom the senate could call in an emergency where swift action was indispensable ; if it found itself compelled to seek their help, it would have to deal with them afterwards as best it could. No law was of any value here, for laws cannot change sentiment, although they may control action ; a senate placed in power by the sword might be overthrown by the sword if circumstances should force it to entrust the command of powerful armies to generals whose loyalty it was unable to secure.

## CHAPTER IX

# THE RISE OF POMPEY

### § 1. SERTORIUS AND METELLUS

SULLA had brought the entire Roman world to acknowledge the authority of his senate with the exception of Spain, where the democratic governor, Q. Sertorius, remained in arms. Sertorius was by far the ablest man among the democrats, but neither Cinna nor his successors in the control of the party had known how to make use of him, and during the Civil War in Italy he had been sent as propraetor to Hither Spain. In 82 B.C. he succeeded in getting possession of the province and set himself to secure the goodwill of the natives, but a new governor named by Sulla soon appeared upon the scene, and Sertorius was unable to maintain himself. At the head of some 3000 men he fled to Mauretania, where he began an adventurous career as a free-lance. In Spain discontent was general among the natives; the Lusitanians, a powerful tribe in the region now known as Portugal, who were planning a revolt against Rome, invited Sertorius to become their leader, and he accepted the invitation (80 B.C.). He was soon able to raise an army among the Spanish tribes, which he had enough Romans to officer and drill in the Roman fashion. His position from the first was difficult, for, while posing as the legitimate Roman governor of Spain, he was relying for support upon a national insurrection of the Spaniards against Rome, but for a time he met with remarkable success. Sulla was so much alarmed by the spread of the movement that he despatched Metellus Pius, one of his best generals, to Spain to suppress it. Metellus arrived in 79, but it soon became apparent that he was no match for Sertorius. The latter adopted guerrilla tactics against Metellus himself, defeated the governor of Hither Spain, and occupied the greater part of that province. By 77 B.C. Metellus was confined to Farther Spain and was earnestly calling for reinforcements.

It is difficult to follow the campaigns of Sertorius in any detail, but the broad outlines of his policy are fairly clear. The Roman element among his followers was steadily strengthened by refugees from Italy, so that he was able to give a distinctly Roman appearance to his government by setting up the semblance of a senate, which he consulted on occasion, although it is not likely that he allowed it to exercise much real influence. The Spaniards were conciliated by every means available, the severest punishment being inflicted upon any Romans who were guilty of misconduct towards them. He founded a school for the sons of native chiefs, in this way indirectly securing hostages for the loyalty of their fathers. While he introduced Roman discipline among his Spanish soldiers, he was careful not to destroy their aptitude for guerrilla warfare, to which the character of the country was particularly adapted. The superstitions of his followers were also turned to account by means of a white fawn, which he pretended had been given to him by Diana. The fawn became so tame that it followed him everywhere, and whenever he received any secret information he announced it as coming from the goddess through the animal. By these and other means, joined to the clemency, justice, and moderation with which he governed, he won the enthusiastic devotion of the Spaniards and was able to keep the Romans firmly in hand, since their hopes of a return to Italy rested wholly upon his success.

## § 2. THE REVOLT OF LEPIDUS

In the first consular elections after Sulla laid down the dictatorship the results had been unsatisfactory to him, for Catulus and Lepidus had been chosen for 78 B.C. Catulus was a dependable man belonging to the old nobility, but Lepidus, although also of a noble family, was ambitious and untrustworthy, and was elected in spite of the warnings of the ex-dictator. The death of Sulla seemed to Lepidus to furnish an opportunity to imitate the career of Cinna, and he lost no time in making a bid for the leadership of a counter-revolution to undo the work of Sulla. He sought support from the discontented elements in Italy by proposing to recall exiles, to restore the corn law, and to give back to the Italians the lands which Sulla had confiscated. The senate did not venture to oppose the revival of the corn law, but the other measures of Lepidus were successfully resisted. In Northern Etruria, however, the Italians took matters into their own hands, driving out the veterans whom Sulla had settled at Fæsulæ. This was armed rebellion, and the senate was compelled to order the consuls to suppress it. Such a commission gave Lepidus an excuse to raise an army, with which he promptly put himself at the head of the insurgents. Appealing to all who had suffered under Sulla and desired the overthrow of the existing government, he was soon at the head of a large force. Leaving a lieutenant, M. Junius Brutus (the father of Cæsar's murderer) in the North, he marched on Rome to demand a second consulship and the restoration to the tribunes of their former powers. The situation was obviously critical, so much so that the senate's only hope of averting the rule of another Cinna lay in checking Lepidus at once. Catulus was faithful to the government, but he was no soldier, so when Pompey, who had supported Lepidus in the elections for 78, offered his services, the terrified senate eagerly accepted them. Catulus, no doubt with the help of Sulla's veterans, drove Lepidus back from Rome, and he retreated to Etruria.

In appearance the rebellion was still formidable, but in reality it was doomed, since the name of Pompey was sufficient to put an end to any serious danger. From his father the young general had inherited a great popularity in Picenum, one of the best recruiting grounds in Italy, and in the Civil War he had gained a reputation out of all proportion to his actual achievements. The news that he was taking the field on the side of the government checked the spread of the movement, for the discontented elements took his success as a matter of course, and no one desired to enlist on the losing side. Pompey had no trouble in finding soldiers and marched at once into Cisalpine Gaul, where he blockaded Brutus in Mutina and soon forced him to surrender. Pompey put his prisoner to death, somewhat treacherously we are told, and then moved southward into Etruria, where he defeated Lepidus in a battle near Cosa. Seeing that his cause was lost, Lepidus embarked his forces and sailed to Sardinia, which he attempted to seize, but the governor beat off the attack. Lepidus died soon after, leaving the command of what remained of his army to M. Perperna, who sought refuge in Spain, where he and his men joined Sertorius.

The revolution had been successfully stamped out in Italy before it could get fairly started, but to accomplish this the senate had placed Pompey in command of most of its troops. Refusing to disband his soldiers, he suggested that he be sent with them to Spain to reinforce the army of Metellus. The conscript fathers grasped at this chance of getting rid of him, and he was invested with the proconsulship of Hither Spain.[1] Having gained his wishes, Pompey departed on a mission which was destined to prove longer and more difficult than he probably expected.

### § 3. THE END OF THE SERTORIAN WAR

Pompey did not arrive in Spain in time to begin active campaigning until 76 B.C. Some of the Celtiberian tribes were friendly or readily submitted, but neither he nor Metellus was able to accomplish much against Sertorius, who, reinforced by Perperna, captured the town of Lauro under Pompey's very eyes. Both Pompey and Metellus were forced to spend the winter in the north of Spain, where they could get supplies
* from Transalpine Gaul. Early in 75 Pompey pushed southward again, defeated Perperna near Valentia and captured the town, while Metellus inflicted a crushing defeat upon another of the lieutenants of Sertorius near Segovia, and then turned to join Pompey, against whom Sertorius himself was now advancing. Pompey risked a battle, in which he was probably saved from defeat only by the timely arrival of Metellus. Although Sertorius was still powerful, his influence had been much shaken by the disasters of his lieutenants, and he was forced to fall back upon guerrilla tactics. Pompey and Metellus found themselves so much hampered by the want of food that Pompey wrote to the senate in a tone little short of despair.

[1] How is not certain. We are told that he was sent by the senate. Legally he could only be given the *imperium* by a special law passed by the assembly, and the senate's approval of the bill was necessary before it could be voted on. Perhaps this is what happened.

He complained bitterly of the inadequate support which he had received from Italy, and declared that unless the government gave him prompt assistance his army would return home, abandoning the struggle, and that Sertorius would invade Italy. The seriousness of the situation may have been exaggerated, but reinforcements and money were sent from Rome. Sertorius also sought outside help and concluded a treaty with Mithridates, but nothing came of it.[1]

The success of Pompey and Metellus in 75 B.C., such as it was, definitely turned the tide against Sertorius. However much he harassed his opponents, his forces were outnumbered and he lost ground steadily. Worst of all, dissensions broke out among his followers; the Romans began to desert him as his prospects of invading Italy vanished, and those who remained quarrelled with the Spaniards. Sertorius was likewise forced to make heavier demands upon the natives, whose enthusiasm diminished as his fortunes waned. Perceiving his loss of prestige, he was driven to stern measures in order to intimidate the wavering. As his authority diminished, he leaned more and more upon the natives, so that the discontent of the Romans in his camp rapidly increased. Taking advantage of this, Perperna finally formed a plot against his life and succeeded in murdering him in 72 B.C. With the death of the great leader the insurrection collapsed. Perperna tried to save himself by handing over to Pompey the papers of Sertorius, among them a number of letters from prominent men in Rome, but Pompey put Perperna to death and burned the papers. The war in Spain was over, and public opinion in Italy gave Pompey the credit for having ended it.[2] Perhaps more important for his future was the fact that he was proconsul of Hither Spain, while Metellus had the Farther province, so that, when the senate, terrified by a new danger, was again seeking a protector, Pompey rather than Metellus was summoned to return to Italy with his army.

[1] During the entire war he had an understanding with the pirates then plundering throughout the Mediterranean, and they gave him a good deal of help by intercepting the supplies of his opponents.

[2] Plutarch, *Pompey*, ch. 21. This seems to be borne out by the course of events later.

## § 4. ITALY IN THE ABSENCE OF POMPEY

After Pompey's departure for Spain the senate had settled back to its appointed task of governing Rome. The machine permitted the revival of the corn law,[1] and it also consented to the repeal of Sulla's law forbidding the tribunes to hold any other office. Probably this restriction was not regarded as of vital importance, and it may have been hoped that a concession on this point would do something to allay the popular discontent.

The first serious difficulty arose when a new war with Mithridates broke out in the East. In 75 or 74 B.C. Nicomedes, king of Bithynia, died and bequeathed his kingdom to Rome. The acceptance of the legacy by the senate so alarmed Mithridates that he at once took up arms and advanced into Bithynia with the bulk of his forces, sending smaller armies against Asia, Cappadocia, and Phrygia. The work of Sulla had now to be done over again, and the senate was obliged to seek a general. One of the consuls for 74 was L. Licinius Lucullus, who was probably the ablest general among the officers of Sulla and who was devoted to the senate; he was eager for the command, but there were legal difficulties in the way. After some trouble these were overcome, and he was sent to the East to take charge of the war. As a result of his departure the senate was left with but one capable general at hand in the person of Crassus, of whose loyalty the conscript fathers entertained justifiable doubts. Yet if a new storm broke out they might find themselves compelled to turn to him in spite of their distrust.

Hardly had Lucullus gone before the clouds began to gather. In 73 B.C. a band of gladiators led by a Thracian named Spartacus broke from their barracks at Capua and began a career of brigandage. In Lucania they were joined by many of the slaves employed in herding the sheep and cattle of the wealthy ranchers. Troops hastily raised were sent against them under one of the prætors, but they were routed by Spartacus. In 72 B.C. the servile insurrection had grown so menacing that both consuls took the field, only to be defeated.

[1] The law of Lepidus was probably cancelled after his overthrow, and the corn law was finally revived in 73 B.C. by the *lex Terentia-Cassia*. (See Holmes, *The Roman Republic*, I, pp. 363–64.)

The rebels now ranged unchecked over Italy, and it was clear that the ordinary machine politicians at the head of hasty and ill-trained levies were worse than useless. In panic the senate assigned the charge of the war to Crassus, who was one of the prætors for 72.

Crassus at once set himself to gather recruits and to restore discipline among the demoralized troops whom the senate handed over to him. When he took the field, he drove Spartacus into Bruttium and there sought to blockade him. Spartacus, however, succeeded in breaking the lines, so that Crassus seemed no more successful than his predecessors, and the conscript fathers, more frightened than ever, summoned Pompey with his army to assist in crushing the rebel. Pompey responded gladly, but he found little to do except to intercept and cut down a number of the fleeing slaves,[1] for Crassus was able to bring on a pitched battle, wherein he won a victory which was rendered decisive by the death of Spartacus. Rome might have breathed freely again had it not been for the fact that there were now in Italy two generals of somewhat uncertain convictions at the head of victorious armies. It remained for the senate to deal with them, and for them to decide upon their attitude toward each other and the senate.

## § 5. THE FALL OF SULLA'S CONSTITUTION

Both Pompey and Crassus had fought on Sulla's side in the Civil War, but neither had any sincere attachment to his constitution or the political machine which he had set up. In this there is no necessary inconsistency, for when Sulla first landed in Italy he posed as a moderate, and he might well seem to many the only man who could deliver the Republic from the grip of the gang which had come into power with Cinna, and which had since ruled by force very thinly disguised by constitutional forms. Until Sulla had beaten down all opposition, he had given no hint of the ruthless and drastic use he meant to make of power. It would be quite possible, therefore, for men of moderate views to join him out of disgust at the crimes and blunders of the self-styled democrats, and to feel almost equal disgust at the proscriptions and the sweeping changes which followed his victory. Both Pompey and

[1] According to Plutarch (*Pompey*, ch. 21) the number was 5000.

Crassus had ended by incurring his displeasure, Pompey by demanding an illegal triumph for his success in Africa, and Crassus by some tampering with the proscription lists. Although the dictator had indulged Pompey's vanity, and had inflicted no punishment on Crassus, they had aroused his distrust, and he permitted them no further part in public life. His senate shared his view of both, and they must soon have seen that they were likely to get little from the reorganized machine. Events soon enabled Pompey to force his services upon the reluctant senate, but Crassus remained longer in the cool shades of retirement. He occupied his leisure with business and amassed the fortune which was afterwards a byword. The foundation of this fortune was laid in the time of the proscriptions. An immense amount of property was then confiscated, and much that was not needed for his veterans Sulla sold at public auction. Under the circumstances it is clear that any man with ready money could buy to great advantage in a market glutted by the goods of the proscribed, but, if we take into account the awe and terror which Sulla inspired, it is evident that a man known to be one of his friends and lieutenants would find few who dared to bid against him. Crassus used his opportunities so well that he had made himself rich before the discovery of some of his methods provoked the anger of the dictator. In the years that followed he increased his wealth by successful speculation, in the course of which he must have been brought into more or less close contact with the new capitalist class which was fast arising. He was, perhaps, already the richest man in Rome when the danger to the whole fabric of Roman society from the revolt of the slaves compelled the senate, much against its will, to seek his help.

Neither Pompey nor Crassus, therefore, had any reason to love the senate, and both had reason enough to wish to break its complete control over the government. Their course might have been anticipated with ease, but for the fact that they happened to be personal enemies. It was probably the knowledge of this enmity which led the senate to blunder in its handling of the situation. Confident that they would never unite their forces, it saw a chance to play them off against each other and in this way to avoid unwelcome concessions to either. Had the conscript fathers been more far-sighted they might have conciliated Pompey, who could have been secured without much difficulty and whose army was the stronger of the two. For himself that general demanded the consulship, a demand which was at once perfectly natural and entirely illegal. He had never held any of the lower offices required as a qualification, and before he could legally become a candidate he would have to work his way up from the quæstorship. One can hardly blame Pompey, who had already enjoyed a triumph and held the rank of a proconsul in Spain, if he felt no inclination to go through such a long and humiliating process, for the subordinate office of quæstor would have been a curious anti-climax at this point in his career. He felt not unreasonably that since he had risen in an exceptional way a further exception ought to be made, and that he should be allowed to hold the consulship without the legal preliminaries. Such an exception the senate could grant, for it had assumed the right to confer dispensations upon favoured individuals. Crassus had been prætor, but he could not legally hold the consulship until 69 B.C. Under other circumstances he might have been content to wait until he was eligible, but he was jealous of Pompey and anxious to place himself as nearly as possible on an equal footing. If Pompey was to receive an exceptional privilege, he was determined that he also should receive a similar distinction by being allowed to become a candidate at once.

It was soon apparent that neither was at all likely to obtain any special privileges from the senate unless they applied pressure to that body. We may conjecture that the senate counted on their inability to work together, and expected that Sulla's disbanded veterans would rally to whichever of the two appeared to be supporting Sulla's constitution. If such hopes were entertained, their vanity was soon demonstrated. Although Pompey and Crassus disliked each other, neither was prepared to pay too high a price to gratify his animosity. If they fought, there was the risk that the senate would be able to eliminate the victor, so they decided to combine to secure what they wanted. Under the pretext of celebrating triumphs for their victories they marched their armies to the neighbourhood of Rome,[1] and presented themselves as

[1] Some of the troops always took part in a triumph. The soldiers were of course disarmed, but were kept together, and their arms were doubtless

candidates for the consulship. The senate found itself helpless, for Sulla's veterans cared only for their lands, and the fact that both men had been his officers doubtless allayed any fears they might have had on that score.

Once the two generals had extorted the senate's sanction for their candidacy there could be no doubt of their success, but it was obviously desirable to surround their election with as much enthusiasm as possible. An agreement with the democrats was a simple expedient and one which harmonized with the personal interests of both men, perhaps also with their convictions.[1] The support of the people was gained by the promise of restoring the powers of the tribunes, while the knights were won by the hope of regaining their control of the courts; the machine was too thoroughly cowed to offer any opposition, so that Pompey and Crassus were elected * consuls for 70 B.C. with apparent unanimity and enthusiasm.

Having carried their point, the consuls elect were by no means ready to disband their armies; Pompey postponed his triumph on the ground that Metellus must share it with him, and Crassus could plausibly claim that Pompey should act first in the matter. Even after they had taken office they found excuses for keeping their men together,[2] and were thus able to continue their coercion of the senate. The conscript fathers were obliged to permit the election of censors and the repeal of Sulla's law by which the senate's sanction was made necessary before a bill could be submitted to the assembly. By this last measure the control of the senate over legislation was destroyed, and the tribunes recovered almost all the powers which they had formerly possessed.

The motives for the revival of the censorship seem to have been two, to cleanse the senate of some of its unworthy members and to complete the registration of the new citizens. Both purposes were more or less thoroughly carried out; sixty-four senators were deprived of their seats, and the number of citizens enumerated in the census rose from 463,000 (in 85 B.C.) to 900,000. The figure is still too small to have

within easy reach. Pompey claimed the full honour of a triumph as the conqueror of Spain, while Crassus only claimed an ovation, practically the same thing but celebrated with less pomp and conferring less honour.

[1] Pompey may have been an honest moderate, but it is difficult to credit Crassus with any real convictions.

[2] See Appendix 5.

included all the new citizens, but it is probable that only those who could claim a place in the centuries of the three or four higher classes in each tribe would take the trouble to register, and it is not unreasonable to assume that most of the former Latins and Italians who met the property qualification for these classes were now enrolled in the centuries and for the first time acquired a vote in the election of the higher magistrates.

Another reform which, although not proposed by the consuls, was doubtless carried with their support was a reorganization of the courts. Henceforth the juries were to be composed of senators, knights, and *tribuni ærarii* in equal numbers. Just who the *tribuni ærarii* were is a much disputed point, but they seem to have voted generally with the knights, so that they were probably the lesser business men whose property fell short of the equestrian rating. In practice the change amounted to giving the knights control of the courts once more, but a control less absolute than they had enjoyed under the system of C. Gracchus.

We may reasonably assume that during the year some provision was made for the armies. No mention of this is to be found in our sources, but it is difficult to believe either that the soldiers made no demand for land or that no attention was paid to their demands. It is possible that the soldiers of Crassus were mainly small landowners who had rushed to arms to protect their property from the ravages of Spartacus and his slaves, and that they were willing to return to their homes without reward. On the other hand, some of the soldiers of Pompey must have served for eight or nine years, and it would be truly extraordinary if they had advanced no claims. The silence of the ancient writers whose works have survived should probably be interpreted as showing that whatever measures were adopted to provide for them encountered no opposition. Perhaps many were satisfied with lands in Spain, and the ravages of the servile war may have left some lands in Italy vacant. All that is certain is that the consuls ultimately disposed of their soldiers in some way without serious difficulty.

Even when Pompey and Crassus had extorted the senate's sanction for their programme and had seen it duly enacted, they were still unwilling to dismiss their armies. In fact, the consuls were rivals, and differed on every matter which was not covered by their pre-election agreements. As the year wore on their constant dissensions caused growing alarm lest a new war should break out between them. Finally, toward the close of the year they yielded to public appeals, went through the form of a reconciliation, and disbanded their troops. In fact, the armies were now useless, for neither Pompey nor Crassus really wished a civil war. Probably both had kept strictly within the letter of the law, however much they had violated its spirit. Until they had celebrated their triumphs they could legally keep their armies together, and after this they could find pretexts without difficulty which the senate was obliged by fear to accept. What the sword had established by open violence the sword now overthrew under the outward forms of law; when Pompey and Crassus laid down the consulship, they left the Roman constitution very nearly as it had been before Sulla. In many details, such as the increase in the size of the senate, the dictator's work survived, but no trace remained of the ingenious constitutional devices by which he had sought to make the senate the supreme governing body of the Republic.

## § 6. LUCULLUS AND MITHRIDATES

While these events were passing in Rome, Lucullus was winning glory in the East by his conduct of the new war with Mithridates, which had arisen over the annexation of the kingdom of Bithynia by Rome. The colleague of Lucullus in the consulship, M. Aurelius Cotta, was sent with a fleet and some troops to occupy the new province, while Asia, Cilicia, and the general command on land were assigned to Lucullus. They both left Italy while still consuls in order to deal with the critical situation in Asia Minor, but before they arrived on the scene, toward the end of 74 B.C.,[1] Mithridates had taken possession of Bithynia and was threatening other districts; many cities had joined him, and unrest was general throughout Asia. Lucullus brought with him one legion which he had raised in Italy, and took over the command of the Roman troops in the East. About half of these were the old soldiers

[1] The chronology is disputed. Reinach (*Mithridate Eupator*, p. 321) holds that the war did not begin till 73 B.C. On the other side, see Holmes, *The Roman Republic*, I, pp. 398–403.

of Fimbria, whom Sulla had left as a garrison in Asia. Lucullus found that his first task was to restore discipline in the army under him, and to check the spread of disaffection among the provincials by compelling the knights to moderate their exactions. While he was thus occupied, Mithridates defeated Cotta at Chalcedon and pushed on to Cyzicus, which he besieged with the bulk of his army. Hastening to the rescue of his colleague, Lucullus succeeded in cutting off Mithridates' communications by land, while the citizens of Cyzicus held out stubbornly. In the winter the position of the king became untenable, and when he attempted to retreat a large part of his army was cut off and destroyed, although he himself with some of his troops made his escape by sea. Lucullus could not press the pursuit, for he was delayed for some time in Cyzicus, gathering a fleet from the cities of Asia.

In the spring of 73 B.C. active operations were resumed. The new Roman fleet with little difficulty cleared the Aegean and practically destroyed the fleet of Mithridates. Leaving Cotta to capture Heraclea, Lucullus invaded Pontus and besieged Amisus, but the town held out for a considerable time, so that at length Lucullus with part of his army pushed on into the interior. Mithridates had gathered his forces at Cabira, where he met Lucullus in a battle which resulted in a complete success for the Romans. Abandoning his kingdom, Mithridates fled to Armenia in the hope of obtaining aid from Tigranes, the king of that country. Tigranes, however, was not disposed to take risks and so contented himself with sheltering Mithridates. Lucullus and his lieutenants captured the Greek towns of Pontus one after another, and by the middle of 70 B.C. practically the entire kingdom had submitted. During these operations Lucullus found time to regulate the affairs of Asia, where the exactions of Sulla had forced the cities to borrow heavily from the Roman capitalists. They had since fallen still more deeply into debt, so that they were now on the verge of ruin. Lucullus was enough of a statesman to see clearly that the bankruptcy of Asia would be a disaster to the Roman treasury, and that to drive the provincials to despair was to invite rebellion. He adopted drastic measures to meet the situation, reducing the interest on debts and cancelling part of the principal, and in this way succeeded in restoring the prosperity of the province, but at the cost of incurring the bitter enmity of the knights. For the moment the senate was strong enough to protect him from the rage of the capitalists, who were forced to bide their time.

Lucullus may have underestimated the power of the equestrian class in Rome, where many changes had taken place in his absence, but he understood perfectly that his success against Mithridates would prove temporary if the king himself remained at large. The Pontic monarch, like Jugurtha, had a strong hold on his former subjects, so that his restoration to power was likely to follow any weakening of Rome's position in the East. Lucullus was determined to effect a permanent settlement, and was as indifferent to the wishes of the senate as to the feelings of the knights. He accordingly demanded that Tigranes surrender his guest, and on the rejection of this demand he at once attacked Armenia.

In appearance Tigranes was a formidable antagonist, for in recent years he had greatly extended his kingdom. A temporary weakness of the Parthians had enabled him to seize the northern part of Mesopotamia, where in 77 B.C. he founded a city called Tigranocerta, which he made his capital; he had also taken nearly all of Syria from the last of the Seleucid kings. In 69 B.C. Lucullus invaded these newly annexed territories, besieging Tigranocerta before Tigranes had completed his preparations for war. When the king came up at the head of a large army to raise the siege, Lucullus met him with a portion of his troops, while the rest continued the blockade. Disregarding the advice of Mithridates, who had learned wisdom by experience, Tigranes attempted to overwhelm the Romans by weight of numbers, but was completely defeated by the tactical skill of Lucullus and the superior quality of his men; Tigranocerta fell, and Syria accepted the supremacy of Rome. So far Lucullus had been brilliantly successful, but the army which he commanded was largely composed of the Fimbrian veterans, who were anxious for their discharge[1] and who disliked the haughty manners and stern discipline of their general. The refusal of Lucullus to

[1] They had been brought to Greece by Valerius Flaccus in 86 B.C. and had been in the East ever since. They were later willing to enlist under Pompey, probably because he promised them a reward in land. Unless they thought that Lucullus both could and would secure such a provision for them they might naturally wish their discharge, especially since his campaigns brought danger and hardship but little booty.

permit the unrestricted pillaging of captured towns did not increase his popularity with his troops, so that henceforth he had to contend not only with the enemy in the field but with disaffection in his own camp as well.

Lucullus spent the winter in the country which he had won from Tigranes, and in 68 B.C. advanced into Armenia itself. What he might have accomplished can only be guessed, for the discontent of his men now grew into open insubordination ; they refused to endure the hardships of a campaign in the Armenian mountains and compelled Lucullus to fall back on Mesopotamia, where he captured the city of Nisibis and made it his winter quarters. Disasters now came thick and fast ; Tigranes recovered most of his kingdom, Mithridates defeated Lucullus' lieutenant in Pontus, Cappadocia was threatened, and all that had been gained in the preceding years seemed lost. Lucullus, no longer able to control his army, was obliged to look on helplessly, and it was clear, not only that the war against Mithridates must be begun again, but that another general must be found to conduct it.

## § 7. THE GABINIAN AND MANILIAN LAWS

Mithridates was not the only foe who was giving trouble to the Romans at this time. Rome had more or less completely destroyed the other maritime powers in the Mediterranean, but she had been too preoccupied at home to make any serious attempt to police the seas, and in consequence piracy had grown rapidly. Encouraged by impunity, the pirates became bolder and built up a regular organization with strongholds on land and powerful fleets which swept the Mediterranean in all directions and plundered the coasts at will. At length, after Sulla had restored order in Italy, the senate undertook to deal with a condition which was becoming unendurable. In 78 B.C. Servilius Vatia, one of the consuls for the preceding year, was sent with an army to Cilicia, one of the chief pirate centres. Here he carried on a war against the strongholds of the freebooters with some success, but his campaigns seem merely to have dislodged the pirates, who transferred their base of operations to Crete. It was obvious that further measures were necessary, so the senate appointed M. Antonius, prætor for 74 B.C., to the command of the fleet; he was to have complete control over the seas and concurrent authority with the governors in all the provinces. He invaded Crete, where he died in 72 B.C. without having accomplished anything of importance. For a time the senate allowed matters to drift, but at length in 68 B.C. it sent Q. Cæcilius Metellus, consul for 69, to Crete. He conquered the island in two campaigns, but his success merely aggravated the evil, perhaps, by dislodging the pirates once more, the seas becoming so unsafe that the cornships, on which the food of Rome depended, no longer dared to sail. This was too much to be borne; since the senate had failed to improve the situation, the people felt that it was time for the assembly to assert itself.

At the close of their consulship both Pompey and Crassus had retired into private life. The former held aloof from public affairs, waiting for some new emergency serious enough to require his services, and in 67 B.C. the shortage in the food supply gave him his opportunity. From the senate he could expect nothing, but one of his friends, Gabinius by name, who was one of the tribunes for the year, took advantage of the newly recovered powers of his office to lay before the people a law giving Pompey an extraordinary command against the pirates. The machine was helpless in face of the hungry people,[1] and, when one of the other tribunes tried to interpose his veto, Gabinius at once proposed to depose him from office. After 17 tribes had voted in favour of his deposition the tribune withdrew his veto and the bill was triumphantly carried. The Gabinian law conferred on Pompey the most sweeping powers; he was given complete command of the sea, and in all provinces which bordered it an *imperium* equal to that of the governor for fifty miles inland; also the right to raise a fleet of 500 ships and an army of 120,000 men, and to draw on the treasury for money to meet all expenses. Last of all he was permitted to name twenty-four legates from among the senators. As a slight concession to appearances the law did not actually name the person to be invested with these powers, providing that the senate should choose him from among the consulars, but the conscript fathers were wise enough to bow to the inevitable and to name Pompey.

[1] Probably the knights supported the bill both as a step toward getting rid of Lucullus and because the insecurity of the seas affected business adversely.

The new "dictator of the seas" set about his work promptly but methodically. He divided the Mediterranean into districts, each with a squadron under one of his lieutenants and systematically set out to clear the seas. The pirates were soon forced to retire to their former strongholds in Cilicia, where they turned at bay, risking a battle with their main fleet, in which they were crushingly defeated by Pompey. He followed up his victory by an offer of pardon to all who submitted, and most of the pirates made haste to take advantage of it. The Gabinian law had allowed him three years for his task, but in three months it was practically accomplished. It still remained to make sure that the results would be permanent, and for this purpose it was necessary to capture the strongholds of the pirates on the coast, so that they could find no point where they could rally again. Pompey, therefore, besieged such strongholds as still held out, while he settled the pirates who had surrendered in colonies where it seemed unlikely that they would relapse into their former evil ways.

The enthusiasm at Rome over Pompey's swift success was great, and it came at the very moment when the war with Mithridates flared up again and when it was clear that Lucullus must be superseded. There could be no doubt as to who must be his successor, for Pompey was on the coast of Asia with an army and a fleet, so that if he took over the command there would be no need of reinforcements. Moreover, his desire for the command was well known, and a refusal might lead him to embark his troops and sail for Italy. His appointment was therefore inevitable, and the only question was whether it should come from the senate or the people. A tribune named Manilius surprised Rome and solved the problem by bringing before the assembly a bill conferring on Pompey the complete control of Asia Minor and all wars there. Many senators, although prepared to bow to the necessity of naming Pompey to succeed Lucullus, were dismayed by the sweeping character of the Manilian law, but few ventured to speak out and run the risk of offending the most powerful man in the Roman world by an opposition which was obviously futile. A few politicians spoke in favour of the bill, among them Cicero and Cæsar, but their eloquence mattered little. The law was passed, and would have been passed no matter what was said either for or against it, and Pompey proceeded to take over the command against Mithridates.

### § 8. POMPEY AND MITHRIDATES

It was Pompey's good fortune to reap the fruits of Lucullus' victories. These victories had had a deeper effect than appeared upon the surface, since they had shattered the prestige, so all-important to an Oriental ruler, of both Tigranes and Mithridates, and thus greatly weakened their hold upon their subjects; they had, indeed, regained much of what they had lost, but the circumstances had not been such that their recent successes could efface the impression of their earlier disasters. Pompey induced the king of Parthia to give support to a son of Tigranes who was seeking to supplant his father, while he turned his own attention to Mithridates. In the spring of 66 B.C. the invasion of Pontus was begun, and Pompey defeated the last army of the king at Nicopolis. Mithridates escaped to Armenia, but found that he could expect no aid from Tigranes, who was fully occupied in dealing with his son and the Parthians. In no long time Mithridates was forced to flee to his possessions in the Crimea, and Tigranes to make humble submission to Pompey and to acknowledge the suzerainty of Rome.

Pompey seemed triumphant, but the war could never end while Mithridates was at large. What remained to do was really the most difficult part of Pompey's task. He attempted to reach his foe by marching overland through the Caucasus, winning two victories over the hardy mountaineers, but the difficulties were so great that he abandoned the enterprise. Fortune, however, again favoured him, and the death of Mithridates suddenly ended the war. The king's cruelty and suspicion, which had grown with his misfortunes, had become intolerable so that his subjects in the Crimea broke out in insurrection, finding a leader in the old man's favourite son. Shut up in his palace with all chance of escape cut off and all hope of mercy gone, Mithridates, after murdering such of his family as were within his reach, had himself slain by one of his attendants (63 B.C.). Pompey, who had done nothing directly to secure this result, received the body of the king with respect, and had it interred with those of his ancestors in the royal tombs. It was Lucullus who really conquered Mithridates, but it was Pompey who received the credit and the glory.

All that remained was to settle the affairs of the East and to return to Rome. In this task Pompey seems to have shown himself a competent organizer and administrator. Bithynia had already been annexed by the senate, and Pompey added to it some districts of Pontus, forming the new province of Bithynia-Pontus, while other portions of the conquered kingdom were handed over to the neighbouring princes; Syria was annexed and organized as a province with Judæa as a dependency under the rule of the high priests; the interior of Asia Minor remained under the rule of client kings, the boundaries of their kingdoms and their relations to Rome being determined by Pompey. He also sought to promote civilization by founding colonies and granting special privileges to the existing cities. Since his settlement of the East seems to have been wise and reasonable, and since he had taken greater pains than Lucullus to respect the interests of the knights, Pompey probably thought that he would have little difficulty in securing the formal ratification of his arrangements, but in this regard he was destined to be bitterly disappointed.

## CHAPTER X

# INTRIGUE AND CONSPIRACY

### § 1. CRASSUS AND THE DEMOCRATS

WHEN Pompey sailed from Italy to clear the Mediterranean of pirates he left behind him a jealous rival in the person of Crassus. The latter had amassed a great fortune, but mere wealth was far from satisfying him, for throughout his life he cherished political and military ambitions, to advance which he never hesitated to spend money with reckless profusion. He had shown himself an able general, and it was with much bitterness of spirit that he saw himself eclipsed by Pompey. When the Manilian law was passed (in 66 B.C.) he began to feel not merely envy, but fear. Few in Rome doubted that in a few years Pompey, having disposed of Mithridates, would be at the head of the most powerful fleet and army in the Roman world. What he would do in such circumstances no one could predict with certainty, but there would be nothing to hinder his repeating Sulla's career. If he should do so and should draw up a proscription list, Crassus felt no doubts that his name would stand among the first. The way to ensure his own safety under these conditions was clear: he must contrive to place himself at the head of an army strong enough to extort terms from his rival by the threat of civil war. Since only such an army could protect him, to get control of one in some fashion and under some pretext was the primary object of Crassus during the next few years.

The millionaire had long been spending freely in the attempt to secure as much influence as possible. He was always ready to loan money to any man who had, or who seemed likely to gain, any influence, and he was careless of security and indifferent to payment, since in such transactions it was political and not financial profit which he had in view. He paid no attention to party lines, aiming to acquire a hold on men in all factions, and so it came about that, while many of the senators were in debt to him and hence unwilling to offend him if it could be avoided, many of the popular leaders were in the same situation. In this way he had succeeded in acquiring an influence of varying extent over a large number of persons. Some of his debtors were completely at his mercy, for if he demanded payment they would be utterly ruined. There were others, however, who could pay, although at more or less inconvenience, and such men might set limits to their compliance. Still, through his political loans Crassus could pull many wires, and on occasion he did not hesitate to do so.

He had of course other and less obvious means of gaining influence. A Roman advocate was not supposed to accept a fee for his services, but he did expect gratitude from his client, and this gratitude usually took the form of political support. Crassus was no orator, but he was a good lawyer, and appeared constantly in the courts for people of all sorts. In this way he placed many under obligations to him, while his investments gave him a considerable influence in business circles.

Crassus had become powerful in these and other ways, but when Pompey left Rome in 67 B.C. he redoubled his activity. In spite of the number of his debtors in the senate he appears to have realized that he could not secure an army through the conscript fathers, who regarded him with as little love and as much suspicion as they did Pompey, and who had probably abandoned all hope of using him to balance his rival to their advantage after their experience in 71 B.C. The millionaire speedily made up his mind to seek what he wanted with the help of the democrats, and set out to secure control of the popular party, caring little for the cost if he could achieve his purpose. He had already enlisted the support of many of the leaders of the rabble, and he was ready to buy more. Lacking the qualities of a mob orator himself, he preferred to work through others, and he had the good fortune or the keen discernment to secure as his political manager the ablest man in Rome, the young C. Julius Cæsar.

The subsequent greatness of Cæsar has led many historians

to paint his early career in far too flattering colours. There is nothing to show that he had any part in the overthrow of Sulla's constitution, and he first came forward as a prominent figure in politics as the henchman of Crassus. In this there is nothing discreditable to Cæsar. By the marriage of Marius into his family and by his own marriage to a daughter of Cinna he was early bound to the side of the democrats. To these affiliations he was resolutely steady, and all his days he was a consistent opponent of the senatorial machine. He refused to divorce his wife at the bidding of Sulla, but his friends succeeded in keeping his name off the proscription list in spite of this open defiance. Nevertheless, Cæsar felt it wise to leave Rome and spent some time in the East, perfecting his education under the famous Greek teachers of the day. When he returned to Rome after Sulla's death, he began his career in the usual way. Politics had become an expensive business, so that Cæsar easily contrived to get rid of his fortune. Needing money for his career, there was no reason why he should not combine with Crassus, if the millionaire was disposed to support the democratic party. There is no evidence to show that Cæsar sacrificed any of his principles, for Pompey's dictatorship was likely to be almost as distasteful to the popular party as to the machine. To Crassus he was an invaluable assistant, for he was a handsome and affable young aristocrat, one of the best orators of his day,[1] with a singular gift for the management of men. He was thus superbly equipped to take the lead in the forum, while Crassus sat at home and supplied the funds. Throughout Pompey's absence in the East Cæsar's brains and Crassus' gold were alike devoted to securing control of the democrats and through them of an army.

The first moves in the game are naturally obscure. Bribery of the voters was becoming a more and more prominent feature of Roman political life, a fact which has generally been taken as evidence of a profound deterioration among the Roman people. It shows nothing, however, as to the character of the majority, for the bribery was probably limited to that portion of the rabble which voted in the rural tribes and to that section of this group which was registered in those

[1] None of his speeches has survived, but we know his reputation with his contemporaries.

tribes where the result was more or less uncertain. The senatorial machine may have had too firm a hold on a number of the tribes through the dependents of the noble families to leave the opposition any hope of carrying them, while the knights could doubtless count on others, but there must have been some where the different elements were so evenly balanced that the result was more or less doubtful, and it is probable that the bribery was mainly employed to carry these tribes. The same thing would, of course, be true of the centuries, and the increase in bribery would only show that the number of doubtful groups was increasing.

Such facts as we know would fit very well with this conception of the situation. The Roman law forbade all organizations, with a few exceptions, among the common people, but during this period there were numerous illegal and semi-legal clubs, which, whatever their ostensible purpose, had as their main reason for existence the selling of the votes of their members. Their leaders negotiated with the politicians and delivered the votes of the clubs on receiving a satisfactory consideration in money. Such clubs may have been formed chiefly among the section of the rabble which voted in the rural tribes, especially in the doubtful ones. In any case, it is certain that there were many votes which could be bought, whether singly or in groups, and some impecunious nobles or knights who were ready to sell the votes of their retainers as well as their own. By the lavish use of money it was possible, therefore, to build up a powerful democratic machine, but it proved to be impossible to buy a sufficient number of voters to enable this machine to control the assembly whether voting by tribes or centuries. There always remained enough voters who could not be bribed or who were retainers of nobles and knights who could not be influenced to prevent Crassus and Cæsar from accomplishing their programme, as will shortly appear.

In 66 B.C. Crassus seems to have made his first attempt to use the machine which he had constructed at so much expense, and was so far successful that he was elected one of the censors for 65. In the consular elections Cornelius Sulla, who was probably a nephew of the dictator, and Autronius Pætus were chosen, but were convicted of bribery and in consequence forfeited their offices and were rendered ineligible for the future. They were not disposed to submit, and with Catiline, a reckless politician of whom we shall hear more presently, they entered into a plot known as the First Conspiracy of Catiline. The whole episode is very obscure, and all we can say with any degree of certainty is that Sulla and Autronius planned to seize by violence the office of which they had been deprived, and probably to murder the two consuls who had been chosen at the supplementary elections to take their places. There were suspicions, then or later, that Crassus and Cæsar were somehow involved, but this is very unlikely. The plot was a complete failure, for the design was suspected, and the senate made any action on the part of the conspirators impossible by voting a bodyguard to the new consuls. Although Crassus probably had nothing to do with the conspiracy, it seems practically certain that after its collapse he exerted his influence to prevent an investigation, and so effectively protected the plotters. His motive may easily be guessed, for he later tried to use some of those implicated, and it must, therefore, be assumed that he regarded them as more or less valuable tools in spite of their bungling on this particular occasion.[1]

## § 2. THE CENSORSHIP OF CRASSUS

In 65 B.C. Crassus as censor made a bid for democratic support by bringing forward two measures. He proposed to register the people of Cisalpine Gaul living on the farther side of the Po (the Transpadanes) in all the tribes as full Roman citizens. Those on the nearer side of the river had already been so registered, but the Transpadanes had been granted only the status of Latins. This move was blocked by the other censor, who was an adherent of the senate, and perhaps Crassus was not displeased at this result, for he had gained his object by securing popularity in an extensive region where recruits for an army were easily to be found. Perhaps he was more popular in failure than he would have been if successful, since the Transpadanes who wanted citizenship had been taught to look for it to him rather than to the senate.

A recruiting ground was of little use without the authority

[1] In regard to this plot I have accepted the views of M. Cary in *Camb. Anc. Hist.*, IX, pp. 475–80.

to raise an army, and the second measure of Crassus was a scheme to secure this. The Roman populace had very recently (67 B.C.) suffered from a shortage in the food supply, so that the millionaire hoped to be able to obtain their sanction for a project which would provide an abundance of grain for the future. Egypt, which was the richest grain producing country of the Mediterranean region, was now in a condition of disorder, one Ptolemy after another being set up and pulled down in Alexandria. There was in existence a document which purported to be the will of one of these ephemeral monarchs bequeathing Egypt to the Roman people. Whether the will was genuine or a forgery was never determined, nor was the matter ever investigated, the politicians of Rome preferring to believe whatever suited their interests. Crassus, assuming it to be valid, proposed to accept the legacy, and a bill was prepared appointing Cæsar, who was then ædile, governor of the new province. The fact that Ptolemy Auletes, the father of Cleopatra, was actually on the throne would make an army necessary to secure possession.

The design was a clever one, for it might be expected that the Roman people would welcome the prospect of an increased supply of grain, and that the knights would look with favour on a new field for money-making, while Cæsar's lavish expenditure on public games had made him popular. An army in Egypt would occupy a position on Pompey's flank, where it could either hinder his return unless he agreed to terms or, at the worst, secure a safe retreat for such Romans as felt it dangerous to remain in Italy under his government. Nevertheless the scheme failed; the rabble, once more supplied with food, took little thought of the future, and a large section of the knights probably felt that Pompey's conquests in the East would give them sufficient opportunities for the present. *

## § 3. THE AGRARIAN BILL OF RULLUS

Foiled in these projects, Crassus cast about for other means to achieve his object. He now set himself to secure control of the executive of the Republic by having two of his tools elected consuls for 63. In the election (in 64), with five candidates in the field, Crassus and Cæsar supported Catiline and Antonius. Of the other aspirants the most important was

Cicero. C. Antonius Hybrida was personally insignificant, although a member of a distinguished family,[1] but Catiline and Cicero merit a brief consideration.

L. Sergius Catilina was a man of patrician descent. A former partisan of Sulla, he had risen to the prætorship and had served as proprætor in Africa. On his return to Rome he tried to stand for the consulship in 66 B.C., but was disqualified by a prosecution for extortion in his province. Cicero thought seriously of defending him, but fortunately for himself did not do so. However, Catiline was finally acquitted without the orator's help, although too late for the elections in 65, so that it was not till 64 that he could become a candidate. He was probably no worse than many politicians of his day, and was ready enough to accept the support of Crassus. That he was able and daring there can be no doubt, but he was also reckless and unscrupulous. He had incurred the suspicion of the aristocracy, partly perhaps because of the abortive plot in 66, partly no doubt because of his alliance with Crassus and Cæsar, so that many of the nobles resolved to defeat him at all costs. It soon became apparent that the only way to accomplish this was by backing Cicero in spite of the fact that he was a new man, for he was the only other candidate who had a serious chance.

M. Tullius Cicero was a native of Arpinum, and began his career as an advocate. By his speeches in the courts he soon acquired a reputation as an orator, and at the same time a wide circle of friends. His most spectacular case was his successful prosecution of Verres (in 70 B.C.) for maladministration in Sicily. Cicero, like most Roman advocates, used the courts as a stepping-stone to politics, and rose as rapidly as the law permitted through the lower offices. He had up to this time leaned to the democratic party and had spoken eloquently in favour of the Manilian law. It has often been said that, when he stood for the consulship and the nobles rallied to his support, he changed sides and went over to the senatorial party. This is in some degree a misstatement of the case. In the first place it assumes the existence of well-organized parties with definite programmes, whereas there were no such

[1] He was a younger son of M. Antonius the orator, a brother of the M. Antonius who held the command against the pirates, and, incidentally, an uncle of the Triumvir.

parties. There was on the one side the senatorial machine and on the other those elements, mostly the rabble, which were more or less consistently opposed to this machine. Between these two groups were the knights, who inclined sometimes to one and sometimes to the other. Now Cicero was by birth a knight, and in the earlier years of his political life the knights were as a class allied with the rabble, at first against the constitution of Sulla and later against Lucullus and in favour of Pompey. In opposition to the schemes of Crassus a considerable section of the knights, probably a majority, were led by their support of Pompey to join hands with the senate, and Cicero went with this group. Although his course may have been to some extent dictated by self-interest, there is nothing inconsistent in it, and the key to his whole future policy was to maintain a working alliance between the senate and the knights. It was a sensible and practical policy, by which he might have prolonged the life of the Republic if the Roman nobles had been willing to follow him, but they never divested themselves of a certain prejudice against the new man whom they had been forced by a combination of circumstances to accept as their champion. When he thought of standing for the consulship Cicero seems to have expected little help from the aristocratic machine, and for a moment at least thought of a combination with Catiline.[1] He soon abandoned this idea, perhaps when he discovered that Crassus and Cæsar were supporting Catiline and Antonius.

The election was hotly contested, and resulted in the choice of Cicero and Antonius, Catiline running third. On the surface this result appeared a partial victory for Crassus, but in reality it was a complete defeat, since his object could only be attained by positive action, and Cicero could block every move of Antonius. The latter, therefore, abandoned his supporters in order to make a bargain with Cicero, who had drawn the better of the two consular provinces. By agreeing to exchange with Antonius, Cicero secured his colleague's acquiescence in whatever policy he chose to pursue.

Seeing clearly that their half victory in the consular elections was worthless to them, Crassus and Cæsar devised a fresh plan. The tribunes took office in December, and one of them,

[1] *Att.*, i, 1 and 2.

P. Servilius Rullus, at once introduced an agrarian bill of startling scope and character. Its alleged purpose was to inaugurate an extensive distribution of land in Italy among the poor. To get the land all properties of the Roman state outside of Italy were to be sold and the money so raised was to be expended in the purchase of Italian land for allotment. To carry out the provisions of the law an agrarian commission of ten members was to be appointed, who were to be given the *imperium* and the right to raise an army if necessary to enforce their decisions; the ten commissioners were to be chosen by 17 tribes selected by lot from the 35,[1] and candidates were required to give in their names in person, a provision undoubtedly intended to exclude Pompey. Crassus and Cæsar probably hoped that the old cry of lands for the poor would gain support for the bill, and when it was passed, the commission could at once declare the entire kingdom of Egypt the property of Rome under the alleged will already mentioned, and could then raise an army to take possession of it, thus reviving the project which Crassus had failed to carry during his censorship in 65 B.C.[2]

Cicero at once attacked the bill in a series of speeches in which he exposed its real intent. This was, perhaps, enough to secure its defeat, for the bill was aimed at Pompey, so that his friends would join the senate in opposition, and would be reinforced by all who feared a civil war. It is possible that another influence made itself felt. When the bill was proposed, Pompey was fighting in the Caucasus, but in the winter of 64 he returned to Syria. It is impossible to determine when the news of his return to the coast reached Rome, but, if it arrived before the eloquence of Cicero had killed the bill, it must have reinforced his arguments powerfully. With Pompey in a position to return promptly to Italy further attacks upon him, however disguised, were so dangerous that

[1] This provision was probably devised to facilitate packing the commission. Cicero (*de lege agr.*, ii, ch. 8–9) asserts that the lots could be drawn by Rullus himself without witnesses.

[2] If the bill was passed and could be carried out, Pompey would have to get the land for his soldiers from the new agrarian commission. It would also place an immense amount of patronage in the hands of this commission and make possible an immense amount of jobbery. Nevertheless, I believe the main object in view was to get an army in Egypt, for if Pompey returned at the head of his army he could easily have the law annulled, and the commission would be helpless unless backed by a military force.

Crassus resigned himself to wait quietly and see what course his rival would take.

## § 4. THE CONSPIRACY OF CATILINE

When Crassus abandoned his intrigues against Pompey, Cæsar and most of the other democratic politicians followed the example of their leader. Since they no longer dared to attack Pompey, their one object was to avoid giving him any excuse for returning at the head of his army, but there were some, among them Catiline, who could not afford to wait. He was heavily in debt, and when he was a second time defeated for the consulship (in 63 B.C.)[1] he became desperate. We may surmise that Crassus, having found him useless as a tool, was unwilling to furnish him with additional funds as he did Cæsar and others who might yet be of service. At any rate, Catiline embarked upon a conspiracy which the speeches of Cicero have immortalized, and at the same time somewhat obscured. That the conspiracy was a dangerous one may be granted, so that, in trying to arouse the senate and people to a realization of the peril, Cicero had a strong motive for painting Catiline and his followers in the blackest colours and for exaggerating the atrocity of their designs.[2] It is obviously necessary to make some allowance for the fervour of his eloquence, but to determine just how much is far from easy. Moreover, Cicero's vigilance forced Catiline to modify his original plans, and there is evidence of divergent views among the conspirators.[3] Probably Catiline throughout aimed simply at repeating the career of Cinna by setting up a so-called democratic government with himself as the head, and his final plan was to stir up revolt in Italy and to march on Rome with the insurgents. His friends in the city were to help him by murdering some of the leading men, Cicero, of course, included, and to set the city on fire in several places at once, so that in the resulting confusion Catiline could take possession of Rome without serious opposition.

Both Crassus and Cæsar were suspected of some degree of

[1] In this election neither Crassus nor Cæsar seems to have supported him.

[2] Sallust in the main repeats the Ciceronian version and is little more trustworthy than the orator.

[3] The conspirators in Rome sent a message to Catiline in Etruria asking why he refused to recruit slaves (Sallust, ch. 44).

complicity in the plot, but the suspicion was almost certainly unjust, for they were far too intelligent not to see that Catiline had no real chance of success. He might indeed be able to seize Rome and to proclaim himself consul, but this would at once bring Pompey back to Italy at the head of his army to restore order, and there would be no time for the new government to organize its defence. The consulship of Catiline could be nothing but a brief prelude to the dictatorship of Pompey, the thing above all others which Crassus dreaded, and which with Cæsar's help he had been trying to avert. The conspiracy must, therefore, be regarded as a desperate venture in which a few reckless men engaged without the knowledge, connivance, or encouragement of either Crassus or Cæsar.

At first Cicero found great difficulty in dealing with the situation, for, although he was well informed by spies of what was going on, he dared not strike until he had legal proof against the conspirators, which for a considerable time he was unable to secure. He succeeded in arousing enough alarm to induce the senate to pass the last decree, and he finally forced Catiline to leave Rome and take command of the insurgents in Etruria, where a considerable force had been recruited. With their leader gone the conspirators who remained in the city blunderingly supplied Cicero with the necessary evidence, and as a consequence they were promptly placed in custody. The danger was not yet over, but at least the government had no longer to fear a stab in the back as well as an open attack.

The next question was what should be done with the men under arrest. On this point Cicero naturally and properly consulted the senate. Its advice had no legal force, for when it passed the last decree it had done its utmost; whatever was done now must be done by Cicero under that decree, and the responsibility for any measures he took was his alone. Yet to ask the advice of the senate was the customary course, and its solemn judgment would relieve the consul of some of the moral responsibility at all events. In the debate Cæsar delivered a powerful speech maintaining the old democratic doctrine that no citizen could lawfully be put to death without a trial and recommending life imprisonment. Such a penalty may have been as illegal as death, but Cæsar and his party had never taken any stand on the matter. So great was the impression produced by his speech that the senate wavered until Cato turned the scale by pointing out that to imprison the culprits, whose guilt was beyond dispute even though they had not been tried and convicted in court, would be a disastrous blunder. Throughout Italy the discontented were waiting to see what the government would do. If it showed any sign of fear they would flock to Catiline's standard, and the mere imprisonment of the conspirators would be accepted as proof of timidity, whereas their immediate execution would be taken as the clearest possible evidence of the confidence of the government in its ability to cope with the situation. As to legality, Cato argued that the conspirators had ceased to be Roman citizens. No one disputed that Catiline could be legally put to death by any general who might capture him, and Cato contended that men caught plotting against their country were equally outside the pale of the law. This view soothed any scruples among the conscript fathers, but it was a superficial one which overlooked a vital distinction: Catiline *had* drawn his sword against the government and so could properly be treated as a traitor and a rebel, but his friends in the city had *not* murdered Cicero or anybody else. They had planned to do so, but they had as yet committed no overt act. Nevertheless, the senate voted in favour of the execution and Cicero at once carried out the decree.

Whatever the force of Cato's argument about the legality of the execution of the conspirators, there is no doubt that he was right on the question of expediency, for the boldness of the government put an end to the rebellion. At the news of the execution Catiline's army began to desert, and Cicero's colleague Antonius soon crushed such forces as still kept together. Catiline himself died on the field of battle, fighting valiantly to the last. In Rome Cicero was hailed as the father of his country and for the moment seemed to be a hero with all classes. Unfortunately he could never forget his achievement or cease to boast of it, with the natural result that some historians, disgusted by his vanity, have denied him the credit he had really earned. He did not save Rome from destruction, but he did meet a dangerous crisis with coolness, energy, and courage. He succeeded in uniting the senate and the knights, thus establishing a strong government. No one could be as great a man as Cicero thought himself, but he was really a great man, an orator of the first rank, and an honest and far-sighted statesman as well.

### § 5. THE RETURN OF POMPEY

If Cicero was far-sighted, he was sometimes oblivious to what was near and obvious. He was quite mystified to find that Pompey did not share his own exultation at the suppression of the conspiracy. It seems never to have occurred to him that Pompey would have welcomed such success on the part of Catiline as would necessitate his return to Italy at the head of his army. Yet this should have been clear from the course of Metellus Nepos, an officer whom the general sent to Rome to stand for the tribuneship. Having been elected without difficulty, as soon as he had taken office in December, just after the execution of the conspirators, he demanded the recall of Pompey to suppress Catiline, who was still at the head of the insurgents in Etruria. This demand was rejected by the senate, and Catiline was disposed of without Pompey's help, but the move showed plainly enough what the great general desired.

After being rebuffed by the senate, Metellus brought the question of recalling Pompey before the assembly. Cæsar, who had just taken office as one of the prætors for 62 B.C., actively supported the bill, although he can have had no wish to see it passed. Doubtless he counted on the aristocratic machine to find some means of killing it and thereby alienating the great general. His expectations were justified by the event. Cato, who was a colleague of Metellus in the tribunate, interposed his veto, and the assembly broke up in disorder. The senate seized the opportunity to pass the last decree, whereupon Metellus at once left Rome and hastened to Pompey's camp, hoping to provide his master with a pretext for armed intervention. Pompey had been waiting for some pretext for such intervention, but the flight of Metellus was too transparent a device, and he made no attempt to take advantage of it. He postponed his return as long as possible, however, evidently clinging to the hope that something might yet occur, but even the slowest journey ends at last, and toward the close of the year he landed at Brundisium. To the surprise of many, if not most, of the politicians Pompey at once disbanded his army, and after celebrating a splendid triumph, retired into private life. His conduct not only surprised his contemporaries, but has also puzzled modern historians,[1] yet the explanation is probably very simple. It is unlikely that any one at that time dreamed of subverting the Republic and establishing a monarchy upon its ruins, but if there were any who cherished such dreams Pompey was certainly not among the number. He had desired to return at the head of his army, for this would have enabled him to provide for his veterans without trouble or difficulty; when he could find no decent pretext for this he accepted the inevitable with what grace he could. It is by no means certain that his army would have followed him if he had ordered a march on Rome, because he could offer no serious justification for such a step, and Roman soldiers, however devoted their general, were after all Romans with some respect for law and constitutional government.[2] To employ such men to establish and maintain a naked and undisguised tyranny would have been a dangerous experiment[3] which probably Pompey never thought of trying. His ambition was to be the first citizen of the Republic, and he may have imagined that he would be accepted as such and could carry out his programme without the help of an army, even though an army would have expedited and simplified matters.

## § 6. POMPEY AND THE SENATE

The programme to which Pompey was committed was the legacy of his eastern victories. He must, of course, secure land for his veterans, and he felt bound to obtain a formal ratification for his settlement in the East. How far this last was legally necessary it is impossible to say. He had made

[1] Hardy (*The Catilinarian Conspiracy*, pp. 106–111) holds that Metellus Nepos was sent to Rome to bring about an understanding with Crassus and Cæsar and that Pompey dismissed his army because he had reached such an understanding. Holmes (*The Roman Republic*, I, pp. 466–67) seems to me to have refuted this view.

[2] Both Sulla and Cæsar had excellent pretexts for taking up arms against the government, in fact they were more or less forced to do so for their own safety and to secure the interests of their men; the course of events made a dictatorship a practical necessity for both.

[3] Augustus took care to disguise his monarchy under republican forms.

numerous treaties with Oriental princes, had organized new provinces, and granted special privileges to many cities. His settlement (*acta*) thus covered the whole of Asia Minor and Syria, and, while much of what he had done was no doubt authorized by the Manilian law, he may in some of his agreements with individuals and communities have exceeded the powers which that law conferred upon him. At any rate, he wished the senate to confirm his *acta* as a whole, thus legalizing anything which was not strictly legal, and giving a pledge to respect all his arrangements. He also desired the senate's approval of a bill to provide for his veterans, since this approval would mean that the aristocratic machine would support the bill in the assembly. Moreover, he was anxious for a reconciliation with the nobles and was quite willing to accept the government of the senate, if it would grant what seemed to him his just and reasonable demands.

Cicero saw clearly that this was an opportunity to harmonize the military and the civil powers. In his consulship he had brought about an alliance between the nobles and the knights, and the one thing lacking to the stability of the Republic was the control of the army, which would be secured if the senate made a friend of Pompey. Although the general owed much of his success to good fortune rather than to his own ability, still he had gained such a reputation that it would be impossible for any other Roman to raise an army to oppose him in the field. The wise course for the conscript fathers was to obtain his backing at almost any price, and the price which he demanded was far from exorbitant.

The senate, however, judged differently, thinking that the general could be safely humiliated and thwarted as soon as he had disbanded his army. Many causes combined to bring about this result. First, and perhaps foremost, Pompey had many personal enemies among the conscript fathers ; he was vain and self-centred, with awkward manners, and entirely lacking in suavity and tact. When he took over the command against Mithridates he seemed to take a perverse pleasure in making the transaction as painful to Lucullus as possible, and Lucullus bitterly resented his conduct. In similar ways he had probably offended many others, and he had always to expect the enmity of Crassus, who through his numerous debtors in the senate wielded a formidable influence. The power of his enemies was greatly increased because they could disguise their personal motives under specious pretexts, deceiving themselves to some extent and gaining the support of others who had no grudge against Pompey, but were simply short-sighted and narrow-minded legalists. To such men as these Pompey's demands could be presented in the light of dangerous and unconstitutional innovations.

When Pompey requested the ratification of his eastern *acta* as a whole, there were obvious objections which could be, and doubtless were, made to such a course. The conscript fathers would be pledging themselves to the observance of a large number of complicated treaties and agreements without examining them in detail, and so without clearly knowing to what they were committing themselves. It could be urged with much plausibility that they ought to consider these arrangements one by one. If Pompey had not exceeded his authority under the Manilian law his *acta* should be ratified as a matter of course, but if he had the senate should exercise its constitutional control over foreign and provincial affairs, approving or disapproving at its discretion. The result of this or some similar line of reasoning was that the senate refused to confirm Pompey's *acta* as a whole and insisted on taking them up separately. This decision was most distasteful to Pompey, who felt that his honour was involved in the fulfilment of his word to the eastern princes and cities, and that the examination of his eastern *acta* in detail would certainly consume a large amount of time and would probably result in the serious modification or rejection of some of them.

In regard to his soldiers, the conscript fathers, professing a willingness to provide for them, left it to Pompey to suggest the means by which it should be done. When he prepared a bill, however, and had one of the tribunes submit it to the senate, an interminable debate began over its provisions. These provisions were that the public land which the state still retained in Campania should be allotted to the veterans, and that the revenues from the new provinces annexed by Pompey should for the next five years be paid into a fund to be used for the purchase of additional land for distribution. The senators objected strongly to the sacrifice of the Campanian land, since it yielded a considerable revenue to the treasury. Cicero agreed with the majority on this point, but he supported the purchase part of the scheme. The conscript fathers, though apparently less open in their objections to this, could not be induced to approve it. In his letters Cicero attributes their attitude to a suspicion that Pompey was seeking some new power for himself.[1] This suspicion is intelligible if we remember that a commission was to be appointed to have charge of the purchase fund and that in the course of five years about £1,400,000[2] would be paid over to and expended by the commission. It is evident that this sum, a huge one for those times, could be so administered as to influence elections for some years to come and the commission would probably be dominated by Pompey. No doubt behind all other motives was the perception that nothing would do more to destroy Pompey's influence than a failure to provide for his men, and the desire of the nobles to weaken his influence as much as possible.

Finding at last that nothing could be accomplished in the senate, Pompey had his tribune bring the bill before the people, and it might have been expected that this move would easily succeed, since many of the veterans were in the city, waiting impatiently for their rewards. The assembly, however, voted by tribes, so that the influence of Pompey's former soldiers would depend upon their distribution among the tribes and not at all upon their number. In view of the fact that he was especially popular in Picenum, which was one of the best recruiting grounds in Italy outside of Cisalpine Gaul, it is probable that most of his men came from this region, the greater part of which was included in one tribe, the Velina. If this were the case, it would go far to neutralize the influence of the veterans, and those who were not massed in this tribe might easily have been so distributed among the rest that they could only determine the votes of a few, too few to defeat the senatorial machine supported by that of Crassus. In the end the opposition and obstruction which the bill encountered so discouraged Pompey that he allowed it to drop. Thus toward the middle of 60 B.C. the triumphant general found himself defeated on both issues. He might perhaps have yielded on the question of his eastern *acta*, but he could not give way in the matter of providing for his veterans, since to

[1] *Att.*, i, 19.

[2] If the figures given by Plutarch (*Pomp.*, ch. 45) are to be trusted.

accept defeat in this would imperil his ability to get recruits in the future, and would leave him, illustrious indeed, but practically insignificant. We cannot wonder, therefore, that he should have been ready to grasp at any means, however personally distasteful, of satisfying his men.

## § 7. THE BREACH BETWEEN THE ORDERS

While the conscript fathers thus refused to follow Cicero's leadership in his attempts to effect a reconciliation with the great general, they destroyed what he considered one of the achievements of his consulship by breaking up the concord of the orders. They contrived to quarrel with the knights on two issues. The equestrian syndicate which had farmed the taxes of Asia, urged on by Crassus, declared that they had bid too high and asked the senate to reduce the amount by a third. In his private letters Cicero called this demand scandalous and impudent,[1] but in public he supported it, because of his earnest desire to avoid a breach between the senate and the powerful financial interests involved.

Cato, with his usual instinct for doing the right thing at the wrong time, seized this moment for proposing that the senate approve a bill which made the acceptance of bribes by knights serving on the juries a criminal offence. It was so already in the case of senators, and Cato wished to put all the jurors on the same footing.[2] It is probable that the measure was brought up because of a resounding scandal in connection with the trial of Clodius for sacrilege,[3] in which case the bribery was particularly open and notorious. It was an outrage on common sense and decency that what was a crime if done by a senator was legally an innocent act if done by his fellow jurors, so that Cato had unanswerable logic behind him. Cicero recognized this, but opposed the bill in the hope of saving the concord of the orders.

As the consular elections for 59 B.C. drew near the senate

[1] *Att.*, i, 17 ; ii, 1.

[2] This curious anomaly in Roman law dates from the time of C. Gracchus. Before he remodelled the juries he seems to have passed a law against bribery so worded as to apply only to senators, who were then the only jurors. When he later gave the juries to the knights he neglected to change the law, which became a dead letter until the senators again secured a place in the courts.

[3] For the trial see § 3 of the next chapter.

had thus contrived at the same time to drive Pompey to despair and to quarrel with the knights. While these events were taking place in Rome, Cæsar was absent in Spain, where he was serving as propraetor. It was here that he first began to win a reputation as a general, his success in fighting the independent tribes in the interior being such that he could claim the honour of a triumph. He returned from Spain on the eve of the consular elections anxious to stand for the office and to enjoy a triumph as well. The attitude of the senate soon showed him that he could not secure both, so he sacrificed the triumph and entered his name as a candidate. This event was destined to have a significance which probably no contemporary, not even Cæsar himself, foresaw, for it was to lead to nothing less than the overthrow of the Republic.

# CHAPTER XI

# THE FIRST TRIUMVIRATE

## § 1. THE ELECTION OF CÆSAR

WHEN Cæsar became a candidate his prospects appeared excellent, although he himself may well have had some misgivings. Probably all Romans recognized him as one of the ablest orators and most adroit politicians of the day, but it is unlikely that his military capacity was rated very highly, for his claims to a triumph for his successes against the mountain tribes of Spain can hardly have made much impression in Rome; triumphs were sometimes claimed and granted on rather slender grounds, and victories over barbarous tribes on the frontiers were decidedly commonplace. There was nothing in his achievements to impress the public of the capital, no Sertorius or Mithridates to strike the popular imagination. In the eyes of Rome Pompey was the great general of the time, and probably no one, except perhaps Cæsar himself, thought of the former propraetor of Spain as in the same class. It was as a politician that the Romans knew Cæsar, and as such the nobles found little in him to admire, for he had consistently opposed them and their machine and had shown himself no negligible opponent. Besides this he was closely connected with Crassus and very heavily in debt to him, too heavily, Rome may have thought, to venture on an independent role. Both he and his chief were more or less discredited by the failure of their efforts to undermine Pompey during his absence in the East, and they were both more or less widely suspected of some sort of complicity in the conspiracy of Catiline. The present aims of Crassus were probably shrouded in obscurity, but that he and Cæsar were a dangerous combination the nobles could have little doubt. If the millionaire still desired the support of an army, the election of Cæsar would under normal circumstances provide it, for Cæsar as proconsul would receive a province, which according to precedent would be one of the most important in the Roman world. To keep an army out of Crassus' hands the senate resorted to an unusual expedient. By a law passed by C. Gracchus and left untouched by Sulla the senate was required to name the consular provinces before the election of the consuls who would receive them. Moreover, they retained from early times the right to declare any department of public business outside of Rome a province for any year, providing in whatever way might seem most convenient for the regular provinces, generally by prolonging some governor's *imperium* for another year. To make possible the designation of the consular provinces before the election, C. Gracchus had deprived the tribunes of any power to obstruct the senate's action by their veto or otherwise. Seeing that Cæsar was likely to be elected, the conscript fathers resolved to relegate him to obscurity as soon as his term was over, and with this object in view they designated the mountain roads and forests in Italy as the provinces of the consuls for 59 B.C. It is possible that they only took this step when alarming rumours began to circulate that Cæsar had effected an unexpected and surprising combination.

Whether Cæsar could have won the election with the support of Crassus alone may be doubted. It is true that he was personally popular and could command many votes which the millionaire did not control, but there was a very real danger that his connection with Crassus would ensure the opposition of Pompey, whose influence in alliance with the senatorial machine might defeat him. To make success certain Cæsar needed the support of both Pompey and Crassus, and he determined to secure it. The difficulties in the way appeared insurmountable, since the two were bitter enemies, and Crassus had lately been doing all he could to thwart and humiliate Pompey. Beneath the surface, however, there were factors in Cæsar's favour, chief among them the fact that Pompey was ready to do anything to redeem his promises to his veterans, even to forgive Crassus if necessary. The millionaire on his side had been taught by experience that money alone could not give him power ; he was discredited by his failures and anxious to escape from a position where all that he could gain was the pleasure of annoying Pompey. Cæsar, unrivalled for courtesy of manner and personal charm, was able to persuade both men that they could gain little by continuing their quarrel and much from a reconciliation. In the end they yielded to his persuasions and combined in his support. This combination is known as the First Triumvirate, but it should be borne in mind that it was simply an agreement between three politicians, two of whom were private citizens and the third a candidate for office, to work together for their own personal advantage.

What each hoped to secure by the help of the others is fairly obvious. Cæsar wanted to be elected consul and to get a province afterwards with the command of an army for a term of years. This was indispensable for him, if only to free himself from the load of debt which hung about his neck. A governor could make money by plundering his province or by a successful war;[1] Cæsar had shown clearly which alternative he preferred, for he had left Spain with an excellent reputation as a ruler, and the profits of his military operations sufficed to meet his most pressing obligations. With his Spanish experience behind him it would seem natural that he should seek to renew his operations on a larger scale as proconsul. It was also true that only by gaining military glory could he hope to become a really important personage in Rome. Cæsar, who always showed a singular power of accurately estimating realities while others were deceived by appearances, must have seen that he could never reach power through the forum or the senate. If he remained content with the role of a mere politician, he would never be more than Cicero, a man whose insight and statesmanship were largely wasted because he had no real force behind him and hence could always be ignored by his party. Whether Cæsar had already selected the province he desired cannot be known, but that his partners promised to help him set aside the arrangements of the senate and to secure *some* province for a considerable length of time can safely be assumed. Pompey had no need of further glory, and all that he desired was land for his veterans and the ratification of his *acta*. Crassus wished to have his equestrian friends granted the reduction

[1] Partly by plunder of the enemy and partly by the sale as slaves of his prisoners according to the laws of war as then observed.

of the price they had agreed to pay for the farm of the taxes of Asia. Beyond this he apparently made no demands, but it may reasonably be conjectured that there was much besides which cannot now be traced. Crassus seems to have been a man who loved power for its own sake ; he was, perhaps, the type of the politician pure and simple who loved the game for itself and was content to distribute offices and rewards and to be looked up to as a sort of boss. It might have been expected that he would seek a military command, but there is no indication that he did so, perhaps because he perceived that such a demand would instantly arouse the suspicions of Pompey. Probably the understanding developed gradually, and almost certainly the course of events carried the Triumvirs beyond their original intentions. It is highly unlikely that their programme was openly announced, but the fact that Pompey and Crassus were both supporting the candidacy of Cæsar could not be concealed, and from this a bargain of some sort was easy to infer.

As the combination became known the alarm of the nobles increased. Cæsar backed by Crassus would have been bad enough, but with Pompey also behind him the prospect was still worse. It was clear that Cæsar could not be defeated, so the agitated senators determined at least to check him with a colleague of their own party. For this purpose they hastily collected a corruption fund, to which even Cato contributed, and by this means succeeded in electing M. Calpurnius Bibulus in place of the candidate supported by the Triumvirs.

## § 2. CÆSAR'S CONSULSHIP

When on January 1, 59, Cæsar assumed office he can have had few illusions as to the difficulties of the task before him. He knew that the senate was hostile, that his colleague had been elected expressly to check him, and that several of the tribunes were ready to fight the battles of the aristocracy. He began by assuming a conciliatory attitude. Whether he really hoped that this would have an effect may be doubted, but whatever happened such an attitude would at least serve to put his opponents more or less in the wrong in the eyes of the public, and would furnish some sort of excuse if he found himself obliged to resort to high-handed methods.

He treated Bibulus with studied courtesy, and made a show of consulting the senate, bringing before the conscript fathers a very moderate bill for the purchase of land for allotment both to Pompey's veterans and to the poor with the money brought into the treasury by the Eastern wars, and professing himself willing to accept any amendments which the senate desired. As he had probably foreseen, the offer of compromise was spurned, for the nobles thought themselves strong enough to defy the Triumvirate and were determined to do so. In the senate Cæsar was met by prolonged and systematic obstruction; the conscript fathers, unwilling to reject his agrarian bill outright, debated endlessly and would not permit it to come to a vote.

When Cæsar felt that he had convinced the public of the impossibility of working with the senate,[1] he took his bill before the assembly, where Bibulus met it with a veto. Legally nothing further could be done, and the programme of the Triumvirs was wrecked at the start. The only choice now open to them was to accept defeat, or to carry their measure in open disregard of the law. This latter course Cæsar was quite prepared to take, but it was both dangerous and useless unless the senate was first deprived of any means of resistance, and then so intimidated that it would not dare to annul his laws after they were enacted. Before going further it was essential that Cæsar should be provided with an army so that he could overawe the nobles while he violated the constitution. From all that is known of him Crassus appears to have been untroubled by scruples of any sort, while Pompey, although he had a conscience which would not allow him to break the law himself, was willing to profit by the illegal acts of others.

For the time being the agrarian bill was dropped, and one of the tribunes, P. Vatinius, who was a henchman of the Triumvirs, presented a bill to the assembly. This bill provided that Cæsar should have Cisalpine Gaul as his proconsular province with an army of three legions, that he should hold *

[1] According to Suetonius (*Div. Jul.*, ch. 20) Cæsar's first step as consul was to provide for the publication of the senate's proceedings. Probably he intended that obstruction and unreasonable opposition on the part of the conscript fathers should be as widely advertised as possible.

it for five years, and that his command should begin immediately on the passage of the bill. The senatorial tribunes had of course the right to use their veto, but on the last occasion when Bibulus had appeared in the assembly to prevent a vote on the agrarian bill the people, among whom there were no doubt many of Pompey's veterans, had shown their feelings so plainly that the opponents of Vatinius had no desire to appear in person at the meeting. There was, however, another way of accomplishing the same result by announcing unfavourable omens, which they could do without leaving their homes. This course they adopted, but Vatinius paid no attention whatever to their omens, put his bill to a vote, and pronounced it carried. The conscript fathers had ample grounds for declaring it null and void, but they could meet only when summoned by a magistrate, and could act only on such matters as he brought before them, so that action on their part could be, and probably was, prevented until it was too late.

As soon as the Vatinian law was passed,[1] Cæsar took advantage of it; he was at the same time consul in Rome and proconsul of Cisalpine Gaul with authority to raise an army. As proconsul he could recruit troops, nominally for service in his province, when he pleased, stationing them anywhere in Italy outside the city limits until he went to Gaul. Recruits were readily found, and Cæsar took care to keep them near Rome, so that he could promptly avail himself of their services if necessary. Thus armed he could safely defy the law, because he was in a position to crush open opposition by military force. The only way in which he could have been checked was for the senate to pass the last decree and call on Bibulus to restore order. Such a course was out of the question with Cæsar's legions camped near Rome, while Bibulus was without troops. Thus his double position of consul and proconsul made Cæsar master of the situation, and he promptly brought forward the agrarian bill again. The nobles determined to resist to the last, so Bibulus with three of the tribunes appeared in the assembly, having realized that Cæsar would pay no more attention to omens than Vatinius had done. Their attempt at obstruction was met by rioting, in which Bibulus was driven from the scene and

* [1] Probably on the last day of February. See Appendix 6.

the tribunes who supported him narrowly escaped with their lives. All opposition having been suppressed by violence, Cæsar declared his bill carried. The next day Bibulus held a meeting of the senate in his own house and complained of Cæsar's conduct, but the conscript fathers did not dare to take any action, although they doubtless shared his indignation to the full. As a last resource Bibulus shut himself up in his house, refusing to appear in public during the remainder of the year, and issuing edicts on every comitial day announcing that he was observing the heavens, thus preventing any legal meeting of the assembly. Although his edicts did not stop Cæsar, they did provide the senate with a perfect justification for annulling every law he passed if it should ever dare to do so. This was undoubtedly what Bibulus aimed at, and in this he was entirely successful.

Not only did Cæsar declare his agrarian bill carried, but, since moderation no longer served a purpose, he followed it by a second bill providing for the distribution of the last public lands in Italy among the poor, meaning no doubt chiefly Pompey's veterans. These lands consisted of a large tract in Campania, from the lease of which the state derived a considerable revenue, in fact, the greater part of the revenue from Italy itself. In the past the senate had successfully resisted all attempts to touch this land, probably because it was generally felt to be unsafe to leave the state entirely dependent on the tribute of the provinces, but with Cæsar's army at hand resistance had become impossible.

Pompey had now at last provided for his men, and he could confidently expect that his *acta* would soon be ratified; nevertheless, he was far from happy. He had probably joined the Triumvirate in the hope that the three together could so overawe the senate as to induce it to accept their programme; when this hope proved vain, he reluctantly supported Cæsar in his career of violent illegality, while at the same time seeking to evade all responsibility. He declared in public that it was not his business to inquire whether Bibulus was observing the heavens, and that, while he approved of Cæsar's laws, Cæsar's methods of carrying them were no concern of his.[1] Such subterfuges were of little use, because it was obvious that Cæsar was trampling on the constitution to gratify

[1] *Att.*, ii, 16.

Pompey, and that a word from Pompey would have stopped him, for Pompey's reputation as a general was then at its height, and Cæsar's soldiers would never have drawn the sword against him.[1] Although Pompey's excuses were really worthless, the fact that he made them showed a wish to separate himself from his partners and to keep open a line of retreat for himself, so that, if the nobles found the despotism of the Triumvirate intolerable, they might come to terms with him by promising to give legal sanction to the measures in which he was interested. Though such a bargain was highly improbable, Cæsar could not afford to take chances, however slight, since Pompey's desertion would have meant utter ruin, and he found a means of binding Pompey to him by arranging a marriage between his daughter Julia and the all-important general. Rome had long ceased to pay much attention to morals in the narrower sense of the word, but family ties and marriage alliances between noble houses still counted for much in politics. In this case the result may have surpassed Cæsar's hopes, for Pompey soon came to feel a strong affection for his young wife, which she returned, so that the marriage turned out happily and created a real bond between her father and her husband.

Assured of Pompey's loyalty, Cæsar saw to it that what remained of the Triumvirate's programme was rapidly enacted with such additions as they or their henchmen chose to make. The rough work of legislation was largely delegated to Vatinius, but it was Cæsar and his army that kept the opposition from attempting to do more than create technical illegalities in the enactment of every bill in the hope of annulling them in the future. Pompey's eastern *acta* were promptly ratified and the equestrian friends of Crassus got all they asked in the matter of the Asiatic taxes. In this last transaction Vatinius was believed, probably with truth, to have made a large sum from shares given him by the syndicate whose contract he amended so generously. After all, he could hardly be expected to do such work for nothing, and he was further allowed to pass some bills in favour of certain minor Asiatic princes, for which no doubt he was handsomely paid. Nor did the Three themselves hesitate to

[1] The rapidity with which the army was raised suggests that it included a large number of Pompey's veterans.

use their power for their own profit; Crassus probably reaped a golden harvest from the Asiatic tax measure, while Pompey and Cæsar secured the formal recognition of Ptolemy Auletes as king of Egypt in return for his promise to pay the enormous sum of six thousand talents. Although such personal legislation and jobbery must have taken most of his time, Cæsar was able to carry a new and drastic law against extortion on the part of provincial governors, for which he deserves high praise. In it he did perhaps all that could be done by legislation to protect Rome's subjects from oppression and to secure their well-being and prosperity under her rule. That he took the trouble to do this in the midst of his preoccupations with other and less creditable matters is enough to raise him far above either of the men with whom he was associated, and to show that, whatever part circumstances might force him to play in Rome, he was at heart a statesman with a real interest in good government.

The Triumvirs were well aware that they could hope to hold what they had gained only so long as the senate was too much afraid of them to cancel their laws. For the moment Cæsar was a dictator in all but name, but with the end of the year he would have to go to his province. Although from Cisalpine Gaul he could march upon Rome in case of need, something more was necessary to safeguard the Triumvirs, since there were rumours of impending disturbances across the Alps, and a war there might give the senate a pretext for so strengthening the army in the Transalpine province that it would be able to hold Cæsar in check. The sudden death of the governor of Transalpine Gaul in April[1] furnished an opportunity to remove this danger. Under pressure from Pompey, and no doubt from Crassus as well, the senate assigned this province also to Cæsar.[2] The conscript fathers yielded only because they feared that in the event of a refusal on their part Cæsar would have the assembly pass a law giving him the province[3] for a term of years. If he received it from them he would hold it only from year to year, so that they could deprive him of it in the near future if events should take a turn in their favour. It should be noted that it was the

[1] See my book, *The Founding of the Roman Empire*, pp. 265–67.

[2] The legion stationed there of course went with the province.

[3] Suet, *Div. Jul.*, ch. 22.

possession of the Transalpine province that made the conquest of Gaul possible, and that giving it to Cæsar was clearly an afterthought of the Triumvirs. Whatever ambitions Cæsar may have cherished, it is unlikely that he confided them to his partners, for Pompey would certainly have felt that if Gaul were to be conquered he and not Cæsar was the man to whom the task should be entrusted.

As Cæsar continued on his course, the opposition grew more bitter and more general. Rome was accustomed to the passage of an occasional bill by more or less illegal methods, but it gradually became apparent that Cæsar was going far beyond this, for he continued to legislate in utter disregard of the constitution and to suppress all opposition by terror. Senate and nobles were kept quiet by fear, not because of what Cæsar actually did, but because of what they thought he might do. They were convinced that the least resistance would be met by the occupation of the city by Cæsar's army, followed by a proscription or a massacre.[1] Scarcely a voice was raised in public, but beneath the surface the fiercest resentment smouldered, and this resentment was directed more at Pompey than at Cæsar, since it was Pompey whose support made the tyranny possible, and who seemed its chief beneficiary. At first Cæsar had enjoyed wide popular support, and had been applauded by the knights and the rabble, but as the year went on there was a marked change in feeling, and the resentment of the nobles spread to all classes. At the games and in the theatre the knights and rabble began to indulge in demonstrations against the Triumvirs, but Cæsar with his army was independent of public opinion, and it was thought sufficient to drop hints that such demonstrations would cost the people their grain and the knights some of their privileges.[2]

The masters of Rome recognized their growing unpopularity and saw clearly the need of protecting themselves against an immediate reaction as soon as the pressure of Cæsar's army was removed. With this object in view they determined to install their tools and henchmen in office for the next year

[1] Cicero (*Att.*, ii, 20) in July says that although everyone complains of what has been done no remedy is applied. "For we do not think it possible to resist without a massacre nor see an end to yielding short of ruin." His letters during July and August (*Att.*, ii, 18–25) furnish eloquent testimony of the helpless rage and terror of the opposition.

[2] *Att.*, ii, 19.

and to silence the men most likely to take the lead in any attempt to restore constitutional government. In the elections Cæsar had little difficulty in securing the return of most of the Triumvirate's candidates. The two men whose opposition was most dangerous were Cato and Cicero. Cato was disposed of by a special mission to Cyprus, to which he was appointed in such a way that it was impossible for him to attack Cæsar's laws without attacking his own appointment and the legality of all his own acts at the same time. Several attempts were * made to deal with Cicero in the same way, but the orator proved more obstinate. He had refrained from open opposition, to avoid which he had for a time left Rome, staying at various country villas and towns near by. He was approached in vain with various complimentary offers; nothing would induce him to accept any honour or office which would debar him from speaking freely in the future. He believed himself too great and popular to be attacked, and the Triumvirs determined to show all Rome that no one could brave their displeasure with impunity.

### § 3. THE BANISHMENT OF CICERO

In putting the Catilinarian conspirators to death without a trial Cicero had violated the law, at least as it was construed by the democratic party. Of this fact the Triumvirs decided to take advantage, and they easily found an instrument for their purpose. P. Clodius Pulcher, a young noble belonging to one of the old patrician families of Rome, was a bitter personal enemy of Cicero. In 62 B.C. he had been involved in a trial which made a tremendous sensation at the time. Every year the Roman women celebrated certain solemn rites in honour of a goddess known simply as the *Bona Dea*, and from these all men were rigorously excluded. In 62 the celebration was held in Cæsar's house, and in the midst of it Clodius was discovered disguised as a woman. Gossip explained his presence by an intrigue which it was alleged that he was carrying on with Cæsar's wife, but it is quite possible that he came merely out of curiosity. In view of the gossip Cæsar divorced his wife, not because he suspected her, but because, as he said, "Cæsar's wife must be above suspicion." Clodius, however, was prosecuted for sacrilege and attempted to set up an *alibi* as his defence. The testimony of Cicero destroyed the *alibi*, so that his conviction seemed inevitable, but at the last moment Crassus came to the rescue and by open and shameless bribery secured a verdict of "not guilty" from the jury. Clodius never forgave Cicero, and had ever since been seeking an opportunity for revenge. The Triumvirs decided to give him what he sought, and to make him tribune for this and other purposes. The fact that Clodius was by birth a patrician disqualified him for the office, but this difficulty was easily surmounted by a mock adoption into a plebeian family, and his election followed as a matter of course.

When Clodius assumed office as tribune in December, 59, he began by abolishing the use of omens to obstruct legislation, and by making the grain distributed to the poor entirely gratuitous.[1] Having secured the enthusiastic support of the rabble by the latter measure, he introduced a bill banishing all magistrates who had put citizens to death without a trial, a measure which, although drawn up in general terms, was aimed solely at Cicero. When this bill came before the people Cæsar had laid down the consulship, but he still lingered near Rome, postponing his departure for Gaul until the bill was passed. The threat of his presence at the head of his army outside the city overawed all factions and parties in Rome, and Cicero, finding no one ready to make a stand in his behalf, accepted the inevitable and left Italy for Greece. He ever afterwards regretted that he had not remained to fight it out,[2] but since he stood alone the regret was probably wasted. The suddenness of his downfall nearly broke his heart, for up to the last he had clung to Pompey's assurances of protection. The desertion of the great general, whom he had supposed to be his friend, was a heavy blow, and he was deeply chagrined to see how readily he was abandoned by the nobility.

As soon as Cicero was out of the way, Cæsar departed for Gaul, and Rome no longer lived in fear of him and his army.

[1] Clodius doubtless aimed simply at popularity with the mob, but the increasing poverty in Rome may have furnished some justification for the measure. Hitherto the grain had been sold at a low price, so it is only after Clodius that we can speak of the corn-dole with strict accuracy.

[2] By pleading that the law did not apply to him because the conspirators had ceased to be citizens. It seems obvious, however, that if Cæsar's army could force the passage of the law it would have prevailed against any such plea.

He left the city, however, under magistrates selected by himself and his partners, so that, if Crassus and Pompey could contrive to act together in his absence, there was no danger from the senate. Once in Gaul he found himself unable to give any continuous attention to politics. Even if he went north without any definite purpose of conquest, war was forced upon him immediately and with it came a swift perception of the opportunity, and Cæsar was a man who always made the most of opportunities.

## § 4. THE QUARREL BETWEEN POMPEY AND CRASSUS

Cæsar had hardly departed before the two Triumvirs who remained behind began to quarrel. They had always been enemies, and once the peacemaker was gone they saw no reason to continue their alliance, since their programme had been carried out in full. Crassus was always eager to thwart and humiliate Pompey if he could do so with safety to himself, while Pompey felt keenly his unpopularity and wished a reconciliation with the nobility. Moreover, Pompey was probably sincerely anxious to make amends to Cicero, and perhaps somewhat ashamed of the manner in which he had treated him. It might be assumed that Cicero, having learned his lesson, would be more pliable in the future, and his recall would serve as an overture of peace to the senate.

Pompey, therefore, soon began to make tentative moves for recalling the orator from exile. Nothing more was necessary to arouse Clodius to fury. He was undoubtedly a demagogue of some talent, and he had made himself the idol of the slums by his corn law. Moreover, he had passed a law legalizing the clubs and associations which existed among the rabble, and had organized them effectively; he could easily collect gangs of ruffians, and as a gang leader he displayed conspicuous ability. When Pompey showed his hand in regard to Cicero, Clodius turned upon him. Whenever Pompey appeared in public he was assailed by the jeers and abuse of Clodius' gangs, so that it was not long before the great general was almost a prisoner in his own house. The magistrates were helpless, since Rome had practically no police, and Clodius could riot with impunity.

It has been generally assumed that Clodius was a tool of

Cæsar and that he got out of hand when Cæsar left for Gaul, but there is no evidence of any such connection between the two men. On the other hand the fact that Crassus bribed a jury to acquit Clodius suggests that the gangster was a henchman of the millionaire. This supposition is strengthened by the fact that Pompey a little later accused Crassus of supplying him with money, so it may be assumed that in harassing Pompey Clodius relied on Crassus to pay the gangs. The millionaire was quite malicious enough to enjoy thoroughly the spectacle of his rival's troubles, and in addition to this motive he disliked Cicero and had no wish for his recall.

While Clodius was tribune no serious move could be made, since he was armed with a veto and was master of the streets. Most of the magistrates for 57 B.C. were favourable to Cicero, however, so a law was proposed for the orator's recall. Although now a private citizen, Clodius was still at the head of his gangs, and raised a riot at every attempt to bring the bill before the assembly. In this way he might have prevented action indefinitely but for the fact that among the tribunes for 57 there was a man of energy and courage, T. Annius Milo, who determined to fight fire with fire and hired a band of gladiators to resist the gangs of Clodius. Street fights became the order of the day, and the senate so far bestirred itself as to call on the Italians to come to Rome to vote. Gradually Milo got the better of his rival to such an extent that the assembly was able to pass the bill for Cicero's recall. The great orator returned to his country in triumph, but he had troubles still before him. His house in Rome having been destroyed by Clodius, the senate undertook to rebuild it at the public expense, but the gangster drove off the workmen, tore down what they had built, and burned the house of Cicero's brother next door.

In securing the recall of Cicero the senate had worked with Pompey, and this fact must have filled Crassus with alarm, for a permanent alliance between them would leave him powerless and discredited. His obvious course was to break up the combination if possible by thwarting Pompey at every turn, and this was comparatively easy, because in spite of Pompey's recent help the nobles had not forgiven or forgotten his past offences and were inclined to view his every move with profound suspicion. Crassus' debtors in the senate might, therefore, be employed very effectively, and outside there were Clodius and other agents to raise embarrassing questions and to create disturbances in case of need. A sudden shortage of grain soon after Cicero's return precipitated a crisis. The senate, frightened by the situation, made haste to confer on Pompey the charge of the food supply. Two bills for this purpose were proposed, one of which gave him all necessary powers, while the other added a fleet and an army. Pompey professed himself in favour of the first bill, but his friends supported the second, so that it was naturally inferred that he really desired this measure. Since there was no real justification for the army, Pompey was taken at his word and got only what he openly asked for. Undiscouraged by this defeat, his friends soon made another effort. The subjects of Ptolemy Auletes had compelled that worthless monarch to flee from Alexandria, and he now sought to recover his throne by the help of Rome. Since his restoration seemed likely to require an army, it was at once proposed to entrust the business to Pompey. The general again took a disinterested attitude in public, but the zeal of his intimates left little doubt as to his wishes.[1] Just at this moment a passage was discovered in the Sibylline books which was construed as forbidding the use of an army to help an Egyptian king, and the senate availed itself of this to let the whole matter drop.

In both of these episodes the ill-will and suspicion of the senate toward Pompey had been so openly manifested that he could entertain no illusions as to the attitude of the nobles. Meanwhile Clodius was assailing him with such violence that he began to have fears for his life, and called in friends from the country to protect him. Behind his assailants he recognized Crassus, and there can be little doubt that he was right on this point. The millionaire had succeeded in isolating Pompey for the moment, but a new combination between him and the senate was possible, and Crassus was probably on the alert to thwart any moves in that direction. He had already discerned the point at which a wedge could most effectively be driven between Pompey and the senate, for in

[1] Probably Pompey desired an army for its political effect. If he was once authorized to recruit troops, he could keep a sufficient number of them in Italy to overawe his enemies. Since it would not have required a large force to disperse the mob, Clodius would not have ventured to continue his attacks if Pompey had had a few cohorts at his disposal.

58 Clodius had raised the question of the validity of Cæsar's laws. It may seem strange that Crassus should have permitted such a move by his henchman, but he probably risked nothing, since the only law in which he seems to have been interested was the one passed by Vatinius in regard to the Asiatic taxes. It is true that the laws of the tribune were no more valid than those of Cæsar, but the senate was not bound by strict logic and might annul the Julian laws while allowing those of Vatinius to stand. Even if they were all swept away together, it is not certain that Crassus would have lost anything, since the syndicate which had farmed the Asiatic taxes may already have distributed its profits and quietly dissolved on the expiration of its contract. Pompey, however, was in a very different position, since it was Cæsar who had proposed the laws which provided for his veterans, and they had not yet been fully executed; in particular it would seem that there was still much land in Campania to be allotted. In 58 the move of Clodius had led to no result, for the nobles needed the help of Pompey to secure Cicero's recall. During 57 they grew more confident of their own strength and also more certain that the Triumvirate had really broken up, though they still moved with some degree of caution, fearing that an indiscriminate attack might revive the union. At the beginning of 56 the senate decided to take up the question of the validity of Cæsar's law regarding the Campanian land, but a thanksgiving of unprecedented length was voted for Cæsar's victories in Gaul, probably as a hint to him that he need feel no alarm whatever might happen to his laws.

The political situation had thus become extremely complicated, and Pompey was in a very difficult position. Although he cannot have been willing to see Cæsar's laws annulled he must have felt that he could not prevent such action by the senate. He may well have thought that his best course was to accept the inevitable with outward equanimity, in the hope that such a concession on his part would placate the nobles. At any rate, the course taken by Cicero strongly suggests such an attitude, for Cicero took the lead in raising the question of the Campanian land law in the senate, and in one of his letters he afterwards declared that at the time Pompey showed no sign of displeasure.[1] We may suspect

[1] *Fam.*, i, 9, § 9. The letter was written in 54 B.C.

some exaggeration in the letter, since Cicero was trying to justify his conduct when his blunder had become patent to the world, but it is impossible to believe that he intended an attack on Pompey. The most probable assumption is that Cicero was aiming at a reconciliation of Pompey with the senate and believed that he could bring it about if Pompey consented to give up the Campanian land, while Pompey, seeing no way to avoid the sacrifice, concealed the reluctance which he felt and allowed Cicero to pursue his policy.

We cannot suppose that Cæsar was left in ignorance of what was happening in Rome, for he must have kept up a correspondence with both Crassus and Pompey as well as many others. Up to this time, however, he had been too actively engaged in his campaigns in Gaul to interfere effectively, although he can hardly have viewed the disruption of the Triumvirate without anxious forebodings. He had been too long an opponent of the senate to believe that the nobles would refrain from an attack upon him once they had broken the influence of Pompey, so he must have been anxious to revive the coalition again, if only as the best and surest means of protecting himself. He spent the winter of 57–56 B.C. in Cisalpine Gaul, and in the spring both Pompey and Crassus met him at Luca, a town within the borders of the province. Whether they came spontaneously or at his invitation it is impossible to determine, for he had obvious motives for wishing to put an end to their feud, and in view of the situation in Rome each of them might naturally wish to secure Cæsar's support against the other. Whatever the origin of the conference, the result could hardly be doubtful. Once in personal touch with his partners it is probable that Cæsar had little difficulty in reconciling them, since both must have realized that their quarrels were restoring the senate to power, and that neither could hope to profit by such a restoration. Under these circumstances, and with Cæsar to act as peacemaker, an agreement was soon reached; the Triumvirate which had seemed dead at the end of 57 was suddenly renewed, but on a new basis and on new conditions. As soon as the agreement had been completed Cæsar crossed the Alps, while Crassus and Pompey returned to Rome to assume the control of affairs there.

# CHAPTER XII

# THE CONQUEST OF GAUL

## § 1. CONDITIONS IN GAUL

AFTER he laid down the consulship Cæsar lingered near Rome to enable Clodius to carry through the banishment of Cicero until the news of serious dangers menacing the Transalpine province obliged him to hasten there at top speed. What followed can be understood only if the general condition of Gaul at the time is borne in mind, so a few words on the subject are necessary.

The vast region between the Pyrenees and the Rhine and between the North Sea and the Mediterranean consisted of two parts. Along the coast of the Mediterranean stretched the Roman province of Transalpine Gaul, commonly referred to by Cæsar simply as the Province ; the remainder of the country was independent, although the Romans had entered into relations with many of its tribes, some of whom had been declared friends and allies of the Roman people. The inhabitants of Gaul were of mixed origin, although throughout the greater part of the country the Celts were the dominant race. They were invaders from across the Rhine, who, entering the country about the seventh century before Christ, had gradually spread over it, conquering and more or less completely absorbing the original population except in Aquitania. They even crossed the Alps and occupied the valley of the Po, which in consequence was known to the Romans as Cisalpine Gaul. The last of the Celtic invaders, the Belgæ, occupied the northern districts along the English Channel and the Rhine ; their language seems to have differed from that of the other Celts, so that Cæsar regarded them as a separate group of people and counted them as one of the three parts into which he affirmed that Gaul was divided.

These three parts were those inhabited by the Belgæ, the Celts, and the Aquitani. The last seem to have been least mixed with the invaders, and had preserved their original language. In race they were more or less akin to the Iberians in Spain, into which country the Celts had also forced their way.

Taken as a whole the Gauls may be described as semi-civilized; they practised both agriculture and cattle-breeding, they had acquired some skill in mining and working metals, and they carried on a considerable commerce and were acquainted with the use of money, striking coins of their own. A few of their towns were wealthy and important, but many were little more than fortified refuges in time of danger. Politically they were ill-organized and obviously in a state of transition. They had originally been divided into clans (the *pagi* of Cæsar), and these clans were still the prevailing unit among the Aquitani. Among the Celts, however, although some of the clans had remained isolated, the great majority had united to form tribes, which Cæsar calls *civitates*. These tribes had until a recent period been governed by kings, doubtless assisted by an aristocratic council composed of the heads of the clans and an assembly of the freemen of the tribe. In most of Central Gaul the monarchies had been overthrown on the eve of Cæsar's arrival, and had been replaced by aristocracies under one or more elected magistrates. The memory of the older monarchies, however, was still so vivid that the new republican governments were very insecure, exposed on the one hand to attempts to restore the old royal line, and on the other to attempts on the part of powerful nobles to seize the throne and set up what the Greeks would have called tyrannies. In nearly all an effective administration was lacking and dissension was rife. Individual nobles, even when not strong enough to make themselves kings, were yet able to defy the constituted authorities. Moreover, the different tribes were continually at odds with each other and often at war. The stronger had reduced the weaker to a condition of complete or partial dependence, and were constantly seeking to extend and maintain their own influence and to undermine or overthrow that of their rivals.

Almost the only element of national unity was to be found in religion. Like the Romans the Gauls worshipped many gods, concerning whom we are very imperfectly informed. Unlike the Romans they built no temples, but held their solemn rites in sacred groves without images of the gods in human form. All religious ceremonies were presided over by a priesthood known as the Druids. These Druids were well organized, assembling every year in a sort of national council, and at their head was a chief Druid, elected for life. Membership in the order was not hereditary, and was eagerly sought by the nobility, for the Druids were exempt from military service and taxation. They had charge of education, and took a large part in the administration of justice, enforcing their decrees by excommunication and interdict. Cæsar was informed that Druidism came from Britain, which had also been conquered by the Celts, and that it was there found in its purest form, so that many went from Gaul to the island to seek further instruction in its mysteries. It seems probable that Druidism was a pre-Celtic institution which was ultimately taken over by the invaders. At any rate there is no trace of it in Cisalpine Gaul, a fact which seems to confirm Cæsar's statement as to its non-Gallic origin. Probably its elements existed in Gaul, but it was first fully organized in Britain and spread from there to the Continent. Of the teaching of the Druids little can be determined with certainty beyond the fact that they inculcated the doctrine of the immortality of the soul. From Cæsar's language on this point we would naturally suppose that they believed in the transmigration of souls,[1] but if so their teaching would seem to have made little impression on the popular mind, for the Celts appear to have conceived the future life as similar to the present but happier and better. Their theological instruction was oral, though they were acquainted with writing, using the Greek alphabet, which they doubtless had acquired through Massilia, for secular purposes. Human sacrifice was sanctioned and practised with some degree of frequency, at which the Romans were much horrified. It might have seemed that this powerful sacerdotal order, extending over the whole of Gaul, would have taken a leading part in resisting the Romans, but we hear of nothing of the kind. Probably like the rest of the Gauls the Druids were divided among themselves and incapable of united action.

[1] Cæsar, *b.g.* vi, ch. 14.

The military system of the Celts was also in a state of transition. The main strength of the Celtic armies lay in the cavalry, and the infantry, drawn from the common people, who were mostly the serfs and retainers of the nobles, played a somewhat subordinate role. The war-chariot had been discarded on the Continent, although it was still used in Britain. The dissensions and rivalries among the tribes made united action difficult for any length of time, and the lack of efficient political organization prevented the development of any adequate commissariat. The result was that prolonged operations were almost impossible for the Gauls, and, although large armies were easily assembled, they were apt to disperse after a short time. To sum up the general conditions from a military standpoint, the Gauls were sufficiently civilized to make conquest profitable, and they were so ill-organized and divided as to make conquest seem comparatively easy.

## § 2. THE HELVETII AND ARIOVISTUS

The situation which called Cæsar in haste to Gaul was complicated. When the Romans annexed the Transalpine province in 121 B.C. two tribes, the Ædui and the Arverni, were rivals for the supremacy in Central Gaul. In this struggle the Romans aided the Ædui and enabled them to gain the victory. Some forty years later the Arverni regained the lead under a king named Celtillus, the father of the famous Vercingetorix. The Ædui, however, soon got the upper hand again and held it until 61 B.C. Their hegemony was naturally resented by some of the other tribes, so that the Sequani, unable to resist them, sought the help of the Germans across the Rhine. At their invitation Ariovistus with a large body of warriors came to their assistance, and in 61 the Sequani and their allies inflicted a crushing defeat upon the Ædui. The latter appealed to Rome in vain, for, though the senate instructed the governor of Transalpine Gaul to give them what help he could, he was too fully occupied in suppressing a revolt of the Allobroges to do anything at the moment. The Sequani soon found that they had gained little by their victory, for they were obliged to hand over their lands in Alsace to Ariovistus, whose strength grew rapidly as fresh bands of Germans joined him, and they began to discover that they had merely exchanged one yoke for another.

Meanwhile a faction among the Ædui was looking for help elsewhere than from the Romans and was intriguing with the Helvetii. This people, living in what is now Switzerland, already hard pressed by the Germans, were alarmed at the establishment of Ariovistus in their neighbourhood and were planning to abandon their country and seek a new home in Western Gaul. This migration the Ædui hoped to turn to their own advantage by securing new and powerful allies. The movement was one which required long and careful preparation, and the Helvetii determined to start in the spring of 58 B.C. At the appointed time they began gathering near the modern city of Geneva, and it was the news of their muster at this point that brought Cæsar hurrying from Rome across the Alps.

To reach Western Gaul the Helvetii desired to march across the northern part of the Province, so they sent ambassadors to Cæsar to ask his permission. He had no intention of granting their request, for their settlement in Gaul was bound to cause widespread disturbances which would endanger the position of Rome, but, having only one legion at hand, he wished to gain time. Accordingly he informed the Helvetii that he would consider their demands and give them an answer on April 13. He employed the interval in fortifying the south bank of the Rhone, and when their ambassadors returned he refused to allow the Helvetii to enter the Province. They made no serious attempt to defy him, but succeeded in persuading the Sequani to permit them to cross their territory. Against this Cæsar had no technical right to protest, for the Sequani were an independent people ; nevertheless he was determined to put a stop to the migration. Since his forces were insufficient for this purpose, he hastened to Cisalpine Gaul, where he had three legions in winter quarters together with a large number of recruits. Forming the recruits into two new legions and bringing the three old ones with him, he recrossed the Alps prepared to deal with the situation.

During his absence the Helvetii, numbering about 360,000, a fourth of whom were warriors, had crossed the territory of the Sequani and entered that of the Ædui. Among the latter

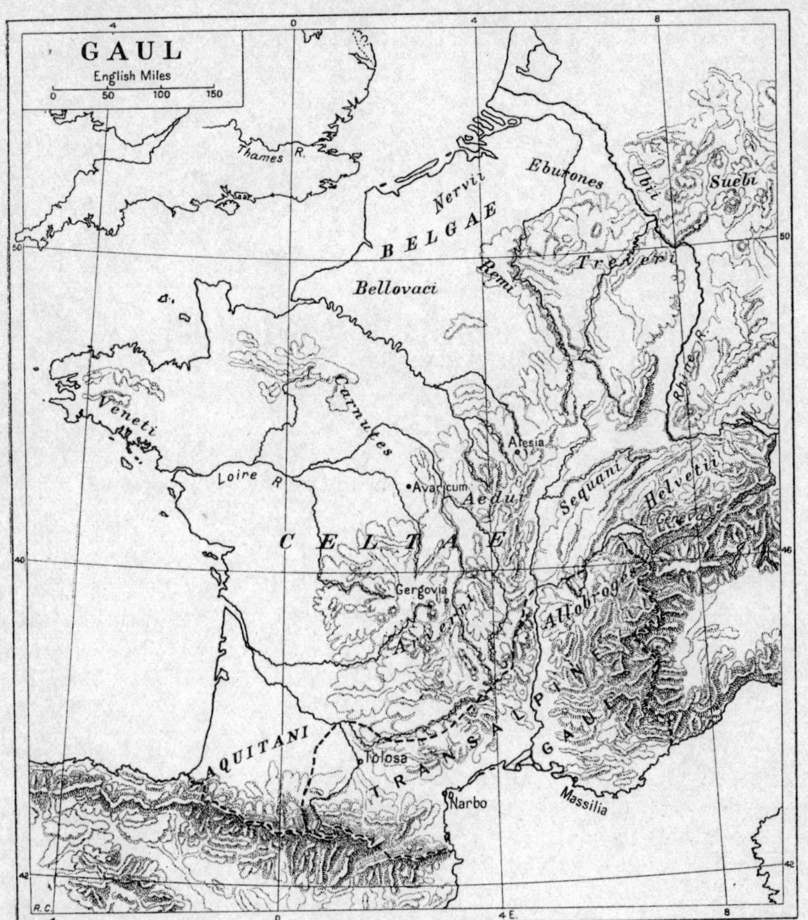
GAUL
English Miles
0 50 100 150
Thames R.
Nervii
Eburones
Ubii
Suebi
BELGAE
Remi
Treveri
Bellovaci
Rhine R.
Veneti
Carnutes
Alesia
Loire R.
Avaricum
Aedui
Sequani
Helvetii
L. Geneva
CELTAE
Gergovia
Allobroges
Arverni
TRANSALPINE GAUL
AQUITANI
Tolosa
Narbo
Massilia
R.C.
4E.

people the pro-Roman party, which was in control of the government, appealed to Cæsar for protection. This appeal gave him the formal pretext he desired, and he marched to the help of the Ædui with his army. For a time he followed the Helvetii, seeking an opportunity to strike a decisive blow. His difficulties soon began to multiply, for the cavalry, furnished by the Ædui, proved to be untrustworthy, and the supplies which they had promised failed to arrive, so that Cæsar was finally obliged to abandon the pursuit in order to secure food for his army. The Helvetii, however, followed him, having suddenly determined to force a battle. Cæsar drew up his army on a line of hills near Bibracte (modern Autun). The Helvetii fought fiercely, but by night the Romans were victorious, and the remnant of the defeated host was in flight. Owing to the exhaustion of his men Cæsar was unable to pursue them, but the Gauls, unwilling to incur the wrath of the conqueror, refused supplies to the fugitives, who were soon forced to surrender. The greater part of the survivors Cæsar sent back to their former country, though some were sold as slaves on the ground that they had violated the terms of the surrender, and one considerable group was allowed to settle in the territory of the Ædui at the request of that people.

The success of Cæsar made such an impression on the tribes of Central Gaul that most of them sent envoys to congratulate him on his victory and to invoke his help against Ariovistus. Until this time Cæsar seems to have troubled himself very little about the German, but he now learned that the rapid growth of his power had produced widespread alarm in Gaul. The invasion of the Cimbri and Teutones was still well remembered, and both the Celts and the Romans feared that Ariovistus might repeat their exploits. Cæsar was easily persuaded, therefore, that the situation must be dealt with promptly and at once opened negotiations. Probably he had no hope of accomplishing anything by diplomacy, but since Ariovistus had recently been declared a friend and ally of the Roman people, a pretext for attacking him was necessary. The negotiations, as Cæsar doubtless intended, merely resulted in supplying a pretext for the inevitable war. After some manœuvring Cæsar succeeded in forcing the Germans to fight a pitched battle at the foot of the Vosges in which they were decisively defeated, and the survivors were driven back across the Rhine.

Cæsar had now come to the parting of the ways. If he followed the traditional Roman policy he would withdraw his army to the Province, leaving the Gauls to go their own way without further interference. Such a course, however, would merely invite fresh trouble in the near future. Ariovistus himself had been disposed of, for he died soon after his defeat, but the tribes of Central Gaul were so disunited and ill-organized that a fresh invasion of the Germans might be confidently expected. Since they could be efficiently protected only by the definite establishment of Roman rule, Cæsar decided on this policy, and soon made his intentions sufficiently clear by quartering his legions for the winter at Vesontio (Besançon) among the nominally independent Sequani, and by recruiting two new legions in the Cisalpine province.

## § 3. THE CONQUEST OF THE BELGÆ

There were many chiefs in Central Gaul who resented Cæsar's interference and feared the probable consequences. There was no doubt much real patriotism, but it was mixed with many less noble motives, for it was impossible for Cæsar to avoid meddling with the internal affairs of the tribes, even if he desired to do so, and this was bound to give bitter offence. He naturally threw the weight of his influence in favour of the pro-Roman party among the Ædui, and this as naturally alienated those who had intrigued with the Helvetii and now found themselves deprived of much of their influence by Cæsar's victory. Similar conditions in other tribes led a number of the discontented chiefs to intrigue for the purpose of fomenting trouble, and the Belgæ, who were alarmed by Cæsar's advance, were persuaded to take the field against him in 57 B.C.

Cæsar had spent the winter in Cisalpine Gaul, but in the spring he rejoined his army, which he had reinforced with the two new legions. He quickly realized the situation and marched north before the Belgæ had completed their preparations. One of their tribes, the Remi, from whom the modern city of Reims derives its name, at once submitted to him.

They were vassals of another tribe and hoped that by an alliance with the Romans they could recover their independence. Their adhesion gave Cæsar a good base for operations, and he took up a strong position, from which the Belgic army when it appeared upon the scene was unable to dislodge him. Cæsar sent his Æduan allies to ravage the country of his enemies, and the unwieldy host, whose supplies were soon exhausted, began to break up, each tribe being anxious to protect its own lands. Cæsar pursued the retreating army, and the retreat became a flight. Some of the tribes, thoroughly discouraged, submitted to him, but the Nervii with some others in the North determined to resist. Cæsar marched against them, but they succeeded in taking him by surprise and nearly defeated him on the banks of the Sambre. With desperate energy he rallied his army and finally won so complete a victory that the Nervii surrendered. The tribes of Normandy and Brittany also submitted to young Crassus, the triumvir's son, so that almost all of Northern and Central Gaul was apparently at the feet of the conqueror. The appearance was delusive, however, and the Roman supremacy rested on no solid foundation. Cæsar was probably aware of this and realized that further struggles were to come.

Meanwhile, as we have seen, Pompey and Crassus had been quarrelling at Rome, where everything seemed to indicate a senatorial revival, which Cæsar was anxious to prevent. He was, indeed, secure in his possession of Cisalpine Gaul till the end of 54 B.C., but the Transalpine province, having been given him by the senate, could be taken from him at the end of 56, and in that event all that he had accomplished might be speedily undone. The situation in Gaul, therefore, gave him the strongest reason for seeking a renewal of the Triumvirate as the only means by which he could make sure of the time necessary to consolidate and complete his conquest.

## § 4. BRITAIN AND GERMANY

When Cæsar crossed the Alps in 56 after the conference at Luca, he found that a revolt had already broken out. In the preceding year he had become interested in Britain, of which the Romans as yet knew very little, for some of the tribes of Gaul had lands on both sides of the Channel, and there was an active trade between the island and the Continent. This trade was mainly in the hands of the Veneti, a tribe living in Brittany, who were alarmed at the rumours which reached them that Cæsar was intending an invasion of Britain. They had submitted after the defeat of the Belgæ, but fear for their commerce now induced them to revolt. Some of the other maritime tribes joined them, the Belgæ were restless, and the Germans seemed to be preparing a new invasion. It was with this situation that Cæsar had to cope when he arrived in Gaul; he despatched his ablest lieutenant, T. Labienus, to guard the Rhine and overawe the North, while P. Crassus, a son of the millionaire, was sent south to subdue Aquitania. Both were successful. Labienus kept the northern tribes quiet; the Germans made no move, and the Aquitani submitted without offering any serious resistance.

Cæsar had already begun the construction of a fleet in the Loire, but it was apparently not yet ready. Without waiting for it, he marched in person against the Veneti, sending one of his officers with three legions to crush the revolt in Normandy. The officer was successful, but Cæsar himself had undertaken a more difficult enterprise, for the nature of the country occupied by the Veneti enabled them to defy all his efforts as long as they remained masters of the sea, so that, after spending much time in operations which were barren of any serious results, he was finally obliged to wait for his fleet. When it arrived the war was speedily decided by a naval battle, in which the Romans completely destroyed the maritime power of the Veneti. That people were now at Cæsar's mercy, and he determined to give the other Gauls a warning of the danger of rebellion, so he put the leading men to death and sold the rest of the people as slaves. Some of the Northern coast tribes still held out, and Cæsar marched against them, but the season was too far advanced for him to accomplish anything, and he was forced to postpone their subjugation till the next year.

During the winter (56–55 B.C.) two German tribes, the Usipetes and the Tencteri, crossed the Rhine, and this event led Cæsar to return from the Cisalpine province earlier than usual, since he feared that the discontented elements in Gaul might unite with the invaders. When he took the field against them, the Germans sent envoys to request that he allow them to settle in Gaul. This request Cæsar refused, but he offered to secure lands for them on the other side of the Rhine. A truce of three days was arranged to enable the Germans to consider this offer, but it was immediately broken by an attack on Cæsar's cavalry. The next day the German chiefs hastened to the Roman camp with apologies for the attack, claiming that it was unauthorized, but Cæsar had little faith in their apologies and concluded that they were simply trying to gain time. Probably he had already determined to make an example of them and was ready to seize upon the first convenient pretext. He arrested the chiefs forthwith and marched rapidly against the offending tribes, who, taken by surprise and without leaders, fled precipitately with little attempt at resistance. Cæsar pursued them relentlessly, and their flight became an indiscriminate massacre. The tribes, whose number Cæsar estimated at over 400,000, were practically annihilated, the few survivors being scattered to the four winds.

The invaders destroyed, Cæsar resolved to strike further terror into the Germans by threatening them in their own homes. To accomplish his purpose he built a bridge across the Rhine and advanced into Germany, ostensibly for the purpose of assisting the friendly Ubii, who were being attacked by the powerful tribe of the Suebi. The latter withdrew into the interior without risking a battle, and Cæsar, who had no desire to pursue them, returned to Gaul, destroying the bridge behind him, after a stay of eighteen days in Germany.

Although the summer was nearly over, Cæsar determined to make a brief preliminary expedition to Britain. He assembled a fleet and with two legions sailed across the Channel to the coast of Kent, where he succeeded in landing in spite of the resistance of the Britons. This so discouraged the tribes in the vicinity that they seemed disposed to submit, but when Cæsar's fleet was badly damaged by a storm they recovered confidence and attacked his camp; after a sharp repulse, however, some of the Kentish chiefs made their submission, so that Cæsar was able to retire without loss of prestige.

Cæsar was well aware that this expedition had accomplished little, and during the winter (55–54 B.C.) he made preparations for a more serious invasion of the island. From the extent of these preparations it has been inferred that he intended the conquest and permanent occupation of Southern Britain, but the inference seems hardly warranted, since the events of 55 were more likely to provoke the resentment of the Britons than to leave a lasting impression of Rome's greatness and power, and it might, therefore, seem desirable to revisit the island at the head of a large army in order to terrify the inhabitants to such a degree that they would refrain from any attempt at interference on the Continent. Perhaps also Cæsar hoped that the invasion of the island, whether resulting in its annexation or not, would impress the imagination of the Romans and contribute to his reputation in Italy. At any rate, after prolonged delays, he finally landed in Kent with five legions and some 2000 cavalry furnished by the Gauls. Finding the Britons unprepared, Cæsar advanced hastily, hoping to defeat their forces before they could be concentrated. He won a victory near Canterbury, but in his haste he had left his fleet at anchor instead of securing its safety by drawing the ships on shore. A sudden storm which destroyed many of the ships deprived Cæsar's victory of results, for he was forced to return to the coast to make arrangements for the future security of his fleet. This circumstance enabled the Britons to rally, and they chose as their leader in the coming struggle a chief by the name of Cassivellaunus, who persuaded his followers to adopt guerrilla tactics and to avoid a pitched battle, a policy which might have been successful if it could have been maintained. In spite of difficulties in procuring supplies Cæsar pushed on and succeeded in crossing the Thames. Several of the British tribes now came over to his side, and he captured the chief stronghold of Cassivellaunus. This, combined with the defections, so discouraged the British leader that he sued for peace. Since Cæsar was ready to bring the war to an end, terms were soon arranged by which Cassivellaunus gave hostages and promised tribute to Rome. Cæsar at once returned to Gaul with his army, leaving no garrisons in Britain to ensure the fulfilment of the terms. Since he can hardly have felt much confidence in the promises, his failure to take any steps to occupy the territory which he had nominally subdued would seem to show that he had achieved his purpose, or that, disquieted by news of unrest in Gaul, he had decided to abandon it for the present.

## § 5. THE REVOLT OF AMBIORIX

When Cæsar was preparing for his second expedition to Britain, he was so well aware of the widespread discontent in Gaul that he had forced the principal Gallic chiefs to accompany him. Such a step was not likely to increase his popularity, although by depriving the Gauls of their leaders it prevented them from taking advantage of his absence to revolt. When he returned in the autumn of 54 B.C. he found that it was necessary to disperse his legions over a somewhat wide area, since the harvest for the year had been poor and supplies were difficult to obtain in consequence. Judging the discontent greatest among the Belgæ, he quartered his entire army among them with the exception of one legion which he sent into Normandy. He himself took up his position near the modern city of Amiens with three legions in the immediate vicinity, while Cicero's brother Quintus was stationed among the Nervii, Labienus was sent to watch the Treveri, and two other garrisons were placed at other points, one of which was under Sabinus in the country of the Eburones.[1]

This scattering of the Roman forces proved an irresistible temptation to the Gauls. The Eburones suddenly rose at the instigation of a chief named Ambiorix and besieged the Roman garrison. The camp could probably have held out, but Sabinus allowed himself to be deceived by the promise of the rebel leader, who had hitherto been friendly to the Romans, that if they would leave the camp and march to join Labienus they would not be attacked on the way. Trusting the pledges of Ambiorix, Sabinus gave orders for a retreat, but the Romans almost immediately found themselves surrounded, and most of them perished in the trap, only a few contriving to escape. Encouraged by this easy victory, the rebels marched at once upon the camp of Q. Cicero. The Nervii readily joined them, and Cicero, who had had no warning of the storm which was about to burst upon him, was blockaded on every side. He defended himself valiantly and managed, though with great difficulty, to inform Cæsar of his

[1] Probably somewhere in the neighbourhood of Liège, but the exact location is uncertain.

perilous situation. As soon as the news reached him, Cæsar hastily collected such forces as he could at a moment's notice, amounting to about 7000 men, and marched to Cicero's relief. He was just in time, for the position of the garrison was desperate when Cæsar appeared and easily routed the Gauls. While these events were in progress a revolt had broken out among the Treveri, who appealed to the Germans for assistance and assailed the camp of Labienus. That able officer, however, defeated them and slew their leader. As a result of these two victories many of the rebel bands dispersed, and the unrest appeared to subside.

Cæsar knew well enough that further revolts were being hatched, and that the rebellion, though checked, was not yet subdued, for Ambiorix was still in arms and the Germans might cross the Rhine in spite of the defeat of the Treveri. Little could be done during the winter (54–53 B.C.) except to prepare for active operations in the spring, and Cæsar employed the time to strengthen his army. To replace the division that had been destroyed under Sabinus he recruited two new legions, and Pompey, with whom he was still on friendly terms, loaned him a third, so that he now had ten in all.

In 53 Cæsar marched through Northern Gaul and received the submission of all the tribes there, while Labienus again defeated the Treveri. To overawe the Germans Cæsar built another bridge across the Rhine and again invaded Germany. As before the hostile Germans fell back into the wilder parts of the country, and Cæsar soon retired to Gaul. Having deprived Ambiorix of all possible allies, Cæsar turned finally on the Eburones, determined to take pitiless vengeance upon them for the disaster which his lieutenant had suffered at their hands. They offered no serious or united resistance, but Cæsar devastated their country with relentless thoroughness, intending that all who did not perish in battle should starve. He was especially anxious to capture Ambiorix, but in spite of all his efforts the rebel leader managed to escape. The revolt having been completely crushed, Cæsar felt it safe to cross the Alps in order to attend to his duties in the Cisalpine province.

## § 6. VERCINGETORIX

In the revolt which had just been suppressed the tribes of Central Gaul had taken no active part. There had been some unrest among them, but Cæsar had promptly checked it, so that they had rendered no aid of importance to the Northern rebels. Nevertheless, in checking the discontent among them, Cæsar had not allayed it, but had made it more acute, and after his departure a definite conspiracy rapidly took shape, the conspirators deriving added confidence from reports of the disorders in Rome which followed the death of Clodius. The Carnutes led the way by massacring the Romans in their country, chiefly traders, and the news was swiftly carried over the whole of Gaul. The Arverni quickly followed the example under the leadership of a young noble named Vercingetorix, who was the son of a former Arvernian king. The aristocratic government was hostile to him, but he roused the common people by his eloquence, and with their help he overthrew the government and was proclaimed king by his followers. He at once set to work to win the support of other tribes and met with such success that in a short time nearly all Central and Western Gaul had joined the insurrection and had accepted him as their leader. The Belgæ and Aquitani, however, took no part in the movement, and the Ædui, old rivals of the Arverni, hesitated and held back.

To prevent Cæsar from rejoining his army, the greater part of which was stationed in Central Gaul under the command of Labienus, the insurgents planned to invade the Province in the vicinity of Narbo, hoping that Cæsar would consider it necessary to defend the old Roman possessions and would thus be detained in the South. This plan met with success at first, for some of the tribes on the frontier were won over, and the Gauls were preparing to advance when Cæsar arrived upon the scene. He had crossed the Alps as soon as possible after he received the news of the revolt and hastened at once to Narbo. He reassured the provincials, collected some detachments which served as a garrison for the Province, and posted them so as to ward off the threatened invasion. This done, he determined to reach his army at all costs. Although the Cevennes were still covered with snow, Cæsar with some new recruits made his way with great difficulty across the mountains into the country of the Arverni. Vercingetorix, with the armed forces of the tribe, was nearly a hundred miles away, so Cæsar began devastating the undefended country. As he had expected, Vercingetorix was forced by the clamours of his men to return, giving Cæsar the opportunity to push rapidly north and join his army without serious difficulty. He found it weak in cavalry, since he had relied for this upon the Gauls, and many tribes who had hitherto furnished contingents were now in revolt. To replace their horsemen Cæsar recruited a body of German mercenaries and marched against the rebels.

Vercingetorix, convinced that it was hopeless to fight pitched battles with the Romans, or to try to hold towns against their attacks, persuaded the Gauls to attempt to starve out their enemy by laying waste their own country, sparing only such towns as were impregnable. Although he was able to prevail on his countrymen to adopt the general principle, they refused to sacrifice Avaricum (Bourges) despite the earnest warnings of their leader. Cæsar promptly invested the town and succeeded in capturing it in spite of the efforts of Vercingetorix and the difficulty of procuring supplies. His men butchered all whom they found within the town without pity, so that only a handful escaped.

It was now the beginning of spring, and Cæsar sent Labienus with a part of his army to the North, while he himself invaded the territory of the Arverni and attempted to capture the town of Gergovia, which Vercingetorix undertook to defend. Cæsar saw at once that the place could not be taken by a direct assault, and he attempted to blockade it, but it proved impossible to surround it on every side with the six legions which Cæsar had with him as long as Vercingetorix held strong positions in the vicinity, so that in the end Cæsar was forced to abandon the siege and retreat. This defeat, the first which he himself had suffered, greatly encouraged the Gauls. The Ædui, who had long wavered in their allegiance, now joined the revolt and tried to intercept Cæsar's retreat by breaking down the bridges on the Loire. Cæsar, however, managed to cross the river and hastened north to unite his forces with those of Labienus, who, in the meantime, had defeated some of the Northern tribes near Paris.

As soon as he had reached Labienus, Cæsar procured additional German horsemen and again turned south with his whole army. Vercingetorix took the Romans by surprise and attacked them with his cavalry. Cæsar's Germans, however, routed the Gauls, and Vercingetorix with his infantry, which for some reason had taken no part in the battle, was driven into the town of Alesia, where Cæsar immediately besieged him. The situation of Alesia and the larger force at Cæsar's disposal made a complete investment possible. Knowing that the Gauls would make a desperate attempt to rescue their leader, Cæsar constructed a double line of entrenchments, one to blockade the town and the other to defend his position against the relieving army which was certain to appear before long. The Gauls realized the necessity of action, but it required time for them to collect new levies, and in the absence of Vercingetorix they divided the command among several chiefs. When they finally arrived, the forces of Vercingetorix were already in the grip of famine, and it was clear that unless the Roman lines could be broken Alesia must soon fall. The relieving army made several furious attacks on Cæsar's entrenchments, while the besieged garrison supported them by assailing the inner lines, but Cæsar succeeded in beating off the attacks. The relieving army, abandoning all hope, dispersed, and Vercingetorix surrendered in order to save the lives of his men. He was sent to Rome, where he was kept in prison for six years and finally put to death, after appearing in Cæsar's long-delayed triumph.

## § 7. THE COMPLETION OF THE CONQUEST

The fall of Alesia decided the fate of Gaul. The Ædui and the Arverni submitted and were leniently treated. The Roman supremacy was soon restored throughout most of the region which had taken part in the revolt, but there was much discontent and some tribes still refused to accept the inevitable. Cæsar was anxious to pacify the country completely and as quickly as possible, since his relations with Pompey were becoming more and more strained. He decided, therefore, to spend the winter (52–51 B.C.) in Gaul, and it was well that he did so, for he had hardly distributed his army in its winter quarters before he was obliged to take the field once more. The Bellovaci, one of the most powerful of the Belgic tribes, rose in arms, and Cæsar had some difficulty in suppressing the rebellion. Sporadic outbreaks also occurred in other parts of Gaul, and not until the middle of 51 B.C. were the last embers of revolt stamped out. During the remainder of that year, and the summer of the next, Cæsar was busy organizing his conquests and attempting to reconcile the Gauls to Roman rule. In this work he was so successful that the country remained at peace for many years.

The conquest of Gaul was a long and arduous task, but when it was finally accomplished it was complete and permanent. Some of the causes which rendered it possible are obvious from the foregoing narrative. The main one was undoubtedly the deeply rooted dissensions among the Gauls themselves; tribe was jealous of tribe, and all were torn by opposing factions, so that at no time in the entire struggle could the Gauls lay aside their internal dissensions and unite against the invader. Nevertheless, the revolt under Vercingetorix was general enough to have defeated the Romans if the Gauls had possessed a better civil and military organization, for the fall of Alesia need not have been decisive if the relieving army could have been kept together and if the rebellious tribes had remained united. Yet with all their defects, and in spite of their continual strife among themselves, the Gauls would have been able to maintain their independence but for the genius of Cæsar, who knew how to take the uttermost advantage of their weaknesses, both civil and military. A less able general would certainly have failed, and a less able statesman could not have so completely pacified the country that the Civil War would not have seen the work in danger of being undone.

The results of the conquest were of supreme importance both to Rome and to Cæsar. It gave Cæsar a military reputation which rivalled that of Pompey, it enabled him to build up a splendid army and to secure its enthusiastic devotion, and it furnished him with so vast an amount of plunder that he could buy supporters in Rome in his political struggle with his great rival. It added a vast and fertile region to the empire of Rome and greatly increased her resources and strength, although the necessity of defending the Rhine partly offset the gain.

For the Gauls themselves the conquest was probably a blessing. It seems very unlikely that they could have preserved their independence for any length of time if they had defeated Cæsar, for the Germans were pressing hard on their frontier, and it is difficult to believe that the jealous and disunited tribes could have successfully resisted their advance. Whatever the Gauls had to suffer at Cæsar's hands, they would probably have suffered more from the Germans. The victory of Cæsar meant the opening of Gaul to the spread of Roman civilization, while subjugation by the Germans would have destroyed much of the progress which the Celts had already achieved and plunged them back into barbarism.

# CHAPTER XIII

# THE PRELUDE TO THE CIVIL WAR

## § 1. THE CONFERENCE AT LUCA

WHEN the Triumvirate was renewed at Luca, Cæsar's position in Gaul was very unsatisfactory. He had undertaken the conquest of the entire country with great apparent success, but he was well aware that he still needed a considerable time to consolidate the Roman supremacy, so that he was anxious to have his tenure of his provinces prolonged. Crassus had once cherished an ambition for military glory, and Cæsar's victories had fired his imagination ; he knew that he could get nothing from the senate and was ready to pay almost any price for an opportunity of winning a spectacular triumph. Pompey, also anxious to secure an army, had found the senate definitely opposed to his wishes. Cæsar was, therefore, able to come to an understanding with his partners. It was speedily arranged that they should be the consuls for 55 B.C., and that after their year of office they should receive armies and provinces for five years. They on their side agreed that Cæsar's proconsulship should be extended to include Transalpine Gaul and should be prolonged for another quinquennium. Cæsar has often been censured for consenting to such conditions by those who overlook the fact that a combination of Pompey and Crassus against him was impossible on account of their mutual enmity. Their armies, therefore, could hardly be dangerous to him because they would serve to neutralize each other. That Crassus would lose his life and his army in the East was an event which could not be foreseen, and but for this there would have been little risk to Cæsar in the arrangements made at Luca.

The fact that the Triumvirate had been renewed was well

enough known in Rome, although its programme was still a secret. The revival of the coalition was enough to produce a complete change in the attitude of the senate, which hastily dropped the question of the validity of Cæsar's laws and waited anxiously to see what would happen. The first development was a postponement of the consular elections by means of systematic obstruction, since Pompey and Crassus were unwilling that either of the consuls should preside over the voting. When the year ended without an election the conscript fathers were obliged to appoint *interreges*, each of whom held office for five days, and, when at length a friendly *interrex* had been secured, Pompey and Crassus were formally elected early in 55 and immediately took office.

## § 2. THE SECOND CONSULSHIP OF POMPEY AND CRASSUS

The most important business of the year was to carry out the arrangements in regard to the provinces. A tribune named Trebonius promptly passed a law providing proconsular commands for the two consuls which were to be held for five years. Under this law Pompey secured the two Spains[1] with an army, while Crassus received Syria with another army. Cæsar's proconsulship was then prolonged by the Pompeian-Licinian law, proposed by the two consuls themselves. Its exact provisions are unknown and have been a matter of much controversy, controversy which is mostly concerned with points of little practical importance. The theory usually accepted by English historians is that Cæsar's term was extended for five years, beginning with the expiration of the term fixed by the Vatinian law. This would make his proconsulship end on March 1, 49. It seems more probable, however, that his second quinquennium began in 55 and that it, therefore, ended some time in 50.[2]

These two measures were passed without serious difficulty, most of the senators being so cowed that Cato was left almost alone in his futile protest. Cicero, who had learned by bitter experience the hard realities beneath the shams of Roman politics, kept silent as far as possible. Some bickering between such old enemies as Crassus and Pompey was natural,

[1] Perhaps with some jurisdiction over Africa as well. The Trebonian law was proposed before April 27. (*Att.*, iv, 9.)

[2] See Appendix 7.

but it amounted to little, for Crassus had other things in mind. Having at last obtained an army, he was dreaming of eclipsing both Pompey and Cæsar by a brilliant career of conquest in the East. His time was largely occupied with military preparations, and before the end of the year he left Rome for Syria.

### § 3. THE END OF THE TRIUMVIRATE

As soon as he arrived in Syria Crassus set himself to provoke a war with Parthia. The moment seemed favourable and a pretext was easy to find, for Parthia was then at war with Armenia and was torn with internal strife between rival pretenders to the throne. After some delay Crassus invaded Parthia, but unfortunately for himself he knew little of the enemy's mode of warfare and little of the geography of the country. Instead of skirting the mountains of Armenia, and using that country as a base of operations, or of descending the Euphrates, he marched directly across the desert. He had not advanced far when he encountered the Parthians. Their cavalry, armed as archers, was their main reliance, and a single engagement showed that the legions were unable to cope with it. The Romans were familiar with mounted archers, but in their experience such horsemen carried only a few arrows, so that their attacks were mere preliminaries to the real fighting. The Parthian army, however, was accompanied by a train of camels laden with arrows, which kept their cavalry constantly supplied. When Crassus, after a hard march through the desert, arrived on the banks of a small river, the Parthians attacked. He at once began to form his army into a square near the river and ordered his son Publius, who had served under Cæsar in Gaul and now commanded his father's cavalry, to drive back the enemy so as to give time to complete the formation. The Parthians retreated until Publius had been drawn away from the infantry, and then surrounded him. He and his men fought desperately, but they were outnumbered and practically the entire force perished, Publius among the rest. The remainder of the army under Crassus himself held out till night, suffering heavily under a constant hail of arrows from the Parthian horsemen and helpless to strike a blow in return. That night Crassus determined to fall back on Carrhæ and from there to the Armenian mountains, where the Parthian cavalry could not act effectively. He succeeded in reaching Carrhæ, but his further retreat was intercepted, and he found himself again surrounded by the enemy. The morale of his army had been completely destroyed by defeat, so that when the Parthians offered to negotiate Crassus was forced by his men to agree to a conference. He and his officers went to it with gloomy forebodings, recognizing a trap, and their worse anticipations were realized, for they were all treacherously cut down. The army soon paid the penalty for its insubordination, the greater part of it being either killed or captured, and only about one-fourth succeeded in escaping to Syria with the news of the disaster.

For a time it seemed that the victorious Parthians would attack the Roman possessions in the East, but, although there was something of a panic at Rome, the danger passed away. The importance of Carrhæ lies chiefly in the death of Crassus and the destruction of his army. Pompey and Cæsar were now left face to face, and Cæsar could no longer hold Pompey in check with an army in the East. After Carrhæ (in 53) no far-sighted statesman could fail to perceive that sooner or later a struggle for supremacy between Cæsar and Pompey was in the highest degree probable, and this probability was increased by the fact that Julia, Cæsar's daughter and Pompey's wife, had died in the preceding year, so that there was no longer any close personal tie between the two. The Triumvirate being at an end, Pompey and Cæsar drifted inevitably into the position of rivals. Pompey, however, realized that he alone could not resist Cæsar and that to have any chance of success he must secure the support of the senate.

## § 4. CLODIUS AND MILO

If an alliance with the aristocracy was essential for Pompey, an alliance with him was equally so for the senate. Cæsar's victories in Gaul had brought him such fame and glory that it was obviously impossible to persuade Roman soldiers to take the field against him except under a leader of equal reputation. For the nobles it was simply a choice between two evils, although they had little doubt that Cæsar was a worse alternative than Pompey. Nevertheless, there were many difficulties in the way of a reconciliation with the indispensable man, the bitterness of their old resentments, suspicions of his intentions, and fears that, having used them for his own purposes, he would cast them aside and make some new bargain with his former partner. Their doubts were increased by the natural hesitation of Pompey, who did not wish to break altogether with Cæsar until he was sure of the senate.

At the close of his consulship in 55 B.C. Pompey did not go to Spain, but sent legates to govern it in his name, while he remained in Italy on the pretext of looking after the corn supply. This course was not actually illegal, for the Roman law set no particular date when a governor must go to his province, but it was expected that he would do so without unnecessary delay. It was certainly never contemplated that he would spend his entire term in Italy and to do so was unprecedented and hence unconstitutional, but Pompey saw advantages in the innovation, and his conscience was not likely to disturb him if he refrained from violating the strict letter of the law. Remaining in Italy, he could recruit troops, ostensibly for service in Spain, and some of them he could always keep at hand, so that the senate could not deal with a critical situation in Rome without calling on him for help. He waited and watched the course of events, hoping undoubtedly that sooner or later he would be able to force the nobles to accept him as their champion.

His presence effectually prevented the senate from maintaining order, for the magistrates could raise no troops without the senate's authority and the conscript fathers dared not sanction this for fear of Pompey. The result was a complete paralysis of the government, with riots, bribery, and intrigue the order of the day. Under Pompey and Crassus consuls had been chosen for 54 B.C., but these consuls were unable to hold any elections because of the discovery of a corrupt bargain between them and two of the candidates. As a result the elections were postponed, and Rome entered on the next year without consuls. Finally, in the course of 53, Pompey, at the request of the senate, approached the city, and his proximity so far overawed the disorderly element that consuls were at length elected for what remained of the year, but when he moved away the rioting broke out afresh.

The obvious cause of the disorder was the simultaneous candidacy of Clodius for the prætorship and Milo for the consulship. Milo had the support of the senatorial machine and his prospects were excellent. This was not at all satisfactory to Pompey, who probably feared that if Milo were elected the senate would recover some freedom of action. Clodius reappeared at the head of his gangs, and it seems altogether likely that Pompey secretly footed the bills; at any rate he was publicly reconciled with his old enemy[1] and privately opposed to his former friend. Clodius aimed to prevent the success of Milo by making elections impossible, and Milo resorted to his old tactics of employing rival gangs. Street fights became a matter of daily occurrence, although they were confined largely to the gangs themselves and probably the law-abiding citizens were not much disturbed. Nevertheless, the constant clashes of the gangs made a meeting of the assembly impossible, and the senate sat by helplessly.

Finally the situation became unendurable. At the beginning of 52, the city being without magistrates, Milo encountered Clodius by chance on the Appian Way. A fight between their followers ensued in which Clodius was wounded and his men scattered. Milo, who had not recognized his foe in the melee, was proceeding on his way when he was informed that Clodius had been carried into a tavern near at hand. He turned back and had the wounded man dragged from the inn and murdered. The news of Clodius' death created pandemonium in Rome. The populace burned his body and used the senate-house for a funeral pyre; his gangs, no longer controlled by their leader, began to murder and pillage at random. The conscript fathers could not continue to dally with the situation and were forced reluctantly to appeal to Pompey. That he must be made dictator to restore order was evident to all, but the senate shrank from the word and finally compromised by passing a decree that he should be named sole consul with power to take a colleague when he chose.

[1] In his speech for Milo (ch. 8 and 29), Cicero refers to a reconciliation between Pompey and Clodius. There was probably something of the kind in 56 B.C., but if this were all Cicero would hardly treat the matter so seriously. His elaborate argument seems to me to suggest that the two were actually allied in 52.

## § 5. THE THIRD CONSULSHIP OF POMPEY

Backed by the troops already under his command and by those whom the magic of his name immediately brought to his standard, Pompey experienced no difficulty in restoring order, for the gangs dispersed without resistance and left him undisputed master of the city. The courts were promptly reorganized, and Milo was brought to trial for the murder of Clodius. Cicero defended him[1] but could not save him from exile. Others soon followed him, for Pompey was determined that Rome should have a thorough house-cleaning. With this object in view he had laws passed against disorder and corruption which were so framed as to be retroactive as far back as 70 B.C. When objections were raised to this feature of the laws on the ground that Cæsar might be indicted under them for bribery in the elections for 59, Pompey retorted that his own second consulship was equally included and treated the objection with contempt. Such an attitude was safe enough for him, since he drew up the lists from which the non-senatorial jurors were to be chosen, but under certain circumstances Cæsar might feel that he was far from being equally secure. Nor did Pompey wait long to demonstrate his control of the courts, for, when his father-in-law, Metellus Scipio,[2] was prosecuted, he invited the entire body of prospective jurors to his house and interceded with them in favour of the accused with the result that the prosecution was dropped. Such an act inevitably tended to destroy confidence in the impartiality of Pompey and of the courts as well, in spite of the fact that his wishes were not always obeyed.

Pompey, however, did not confine his attention to Rome, but proposed and carried a law completely changing the method of selecting the provincial governors. Hitherto the consuls and prætors had received their provinces in the year following their term of office in the city. By Pompey's law there was henceforth to be an interval of five years between

[1] Cicero's speech *pro Milone* is not the one he delivered in court, but one which he published afterward.

[2] He was a Scipio who had been adopted by Metellus Pius, Pompey's old colleague in Spain during the Sertorian war. Pompey married his daughter after the death of Julia.

the magistracy and the promagistracy, so that a consul would retire into private life at the end of his consulship and five years later would be reinvested with the *imperium* and sent out to govern a province. To provide governors for the first five years under the new system, the senate was to make use of such ex-consuls and ex-prætors as had never held provinces, either because, like Cicero, they had not wished to take one, or because they could not get one owing to the prolonged tenure of several provinces by the Triumvirs and others.[1] The avowed purpose of the law was to check the violence and reckless expenditure which had become usual at the elections. A candidate for the consulship would not hesitate to plunge himself in debt to any extent if he could hope to regain all and more than all he had spent in the next year, but if he must wait five years he might pause before incurring too heavy liabilities, and he would find it much more difficult to borrow. Behind this purpose there was almost certainly another object in view, for the law weakened Cæsar's position in Gaul by rendering it possible for the senate to supersede him as soon as his term expired, which under the Sempronian law, passed by C. Gracchus and still in force, the senate was unable to do.[2] Cæsar was counting on being able to retain his provinces for a considerable time after the legal termination of his proconsulship, since a governor had the right to continue at his post until his successor arrived to take over the command, so that the new system by repealing the Sempronian law seriously endangered the success of his plans.

In spite of his achievements Cæsar's position was one of real danger. As soon as he laid down the *imperium* and became a private citizen he could be prosecuted for any illegal acts he had committed. These had been so numerous and so flagrant during his consulship that his conviction was certain if the jury paid the slightest attention to the facts. To protect himself Cæsar was anxious to secure his election to a second consulship while he was still in Gaul, since as consul elect he would be safe from prosecution except for offences in the election itself. His immunity would be absolute if he could find a way to retain his command in Gaul not only until after the election but until the time came to enter upon his second

[1] Both Gabinius and Piso, consuls for 58, held their provinces for more than a year.

[2] See Appendix 7.

consulship. In this case he would step directly from the proconsulship to the consulship, and his enemies would have no opportunity to call him to account on any charge.

Cæsar undoubtedly expected to protect himself in this way, and Pompey, in repealing the Sempronian law, probably acted with the deliberate purpose of blocking this design. From Pompey's standpoint there were very good reasons for such a course, and it is quite unnecessary to suppose that he had any intention of permitting a prosecution of Cæsar, or of using his laws and his control of the courts to ensure its success. Cæsar's plan of passing directly from the proconsulship of Gaul to a second consulship involved a serious menace to the Republic, for if he was still in actual command of an army when he left Gaul to come to Rome he could bring such part of that army as he chose with him to take part in his triumph, and after that was celebrated he could easily find pretexts to keep them near Rome, technically perhaps disbanded, but ready for service at a moment's notice. In 70 B.C. Pompey and Crassus had done this very thing, and Pompey did not intend to let Cæsar copy his performance, for the means which had destroyed Sulla's constitution could be used with equal effectiveness against any other. No one who remembered his first consulship could believe that Cæsar would be restrained by constitutional scruples, and Pompey was resolved that he should not again have the state at his mercy. That Pompey was jealous of Cæsar is possible enough, but it seems unlikely that this was the decisive motive in determining his attitude. Probably he was much more deeply influenced by fear of what Cæsar might do and a very natural reluctance to trust another to the same extent that he was prepared to trust himself. Pompey's aim, therefore, was to find some means of superseding Cæsar in Gaul before he became consul. While steadily insisting on this point, Pompey at first was willing to let Cæsar have a second consulship on condition that he was deprived of his army[1] and thus prevented from bringing any troops with him into Italy. If as consul Cæsar had no soldiers in Italy while Pompey, as proconsul of Spain, had a large force there, the situation would be one which Pompey thought he could control. Since the

[1] Later he came to fear a second consulship for Cæsar on any terms. (*Att.*, vii, 8.)

Sempronian law created difficulties in the way of superseding Cæsar as promptly as Pompey wished, he was ready to repeal it, but he was not yet ready for a complete break with Cæsar; probably he did not yet foresee that such a break was inevitable.

Cæsar on his side could not accept a second consulship on Pompey's terms, for to do so would be to place himself at Pompey's mercy. Even if he were allowed to retain his army till after his election, he would have no security that his election would not be annulled for bribery as soon as he had laid down his command. If such a charge were brought against him, it must have seemed only too clear that the verdict would depend upon Pompey's wishes rather than the evidence. Cæsar could hardly feel much confidence in Pompey, for he must have remembered how Cicero had trusted Pompey's promises of protection in 59 B.C. and had fled sorrowfully into exile in the next year. Granted that Pompey had deserted his friend under pressure from his partners, might he not in the same manner desert Cæsar under pressure from Cæsar's enemies? Even if Cæsar had been willing to trust Pompey's intentions, there was still the question of whether Pompey could control the senatorial party, with which he was now in alliance, and it was not unlikely that so clumsy a politician might be dragged on by his allies much further than he either wished or meant to go. One can hardly blame Cæsar, therefore, if he refused to stake his political fortunes on the chance that Pompey would be faithful to his engagements and would be able to fulfil them. Moreover, it was not only his own political future that Cæsar would have put to the hazard, but the interests of his army as well. He was morally bound to see that the soldiers who had served him so long and so devotedly received the rewards which had been promised them. If he were eliminated from Roman public life, or if as consul he was rendered powerless to deal with obstruction, there was little reason to expect that the senate would be more ready to provide for them than it had shown itself in the case of Pompey's veterans. Thus Cæsar's obligations to his men made it impossible for him to sacrifice himself and forced him to insist that he should hold his second consulship upon his own conditions.

In 52 B.C. Pompey's reconciliation with the senate was still too recent and imperfect for him to wish to burn his bridges behind him. He therefore yielded to the protests of Cæsar's partisans and exerted his influence to induce the ten tribunes to pass a law granting Cæsar the special privilege of standing for the consulship without making a personal canvass in Rome. This was a concession which was essential to Cæsar if he were to carry out his plans, but its value would depend entirely on whether he could contrive to retain his position as proconsul down to the time of the election. If he were superseded before he had become consul elect, the right to be a candidate while absent from the city was worthless to him. The new system of selecting the provincial governors would make it possible to send a successor as soon as his term expired, but it was not in any way obligatory on the senate to do this, so that the possibility of continuing negotiations with Cæsar was left open. In fact, it is highly probable that Pompey agreed to the passage of both measures because he believed that their joint result would be to make him so far master of the situation that he could impose his own conditions on either Cæsar or the senate. Only one thing seemed necessary to the strength of his position, and that was to make sure that he could retain his proconsulship in Spain while Cæsar was consul, that is, if Pompey finally decided to concede him a a second consulship. Under the Trebonian and the Pompeian-Licinian laws Pompey's term in Spain and Cæsar's in Gaul would expire at about the same time. Pompey, therefore, induced the senate to prolong his *imperium* for some years.[1] Having completed his arrangements he was ready to bring his sole consulship to an end by taking as a colleague his father-in-law, Metellus Scipio, and he probably faced the future with serene confidence.

### § 6. THE POLITICAL STRUGGLE BETWEEN POMPEY AND CÆSAR

Pompey had utilized his third consulship to put himself in a far stronger position than had been contemplated by the agreement at Luca, and Cæsar had been too much occupied

[1] Dio (xl, ch. 56) says that his *imperium* was prolonged for five years, while Plutarch (*Pomp.*, ch. 55) says four. Appian (*b.c.* ii, ch. 24) says that the senate prolonged it.

with the revolt of Vercingetorix to do more than exact the concession of the law of the Ten Tribunes. How much this would prove to be worth it was for the future to reveal, and Cæsar, still engaged in stamping out the last embers of revolt, discreetly waited for his former partner to show his hand by making the first move. Pompey on his side was in no hurry to force the issue. Not yet sure of his new allies, he realized that to assume the role of the aggressor might frighten them into abandoning him. There were many senators, Cicero among them, who dreaded a civil war as the worst of all evils, and were prepared to make any concessions to avert it. This sentiment was very general in Italy, so that whoever seemed responsible for war was certain to lose the support of public opinion. It is true that public opinion no longer governed the Republic, but it was still a power which neither Cæsar nor Pompey cared to disregard. For this reason each endeavoured to throw the odium of a resort to arms upon the other, and the result was a political duel between them, Pompey striving to secure the legal appointment of a successor to Cæsar who would take over his provinces before his election to a second consulship, and Cæsar fighting with every weapon at his disposal to prevent such an appointment until after his election. In such a contest it was to the obvious interest of each to keep within the law himself and to force his adversary to violate it.

The duel began in 51 B.C. when some of Pompey's allies urged immediate action. One of the new consuls, M. Claudius Marcellus, was a bitter opponent of Cæsar, and proposed to supersede him in Gaul before his legal term expired on the ground that the war there was now over and that Cæsar's army should, therefore, be disbanded, but the other consul and some of the tribunes blocked any action. Pompey's attitude seemed for a time very uncertain, and it was believed that he intended to go to Spain. If he ever had any such intention it was given up, and toward the end of the year he induced the senate to pass a resolution that no action should be taken in regard to a successor to Cæsar until March 1, 50, but that after that date the question should take precedence over all other business. In the debate Pompey revealed his hand fully. The Sempronian law had deprived the tribunes of the right to veto the assignment of the consular provinces, but the repeal of that law had removed this limitation,[1] so that tribunes friendly to Cæsar could now prevent all action by the senate in regard to the provinces. Pompey declared that for Cæsar to obstruct the passing of a decree on the subject was the same as a refusal to obey the senate. Such an attitude was not without some show of justice. It could be argued that, by using his agents to render it impossible for the senate to exercise its constitutional right to appoint a successor, Cæsar was practically refusing to give up his provinces, and that he was, therefore, in rebellion against the state. Whether the argument was sound or not, it was plausible enough to serve the purpose of impressing public opinion. Cæsar, however, found a means of evading the issue which Pompey sought to force upon him.

In the tribunician elections for 50 B.C. most of the successful candidates were known to be Cæsar's partisans. One of them was promptly convicted of bribery, and his election annulled in consequence. The nobles were exultant when a young aristocrat, C. Scribonius Curio, who presented himself as a bitter opponent of Cæsar and an ardent supporter of Pompey, won the vacant place. They soon had the amplest reason to regret their victory, for Cæsar succeeded in bribing Curio by paying his large and varied collection of debts. Under the circumstances the desertion of Curio left Pompey helpless. It might seem reasonable to hold Cæsar responsible for what his avowed henchmen did to obstruct action by the senate, but it was obviously absurd to hold him accountable for what his enemies might do. As long as Curio avoided openly changing sides, and as long as the fact that he had sold himself to Cæsar was not clearly proved, Pompey could not follow up his threat without putting himself hopelessly in the wrong. In playing Cæsar's game the venal tribune proved himself a masterly politician, and throughout 50 he successfully thwarted every attempt to supersede Cæsar, but always on such pretexts that he did not appear to the public to have abandoned his original party.

To accomplish this Curio posed as a strict republican, aiming at freeing the senate from the fear of the military power. He pointed out that the state would be at Pompey's mercy if he

[1] Pompey may have overlooked this when he repealed the Sempronian law, or he may have counted on meeting an attempt to use the veto in the way in which he actually tried to meet it.

remained in Italy at the head of an army while Cæsar was disarmed, and on the other hand that Cæsar would be supreme if he retained his command while Pompey was deprived of his. The existing semblance of liberty was due to the fact that as things stood the two generals held each other more or less in check. The real cure for the ills of the state was to restore effective control to the senate, and the only way in which this could be done was for Pompey and Cæsar to resign their extraordinary commands simultaneously. Such a solution would have been enthusiastically welcomed and its absurdity may not have been generally perceived. In any case, it put Pompey in an embarrassing position. He was in Italy, so that, if he surrendered his *imperium*, he would have to do so before he could be certain that Cæsar had done the same. Even if Cæsar promised to give up the command of his army on a specified day, there was always the chance that he could contrive a revolt in Gaul sufficiently serious to justify him in breaking his promise, and that Pompey would have disbanded his army before he learned that his rival had failed to carry out the agreement. Pompey, therefore, was naturally unwilling to accept Curio's proposal, but to refuse would be to play into Cæsar's hands. He evaded as best he could, thereby laying himself open to bitter and telling criticism. Curio made full use of his opportunity; he reviewed Pompey's career, easily showing that he had been no more loyal to the constitution than Cæsar. In view of Pompey's record Curio declared that he would never consent to leave the state at Pompey's mercy, but would resolutely insist that Cæsar should remain in Gaul as long as necessary to avert a dictatorship by Pompey. Curio's motives might be clear enough to those behind the scenes in politics, but his pose as a patriotic and independent citizen told with the general public and made it difficult to deal with him. Moreover, the solution he proposed was so obviously desirable that the senators who saw through his motives could not very well oppose him. In addition to this there were many knights and nobles, like Cicero, who feared civil war more than Cæsar, and who were ready to do anything to avert it.[1]

[1] Under Pompey's new law Cicero was compelled to go to Cilicia as governor in 51 B.C. He only returned to Rome late in 50, too late to exert any influence, but his attitude is made perfectly clear in his letters.

Throughout his year of office (50) Curio continued to veto every attempt to appoint a successor to Cæsar, so that Pompey's friends were unable to accomplish anything. The senate had only two weapons with which to overcome such obstruction. The first was to remonstrate with the tribune and to put pressure upon him by declaring that his course was harmful to the public interest. If this failed, the conscript fathers could pass the last decree under which the tribunician veto was suspended. In June an attempt was made to induce the senate to remonstrate with Curio, but the motion was rejected so that nothing further could be done.[1] Perhaps Pompey submitted to Curio's victory the more readily because he thought that he could carry his point in the next year. For 49 B.C. Cæsar had two partisans among the tribunes, but, if he were forced to employ their veto in order to retain his provinces, Pompey would be able to act upon his former threat and to treat such obstruction as rebellion against the Republic.

If Pompey had such a plan, it was ruined by the haste and violence of his supporters. Rumours of all kinds were rife, among them that Cæsar's army, weary and disaffected, would desert him at the critical moment. Moved, perhaps, by overconfidence as a result of this report, or perhaps anxious to force Pompey's hand and commit him irrevocably to the senate's cause, C. Claudius Marcellus,[2] one of the consuls, brought matters to a head by forcing a vote in the senate on two questions, the first as to whether successors to Cæsar should be appointed, and the second as to whether Pompey should be deprived of his command. He thus made a pretence of putting Curio's policy to a test, but contrived to put it in a way that made its acceptance impossible, for the senate could not reject the first proposal without refusing to perform its constitutional duty, nor accept the second without repudiating Pompey and ending its alliance with him. The conscript fathers were obliged to vote as the consul desired, and he was about to adjourn the meeting, when Curio arose and offered a motion of his own which, as tribune, he had a right to do. He demanded that a vote be taken on the proposal that both Pompey and Cæsar should lay down their commands, and this

[1] See the letter of Cælius Rufus to Cicero. (*Fam.*, viii, 13.)

[2] He was a cousin of M. Claudius Marcellus, consul for 51 B.C., who had tried to have Cæsar superseded before his term expired.

motion was carried by 370 to 22. Marcellus dismissed the senators, congratulating them with bitter irony on having made Cæsar their master.[1]

A new rumour that Cæsar was marching on Rome produced a panic, taking advantage of which Marcellus made a last attempt to force the senate into action. Earlier in the year Cæsar had been compelled to send two legions from his army into Italy on the pretext that they were needed for a Parthian war.[2] They were then stationed at Capua, and Marcellus proposed that Pompey be given command of them for the defence of Italy against Cæsar, who was thus, implicitly, at least, declared a public enemy. Curio, emphatically denying the truth of the rumour, vetoed the motion, and Marcellus, recognizing his defeat, announced that he would save the state on his own responsibility. He and his colleague went at once to Pompey, who was staying outside the city, placed a sword in his hands, and urged him to take over the legions, to recruit fresh troops, and to lead his forces against Cæsar, all on the authority of the consuls. Although such a commission was clearly unconstitutional,[3] Pompey accepted it. He could, perhaps, hardly refuse, for to repudiate the consuls would have left him at the mercy of the peace party in the senate which seemed disposed to yield to Cæsar rather than fight. Nevertheless, in accepting he appeared as the aggressor, so that the long political struggle was decided in favour of his rival.

Cæsar took full advantage of his opportunity to put Pompey as completely as possible in the wrong. He professed his willingness to obey the decree of the senate if Pompey would do the same. If the decree could not be carried out owing to Pompey's refusal to resign, he offered to accept almost any compromise. There can be little doubt that the conscript fathers would gladly have agreed to his terms, but they were

[1] Appian, ii, ch. 30.

[2] While allied with Cæsar Pompey had loaned him a legion which was still with his army when the senate decreed that each should contribute a legion for a Parthian war. Pompey recalled this legion and Cæsar had to send one of his own in addition. Both were, therefore, taken from Cæsar's army.

[3] It may be that the consuls did not exceed their legal powers, but the traditions and principles of the senatorial party were certainly repudiated. To take such a step when the senate was unable to act was an entirely different thing from taking it after the senate had refused to sanction it.

unable to act freely, for the city was surrounded by Pompey's troops, and a minority determined on war had control of the situation. Under pressure the senate reluctantly voted that Cæsar must surrender his army and provinces by a certain day or become an outlaw, and passed the last decree to overcome the veto of his tribunes, who immediately fled from Rome to join him.

Cæsar met the challenge with his usual promptness and decision. He called together such of his soldiers as were at hand and informed them of the last measures of the senate. On their part there could be no hesitation, for their interests were bound up with those of their general whose foes were violating the constitution in order to attack him. Assured of their enthusiastic support, Cæsar crossed the Rubicon, a river which formed the southern boundary of Cisalpine Gaul, and began the Civil War by invading Italy.

# CHAPTER XIV

# THE CIVIL WAR

## § 1. THE OUTBREAK OF THE WAR

ALTHOUGH Cæsar and Pompey had realized for some time that a war between them was inevitable, yet when it came neither was ready for it. For over a year they had been playing a complicated game in which each was seeking to make the other seem the aggressor, and while this continued they could make no adequate preparations. For Cæsar to bring his legions across the Alps would have been to put himself in the wrong, unless Pompey gave him an excuse by beginning to raise an army, while for Pompey to take this course without the sanction of the senate would have been a plain declaration to all the world that he meant to fight under any circumstances. The actual outbreak of the war seems clearly to have taken Pompey by surprise, for as late as December 25[1] he expressed to Cicero his belief that Cæsar would not fight, and his confidence in his own ability to deal with the situation should he be mad enough to do so.[2] Even after the senate had passed the last decree he sent envoys to Cæsar[3] in the hope of continuing negotiations. In fact, no step had yet been taken which made war inevitable. The senate had declared Cæsar a traitor if he did not surrender his provinces and army by a " certain day," and had passed the last decree to overcome the obstruction of his tribunes in order that successors to him might at last be appointed.[4] The

[1] Dates are given according to the official Roman calendar without correction. Thus Dec. 25 was really Nov. 5.

[2] *Att.*, vii, 8.

[3] See Appendix 8.

[4] Perhaps also in order to validate the commission which Pompey had received from the consuls.

"certain day," however, had not yet been fixed,[1] so that a compromise was still among the possibilities. Under Pompey's new law the selection of the provincial governors was a somewhat complicated matter.[2] The senate first decided which provinces should be consular and which prætorian and designated the ex-consuls and ex-prætors who were to draw lots for them. After the new governors were thus chosen, it was necessary to invest them with the *imperium* by a formal law, which no doubt simply repeated the provisions of the senate's decrees as to when their terms should begin and end. They could not start for their provinces until some date specified in it, and apparently their terms were reckoned as beginning at the time of their actual arrival in their provinces. It had not yet been determined to whom Cæsar's provinces were to be assigned, nor when the necessary law should be brought before the assembly, and it was this law which would fix the day when Cæsar must give up his proconsulship. It was still possible for the senate to delay the passage of the law until after the consular elections, or, while insisting on an early surrender of his provinces by Cæsar and refusing to admit his candidacy *in absentia*, it might grant him permission to enter the city for his canvass without forfeiting the *imperium*, which he could legally retain until he had celebrated his triumph. In this way he would be protected from prosecution and practically assured of a second consulship. There was room, therefore, for further negotiations, although there was little chance that they would lead to any result, for Pompey, who now dominated the senate, no longer desired peace,[3] but was simply trying to gain time in order to collect and organize his forces, which were widely dispersed in Italy, as well as to recruit additional troops. Though his motives were obvious, he believed that Cæsar would be anxious to delay hostilities until he could bring his legions across the Alps and that he would, therefore, welcome a pretext for avoiding an immediate break. It seems certain that Cæsar's prompt offensive took Pompey by surprise, although he was too experienced a

[1] I think there can be little doubt on this point. See E. T. Merrill, *On Caes. B.C. I*, 2, 6 *Ante Certam Diem*. Cæsar (*b.c.* i, 9) speaks as though he were being superseded immediately, but he is more or less justified in so doing because such was undoubtedly the intention of the authors of the decree.

[2] For a discussion of the procedure see P. Willems, *Le sénat*, II, pp. 588–98.

[3] *Att.*, vii, 8.

soldier not to have foreseen the possibility that Cæsar might be able to concentrate a strong enough army in Cisalpine Gaul to invade Italy before he himself had completed his preparations for defence. It is highly probable, therefore, that Pompey had considered the abandonment of Rome as something which might be forced upon him when the war actually began, but he seems to have thought that such a course was not likely to be necessary. Perhaps his confidence was due in part to the rumours of disaffection in Cæsar's army, rumours which were doubtless confirmed by Labienus, Cæsar's ablest lieutenant, who deserted to the senate's side at the outbreak of hostilities, but besides this Pompey was convinced that he could count upon the firm support of the Italians. If the towns in Northern Italy held out resolutely against Cæsar, it might be possible to check him with such forces as could be assembled in a comparatively short time.

Cæsar on his side seems to have striven sincerely for peace as long as he thought that peace was possible. When the senate passed the last decree he saw clearly that further negotiations were useless unless his adversaries could be frightened into a mood for compromise, and that he could not hope for a better pretext for war than was now provided for him. He was not the man to lose an opportunity through caution, and he knew that Pompey was even less ready for the struggle than he was himself. By striking at once he could take advantage of any change in Italian sentiment which the course of events might have produced, and if he kept a line of retreat open he could always fall back to wait for his main army in case his enemies proved unexpectedly strong. Pompey's reliance on the support of the Italians proved a complete miscalculation; the outbreak of the war had alienated their sympathy, since they could not interpret what was happening in Rome in the light of inside information concerning the political struggle going on there. What they saw was that the senate had demanded the resignation of both Pompey and Cæsar, that Cæsar had announced his willingness to obey, and that Pompey had, without the authority of the senate, assumed command of two additional legions and begun recruiting. Moreover, he had followed this defiance by surrounding the senate with his soldiers and coercing the conscript fathers into rejecting Cæsar's offers of a liberal compromise, and had extorted from them what seemed to be practically a declaration of war. Thus it was natural that Pompey's conduct should be widely and bitterly condemned[1] and that public opinion should veer abruptly toward his rival. Cæsar determined to give Pompey no chance to repair his blunders, and so, while responding to the attempts to continue negotiations with offers of peace upon the most reasonable terms, he pressed forward without delay or hesitation. After crossing the Rubicon he invaded Umbria and Picenum, the latter of which had always been peculiarly devoted to Pompey. Yet the towns opened their gates to Cæsar, and Pompey's officers, who were recruiting soldiers there, fled in panic, leaving the recruits they had gathered to take service under his adversary, so that in a few days the two districts were in Cæsar's hands and the way to Rome lay open.

## § 2. POMPEY'S FLIGHT

The news that Cæsar had crossed the Rubicon and occupied Ariminum caused consternation and dismay in Rome. The senators put searching questions to Pompey about his military forces, and his answers only revealed his complete unreadiness. On learning that he had only the two legions taken from Cæsar, but thought that he could soon assemble some 30,000 recruits already raised, one senator exclaimed bitterly that they had been deceived, and advised sending envoys to Cæsar.[2] Pompey put an end to discussion by leaving Rome and ordering the senators and magistrates to follow him, declaring that he would regard as enemies all who remained in the city. The conscript fathers, disillusioned but panic-stricken, trailed obediently after him, the magistrates in their haste and confusion leaving a large sum of money in the treasury.

Pompey's abandonment of Rome was in itself necessary, although it seems to have been badly managed; it was impossible to defend the city with the forces at his disposal, and to make the attempt was to invite complete disaster. His only chance was to retreat southward, where he could effect a concentration of his troops. He was too experienced a general to imagine that his new recruits could face the

[1] *Att.*, vii, 5. [2] Plutarch, *Pomp.*, ch. 60.

veterans of Cæsar, and he dared not trust the two legions which had so recently formed part of Cæsar's army. When he saw that Rome must be abandoned, it is probable that he determined to abandon Italy as well and to take refuge in Greece, where he would be safe until he could put his army into shape. His decision may have been wise, but his supporters seem to have been quite unprepared for it, for up to the last moment he had talked confidently, so that they were amazed and furious at his flight. When Pompey's envoys returned from Ariminum, many of the senators at Capua discussed the terms of peace which Cæsar offered and were eager to accept them, even the rigid Cato having now become convinced that submission was preferable to war.[1] Such a change of heart was naturally accompanied by bitter resentment against Pompey, who was chiefly responsible for the crisis, and who had signally failed to cope with it. It had been supposed that he was staying in Italy in order to organize a defence of Rome,[2] but now it seemed that he had done nothing of any consequence.

The peace negotiations came to nothing, for neither side was willing to trust the other, and, although for a time messages were sent back and forth, Cæsar continued his advance with little, if any, delay. Pompey pressed his preparations for a retreat to Greece, and the consternation of his followers increased as his intentions were more and more clearly perceived. It was a new Pompey whom they saw, one who had neither courage nor plan, neither troops nor energy, one who was ignorant not only of his enemy's forces, but also of his own,[3] one who fled before he knew from whom he was fleeing or whither, who had betrayed them and was about to abandon his country.[4] In spite of all, however, they were committed to his cause, and the fear of Cæsar kept them loyal to a leader who had forfeited their confidence.

Cicero, who had been sent to superintend the levy of troops in Campania, watched the course of events with intense anxiety, for he was left uninformed of Pompey's plans and intentions and had to guess them as best he might. He did not comprehend the necessity of the flight from Rome, which he considered disgraceful and cowardly, and for a time he hoped that peace might yet be secured by accepting Cæsar's

[1] *Att.*, vii, 15. [2] *Att.*, vii, 13. [3] *Att.*, vii, 21. [4] *Att.*, viii, 7.

offers. When he realized that Pompey meant to abandon Italy his dismay was complete, and he hesitated to follow him. "I already knew him (Pompey) to be the most incompetent of statesmen," he wrote to Atticus,[1] "now I know that he is the most incompetent of generals also." Nevertheless, he set out finally to join Pompey, but he had delayed too long, and Cæsar's forces barred the way. In his mood of bitter disapproval and despair he can have rendered little service to Pompey in Campania, and he seems to have been typical of many in his party. Even the military leaders acted with little harmony, either because they did not understand, or because they disapproved of, Pompey's policy. The largest body of troops, aside from those under Pompey himself, was commanded by L. Domitius, who was not technically subject to Pompey's authority. He took up a position at Corfinium, hoping to be reinforced by the fugitives from the North and to be able to check Cæsar's advance. Pompey urged him to hasten south while the way was still open, but in vain, for Domitius was confident that he could make a stand, or could retreat at will if he found Cæsar's forces too strong. As a result, what Pompey had foreseen happened, for Cæsar blockaded Corfinium, and, when Domitius appealed frantically for help to the leader whose advice he had ignored, Pompey sadly replied that he could do nothing. The end was not long delayed, for the beleaguered troops, who had little enthusiasm for their cause and no confidence in their commander, soon surrendered to Cæsar. Domitius, who had hoped to escape with some of his chief officers, was handed over by his men. Cæsar at once released them and enrolled their forces in his own army, sending them forthwith to Sicily to secure possession of that island, so important for the food supply of Rome.

The clemency which Cæsar displayed in dealing with Domitius and his officers made a profound impression throughout Italy, and this impression was enhanced by the reports which circulated as to Pompey's mood. In his camp there were constant threats of proscription and vengeance, and he himself seemed to have discarded all moderation and to be ardently desirous of imitating Sulla's bloody example. Cicero was horrified at what he heard, and many who had hitherto

[1] *Att.*, viii, 16.

supported Pompey shared his feelings.[1] Public opinion welcomed Cæsar with enthusiasm, partly at least from apprehension of his rival, so that all opposition to him in Italy collapsed, and the only question was whether Pompey could make good his escape from the peninsula.

After the fall of Corfinium the military operations resolved themselves into a race for Brundisium, where Pompey had assembled all available shipping for the purpose of transporting his forces to the East; if he could be intercepted, the war must end at once in a battle or a peace. Cæsar strained every nerve with this object in view, but arrived before the city just too late and was forced to look on helplessly while Pompey embarked his troops and sailed away. Pursuit was for the time impossible, so Cæsar reluctantly turned his attention elsewhere.

## § 3. CÆSAR'S FIRST SPANISH CAMPAIGN

In a little over two months and with scarcely any fighting Cæsar had made himself master of Italy, but the real war was still to come. The flight of most of the magistrates and senators had left Rome in chaos; some sort of government must be improvised at once, and for that purpose it was necessary to have at least the semblance of a senate. On his way from Brundisium to Rome Cæsar had an interview with Cicero and tried in vain to secure his support. The orator's presence would have added greatly to the prestige of the rump senate which was about to be convened, but he could not be induced to attend. Although at parting Cæsar merely asked him to think the matter over, Cicero felt that the great man was annoyed.[2] For two months longer he lingered in Italy, unable to escape and distracted by the fear that he would be thought ungrateful to Pompey, but finally, early in June, he slipped away to Epirus.

At Rome Cæsar respected constitutional forms as far as possible. As proconsul he could not enter the city, so his tribunes gathered together such senators as they could outside its limits. Cæsar addressed them, justifying his course and declaring that he was still anxious to carry on negotiations with Pompey. He wished the senate to send envoys to his

[1] *Att.*, viii, 13; 16; ix, 7. [2] *Att.*, ix, 18.

opponent, but no one could be found willing to accept the mission, since Pompey had declared that all who remained behind would be treated as enemies. Seeing that he could expect little help from the senators, Cæsar arranged matters in Rome as well as the circumstances would permit; he
* placed the city in charge of a prætor, and appointed Mark Antony, a young noble of reckless and dissolute character who had won his favour in Gaul as an able and gallant soldier, as commander-in-chief in Italy in spite of the fact that he was one of the tribunes.

Cæsar's military position was dangerous, for Pompey had escaped to the East with the raw material for an army, and he had already a powerful army in Spain. Since Cæsar had no fleet and so could not follow him to Greece, he resolved to deal with his Spanish legions without delay, hoping to dispose of them before Pompey could organize his forces. Such a plan required prompt action, and Cæsar hastily set out, telling his friends that he was going against an army without a general and would return to face a general without an army.[1]

He was delayed by the resistance of Massilia, which went over to Pompey, but, leaving a force to besiege the city, he hastened on after his army, which had been sent forward in advance, and had crossed the Pyrenees before he caught up with it. Events soon justified his opinion of the Pompeian generals in Spain, Afranius and Petreius; they made little effort to defend the Pyrenees, but decided to face Cæsar on the Ebro, where they occupied a strong position at Ilerda and repulsed Cæsar's first attacks with success. For a moment Cæsar seemed on the verge of disaster, but he extricated himself from his difficulties. The two generals then decided to abandon the Ebro and retreat into Celtiberia, but Cæsar's pursuit was too rapid, and they found themselves surrounded. They surrendered on the promise of pardon if they disbanded their legions, and the promise was kept. The effect was great, for in Farther Spain the provincials forced Pompey's legate, Varro, to surrender, and submitted to Cæsar, so that Pompey's army in Spain ceased to exist.

[1] Suetonius, *Div. Jul.*, ch. 34.

## § 4. DYRRACHIUM AND PHARSALUS

The news of Cæsar's victory in Spain led to the surrender of Massilia, so that on his return the conqueror had only to dictate terms to the city. He deprived it of some of its territory but permitted it to retain its autonomy. At Massilia he received the news that in Rome he had been named dictator in obedience to orders which he had despatched from Spain. He desired the office to enable him to preside over the elections, which were overdue, and which must precede the organization of any regular government. He also learned[1] that Curio, whom he had sent to secure Sicily and Africa, had met with disaster. The former tribune had accomplished the first part of his mission without difficulty, but in Africa his rashness and impetuosity had resulted in his defeat and death.

Having settled affairs at Massilia, Cæsar hastened to Rome, where he held the elections for 48 and was himself chosen consul. As soon as the elections were over he resigned the dictatorship, which he had held only eleven days. Since many other matters required immediate attention, a number of laws were quickly passed by the assembly. The Civil War had produced a financial crisis which frightened creditors and caused debtors to clamour for relief. To meet the situation Cæsar enacted that the interest paid should be deducted from the principal of all debts, and that creditors must accept the property of the debtors on a pre-war valuation in discharge of obligations. This measure, which amounted to a bankruptcy law, seems to have had an excellent effect, so much so that its provisions were made permanent ; it gave some relief to those who could not dispose of their property for anything like its real value, and at the same time it reassured the creditors by showing that Cæsar had no intention of cancelling debts, as many of his followers were demanding. He also recalled most of those who had been driven into exile under Pompey's supremacy and restored their civic rights to the descendants of those who had been proscribed by Sulla. Whatever other arrangements were necessary were rapidly completed, and Cæsar left Rome for Brundisium before taking office as consul.

[1] He may have heard of Curio's death earlier, perhaps while still in Spain.

Meanwhile Pompey had employed his respite in gathering resources in the East and in drilling his Italian recruits into an army. His troops were now in fair condition, but they were far from equal in quality to the veterans of Cæsar. Both generals were aware of this, and Cæsar was anxious to force a battle as quickly as possible. During his Spanish campaign his officers had been busy gathering and constructing ships, but in spite of their efforts Pompey's naval power remained far superior. When Cæsar arrived at Brundisium he was unable to transport his army across the Adriatic in one trip. Without hesitation he embarked with about half his forces and landed safely in Epirus, having eluded the negligent blockade kept up by Bibulus, his old colleague in the consulship, who was now in command of Pompey's fleet. Antony was to bring over the rest of the army at the first opportunity, but Bibulus suddenly became vigilant, so that it was some time before the opportunity presented itself. At length Antony succeeded in crossing and uniting his half of the army with the other under Cæsar, whose problem now was to force his adversary to fight.

Pompey, always a cautious commander, determined not to risk an engagement in the open and entrenched himself on the coast near Dyrrachium in a position where his fleet could keep him well supplied with provisions. Cæsar attempted to blockade him, but Pompey, having the larger army, constantly extended his entrenchments until Cæsar's lines were drawn out too thin for safety, when he succeeded in breaking them by a sudden attack.

After this defeat Cæsar abandoned the blockade and marched into Thessaly, where he had stationed a considerable force under Domitius Calvinus to intercept Metellus Scipio, the governor of Syria, who was hastening with the troops under his command to join Pompey. Cæsar succeeded in rescuing Domitius from a dangerous situation, but he could not prevent Pompey, who had followed him, from effecting a junction with Metellus. The rivals now confronted each other near the town of Pharsalus, and Cæsar was anxious to fight. Pompey, however, at first seemed disposed to stand on the defensive, but the nobles in his camp, rendered confident by the victory at Dyrrachium, were eager to give battle, and Pompey at length yielded to them. It is not likely that he allowed his own judgment to be entirely overruled, but their urgency may have overcome his cautious hesitation. Undoubtedly he expected victory, for his infantry was more numerous than that of Cæsar, even if inferior in quality, and his cavalry much stronger. From his infantry he expected little, except that it would stand firm under Cæsar's attack, and it was on the cavalry that he relied to strike the decisive blow by scattering Cæsar's horse and charging upon his legions from the rear. Cæsar divined the plan, or at least recognized the danger, and met it by placing a picked body of troops behind his lines. When the battle began Cæsar's horse were routed, but as Pompey's cavalry swept round the line the picked troops met them with their spears, and the cavalry broke and fled. Pompey's infantry were already hard pressed by Cæsar's veteran soldiers, and the flight of the cavalry enabled the picked troops to turn their flank, so that under a final attack the Pompeian army broke and the men sought refuge in their camp. Cæsar pursued them, stormed the camp, and pressed so hard upon the defeated army that by nightfall the bulk of the Pompeians had surrendered and the rest were hopelessly scattered.

## § 5. ALEXANDRIA

From the field of Pharsalus, where he had experienced his first serious defeat, Pompey fled to the coast. If he would not accept the result of the battle, his best course would have been to seek in Africa a new base of operations. He conceived the hope, however, that he could retrieve his fortunes in the East, where he believed that his prestige as the conqueror of Mithridates was so great that the recent reverse would have little effect. He accordingly took ship for Egypt in the hope of receiving assistance from the royal house. Ptolemy Auletes was dead, but his children, Cleopatra and Ptolemy XII, had succeeded him and might remember that they owed their thrones to the action of Gabinius in restoring their father at Pompey's order.

Gratitude, however, was not a strong sentiment among the Ptolemies, and the approach of Pompey caused consternation in the royal court. To receive him was dangerous, for at the moment Cæsar seemed all-powerful, and to repulse him equally perilous, for he might yet prove the victor. The best way out of the dilemma seemed to those who ruled in the name of the young king to murder Pompey, thus gaining Cæsar's favour, and at the same time averting Pompey's possible vengeance. When the fugitive arrived off the Egyptian coast he was induced to land by a friendly message, and was treacherously slain as he was about to step on shore.

Such was the tragic end of one who had played a great part in the world without being a great man in himself. It is difficult to estimate him fairly, for till his last campaign good fortune contributed largely to his success. He rendered valuable service to Sulla, but displayed no greater military gifts than Crassus, for the campaign in Sicily and Africa, to which he owed his first triumph and his surname of the Great (Pompeius Magnus), was one against inferior opponents, so that the surname was cheaply and easily won. To put down the revolt of Lepidus needed no remarkable ability, and it was not until he fought Sertorius that he met a real general. In that campaign he was saved from disaster by the timely arrival of Metellus and only succeeded in putting down the Spanish insurrection after Sertorius was murdered. In his Eastern campaigns he reaped the fruit of the victories of Lucullus, while his achievement in clearing the Mediterranean of pirates needed only careful organization of the overwhelming force at his disposal. In Cæsar he encountered a general of the first rank and was totally defeated for the first time, but the result was due rather to the inferior quality of his army than to his own mistakes. There are thus inadequate grounds for calling him a great general, in spite of the immense reputation he acquired. Certainly he was a competent commander and won the devotion of his soldiers. As a politician he has been considered clumsy and incapable, largely on the strength of Cicero's criticisms. Allowances should be made, however, for the feelings of the orator, who was deeply hurt by Pompey's failure to appreciate his great achievement in suppressing Catiline. It is not easy to see how Pompey could have done much better under the circumstances. He was unable to induce the senate to accept the policy he felt bound to carry out, and equally unable to control the assembly, so that he was forced to join the First Triumvirate in order to redeem his promises to his veterans. Perhaps his awkward manners and his aloofness contributed somewhat to this result, but it is difficult to imagine the conscript fathers extending a cordial welcome to the man who had overthrown Sulla's constitution. In private life he was respectable, far more so than many of his contemporaries, and he was an affectionate husband to Julia. He had a conscience, although it was a rather pedantic one, and he resembled Macbeth in that he " would not play the false and yet would wrongly win." He was willing to violate the spirit of the constitution if he could observe the letter, and ready to profit by illegality, if someone else would take the responsibility. Even here, however, no other course seems to have been open to him. The bitterness of the resentment aroused by Cæsar's career as consul apparently took him by surprise, but the unexpected stubbornness of the nobles forced him to allow his partner to go much further than had probably been intended, with the result that he found himself too deeply compromised to draw back and was obliged to persevere. Left to himself it is not impossible that he would have compromised with Cæsar, but, having at last formed an alliance with the senate, he was dragged into war by the hot-heads among the nobles. Cæsar's bargain with Curio, an event which few could have foreseen, left Pompey helpless to supersede his rival during 50 B.C. Could he have held his allies in leash, he might have found a better pretext for war, if war could not be averted, but as it was he forfeited his popularity because he was made to appear as the aggressor. Yet, although he had given much provocation to the senate, his ambitions were moderate, and the nobles had more than one opportunity to make him their friend. Had they done so (and Cicero spared no effort to induce them) the Republic would have been safe for his lifetime at least. That it should have fallen when and as it did was due to the blundering of the senate more than to the mistakes of Pompey.

Cæsar had sailed after Pompey with a small force and arrived soon after the death of his rival. He was deeply moved by Pompey's fate, and no doubt sincerely so. Yet, although he may not have allowed his mind to dwell upon it, the murder simplified his problems, for Pompey would always have been a serious embarrassment to his conqueror ; he was too great a man in the eyes of the public to be ignored, and it is hard to imagine him content with a subordinate position. Now that he was gone there was no one left who could dispute the preeminence of Cæsar.

At the moment the court of Alexandria was torn by dissensions, one faction supporting Cleopatra and the other her brother Ptolemy. Cæsar determined to arbitrate between them and to obtain large supplies of money from the Egyptian treasury at the same time. Whether he judged Cleopatra the more competent to rule as the elder of the two, or whether he was fascinated by her youthful charm, it was soon evident that he was leaning to her side. The faction of Ptolemy having gained the support of the royal guards and of the turbulent mob of Alexandria, an unexpected uprising left Cæsar barely time to fortify himself in a strong position. His forces were too few to do more than hold their own and wait for reinforcements. When these finally arrived from Asia they released Cæsar and defeated the guards of Ptolemy, and the young king, whom Cæsar had allowed to join his partisans, was drowned in his flight. Cæsar, now at liberty to settle affairs as he chose, made Cleopatra queen of Egypt with Ptolemy XIII, a still younger brother, as her colleague.

While Cæsar was in Egypt Pharnaces, the son of Mithridates, whom Pompey had permitted to retain some portions of his father's kingdom, seized the occasion to claim the whole and defeated Cæsar's lieutenant, Domitius Calvinus. Determined to end this war before it became serious, Cæsar hastened to Asia Minor with such forces as he had at hand. Meeting all attempts at negotiation by a demand for immediate submission, Cæsar destroyed the army of Pharnaces at Zela after a campaign of five days, announcing his victory to a friend in Rome with the famous phrase, " I came, I saw, I conquered."

## § 6. THAPSUS AND MUNDA

When the news of Cæsar's victory at Pharsalus reached Rome, he was at once declared dictator again for an indefinite period, and most Romans believed that the war was over. In this the public was deceived, for the Alexandrian entanglement had important consequences. The delay which resulted from that episode gave the surviving adherents of Pompey an opportunity to concentrate their scattered forces in Africa, so that, when Cæsar finally extricated himself from his

Eastern difficulties and returned to Italy, he found it necessary to begin preparations for a new campaign. The year (47 B.C.) was too far gone for immediate action, so it was not until 46 that he was able to embark.

In Africa were gathered all his most stubborn opponents, the rigid Cato, who preferred to die with the Republic rather than outlive it, the deserter Labienus, and the two sons of Pompey. Cæsar's fleet was dispersed by a storm, so that he reached Africa with so small a force that he was compelled to entrench himself and wait for the arrival of his veterans. As soon as he was able to take the offensive, he marched on Thapsus and lured his enemies into a battle, in which they were disastrously defeated. Some of the leaders were slain by Cæsar's infuriated soldiers, over whom he lost control, some died by their own hands, but the young Pompeys and Labienus managed to escape.

Among the suicides was Cato, whose death cast a glamour over his whole character and career and made him a hero to later generations of Romans. Throughout his life he had shown himself honest and fearless, but narrow-minded and pedantic. Once only, so far as can be determined, had he compromised with his conscience, namely, when he subscribed to the corruption fund raised to secure the election of Bibulus as Cæsar's colleague in the consulship. At other times his untimely scruples and his rigid integrity involved his party in considerable difficulties. He was partly responsible for the disaster of Thapsus because he had insisted that the command should go to the man of highest official rank instead of to the ablest soldier in the army which had rallied in Africa. That he killed himself rather than accept the clemency of Cæsar atoned for all in the minds of later Stoics, to which school of philosophy he belonged, but pride and obstinacy seem to have prompted him to this act, and to modern eyes it will seem a poor title to glory. In any case, it can hardly wipe out the plain fact that in life he was always a source of weakness to the party he supported.

After settling affairs in Africa Cæsar returned to Rome and celebrated a triumph. Of course, no hint was given in the celebration that Cæsar had defeated Romans in the field, for a Roman could not triumph over Romans ; the ceremony was supposed to be in honour of his victories over Gauls,

Egyptians, and Numidians. After the triumph Cæsar was able to devote a few months to the task of government, and then was called away to undertake his last campaign and win his final victory.

After he had crushed the army of Pompey in Spain, he had left that country in charge of Q. Cassius. The choice proved a bad one, for the misgovernment of Cassius soon provoked a revolt. Trebonius had been despatched to supersede him and restore order before the African campaign, but Labienus and the two young Pompeys by taking advantage of the disaffection were able to put themselves at the head of a serious insurrection. This soon attained such proportions that Cæsar felt it necessary to leave his work in Rome and take the field in person. The details matter little, for the war was soon ended by the battle of Munda (45 B.C.) in which Cæsar crushed his opponents. Labienus was killed in the battle and Cn. Pompeius soon afterwards, but Sextus Pompeius made his escape. Although the refugee could do nothing of importance while Cæsar lived, after the Ides of March he was able to make serious trouble.

The battle of Munda at last terminated the long Civil War. On the news of it Cæsar was voted further honours (and a perpetual dictatorship in 44), and the Roman world waited with such patience as it could for him to reorganize the shattered Republic and restore again some semblance of constitutional government. This Cæsar was in no haste to do, and on his return to Rome he began, instead, to make preparations for a war with Parthia. Although he had pardoned his enemies freely, he had not and could not satisfy them. The last months of his life were spent in Rome surrounded by smouldering hatred which, unable to draw the sword against him, gradually turned the minds of some to the dagger.

## CHAPTER XV

## THE DICTATORSHIP OF CÆSAR

### § 1. CÆSAR'S REFORMS

IN any discussion of Cæsar's work as a statesman, it must be remembered that what he accomplished was done during the comparatively few months which he spent in Rome amid wars and preparations for war. Under such circumstances his reforms were necessarily incomplete, and the solution of many problems had to be postponed to that future which never came for him. Yet he achieved enough to extort the admiration of the most reluctant and to inspire a profound regret that he was not spared to finish his task.

From the day he crossed the Rubicon he found himself confronted by difficulties of every sort, and perhaps one of the most immediate and pressing was to control his own partisans, some of whom wished to go much further than he desired and made trouble whenever his back was turned. His measures in regard to debt have already been described. Their success in relieving the situation was neither so immediate nor so complete as to put a stop to agitation in favour of something more drastic, since with Pompey in possession of the East it was impossible for business to revive. Naturally enough, Cæsar had been joined by many reckless and desperate characters, and during the campaign of Pharsalus there were disorders in Italy, instigated by men closely connected with Cicero, although he was in no way responsible for their actions. Cælius Rufus, an intimate friend of the orator, had gone over to Cæsar at the outbreak of the Civil War, espousing what he considered the stronger party. He obtained the prætorship, but did not receive the financial rewards which he apparently expected. Angry and disappointed, he attempted with the help of Milo, who had returned from exile, to provoke a disturbance in Southern Italy. The pair failed to accomplish anything, however, and both lost their lives in the attempt. Dolabella, Cicero's son-in-law, took up the cry for the cancellation of debts, which Cælius had raised, with much better success. After a good deal of hesitation Antony suppressed the agitation, which finally subsided with the return of Cæsar from the East in 47. Cæsar refrained from punishing the offenders and conceded some measures of temporary relief to those in financial difficulties. Now that the control of the East had been recovered the economic situation improved, so that no further legislation concerning debt was necessary. Moreover, since Cæsar's absences from Italy were henceforth shorter, he was able to keep his partisans better in hand.

Everything in Rome and Italy was in disorder after the long political struggle which had terminated in the Civil War. The calendar was out of harmony with the seasons, for the necessary intercalation of an extra month every two years had been neglected, so that Cæsar found a thorough-going reform necessary. With the help of an Alexandrian astronomer the Julian calender was framed and introduced. In Italy there was also much legal confusion, for before the extension of the franchise each of the allies had possessed its own municipal government, and when citizenship was granted to the Italians they retained their local institutions. Cæsar seems to have sought to introduce some degree of uniformity among these local constitutions and to provide for a revision of them.[1]

More difficult problems confronted him in Rome and in his army. In Rome the rabble who were fed by the corn-dole had reached the number of 320,000, while in the army were thousands of veterans who demanded land in payment for their services. Some of the land was secured in Italy, but Cæsar founded in the provinces a number of colonies for his veterans, to whom were added many of the city rabble. For others of the rabble he created employment in Rome by the erection of public buildings, and in Italy by other works on a large scale. He planned to drain the Fucine Lake and

[1] The *lex Julia municipalis* has been a subject of much controversy. For a discussion of the matter with references see Holmes, *The Roman Republic*, III, pp. 553–64.

the Pomptine marshes, as well as to construct a new road through the Apennines to join Central and Northern Italy. To reduce still further the number of unemployed, probably mostly rural, he obliged the ranchers to employ freemen to the extent of one-third of their herdsmen. He also decreed that all capitalists must invest half their money in land in order to raise its value and to diminish the economic antagonism between the nobles and the knights. By these measures he greatly reduced the size of the city rabble, and by stricter regulation of the distribution he succeeded in cutting down the number of those dependent on the corn-dole to 150,000.

For the provinces he accomplished little, however much he planned. He conferred Latin rights on the Greeks in Sicily and on a number of communities in Gaul and Spain. Without regard to the feelings of the knights he abolished the system of tax-farming in Asia, and planned a new adjustment of the tribute throughout the empire. For this purpose he made preparations for an elaborate census of all property, but he did not live to see its completion. From what he did and what he began to do, it is obvious that he would have tried to introduce a better system of government in the provinces, and that he aimed at promoting the prosperity, not of Italy alone, but of all Rome's subjects.

### § 2. POLITICAL RECONSTRUCTION

Reforms of the kind mentioned, however far-reaching in their effects, were easy compared with the task of reconstructing the shattered Republic, and here Cæsar's clemency contributed to his difficulties. At first his government was obviously provisional, and no one could seriously object if, in the midst of the Civil War, he gathered all the powers of the state into his own hands. This character his government never lost, because, as soon as the Civil War was ended with the battle of Munda, he began planning a war with Parthia, for which he was on the point of leaving Rome at the time of his murder. Perhaps he designed this Parthian expedition partly as an excuse for postponing the work of political reconstruction until the passions engendered by civil strife had died away, but the delay increased the resentment of his secret enemies. The bitterness of this resentment Cæsar does not seem to have realized. Although he was well aware that he was hated by many of those about him, he was careless of danger, and exposed himself to the daggers of possible conspirators by dismissing his guards.

By virtue of the various powers and offices which were from time to time conferred upon him, he was at once perpetual dictator, consul, and *pontifex maximus*, and was also invested with the tribunician power and the authority of a censor.[1] Last of all, in view of his expected absence from Rome on the Parthian war he was given the right to name the consuls and half the other magistrates for some years in advance. He was thus absolute master of Rome, an autocratic sovereign in all but name, and he could not safely lay down any of his powers or limit his autocracy.

Sulla had prepared the way for his political reconstruction by clearing the senate of his enemies and filling it with his friends, but Cæsar had chosen to pursue a different course and found himself, in consequence, confronted by a senate in which a large majority was secretly hostile to him. To permit such a body to hold any independent authority was to invite trouble the moment his back was turned. He tried to introduce new members on a considerable scale, but only provoked such derision for his new senators that he was induced to stop, for if the senate lost the public respect, its support was useless. He then sought to modify its composition in another way by increasing the number of the prætors to sixteen and of the quæstors to forty, so that the senators from new families would hold their seats by the same title as those from the old noble houses. In a few years the effect would be considerable, and when Cæsar returned from the East he could hope to find a senate with which he would be better able to work. As it was he could not trust the conscript fathers, yet no government in which they did not hold an important place would seem constitutional in Roman eyes, and this fact constituted the chief difficulty in the way of reconstruction.

[1] The last under the title of prefect of morals. As to the tribunician power, he may have received only the sacrosanctity of the tribunes.

## § 3. CÆSAR'S INTENTIONS

What Cæsar would have done if he had lived to conquer Parthia can only be guessed. It is probable that he would have undertaken a reorganization of the whole system of government, but in what precise form it would have emerged from his hands must always remain a matter of conjecture. There are, however, one or two points which seem reasonably clear. There can be little doubt that under some title he meant to remain in control, though it is possible that he might have shared his power, in appearance at least, with the senate and have left some place for the independent action of the people and magistrates. Of any such intention he certainly gave no sign, and it seems very doubtful if the diarchy of Augustus, with its elaborate shams, would have appealed to him as a desirable solution. His enemies were constantly whispering that he meant to establish an avowed monarchy, and some of the incidents of his last days can be interpreted as feelers put out to see if public opinion was ripe for such a change. On the other hand, they may equally be construed as attempts on his part to silence such rumours. When Mark Antony, during the Lupercalia, sought to place a diadem upon his head and Cæsar thrust it aside, he may have been testing popular feeling, or he may have intended by his ostentatious refusal to allay the popular suspicion. The last supposition is, perhaps, the more probable, but its acceptance does not carry us far. Cæsar may have had no design of changing his title at the moment, and have thought it politic to reassure the people whatever his ultimate plans may have been. It is hardly likely that he would choose a time when he was about to leave for a long Eastern war for an unpopular innovation. If he returned as the conqueror of Parthia he may have believed that he could take the crown with general acquiescence.

If Cæsar dreamed of establishing a monarchy, it must have been a monarchy of the Hellenistic type, for that type was the one most familiar to his contemporaries and would have been the only one open to him. A national monarchy like that of Macedon was impossible, because it could find no support in the national traditions and sentiments of the

Romans, whose ancient kingship was long since forgotten, except by antiquarians. If a monarchy was to be created, a basis for it could be found only in the assertion of some form * of divine right. A claim of this sort in a polytheistic age naturally took the form of the deification of the ruler, and the Eastern world had long been accustomed to regard their kings as earthly divinities and to worship them as gods. To the Romans, the idea of worshipping a living man was not only foreign, but repugnant,[1] for they still clung to their republican tradition, and a ruler who was also a god was utterly incompatible with any sort of constitutional government. Unless Cæsar became a god in the eyes of his subjects, the mere title of king was useless, and he must have realized that in 44 B.C. the Romans were not yet ready to accept him as a divinity. There was, however, a vast reserve of superstition and of genuine religious feeling in Italy, to which the conquest of Parthia might make a successful appeal, appearing to lift the conqueror above mere humanity. Even so, the acceptance by the West of Cæsar as a divine king was so far doubtful that those who represented him as aiming at a crown alleged that he intended to transfer the seat of empire from Rome to Alexandria, and such a step might seem not only logical, but necessary. It is difficult to believe, however, that Cæsar ever contemplated this course, for his power rested on an army which was thoroughly Italian. Probably he had no very definite plan, but left the future to take care of itself. His next task was to conquer Parthia, and when that was done it would be time enough to reorganize the government. What form the reorganization should take would be determined by circumstances and the mood of the world.

## § 4. THE IDES OF MARCH

Whatever Cæsar's intentions for the future may have been, his measures in the present stirred his enemies to fury. After Munda many, perhaps nearly all, expected a settlement of the political problem. They may have had no very clear idea of what the settlement should be, but they hoped for a return to some sort of constitutional government, for an

[1] After Cæsar's death his deification presented no difficulty, since there was a precedent in the case of Romulus.

arrangement by which the senate and the magistrates would cease to be mere tools to register and execute the will of an autocrat. When Cæsar gave no sign of relaxing his control but began preparations for a new war instead, such hopes gradually faded and were replaced by sullen resentment. Nevertheless the yoke of his dictatorship might have been borne if he had not laid his hand upon the holy of holies. To the aristocracy liberty meant the independence and supremacy of the senate, and there is little to show that the champions of the Republic were at all concerned for the rights of the people. The sentiments of the nobles were precisely what we might expect in a class which had been dominant so long. They had come to feel that they had an inalienable, almost a divine, right to govern the Roman world, and they had always resented the intrusion of new men into their narrow circle. Consequently when Cæsar doubled the number of the quæstors and prætors he committed an unpardonable offence, for his new quæstors would in a few years fill the senate with upstarts, while his new prætors would give rise to a large number of new noble families. In a word, Cæsar proposed to swamp the senate with new peers, and nothing could reconcile the old nobility to this. Even if, when he returned from the East, he should give the senate a real share in the government, it would be a new senate that would receive it. His measures must inevitably create a new governing class, and the supremacy of the old nobles would be gone for ever. Open resistance being impossible, it was only by the dagger of the assassin that *their* Republic could be saved. As this became more and more fully apparent a conspiracy began to take shape. The majority of the senators had no share in the plot, but they were ready to applaud the deed when a few of the more daring had accomplished it.

The actual conspirators are said to have numbered more than sixty,[1] and many different motives must have been at work to bring together so large a group for such a purpose. No doubt some were honest, narrow-minded nobles discharging what they thought a patriotic duty; others were followers of Pompey on whose animosity the generosity of Cæsar made no impression; probably most were moved, in part at least, by personal grievances or ambitions. While many

[1] Suetonius, *Div. Jul.*, ch. 80.

were former opponents whom Cæsar had pardoned, a majority were drawn from the ranks of his own party,[1] and the leaders were guilty of both ingratitude and treachery. The most respectable figure in the group was M. Junius Brutus, a rigid, intense man who had married Cato's daughter and published a eulogy of the upright and unpractical Stoic. Others of note were Decimus Brutus, one of Cæsar's officers, and C. Cassius, who had fought against Cæsar and had then been pardoned and promoted, although the promotion, many thought, had fallen short of what he conceived to be his merits.

Whatever base motives may have actuated many of the conspirators, most of them might have shrunk from such a crime if it had not been justified by the accepted moral standards of the day. The Romans were not original thinkers, and the educated class had taken over without serious question the ethics of the Greeks. From the old city states of Greece, where tyrannies had been a standing menace to every form of government, there had been derived the maxim that the slaying of a tyrant was not only a righteous act but a positive duty of the patriotic citizen. By a tyrant the Greeks meant a ruler, whatever his character, who gained the supreme power by illegal means and by the subversion of the constitution of his country. The Greeks detested tyranny, however mildly the tyrant might rule, because he was necessarily an autocrat; holding power in defiance of the laws, he could not be bound by them, and his government could only be shaken off by means as violent as those by which it had been established. The early oligarchies and democracies of Hellas, feeling that they rested on an insecure foundation and might at any moment fall before the audacity of some resolute and able leader of the opposite party, sought to defend themselves against such men by holding up as a fundamental principle that in breaking the law the tyrant became a public enemy, and that his murder was not only excusable but in the highest degree praiseworthy. The only question which could occur to a cultured Roman trained in Greek ethics, as practically all were trained, was whether Cæsar came within the definition of a tyrant. On this point the followers of Pompey entertained no doubts, for to have done so would have been to admit that their party had subverted the legal government of

[1] Seneca, *de ira*, iii, ch. 30.

Rome, and that Cæsar had been its defender. Since they would not admit this, they were forced to regard him as a man who had seized control of the state by violent and illegal means. Still, as long as they entertained the hope that he would restore the Republic which he had overthrown, they could accept his dictatorship as a temporary necessity. As this hope faded they began to think of their duty in the light of the accepted ethical systems. The followers of Cæsar were in the same position; they had supported him against his enemies, but, when they saw him lifted by circumstances to supreme power and perceived no sign that he meant to give it up, they were troubled in mind and began to ask themselves whether they could reconcile their consciences to supporting him further. Many, of course, were able to do this on the ground that the powers of the dictator, however extensive they might be, had been conferred by the senate and people, and that he was, therefore, a constitutional ruler. To those who resented his measures and felt that their services had been ill-requited such an argument would naturally seem mere sophistry, since it could be maintained that neither senate nor people had acted freely, but that the decrees and laws in Cæsar's favour and the honours heaped upon him had been extorted from them by the fear of his army. At any rate, some of them brought themselves to regard him as one who had made use of his opportunity to establish a tyranny, and once this point was reached all moral scruples were at an end. Cicero, for example, although he had no part in the conspiracy, seems never to have felt a doubt that the assassination was a noble act and that the assassins were heroes to be admired to the end of time.

Such ethical considerations had so much weight with the conspirators that after due deliberation they decided to spare Antony, who was Cæsar's colleague in the consulship. To slay Cæsar was in their minds a duty because he was a tyrant, but it was not equally clear that the duty extended to the murder of his friends. Antony was not himself a tyrant, but at most merely the supporter and tool of one, and Greek ethics did not include subordinate agents in the same class with the usurper himself. The conspirators, therefore, resolved to confine their action within the bounds of the strictest morality and to make Cæsar their sole and only victim.

One may wonder at the blindness which imagined that the death of Cæsar would restore the Republic, but the conspirators were short-sighted enough to be deceived by appearances. It must be remembered that the machinery of the Republic was still in existence, magistrates, senate, and assembly, although the powers held by the dictator rendered independent action impossible. If he were removed, the conspirators persuaded themselves that the republican machinery would at once begin to function ; the magistrates could summon the senate and the assembly, and there would no longer be any obstacle to their free action. Just how Cæsar's army was to be dealt with was a point which seems to have escaped the notice of the conspirators, or they may have left this matter to be settled by the Republic when it had been restored to life, feeling that any attempt on their part to determine in advance what should be done would be to overstep their role of liberators and to give a handle to Cæsar's supporters by making possible the counter charge that they were simply replacing Cæsar's tyranny with a selfish usurpation of their own.

For whatever reason, the conspirators apparently made no plans for the future. They resolved to strike down Cæsar in the senate-house, where he would be unprotected by attendants, and where most of those present would be in sympathy with them and more likely to applaud the murder than to make any attempt to defend him. Time was pressing, for Cæsar was soon to depart for the Parthian war, and once he had resigned the consulship, as he planned to do before leaving Rome, he would be surrounded by his soldiers, so that it would be difficult or impossible to accomplish their purpose. A meeting of the senate had been called for the Ides of March, and this was the last session of the conscript fathers which Cæsar would attend. It was a case of then or never, so the conspirators made their preparations.

Many stories have clustered about the tragedy, some of which may very well be true in substance if not in every detail. We are told that on the evening before the fatal day Cæsar dined with Lepidus, his master of horse, and that Decimus Brutus was in the company. The conversation turned on the kind of death to be desired and various opinions were expressed, Cæsar alone declaring his preference for a sudden one. That night his wife Calpurnia dreamed that she saw him bleeding and in the morning begged him not to leave his house. When the sacrifices which he offered were unfavourable, Cæsar, though little affected by the prevalent superstitions, was about to yield to Calpurnia's entreaties and to send Antony to dismiss the senate, but Decimus persuaded him that such a course would be disrespectful to the senate and that he ought to dismiss the conscript fathers in person. Cæsar accepted this view and went to the meeting. As he was offering sacrifice before the senate house, a tablet was thrust into his hand containing an account of the conspiracy. He did not stop to read it, however, but entered the house, and after his murder the tablet was found in his hand.[1]

When Cæsar was seated in his chair the conspirators gathered around him with their daggers concealed under their togas except Trebonius, who remained near the door and engaged Antony in conversation. Cæsar's suspicions were not aroused as his murderers drew near, since they were all, as he supposed, his friends. One of them made a pretence of demanding the recall of his brother, and when Cæsar replied that the matter must be deferred for a time he seized the dictator by his robe, in this way exposing his neck. Immediately one of the conspirators tried to drive a dagger into his throat, but missed his aim and wounded him in the breast. As Cæsar sprang to his feet he found himself surrounded by a ring of daggers. For a moment he attempted to defend himself, then gathering his robe about him he fell at the foot of Pompey's statue.

## § 5. CÆSAR'S CHARACTER AND GENIUS

Opinion has varied widely as to Cæsar's character, but his greatness has never been denied. Yet it would seem that even here there might be room for some difference of opinion, for he has too often been credited with qualities of which there is little evidence in the facts of his life. He has been lauded as a sort of super-statesman, who displayed marked originality and daring, and who if he had lived would have solved all problems. Yet as a statesman Cæsar showed little originality ;

[1] These stories are among the most credible given by Appian, *b.c.* ii, chs. 115–17.

his measures were all based upon well-established precedents, and he dealt with the most pressing evils of his time in the traditional Roman way. In the means he took to dispose of his veterans and to reduce the number of the Roman rabble he followed the lines which C. Gracchus had pointed out; in his debt legislation he adopted the solution of Valerius Flaccus in a milder form; in his requirement that the great ranches of Southern Italy should be operated partly by free labour he re-enacted a provision of the Licinian laws on a more limited scale; when he compelled the knights to invest half their capital in land, he tried to accomplish what Sulla actually did by the proscription and the advance of many of the equestrians to the senate; his reform of the calendar was a mere matter of practical common sense, the details of which were worked out by others; in his law concerning the municipalities he seems in the main to have contented himself with giving legal form and system to existing facts.

This, however, is no reflection on his genius. After all, originality is no part of the business of a statesman, and the greatest is he who can find a solution for the problems of his time while keeping within the bounds of common ideas. To depart from these ideas is to ruin his work, for men will not accept what they cannot understand, and they can seldom understand what is wholly unfamiliar. If Cæsar had attempted anything at once important and original, his work would have vanished with himself because his innovations would have been rejected by all classes. He was clear-sighted enough to perceive that novelties forced on a reluctant world were no solution of anything, and to content himself with doing what was possible, refusing to go beyond the limits within which action could prove fruitful. It is his highest claim to sanity and judgment that he did this and accomplished so much in the way of practical reform with so little disturbance of existing prejudices. Some critics have questioned his greatness on this very ground and have blamed him for not discovering and applying all the panaceas of the nineteenth or twentieth century. He should, they think, have modified the system of slavery, invented representative government, or set up some form of Socialism. Even if Cæsar had been thus far in advance of his age, and the ideas involved were by no means unknown to the Romans,[1] he must have failed had he attempted anything of the kind. Even a dictator requires some support to carry out his decrees, and Cæsar could hardly have relied on an army of Roman citizens to enforce measures repugnant to all their fellow citizens. The whole social and economic life of the world then rested upon slavery, so that a serious modification of it might have brought universal chaos. By introducing representative institutions he would have made few friends and many bitter enemies, and as a result he would probably have been murdered sooner than he was, without having solved any problem worth solving. The essential weakness of the Republic lay in the fact that the senate could not control the army, and there is not the slightest reason to suppose that the soldiers would have had greater confidence in a body elected by the towns of Italy. Any profound change in the old constitution would have driven all who cared for the Republic to frenzy and would probably have been regarded with indifference by all others. A representative senate or assembly would have been as futile an experiment as Cromwell's House of Lords, and a Republic founded on these lines would probably have fallen as ignominiously as the Protectorate, while any attempt to set up a system of Socialism would have united all parties, including his own army, against him.

Cæsar's real greatness lay in his clear perception of realities, in the boldness with which he used each opportunity up to the limits of the possible, and in the cool sanity which kept him from exceeding those limits. Although both as a general and as a statesman he often displayed great daring, the event always justified his audacity. That the political problem could not be solved immediately after Munda was his misfortune not his fault, unless we count his clemency a fault. If he had escaped death upon the Ides of March and succeeded in conquering Parthia, he might have undertaken a solution under more favourable conditions. This opportunity was denied him by the nobles, who required another civil war,

[1] Some sort of socialism could easily have been derived from Plato and later Greek philosophers, and representation was used to a limited extent by the Greeks, for example, in the Achæan and Ætolian leagues. As to slavery, some modification of it was surely conceivable by a Roman of that day, and Cæsar did actually try to limit it.

this time accompanied by a proscription, to teach them that their senate had no hold upon the army. Only when they had learned this lesson thoroughly would they be satisfied to accept the rule of one who *could* control the legions and to content themselves with such semblance of power as could be given them by a military autocracy.

As to Cæsar's character it is necessary to be on our guard against the exaggerations and falsehoods of his enemies. The abuse of fashionable society which is reflected in the poems of Catullus should not be taken too seriously. All public men in Rome were freely slandered, and it would have been strange indeed if Cæsar had escaped. It is no doubt true that his morals did not always conform to modern standards, but the same may be said of nearly all his contemporaries. Cicero divorced his wife because he found her temper trying, and the austere Cato gave up his because he found that she preferred another man. Although Pompey did not hesitate to repudiate his wife and marry again at Sulla's order, Cæsar risked his life by openly refusing to obey a similar command. The wife for whose sake he had braved the wrath of Sulla died young, and his other marriages were contracted for political reasons rather than affection, as were most marriages in high society at that time. Cæsar was probably not a model of conjugal fidelity, but we have serious evidence of only one love affair, that with Cleopatra. Cicero in his private letters mentions nothing else to the discredit of Cæsar, although he was opposed to Cæsar in politics, and must have been familiar with the gossip on which Catullus drew for his materials. In short, there is no reason to suppose that Cæsar was more of a libertine than most men of his day, and, while the prevailing standard was not high, it was by no means so debased as it has been pictured by writers who take their Catullus too literally.

In some respects Cæsar cannot fail to command our admiration. He seems to have had little share in the common Roman vice of cruelty. He was quite capable of striking terror into barbarians by acts which to-day would be regarded as savage, but which were permitted by the accepted rules of warfare in his time. Toward his fellow citizens he displayed extraordinary forbearance and generosity. In astonishingly few cases did he manifest the slightest animosity, and in these cases the reason is not wholly clear. He professed regret for

Cato's suicide, yet he published a bitter work against him later on. The motive may have been political, for there was rising a sort of cult in honour of the Stoic martyr in which Cæsar may have seen an obstacle to a reconciliation with the nobility.

In person Cæsar is described as tall and fair with keen black eyes. He is uniformly represented as a man of courteous manners and of great personal charm. While Pompey made bitter enemies by his awkwardness and lack of consideration for others, Cæsar seems to have made few if any in such ways. He was essentially a versatile and many-sided man, not only a soldier but a writer, orator, wit, and poet of a sort. He seems, indeed, to have touched life on every side, winning distinction in widely different fields. His contemporaries regarded him as one of the greatest orators of Rome ; his Commentaries are models of clear and direct narrative ; as a general he was one of the foremost of all time ; and as a practical statesman he lived long enough to reveal the highest qualities. In Cæsar alone were to be found the insight and the daring which with fuller opportunity might have found real solutions for some at least of the evils which his successor was content to smooth over without attempting to cure. That he would have lightened the burdens of the provincials and reorganized the finances of the state he indicated clearly, and it seems likely that he would have stopped with no half-measures. Just what he would have done we cannot say, but it was unquestionably a vast misfortune that a handful of Roman nobles deprived Rome of the services of the greatest man she ever produced.

The chief charge against Cæsar is that to gratify his personal ambition he overthrew the Republic and introduced a military monarchy. He is even endowed with superhuman prescience to fit him for the task, since we are told that he went to Gaul with the definite plan of conquering it and so securing an army to defeat Pompey and make himself the master of the state. This is hard to reconcile with the facts. It seems much more reasonable to see in Cæsar a great opportunist who went to Gaul without definite plans, if only because it would have been folly to make them, but who saw at once that the condition of that country made its conquest possible. Nor is there any reason to suppose that his attempts to compromise with Pompey were insincere.

Some offers he may have made knowing that they would not be accepted and that their rejection would put his rival in the wrong, but it is quite probable that he would have made terms with Pompey if he could.

To say that Cæsar overthrew the Republic is a superficial view, for the army had dominated Rome for many years before he came upon the scene. Pompey, when in 70 B.C. he compelled Sulla's senate to abdicate by the presence of his army outside Rome, was for the moment as much a military monarch as Cæsar. Every successful general had the Republic at his mercy, and the essential difference between Cæsar and Pompey or Sulla was that he used his power intelligently to promote the welfare of the world instead of laying it aside as soon as his personal demands had been satisfied. It is true that after Cæsar's death the Republic could not be restored, but the chief obstacle in the way was the profound distrust with which the army regarded the senate. It was the conscript fathers and not Cæsar who overthrew the Republic, and they had overthrown it before he went to Gaul by refusing to provide for Pompey's veterans. Henceforth every general must either betray his soldiers or dictate terms to the government, and under such conditions the Republic could survive only by accident. Cicero saw the situation clearly when he said before the Civil War that it would end in a tyrant,[1] for had Pompey won he would have been as much the master of the state as Cæsar. When a faction of the nobility forced Cæsar to draw the sword they destroyed their own supremacy forever, whatever the result of the war which they had recklessly provoked.

[1] *Att.*, vii, 5. "Peace is necessary. Victory will bring many evils and certainly a tyrant among them." There are other passages in his letters to the same effect.

## CHAPTER XVI

# THE DEATH AGONY OF THE REPUBLIC

### § 1. ROME AFTER THE MURDER

THE conspirators seem to have expected that when they had slain Cæsar they would be hailed as liberators by the senate and the people, but after the murder they found themselves surrounded by empty benches, for the conscript fathers, taken by surprise, had fled in panic. The assassins hastened out of doors to announce to the crowd before the senate-house that Rome was free, but the crowd, hearing of Cæsar's murder, had scattered in haste, and again they found themselves alone. This situation was so unexpected that they hesitated as to what they should do, but finally with their slaves and retainers they occupied the Capitol to wait upon events and to send out messages to their friends.

Since the machinery of the Republic had not started automatically, it was necessary to find some means of setting it in motion, and the first step was obviously to convene the senate. If the conspirators had been wise they would have summoned it themselves to meet on the Capitol before the friends of Cæsar had recovered from their first alarm, but this would have been unconstitutional, so the chance was allowed to slip, perhaps because they feared that the conscript fathers would ignore a summons which on the face of it was irregular. At any rate they opened negotiations with Antony, the surviving consul. This was a tactical error, for the recognition of Antony as consul implied an acknowledgment of the legality of Cæsar's position in the state. It will be recalled that one of the conspirators had purposely detained Antony at the door of the senate chamber, so that he had probably been too far away to come to Cæsar's assistance. After the murder he had hastily fled to his house, fearing for his own life. He had but a vague idea of who were involved in the plot, for, though he may have recognized some of the murderers, he was very much in the dark as to what support they had or could gain after the deed. He, too, sent messengers in all directions, trying to ascertain the strength of the conspirators, and the information which he received seems to have reassured him to some extent. The friends of the conspirators found him quite ready to convene the senate, but on one point he refused to comply with their wishes, insisting that the meeting should take place not in the neighbourhood of the Capitol but near his own house, where his armed slaves and retainers would furnish him some protection from attack. He accordingly summoned the conscript fathers to meet in the Temple of Tellus, and the conspirators, distrusting him, did not venture to attend.

When the senate met with Antony presiding over its deliberations, it was evident that the absence of the conspirators made little difference, for their friends were present and formed a majority. Antony was cool and impartial in his bearing, for he was shrewd enough to see the dilemma in which the senate was placed. The logical course for the majority would have been to declare Cæsar a tyrant and pass a decree in honour of his murderers, but this would have automatically annulled all his acts as those of a usurper whose government had been utterly illegal. The results of such a repudiation of his acts were likely to be serious in the extreme, and the senators had been forced to realize this by the crowds of Cæsar's veterans who surrounded the temple and through the midst of whom they had been forced to pass. Cæsar had already rewarded many of his discharged soldiers with grants of land, but a large number of them were then in Rome waiting for the fulfilment of his promises. To tell these men that neither his acts nor his promises would be considered binding by the senate was to invite an immediate outbreak, and the only armed troops at hand were under the command of Lepidus, who had been the dictator's master of horse. That the conspirators had never thought of this gives us a clear measure of their political insight, for none but men who were blind to the realities could have imagined that the senate could act freely surrounded by Cæsar's soldiers. The conscript fathers, therefore, did not dare to pronounce Cæsar a tyrant, and probably many of them had no wish to do so, for a large number of the senators owed their seats in that body to the dictator or had been advanced in rank under his rule. If his acts were repudiated such men would be forced to quit the senate-house or to step back to a lower place. Moreover, all those whom he had designated to fill the magistracies for the next few years would have to take their chances at a regular election. In addition to this, if Cæsar were declared a tyrant, all the magistrates in office must at once vacate their places, and the senate must appoint *interreges* to conduct the government until elections could be held. The result of such elections could only be conjectured, for the sentiments of the people had not yet been plainly shown. Perhaps the senate might have taken all other risks, but Cæsar's veterans were a decisive argument which could neither be evaded nor met in any way but one. The conscript fathers, therefore, did the only possible thing when they not only abstained from branding Cæsar as a tyrant but ratified all his acts, whether actually carried out or only intended for the future. This it might be hoped would pacify his veterans, since it assured them not only that they should keep what had been given them but that his promises would be redeemed in full.

After ratifying Cæsar's acts the senate was logically bound to punish his murderers, since if Cæsar had been a legal ruler then his death was a crime against the state. Again the senate shrank from logic and sought to find a way of escape. Cicero proposed that to make an end of civil strife a general amnesty should be proclaimed and Cæsar's death treated as some natural calamity; no questions should be asked his friends as to anything they might have done in the past, and they were to abstain from all inquiries as to his end. Catching eagerly at this suggestion the senate not only decreed the amnesty, but decided that Cæsar should be given a public funeral as though he had died a natural death.

## § 2. CÆSAR'S FUNERAL

When a consul died during his year of office it was customary to accord him a public funeral at which in the absence of near relatives his colleague delivered an oration in his honour,

When the senate voted that the usual honours should be paid to Cæsar, the charge of the funeral naturally fell to Antony, who thus secured an opportunity to test the feeling of the people. Of what happened the ancient writers have given two divergent accounts. In one version Antony is represented as delivering an oration resembling that which Shakespeare has put into his mouth;[1] in the other he said little but contrived to arouse the passions of the crowd without actually committing himself to anything. The general situation at the time makes this second version seem much the more probable.[2] Only five days had passed since Cæsar was struck down, and nothing had occurred to assure Antony of the sentiments of any important class except the senators. It was possible that the veterans, the knights, and the populace might accept the amnesty and the ratification of Cæsar's acts and submit to the resumption of power by the senate. Even if there was widespread and bitter resentment, it was by no means certain that a Cæsarian party could be formed which would be strong enough to offer serious opposition to the conscript fathers. The wisest course for Antony might be to make the best terms he could with the aristocracy, although he must have hoped for the development of a Cæsarian opposition with himself as leader. The funeral, however, was hardly the occasion for a direct bid for the leadership of such a party, since a temporary outburst of popular emotion offered little security for the future. Such an outburst would obviously be of great advantage to Antony, for it might have a profound effect upon the veterans, and it would certainly to some extent intimidate the senate, thus enhancing the price which he could command if he found it prudent or necessary to ally himself with the nobles. To stake everything on the effect of a single speech would have been quite out of harmony with the cautious policy which he had hitherto pursued, and the risk involved was entirely unnecessary. It was possible to test the public feeling without committing himself and to stir the mob to fury, if it could be done, without assuming the responsibility for the result. This is the course which Suetonius represents him as taking,[3]

[1] Dio (xliv, chs. 36–49) gives the most elaborate version of the oration.

[2] See M. E. Deutsch, *Antony's Funeral Speech.*

[3] Suetonius, *Div. Jul.*, ch. 84. See also Appian (*b.c.* ii, chs. 144–47), who agrees substantially with Suetonius.

and in view of the circumstances there is a strong probability that his account is substantially correct.

At the funeral Cæsar's will was first read. In it he bequeathed his gardens to the people as a public park and left to every citizen living in Rome the sum of 300 sesterces (£2 to £3). The bulk of his property was to go to C. Octavius, his sister's grandson, whom he adopted as his son ; if Octavius refused to accept the adoption, Decimus Brutus was named in his place.[1] The crowd were deeply moved by Cæsar's liberality to the people and by the evidence of his confidence in Decimus, who was one of his murderers. When Cæsar's body was brought in, still clad in the robe in which he had fallen, it was received with lamentations. Antony then arose, but instead of delivering the usual funeral eulogy he declared that such an oration for so great a man should be pronounced by his whole country rather than by a single individual. The decrees of the senate and the votes of the people in his honour were solemnly read,[2] and after each Antony added a few words. The climax was reached when the solemn oath taken by the senators to defend Cæsar and avenge him upon all conspirators was read. Here Antony invoked the gods to witness that he stood ready to fulfil his oath, but that, since others had considered it better to decree an amnesty, he prayed that it might prove so. Seeing some agitation among the senators at this, Antony concluded with a few soothing words, saying that the death of Cæsar seemed the work of an evil spirit rather than of men, that it behooved all alike to think of the present rather than the past, and finally invited all to join in the customary hymns and lamentations. He had thus contrived to make a bid for the leadership of those who might wish to avenge Cæsar, yet without saying anything to which the senators could very well take exception.

The crowd had been wrought up almost to the breaking point, and the sight of Cæsar's blood-stained robe amid the lamentations and the dirges reciting his great deeds turned sorrow into fury. The mob burned Cæsar's body in the Forum, and likewise the senate-house where he had been murdered ;

[1] An adoption by will was not uncommon in Rome, and it was probably usual to name a second choice if the first declined to accept.

[2] By a herald according to Suetonius, by Antony himself according to Appian,

then it dispersed to set fire to the homes of the conspirators. The senate was terrified, the assassins fled precipitately, and Antony was left master of Rome to make what use he could of the opportunity.

### § 3. ANTONY'S BID FOR POWER

For the rioting which followed the funeral Antony did not seem intentionally responsible,[1] and the senate continued negotiations with him. The agitation in Rome also continued, for there were plenty of politicians who, having been Cæsar's supporters, knew that they could hope for no advancement from the aristocratic machine if it once got into working order again. Such politicians could have accomplished little except to foment disorder, which would have been of little consequence in itself, if it had not been for Cæsar's veterans. The determining factor in the situation was the profound distrust with which these veterans regarded the senate. Although they were naturally indignant at the murder, they might possibly have submitted if they had felt any confidence in senatorial promises,[2] but they were convinced that the conscript fathers would keep their word only under compulsion. Whether such distrust was deserved it is impossible to determine, but under the circumstances it was inevitable. The majority of the senators were former adherents of Pompey, and Cæsar's soldiers could not readily believe that their beaten enemies would reward them for the beating. Indignation and distrust combined to draw them to Antony, who welcomed their support. As disorder in the city grew, Antony, by pleading his inability to deal with it without an armed force, was able to persuade the senate reluctantly to allow him a bodyguard,[3] which he promptly enlisted from the veterans. The disorder was put down, but Antony remained at the head of an armed force, so that the senate found itself helpless.

He had already taken advantage of the ratification of all

[1] Afterwards, of course, when hostilities were openly declared, he was given the credit, probably justly, of having instigated the outbreak.

[2] They might at least have waited for the senate to show its hand had they felt no indignation. Cicero testifies clearly as to the distrust of the senate (*Att.*, xiv, 10) and as to the use made of it by the Cæsarian leaders (*Att.*, xiv, 22).

[3] Appian (iii, chs. 4–5) implies that the guard was larger than the senate intended.

Cæsar's acts and intentions, for, having obtained possession of Cæsar's papers he was able to do very much as he pleased by producing such as he chose, or alleging that he found this or that rough draft among Cæsar's notes. Cicero declared emphatically that many of these memoranda were forged, and such forgery would have been easy, for Antony had secured the services of Cæsar's secretary, and the documents did not need to be in Cæsar's writing. From what Cicero says it seems certain that there were some forgeries among the papers produced, but it is very likely that the orator was unduly suspicious and exaggerated the number. The senate probably agreed with Cicero, but could do nothing, for proof was difficult, and it would not have dared to act even if the fullest proof had been available. To attack Antony for carrying out the intentions of Cæsar would have aroused the veterans at once ; so like Cicero they could merely lament the situation, groan in private, and wait impatiently for the day when Antony would be obliged to lay down the consulship.

Antony had no intention of being brought to account, and he had been anxious to secure a bodyguard partly in order that he might make satisfactory provision for the future. To do this it was necessary for him to modify some of Cæsar's arrangements which were too well known to be upset by forgery. The provincial governorships for the next year were of vital importance ; Antony had been assigned Macedonia as his province, but he concluded that this was too far from Rome and decided to exchange it for Cisalpine Gaul. After the death of Cæsar Decimus Brutus had taken possession of this province, where he was now busily engaged in raising an army to support the senate. It seemed essential to Antony to deprive his enemies of such a recruiting ground, so after Octavian's arrival in June he proposed a law, which of course would supersede any act of Cæsar or the senate, by which Cisalpine Gaul and Gallia Comata were conferred upon him for six years with four of the legions then in Macedonia, where they had been concentrated for Cæsar's Parthian expedition. With his bodyguard he had no trouble in carrying his law, and the senate saw with dismay that for years to come Rome was destined to live under the shadow of his army.

### § 4. OCTAVIAN

Antony's plans, however, were destined to be upset in an unexpected fashion. As has been already mentioned, Cæsar in his will adopted C. Octavius as his son. He had already shown marked favour to this young man, as yet hardly out of boyhood, and had sent him to complete his education at Apollonia, near the spot where the army destined for the Parthian campaign was assembled. The young Octavius relieved his studies by dining frequently with the officers and watching the men at their drill. He had thus become well known to officers and men alike, and his handsome person and unassuming manners had won him many friends. When the news of Cæsar's murder reached Apollonia, the army was prompt in offering him protection, but he declined the offer, rightly judging his youth a sufficient safeguard, and immediately set out for Rome to claim his inheritance, that is, Cæsar's name and his share of Cæsar's private property, for the dictator's public rank and official powers were purely personal and could not be bequeathed by will. He at once assumed the name of C. Julius Cæsar Octavianus, even before he had a legal right to it.[1]

When Cæsar was murdered he had in his possession a large sum of money, partly his own and partly public money drawn from the treasury. Even if Antony had been a man of strict integrity, he would probably have had difficulty in distinguishing what belonged to Cæsar and what to the state. It is unlikely that he made any effort to do so, and the whole sum was quickly spent in one way or another. Consequently he could not satisfy the claims of Octavian, even if he had wished to do so, with the result that the two soon became enemies.

At first Antony imagined that he could easily brush aside " the boy," as he called him, but he was soon destined to realize his mistake. The name of Cæsar, if borne with any shadow of right, was one to conjure with among the veterans, and Octavian, young as he was, was shrewd enough to comprehend and take advantage of this fact. As soon as Antony

[1] The adoption had to receive formal confirmation in the old *comitia curiata*, and Antony was able to prevent this for some time.

left Rome with his guard to meet the legions coming from Macedonia, Octavian hastened to Campania, where Cæsar had settled many of his veterans, and called for recruits. Although he had no legal right whatever to raise an army, the veterans responded to his appeal, and the force so raised was strengthened by two of the four Macedonian legions, which deserted Antony and joined him.

Antony thus found himself between two foes, Decimus Brutus in the North and Octavian in the South. Deciding that Decimus was the more immediately dangerous of the two, he marched against him, postponing a settlement with Octavian to a more convenient season. Decimus, aware that his raw levies could not face the army of his opponent, shut himself up in Mutina, where he was besieged by Antony. In the midst of the siege the year came to a close, and new consuls, Hirtius and Pansa, took office in Rome by virtue of Cæsar's designation.

## § 5. THE WAR AROUND MUTINA

Hirtius and Pansa, although they had been friends of Cæsar, were both opponents of Antony and were willing to give the senate their full support against him, but their support was very far from sufficient. Since they could not begin recruiting until they had taken office, they had too little time for adequate preparations. They got together such forces as they could, but it was clear that they were not strong enough to raise the siege of Mutina. When, therefore, Octavian made overtures to the senate and offered the help of his army, the offer was accepted. Cicero was now the leader of the senate and was seeking by his Philippics against Antony to arouse the conscript fathers to bold and energetic action. Believing it vital to the cause of the Republic that Decimus should be saved, he was ready to use the only means at hand of accomplishing this result. Circumstances thus made an alliance between the senate and Octavian inevitable, although probably neither party to it had much confidence in the other. Some senators hated the name of Cæsar so intensely that they would have left Decimus to his fate rather than accept help from one who bore it, but Cicero could rise above such prejudices and was able to carry the majority with him. For some time past he had been in correspondence with Octavian, whose reiterated assurances he accepted. That the orator was deceived is possible, but it is by no means certain. Of course, in the senate Cicero vehemently affirmed Octavian's loyalty to the Republic, but he could hardly do otherwise, for to suggest doubts of Octavian and at the same time urge the senate to trust him would have been obvious folly. It is therefore unnecessary to assume that Cicero believed with his whole heart all that he found it expedient to say in public, or to suppose that he fondly imagined that an alliance between Octavian and the senate could be permanent. It was enough that the alliance was possible for a time, and that it was the only means of saving Decimus. Under Cicero's leadership the conscript fathers decreed that Octavian should have the *imperium* and should join his forces with those raised by the consuls for the purpose of relieving Mutina.

No time was to be lost if the relief was to come before Decimus had been forced to surrender, so the united armies hastened northward at once. After some skirmishing and a sharp battle at Forum Gallorum Antony had to abandon the siege and concentrate his energies on attempting to extricate himself by a hurried retreat. Across the Alps was a strong army under Lepidus, who was governor of the two provinces of Hither Spain and Transalpine Gaul, and Antony set out to reach him with the troops still under his command and with all the reinforcements he was able to gather up. Had the victors pressed the pursuit with energy his army might, perhaps, have been destroyed, but the forces of Decimus were exhausted by the hardships they had recently endured, the two consuls were dead, and Octavian did not move. It is possible that the deaths of Hirtius and Pansa at nearly the same moment, one from sickness and the other from a wound received in the battle, delayed immediate action, but another explanation was given by Decimus himself, who, being upon the spot, should have been well informed. In a letter to Cicero, while bewailing the escape of the enemy, he declared that Octavian could not control his men.[1] This seems very likely when it is remembered that the soldiers of both Octavian and Antony were for the most part Cæsar's veterans, who had long fought

[1] *Fam.*, xi, 10.

side by side and might naturally be reluctant to fight each other. While Cæsar's son and heir was treated with contempt and denied his rights by Antony, the veterans might stand by him even if this meant rescuing one of the conspirators, but they must have felt the situation an unpleasant one, and it would not be surprising if they were unwilling to pursue their old comrades or to continue to defend Cæsar's murderers longer than was strictly necessary. What Octavian really wished it is impossible to determine. He would no doubt have been glad to eliminate Antony if he could have been sure that he would then be accepted by the Cæsarian party as their leader, but he may well have felt doubts as to whether Antony's men or the legions under Lepidus would come over to him, and he may not have dared to try the experiment of calling on the veterans about him to hunt down Antony. It is very likely that he understood perfectly the impossibility of inducing the veterans to support the cause of the senate for any length of time, and that he entered on the campaign with the intention of making terms with Antony as soon as the latter had been made to see that terms were necessary.

### § 6. OCTAVIAN AND THE SENATE

If Octavian was really uncertain of his course, the senate was not long in forcing him to a decision. The first news of Antony's defeat exaggerated the extent of the victory, and the conscript fathers imagined that their enemy had been disposed of for ever. In their delight they became over-confident and piled blunder upon blunder until they rendered it impossible for Octavian to support them even if he wished to do so. They proceeded at once to declare not only Antony but all the soldiers who followed him outlaws, thus showing Octavian's men the quality of their mercy and discrimination. When news arrived that the consuls were dead, the senate transferred the command of their forces to Decimus, but the soldiers refused to accept him as their general and rallied around Octavian. As if this were not enough, the senate appointed a commission to determine the legality of everything which Antony had done as consul, and on this commission there was not a single member in whom Cæsar's veterans felt any confidence, although their interests were certain to be seriously affected by its decisions. The soldiers of Octavian in anger and alarm took matters into their own hands, and he was either forced to follow them or feigned to be so forced. They sent messengers to Rome demanding that he be given a place on the commission and allowed to stand as a candidate for the consulship for the remainder of the year. In some quarters the suggestion was made that Cicero should be his colleague, and the orator was not unwilling. No doubt a second consulship would have gratified Cicero's vanity, but it is unnecessary to regard this as the sole or chief consideration which influenced him, for to accept such an arrangement was the best course which the senate could take after the blunders already committed. The conscript fathers, however, would no longer follow Cicero's lead and raised technical objections. This was the final straw, and Octavian, willingly or reluctantly, broke camp and marched on Rome at the head of his army. Cicero's policy had failed and the unnatural alliance between Octavian and the senate had broken down. It is highly probable that it would have done so in any case, but if Cicero could have kept control a little longer the rupture might possibly have been postponed until the circumstances were more favourable to the senate. He was exerting himself to the utmost to secure the support of the provincial governors, while M. Brutus and Cassius were raising armies in the East. Every day gained was a distinct advantage to the senate, and that body should have played for time by avoiding all provocation to Octavian's soldiers and by yielding to all his demands. Although Cicero did not wholly appreciate the situation, at least he saw it more accurately than the majority of the nobles, and after his first enthusiasm at the news of Antony's defeat, he soon awoke to the realities and sought to prevent the final break.

With Octavian marching upon Rome the senate, now that it was too late, made futile attempts to check him by conceding his demands. At the last moment some troops arrived from Africa, and the senate's confidence revived, only to give place to despair when the troops went over to Octavian. Since there was no possibility of resistance, he was forthwith elected consul together with a relative named Pedius. He made but a short stay in the city, only long enough to have a law passed for the punishment of Cæsar's murderers, then, resuming command of his army, he moved northward to deal with Antony.

## § 7. ANTONY IN GAUL

While the alliance between Octavian and the senate was breaking down in Italy, Antony had been rebuilding his shattered power in Gaul. He had made good his retreat from Mutina and had succeeded in reaching Transalpine Gaul at the head of a considerable force. As has been said, Lepidus was the governor of that province and had at his disposal an army which could easily have crushed the fugitive. The newly-conquered parts of Gaul were under the control of Plancus, whose army was much smaller than that of Lepidus but was still strong enough to meet that of Antony if Lepidus did not join him. Cicero had addressed long letters to both, seeking to persuade them to stand by the Republic, and both had replied by ardent professions of loyalty. What Lepidus really intended cannot be known, and it is possible that he had no clear intentions. He was not a man with any strong hold on his troops, who were veterans of Cæsar, and he may not have dared to risk a mutiny by ordering them to fight their fellow veterans under Antony. Perhaps his professions to Cicero were not wholly insincere, and, though the final scenes were in all likelihood a carefully staged comedy, it may have been the conviction that his army would not follow him in any other course that induced Lepidus to play the part he did. At any rate, instead of advancing promptly to fight Antony, he encamped near his supposed enemy and allowed the men in the two armies to communicate freely. They soon made common cause and those of Lepidus clamorously insisted that he receive and protect their outlawed comrades. Lepidus wrote to the senate, declaring himself unable to withstand the demands of his soldiers, and he was probably truthful in this, for he must now have lost any control which he might once have had. The two armies at once united with Antony as the real commander. Since Plancus could not resist such a coalition, he hastened to desert the senate and added his forces to those of Antony.

Thus Octavian, having made himself consul by his march on Rome, found himself face to face with an opponent who was stronger than ever before. It might have been expected that Antony would now return to Italy and crush the young man who had dared to drive him from Mutina. This, however, was not the course which he adopted. For some time negotiations had been in progress between the two, and an alliance had practically been agreed upon before Octavian left Rome for Northern Italy. The motives of the latter seem obvious enough, for he had definitely broken with Cicero and the senate, and his army was decidedly inferior to that of his rival. For him to treat was, therefore, almost the only rational course. Antony's motives for accepting an alliance instead of fighting are not so clear, but they may be divined with some degree of probability. His army was composed mainly of Cæsar's veterans, who would be reluctant to fight against Cæsar's son, especially now that he had repudiated all association with the conspirators and the Pompeian senate. Antony may have hesitated also because of the growing menace in the East, for a war with Octavian would take time, and a victory might be bought at such a heavy cost that his chances in the inevitable struggle with M. Brutus and Cassius would be seriously impaired. Nevertheless, it seems likely that the feeling of his army was the main factor in determining his attitude. Having learned that Cæsar's name was a power which could not safely be ignored, he was prepared to ally himself with the young man who bore it and who by declaring implacable war against the conspirators had deprived him of any reasonable excuse for further hostility.

Decimus Brutus had already been eliminated as a factor in the situation. After his release from Mutina he had pursued Antony to Gaul, and when Lepidus went over to the enemy he had succeeded in joining Plancus. When Plancus also deserted the Republican cause, the soldiers of Decimus abandoned him; he then fled, attempting to reach M. Brutus in Macedonia, but was captured on the way by a Celtic chief, who put him to death at Antony's order.

When Antony and Lepidus at length returned to Italy, they found Octavian at the head of his army in Cisalpine Gaul. Lepidus arranged a conference at Bononia: an agreement was speedily reached. It was determined that the three should assume absolute control of the state under the title of Triumvirs for the Regulation of the Republic (*Triumviri reipublicæ constituendæ*). This Second Triumvirate was to be regularly set up by law and was to constitute a joint dictatorship of Antony, Lepidus, and Octavian; the policy which they would pursue after their appointment was also discussed and decided upon, and with their armies behind them there could be no question of their ability to carry out their decisions.

## § 8. THE FALL OF THE REPUBLIC

The march of Octavian on Rome may be taken to mark the failure of the attempt to revive the Republic after Cæsar's death. Cicero had made an heroic effort to bring it back to life, but the effort had been in vain; all that was left to him was to choose whether he would die with it or survive it. He had always been convinced that if Italy was lost the Republic was lost with it, that the battle must be fought out in the peninsula, and that defeat there would be the end of liberty. In this he judged rightly, for, if the senate abandoned Rome to seek a refuge in the camp of M. Brutus in Macedonia or of Cassius in Syria, its prestige and authority were gone for ever. Brutus and Cassius might be victorious, might bring the conscript fathers back to Rome, and might install them with all outward marks of respect in the senate-house, but no one could any longer imagine that they met there except by the permission of a victorious army. There could be no pretence that they governed otherwise than by the support of their champions, nor could those champions resign their power without leaving the conscript fathers at the mercy of any general with whom they might venture to differ. If the senate could maintain a semblance of authority in Italy till Brutus and Cassius could come to its support, the fiction of its government might still be kept intact, and its real and fundamental impotence concealed from the world at large, so that with time and patience it might regain some measure of control.

When, therefore, Octavian broke with the senate and openly dictated his own terms at the point of the sword, Cicero saw clearly that the Republic was dead and that all hope of resurrection was gone. Although the war between the Cæsarians and the conspirators might go on, it was not a struggle for the Republic in anything but name. The Roman world was to be ruled by a master, and the only question at issue now was who that master should be. A military dictatorship was inevitable, and the senate could not even exert a serious influence in favour of one candidate or another. There was no longer any place for an orator or politician, for only the generals and their armies now counted.

The causes which had undermined the Republic and which at last destroyed it lie on the surface, and for that reason, perhaps, have often been wrongly stated although never wholly missed. It has been said that it fell because the government of a city state could not manage an empire, but this only raises the question of why it could not, and few historians have made any attempt at a reply. In fact, several city states did govern empires, Athens and Carthage, for example, and only fell before external attacks. Rome also succeeded in the attempt for at least a century, and this in itself shows that the thing was not impossible. What really destroyed the Republic was the loss of all control over the army by the constitutional government, for no government which is unable to control its army can long endure. The reasons why the Roman soldiers were prepared to support their general against the state have been explained already, but it may be appropriate to point out here why no remedy could be found. That a remedy was possible is fairly obvious, for the senate had merely to give an adequate guaranty to the soldiers that they would receive their rewards to weaken very materially the power of the general over them. This would, however, have required a well thought out policy persisted in for a considerable length of time, and when such a policy became necessary it had also become impossible. The Roman constitution provided so many and such varied means of obstruction and its magistrates were changed at such short intervals that it could work efficiently only when dominated by a strong political machine, that is, by a class bound together by definite political and economic interests and able to control the assembly so as to ensure the election of magistrates willing to carry out the policy of the governing class and the enactment of the necessary legislation. In early times the senate had been the directing board of such a machine, but the economic and social changes which accompanied the acquisition of an empire undermined it and left it in too precarious a position to carry out, or even to think of, any extensive plans. All that the senate could do, when the supremacy of the nobles might be overthrown at any moment by a combination of the rabble and the knights, was to cling tenaciously to the shadow of power, letting events take their course with little attempt to control them. The Empire solved the problem by establishing a regular standing army and a special treasury where funds were accumulated with which to reward the soldiers when their term of service expired. Under the Republic such a solution was not within the field of practical politics, for the senate was too weak to carry drastic reforms even if their necessity had been perceived. Nothing short of drastic reforms, however, could save the Republic; and the blunders of the conscript fathers merely hastened an end which their weakness made inevitable.

## CHAPTER XVII

## THE SECOND TRIUMVIRATE

### § 1. THE PROSCRIPTION

AT their conference the future Triumvirs determined to begin their government with a proscription. The murder of Cæsar seemed to be the result of his clemency and to justify a reversion to Sulla's policy, while the financial needs of the treasury could be most easily met in this way. Nevertheless, there was a long debate between them, and tradition represents Octavian as opposed to the measure. However this may have been, drawing up the list of victims presented serious difficulties, which were only adjusted by allowing each of the three to put down any names he pleased regardless of the opposition of the others; Octavian thus sacrificed Cicero to the resentment of Antony, who could not be expected to forget or forgive the orator's Philippics, and Lepidus gave up his own brother. Instructions were at once despatched to Pedius, the other consul, who had remained in Rome when Octavian left the city, directing the immediate arrest and execution of the most prominent men whose names headed the fatal list. This matter attended to, the Triumvirs marched rapidly on Rome, each accompanied by a picked body of troops.

The executions which had already taken place had thrown the city into a panic, so that when the three arrived before its walls no difficulty was experienced in persuading the terrified assembly to enact a law by which Antony, Lepidus, and Octavian were named Triumvirs for the Regulation of the Republic and invested with the supreme authority for a period of five years. As soon as they were installed in office their entire list was published with a preamble attempting to justify the proscription. Needless to say, the financial needs of the Triumvirs were not mentioned, though they were the real reason for the inclusion of the majority of the names, but emphasis was laid on the disastrous results of Cæsar's clemency and on the danger to the state of leaving enemies behind to take advantage of any opportunity which might arise while they were fighting M. Brutus and Cassius in the East. Despite such disguises, the confiscations which were an integral part of the measure must have made its main purpose clear enough to all. The Triumvirs had made extravagant promises to their soldiers, and with an empty treasury there was no way of redeeming these promises or even providing the regular pay except by plunder, and to this the proscription gave a show of legality.

All Italy now witnessed a second time the scenes which had made the dictatorship of Sulla a nightmare long remembered and passionately loathed : rewards were offered for the betrayal of the victims and punishment threatened against all who aided or concealed them ; side by side with cases of treachery on the part of slaves (sometimes well deserved) and of friends and relatives were instances of self-sacrifice and devotion. Three hundred senators and some two * thousand knights were included in the list, but a few succeeded in escaping, some to seek temporary safety in the camp of M. Brutus in Macedonia, more to find a refuge with Sextus Pompeius, then at the head of a powerful fleet in the Western Mediterranean.

Cicero sent his family across the Adriatic and might himself have joined Brutus, but he hesitated. He was a broken man and preferred to die with the Republic which he had striven valiantly and unsuccessfully to save. At the urgent solicitation of his friends he finally embarked, but turned back on account of the weather, resolved to wait quietly for death. His friends renewed their entreaties, to which he again yielded and set out in a litter to take ship once more, but it was now too late, and he was overtaken by Antony's soldiers. His slaves and attendants were eager to defend him, but he forbade them and leaned forward in his litter, offering his neck to the sword of the military executioner. His head was struck off and sent to Rome, where Antony placed it on the rostra, and his wife Fulvia, formerly the wife of Clodius, thrust a bodkin through the tongue which had spoken so eloquently in denunciation of both her husbands.

To criticize Cicero is an easy task because we have his private letters, which reveal pitilessly all his weaknesses and all his hesitations, doubts, and miscalculations. Augustus permitted no such revelations in the case of Cæsar, so that we have to judge him solely by his acts. If we were to judge Cicero in the same way, ignoring his letters to Atticus and to the members of his own family, his course would appear in a very different light, and it would be an easy matter to represent it as courageous and consistent throughout. Yet it is better so, and the friends of the great orator judged wisely in publishing his letters. What he loses in greatness he more than gains by the intimacy with which he is known to us, and, while we may admire him less as a statesman, we esteem him more as a man. Cicero was intensely human and had some very obvious weaknesses, of which the chief was vanity, but his faults are trivial beside the finer qualities which are unconsciously displayed. He was honest, humane, and true to his friends at all costs, even if sometimes rather too bitter towards his enemies. The fact that he rated his achievements somewhat too highly should not blind us to their real importance. As consul he did suppress a dangerous conspiracy and did display coolness, resolution, and capacity. After his consulship he tried, perhaps a little clumsily at times, to reconcile the senate with Pompey, and if he could have done so he would have prolonged the life of the Republic for many years. His failure was due to the uncompromising attitude of the nobles far more than to any fault of his. He saw clearly that the Civil War must result in the destruction of the Republic no matter who might be the victor, and he did everything within his power to avert it. Here again he failed because he could not persuade Pompey to follow his advice. He joined Pompey without hope and accepted the result of Pharsalus as final. He lived quietly under Cæsar, and, if his exultation in the Ides of March is repellent to modern ideas, it was in accord with the sentiments and convictions of his own day and class. After the murder he strove with all his might to restore the Republic, by which both he and his contemporaries meant the senate. He was well aware that he risked his life, but he never shrank from danger when he felt certain of the right, and his hesitation between Cæsar and Pompey was largely the result of his conviction that *both* were in the wrong. Many years after his death, which was certainly as heroic as that of Cato, Augustus pronounced a judgment upon him to which history must subscribe. It chanced that the emperor one day found one of his grandsons reading a work of Cicero; the youth tried to conceal it, but Augustus took it from him and stood reading for a time. At last he handed it back, saying gravely, "A great man, my boy, and one who loved his country."[1]

## § 2. PHILIPPI

After the funeral of Cæsar the conspirators had fled from Rome, and finally C. Cassius took refuge in the East and M. Junius Brutus in Macedonia, from which Antony had recalled most of the legions for his war with Decimus. In the redistribution of the provinces which Antony carried out Syria had been assigned to Dolabella, his colleague in the consulship after the murder of Cæsar. Dolabella hastened to his new province, of which Cassius had secured possession. On his way he passed through Asia, where Trebonius, one of the conspirators, was in charge. He attempted to stop Dolabella, but fell into his hands and was murdered. In Syria, however, Dolabella in his turn was captured and put to death by Cassius. In Macedonia Brutus was able to secure the command of the troops remaining in the province, and both he and Cassius set energetically to work to raise powerful armies.

While they were thus engaged the war around Mutina was fought and the Second Triumvirate formed. Cicero made frantic appeals to them to bring such forces as they had to Italy at once. Probably Cassius was too far away to have arrived in time, but Brutus could apparently have given some support to Cicero if he had tried. Perhaps his army was too weak to have affected the result, but the reason which he put forward in his letters to Cicero was his disapproval of the orator's policy. He seems to have been an obstinate and conceited doctrinaire who was wholly convinced that he could judge the situation in Italy better than Cicero. He objected strongly to the latter's alliance with Octavian and would have nothing to do with anyone who bore the name of

[1] Plutarch, *Cicero,* ch. 49.

Cæsar. Moreover, he seems to have cherished the absurd delusion that a reconciliation between Antony and the senate was possible. Disgusted because those upon the spot did not follow his advice, he refused to come to their assistance and left the Republic to its fate. After the Triumvirate was established it was too late to save his friends, and he could only continue his preparations for the inevitable struggle.

As soon as the Triumvirs had crushed all possible resistance in Italy, they undertook to deal with their enemies in the East. Antony and Octavian crossed to Greece, leaving Lepidus in charge at Rome. Cassius had moved westward with the forces which he had gathered, while Brutus retreated to Asia, where they united their armies and led them back to Europe. The issue was decided at Philippi, near the modern Kavala.

Brutus and Cassius occupied separate camps in a strong position, where Brutus was protected from a flanking movement by mountains and Cassius by a swamp. They could afford to stand on the defensive, since they could depend on their fleet for supplies while their opponents had no such resource. Antony attempted to cut off Cassius from his fleet by building a dyke through the swamp, and Cassius tried to stop him by building a counter-dyke. When Cassius' lines had been weakened by the drawing off of a large number of men for work on the counter-dyke, Antony made an unexpected attack and stormed the camp, but he was unable to hold it and fell back. While this was happening the soldiers of Brutus attacked the forces of Octavian and took his camp, although he himself escaped, but they likewise retreated to their original position. The battle, therefore, had no result from a military point of view, but Cassius, discouraged by his defeat and believing that Brutus had also been beaten, gave way to despair and committed suicide. His death proved the ruin of the Republicans. He was a much abler and more experienced general than Brutus, who was left in sole command surrounded by refugees whom he had not the firmness to withstand. For twenty days he held out against the clamour of those about him and refused to give battle, but at length he allowed his own judgment to be overborne. It was a fatal blunder, for winter was at hand, and the Triumvirs were having great difficulty in feeding their armies, so that the weakness of Brutus saved them from a dangerous situation. When he offered battle he threw away his advantage, and after a desperate struggle his army was routed. Brutus, knowing that there was no hope of mercy for him, though like Cato he would probably have scorned to live in any case, killed himself, and most of the proscribed who did not follow his example were put to death by the Triumvirs. A few, however, were spared by Antony, and a few others succeeded in making their escape and later received a pardon, among whom were the son of Cicero and the poet Horace.

The second battle of Philippi placed the world at the feet of the victors, but many serious problems still remained to be solved. Since Cassius had upset all previous arrangements in the East, a general settlement of affairs in that region had to be undertaken at once. Moreover, the Triumvirs were in need of money, for the proscription had yielded much less than was probably expected, and in spite of the fact that Cassius had plundered far and near to get funds for the war, the East was still the richest portion of the Roman world, so that here if anywhere there was a prospect of replenishing the exhausted treasury. Another obvious task which admitted of no delay was to disband a large number of the soldiers then under arms. A reduction in the size of the army was essential to relieve the treasury, but it was impossible to discharge the men without giving them their promised rewards in the shape of allotments of land. Since land for this purpose could not be purchased, there was no alternative to new confiscations, which were certain to entail difficulties and intense unpopularity. The victorious Triumvirs were thus faced by a double task, and there could be no question either as to which part of the work was the easier and the more attractive, or as to which of the two conquerors would have the power of choice, for throughout the campaign which ended at Philippi Octavian had been ill, so that the glory of success fell almost entirely to Antony. The young Cæsar was thus in no position to dispute his partner's wishes, and it was determined that Antony should undertake the reorganization of the East, while Octavian returned to Italy to deal with the veterans as best he might. To this it is possible that Octavian was ready to agree, for he may have had the acuteness to discern that Italy was the real key to the empire, and that to secure control there might in the long run give him a decisive advantage over his partner. There were other arrangements however, to which it is difficult to believe that he would have consented if he had been able to refuse. Antony was not only to take charge of the East, but he was to have all of Gaul except the Cisalpine province as well. Octavian was to receive Spain, Sardinia, Africa, and Sicily, while Cisalpine Gaul was to be incorporated with Italy. Lepidus was contemptuously ignored, and the provinces he had held taken away from him. In the end, however, Octavian thought it wise to placate him to some extent by giving him Africa. Henceforth he subsided into insignificance and was a member of the Triumvirate in name only. He had never had a real hold on his soldiers, so that his stronger colleagues could set him aside at their pleasure.

### § 3. THE PERUSINE WAR

When the arrangements indicated above had been agreed upon, Antony set out for the East, while Octavian returned to Italy with a large body of veterans to begin his work of disbandment and confiscation. He was not long in discovering the difficulties and dangers of his task, for the soldiers demanded that the richest towns should be handed over to them, to which the townspeople objected that it was unfair to make them bear the entire burden of providing for the veterans, and that it should fall upon the country as a whole. Expostulation was soon followed by resistance and disorder, and to make matters worse Antony's wife, Fulvia, and his brother Lucius put themselves at the head of the malcontents, repudiating the written agreement which Antony had signed, so that between the desperate landowners and the irritated soldiers the position of Octavian became one of real danger. L. Antonius, who was one of the consuls for the year, was at the head of a large force of his brother's soldiers, and Octavian was forced to undertake a war against him. Had all the Antonian troops in the West joined Lucius he would probably have won, but both the officers and men were uncertain what to do, for Antony's partner could show a written agreement with him, which it might be as dangerous to disregard as to disobey his wife and brother, who gave verbal assurances that

Antony disapproved of his partner's proceedings. The men, perhaps, felt some sympathy with Octavian, whose difficulties seemed to be due chiefly to his attempt to give them their rewards, so that the situation was one of great perplexity for the Antonian governors in Gaul, and on the whole they seem to have done as little as possible and to have given Lucius no real support.[1] As a result of their inaction Octavian was able to drive Lucius into the town of Perusia and to blockade him there.

After a siege of some duration Lucius was forced to surrender. Octavian, who had every reason to dread a war with Antony, allowed Lucius and Fulvia to depart unharmed, but he put to death some of those who had taken sides with them. Nevertheless, in spite of the care which he had taken to avoid giving Antony any personal offence, Octavian was apprehensive and made haste to secure control of the West as far as possible. Opportunely for him Antony's governor in Gaul, Fufius Calenus, died at this moment, and Octavian at once took over his legions and provinces. Italy, Gaul, and Spain had now come under his authority, but he had ceded Africa to Lepidus and Sicily had been seized by Sextus Pompeius. At length Antony returned from the East to demand an explanation of recent events. Why he had not returned sooner must remain a matter of conjecture. The ancient historians attribute his delay to his infatuation with Cleopatra. The Egyptian queen having incurred the displeasure of the Triumvirs during their war with the Republicans, Antony had summoned her to meet him in Cilicia ; she came and vindicated herself so successfully that her judge accompanied her to Egypt as her lover. Nevertheless, she cannot furnish an adequate explanation of his inaction, for the quarrel between his relatives and Octavian had broken out before he met her, and he soon proved that he was not so deeply in love with her that he could not bear a long separation. His real reason was probably that he felt himself unable to interfere, since Octavian was merely carrying out a bargain to which he had agreed. Moreover, he may well have been doubtful of the attitude of his army in view of the fact that Octavian's difficulties were due to his attempts to reward the veterans. We may conjecture that he would not have been displeased if his

[1] See Reinhold, *The Perusine War*.

wife and brother had succeeded in overthrowing his partner, but that he did not care to take the risk of supporting them in the attempt. The seizure of his legions and provinces, however, he could not ignore, and he returned to settle matters with Octavian.

### § 4. THE TREATIES OF BRUNDISIUM AND MISENUM

At first a war between the two Triumvirs seemed inevitable. Sextus Pompeius sought to ally himself with Antony, but the latter was not ready to commit himself, although a friendly understanding between the two was reached. When Antony arrived at Brundisium he found the town garrisoned by his rival and was refused admittance. He had begun a siege of the place when Octavian appeared at the head of an army. Instead of fighting, however, negotiations were opened in which the representatives of the armies took a prominent part. The two leaders yielded to the pressure of their officers and men, so that a reconciliation was the result. Probably both Triumvirs were more or less willing to give way. Octavian may well have felt doubtful of the loyalty of the legions so recently taken from Antony, without which his army was decidedly the weaker, while Antony had left many things in the East unsettled. Moreover, he had determined to attempt the conquest of Parthia in accordance with Cæsar's plans, and if the attempt were successful there would be little reason to fear Octavian. Probably Antony was willing to arrange a temporary peace in order to secure a free hand in the East, where the Parthians, instead of waiting to be attacked, were invading Syria. A peace, of course, meant a compromise, but a compromise is generally possible when both sides are really desirous of one. After extended negotiations a treaty was finally concluded at Brundisium (40 B.C.), by which Antony allowed Octavian to retain the Gallic provinces, but some of the legions were to be restored to him. This arrangement left Octavian master of the West and Antony of the East, while both were to have an equal right to levy troops in Italy. At the moment Antony might feel that his bargain was not a bad one, since, if he invaded Parthia, Gaul would be of little use to him, and he secured considerable reinforcements for his army. A marriage was also arranged between Antony and Octavia, the sister of his fellow-Triumvir.[1] The position of Sextus Pompeius was left in doubt; Octavian was to try to come to terms with him, but if this proved impossible Antony agreed to lend assistance in a war.

After the treaty of Brundisium was concluded the two Triumvirs proceeded to Rome, where their reconciliation was hailed with enthusiasm. The rejoicings, however, were of short duration. Famine threatened the city as a result of the * occupation of Sicily by Sextus, and the populace was anxious to have some kind of a peace patched up with him, so that the corn supply might be assured. Both Antony and Octavian realized that a lasting peace with Sextus was impossible, and had resolved to put an end to his career, but their announcement of new taxes for a war against him was met by riotous demonstrations which became so serious that they yielded and opened negotiations. Sextus at first demanded that he should replace Lepidus in the Triumvirate, and the negotiations seemed on the point of failure, but he was finally induced to moderate his terms, so that at length an agreement was reached, and a definite treaty, known as the treaty of Misenum, was signed (39 B.C.). By this treaty Sextus was to retain the government of Sicily and Sardinia, but was to furnish Rome with the grain which she had formerly obtained from these islands. He was to be given the consulship in the near future, and all who had sought refuge with him, except the assassins of Cæsar, were to receive a pardon. Those of them who had been included in the proscription were to have one-fourth of their confiscated property restored, while the run-away slaves among his followers were to be set free, and the free men in his service were promised the same rewards as the soldiers of the Triumvirs.

The treaty of Misenum having been concluded, Antony with Octavia proceeded to Greece. Rome, which had been delighted with the prospect of peace and plenty, soon found that the prospect was an illusion. A number of exiles and refugees made haste to return to the city, but the supplies that had been counted upon failed to materialize, and in spite of the treaty Octavian and Sextus Pompeius were soon at war with each other.

[1] Antony's former wife, Fulvia, died very shortly after her release from Perusia.

In this new struggle Octavian might have fared badly if he had still been the same youth who had confronted Antony after the Ides of March, for his antagonist was powerful and his own position in Italy somewhat insecure. From the first he had shown himself shrewd and calculating beyond his years and had cleverly availed himself of the magic of Cæsar's name to push his way to the front. He had played the game with such courage, coolness, and astuteness as to keep his head above water in a storm wherein many others perished miserably. Nevertheless, although his whole importance rested on the allegiance of soldiers, he had shown no particular military talent. His health was delicate and he was frequently ill, sometimes at very inconvenient moments, as at Philippi. In every battle in which he had so far been engaged the credit of the victory had gone to others, and it seemed very possible that the legions would grow weary of a sickly young man with no achievements to his credit. Octavian, however, had grown intellectually in the stormy years he had passed through; he had learned to know men and to recognize his own limitations. He had gathered about him a small circle of devoted friends upon whose loyalty he could rely, among whom were some men of great ability. It is one of the most important gifts of a ruler to know how to use others, and this gift Octavian now began to show that he possessed. In Mæcenas he found an adviser and diplomat of rare disinterestedness and wisdom, while in Agrippa he discovered one of the best generals of the day. In the negotiations with Antony which resulted in the treaty of Brundisium he owed much to Mæcenas, and in the war with Sextus Pompeius he was successful largely because he placed the conduct of the operations in the strong and capable hands of Agrippa. Henceforth Octavian appears more and more as a statesman and administrator, and it was in these directions that his real greatness lay.

## § 5. SEXTUS POMPEIUS

The career of Sextus Pompeius merits a brief survey at this point because his final ruin was to a large extent the natural result of his past. He was the younger son of Pompey, who sent him with his elder brother Gnæus to the East at the outbreak of the Civil War. After the murder of their father, which Sextus witnessed from shipboard, both sons succeeded in joining the remnant of his followers in Africa, but neither took any prominent part in the African war. The Republicans sent Gnæus to Spain, where a rebellion had broken out against the governor whom Cæsar had appointed, and after the battle of Thapsus Sextus made his escape and joined his brother there. After Cæsar's decisive victory at Munda Gnæus escaped for a time, but was killed soon afterwards, and Sextus, who was not present at the battle, succeeded in finding a refuge in Northern Spain, where for a time he concealed his identity and maintained himself as a robber and pirate on a small scale. After Cæsar's return to Rome he grew bolder, and when his identity became known he gradually gained strength. The officers sent by Cæsar to dispose of him were unable to check the steady increase of his power, and soon after the Ides of March he was in possession of Farther Spain with a considerable army and fleet. Neither of the parties then struggling for the mastery in Italy cared particularly for Sextus, yet both sought to secure his alliance against the other. In this contest Antony was upon the whole the more successful; he and Dolabella having bought the property of Pompey, Antony offered to restore it, and the senate voted to recall Sextus, who had been declared an outlaw, and to indemnify him from the treasury. While the war around Mutina was in progress, Sextus moved to Massilia with his army and fleet to observe events. If he had acted with promptness and decision, he might have had an influence on their course, but he contented himself with the role of a passive spectator. Cicero appealed to him, and the senate named him commander of the fleets of the Republic in vain; probably he regarded both parties with well justified distrust, for neither had any real use for another Pompey. Nevertheless, his inaction was a blunder, for as soon as the Second Triumvirate was formed the Triumvirs threw off the pretence of friendliness and included the name of Sextus in their proscription list. This was the end of whatever hopes Sextus had entertained of returning to his country, and he found himself once more a fugitive and an outlaw. The armies of his enemies in Gaul, Spain, and Italy were too strong for him to encounter, so that he was forced with such ships as he had gathered to resume his career as a pirate without a land base for his operations, but this deficiency was soon supplied by the seizure of Sicily. Octavian made some unsuccessful attempts to dislodge him before leaving Italy for the campaign against M. Brutus and Cassius, and after the battle of Philippi the Perusine War made energetic measures against him impossible, so that his power continued to grow unchecked. His following was of a very miscellaneous character ; the most respectable element in it was composed of the refugees who had fled to him after each successive catastrophe : a number of the proscribed, Republicans who had escaped from the ruin of their cause at Philippi, fugitives who had taken the wrong side in the Perusine War, and landowners whose property had been confiscated to provide for the veterans. With these, who may be said to represent the better class of Italians, were joined much larger numbers of pirates, bandits, runaway slaves, and young Italians eager for gain and attracted by Pompey's name. It would seem that Sextus had all the materials for a strong army, as he certainly had the ships for a powerful fleet, but either he lacked organizing capacity or he had to contend with difficulties of which we are ignorant. For whatever reason, he did not place his more respectable Roman adherents in positions of authority, his chief officers being freedmen. He also failed to take advantage of the Perusine War to attack Octavian, although he did enter into negotiations with Antony, forming a sort of half-way alliance with him, and seized Sardinia in addition to Sicily. By the treaty of Brundisium Antony threw him over, but the Triumvirs found it expedient to conclude peace with him by the treaty of Misenum. Although the terms appear very advantageous to Sextus, they were really a disaster for him, since most of the respectable Italians returned home, leaving him more dependent than ever on the worst elements among his followers.

When Antony departed for the East at the end of 39 B.C., Octavian was left face to face with Sextus. Although they were nominally at peace, the situation was an impossible one, for Octavian, being responsible for the grain supply of Rome, could not acquiesce in the control of Sicily by another, and Sextus seems to have had imperfect control over his followers. A war between them was inevitable, and it seems hardly worth while to speculate as to which should bear the chief respon sibility. Octavian was at first severely handicapped by the lack of a strong fleet, so that for a time Sextus seemed to have the better of the war, but Octavian gained an advantage when Sextus attempted to recall his commander, Menodorus, from Sardinia; Menodorus at once deserted and handed over his province and ships to Octavian.[1]

Meanwhile Antony had been busy in Greece, but at length found it necessary for several reasons to return to Italy. He was a party to the treaty with Sextus, and was not disposed to leave him to his fate without receiving some concessions from Octavian as the price; his relations with his partner were becoming strained, for in spite of the treaty of Brundisium, by which both Triumvirs had an equal right to gather recruits in Italy, Antony found that his recruits failed to reach him, being constantly diverted or held back by Octavian on various pretexts; in addition, the five years for which the Triumvirs had been appointed were drawing to a close, and Antony's plans required that their powers should be renewed. Accordingly he returned and concluded at Tarentum a new treaty with Octavian (37 B.C.), by which he abandoned Sextus and agreed to furnish his partner with a fleet to use against him. Convinced by experience that the right to recruit men in Italy was useless, Antony demanded in return for his ships that Octavian should send him 20,000 Roman soldiers for service in the East.

After concluding this bargain the two proceeded to Rome, where they had the Triumvirate prolonged for another five years. Antony then sailed for the East to undertake his long-deferred invasion of Parthia, and Octavian was free to continue his struggle against Sextus. During the winter Agrippa, working with tireless energy, constructed a powerful fleet, which was ready for action by the summer of 36 B.C., when it had been determined that the war with Sextus should be resumed. The plans of Octavian contemplated an invasion of Sicily from three sides at once; Lepidus from Africa was to attack from the south, Statilius Taurus, with the 120 ships contributed by Antony, was to sail from Tarentum

[1] Menodorus was one of the freedmen of the great Pompey. Since Octavian did not give him an independent command, he went back to Sextus and finally deserted again to Octavian, who pardoned his offences but made no use of him.

to the Eastern coast, while Agrippa and Octavian were to operate with the new fleet from the north. At first fortune favoured Sextus, for a storm compelled both Agrippa and Taurus to turn back. Lepidus, however, was able to effect a landing in the West, where he captured Lilybæum, and then marched eastward. Agrippa succeeded in repairing the damage to his fleet and seized the islands to the north of Sicily, from which point he was able to land troops on the island itself. Sextus was at Messana, and he had concentrated most of his fleet and army in the vicinity. Octavian, in Southern Italy, finally secured the Antonian squadron, with which he hoped to land troops on the east coast of Sicily and so pen Sextus up in Messana. Sextus realized the danger of his position, since he was unable to prevent the constant despatch of reinforcements from Italy as long as his enemies had a strong fleet with which to protect the transportation of troops. His one hope seemed to lie in the destruction of their fleet, so that, although their ships greatly outnumbered his, he decided to risk a naval engagement. Accordingly, on September 3, his fleet met that of Agrippa off the promontory of Naulochus in a battle in which it was practically annihilated, of his 200 ships 160 being either captured or destroyed. Sextus himself managed to escape with a few ships and fled to Asia to seek refuge with Antony, who was then engaged in the invasion of Parthia. The representatives of the absent Triumvir at first received him and gave him permission to live quietly as a private citizen, but his old habits proved too strong, and he soon engaged in new intrigues, attempting to gather a following for fresh adventures. Although for a time he met with some success, he could not maintain himself against Antony's officers and was soon captured and put to death, perhaps without express orders from Antony.

One can hardly help feeling a good deal of sympathy for Sextus, however much one may condemn some episodes in his career. Theoretically he should have submitted to Cæsar after Munda, if not before, and there can be little doubt that Cæsar would have pardoned him, but Sextus is hardly to be blamed if he felt less sure of this than we do to-day, and a natural pride forbade it. Refusing to submit, he could be nothing but an adventurer fighting for his own advancement. He must have possessed considerable ability, for otherwise he could not have rallied such forces as he did after Munda and confronted, if only for a time, the victorious Triumvirs upon not unequal terms. Just how great a man he was he had little opportunity to show. His strength was always greater in appearance than in reality, for, though he had ships and men in abundance, neither his land nor his maritime forces were composed of materials from which he was able to create a powerful and trustworthy fleet or army. His success was so largely due to the temporary weakness or preoccupation of others that he fell as soon as he encountered a resolute and well-prepared enemy.

### § 6. THE DEPOSITION OF LEPIDUS

After the flight of Sextus his army had no disposition to continue a hopeless struggle, but Octavian soon found himself confronted by a new enemy in the person of his fellow-Triumvir Lepidus. The latter had come from Africa ostensibly to help in the war with Sextus, but really in the hope of regaining a genuine place in the Triumvirate. He had long impotently resented the contemptuous manner in which he had been treated by his partners, and he now thought he saw an opportunity of reasserting himself. He induced the land forces of Pompey to surrender to him rather than to Octavian and thus found himself at the head of a larger army than the latter had with him in Sicily. Emboldened by this fact, he assumed an independent and even arrogant attitude, but Octavian refused to be intimidated. Knowing that the soldiers of Lepidus had little affection or respect for him, he made overtures to them with such success that they deserted their commander, who was thus left completely at the mercy of the colleague he had ventured to defy. Octavian deposed him from his position as Triumvir, but spared his life and permitted him to reside as a sort of state prisoner in Italy until his death some twenty-three years later. The Triumvirate thus became a duumvirate in fact, although for the moment the change made no perceptible difference, for Lepidus had been practically ignored almost from the first, and his partners continued to style themselves Triumvirs after his fall. Nevertheless, the situation was materially changed by his elimination, since it left Octavian and Antony obvious and inevitable rivals. Octavian was now undisputed master of the West, as Antony was of the East, and a final struggle between them could not be averted, though it might be postponed. Lepidus was not a man of much ability or energy, but if he had remained in command of an army in Africa he would have been a source of grave anxiety to both Octavian and Antony and might have exercised a decisive influence upon the course of history. His disappearance from the scene greatly simplified the situation and so contributed in some measure to the ultimate triumph of Octavian.

## CHAPTER XVIII

# OCTAVIAN AND ANTONY

### § 1. ANTONY'S INVASION OF PARTHIA

AFTER the treaty of Misenum (39 B.C.) Antony hastened with his wife, Octavia, to Greece, for during his stay in Italy the Parthians had invaded Syria and overrun the province. To deal with them he despatched Ventidius Bassus to Syria, while he himself remained for some time in Athens. Ventidius did his work so promptly and well that by the spring of 38 the Parthians had been driven back into their own country. Perhaps from jealousy of his achievements, Antony recalled him and prepared to take command of the Eastern operations in person. Before doing so, however, he returned to Italy, where he made a new arrangement with Octavian (the treaty of Tarentum) and secured the prolongation of the Triumvirate (37 B.C.). Antony then proceeded to Syria to make the final preparations for the conquest of Parthia, sending Octavia back to Italy on account of the impending war.[1] His army was strong enough for his purpose, but money was needed, and he found a ready means of obtaining it by a close alliance with Cleopatra.

When Cæsar was murdered, Cleopatra, who had been living in Rome as his mistress, promptly retired to Egypt, where she was soon freed from her young brother and husband, Ptolemy XIII, very probably by poison. When Antony first came to the East after Philippi she had persuaded him to confirm her position as ruler of Egypt and to take Cæsar's place as her lover; however, the Perusine War soon forced him to return to Italy, and since then he had paid no further attention to her. Now, on the eve of his invasion of Parthia,

[1] Perhaps it would be more accurate to say on the pretext of the impending war.

he summoned her to Antioch and married her according to the customs of the East.[1] Such a marriage, although not recognized by the Romans, made him king of Egypt in the eyes of the Egyptians. It is quite possible that Antony was already in love with Cleopatra, but he had left her for some two years, and it is difficult to escape the conclusion that his close alliance with her at this time was partly due to political considerations. Egypt was the one Eastern land which had not been plundered in the course of the civil wars, and its queen had a well-filled treasury. Antony could have seized the money by violence, but by such a course he ran the risk of provoking a revolt, so that he must have taken a considerable force with him to Alexandria. This would have upset his plans, and when he started for Parthia it might be necessary to weaken his army by leaving a powerful garrison in Egypt. On the other hand the legitimate queen could furnish money and maintain herself against all malcontents with very little help if she had behind her the open and acknowledged support of Rome. The marriage might therefore appear a clever stroke of policy. So far Antony was pursuing Roman aims and seeking to pose as Cæsar's true successor by carrying out his well-known designs. If he conquered Parthia there could be little doubt that he would be able to deal with Octavian and to cast Cleopatra aside if he chose.

In making plans for the Parthian War, Cæsar, warned by the fate of Crassus, had determined to use Armenia as a base for his operations. From there he had planned to descend upon Mesopotamia and to capture the important cities in that region, hoping to force the Parthians to risk a battle in their defence. Only after Mesopotamia had been subdued did he intend to invade the vast semi-arid plateau of Persia, where the prestige of the Parthian dynasty would have been weakened by the loss of Mesopotamia. The plan was well conceived, and in Cæsar's hands it might have been successful; but Antony was not Cæsar, and when he tried to carry out the designs of his great master he failed disastrously.

In 36 B.C. Antony began the long-deferred invasion. His

[1] The date of the marriage is disputed; some scholars think it took place later, perhaps only after the divorce of Octavia. I have adopted the view of Kromayer, which seems to me probably correct. For a discussion with references see Holmes, *The Architect of the Roman Empire*, I, pp. 227–31.

first error was in reposing too much confidence in the loyalty of the Armenian king, who deserted him, with the result that the Parthians succeeded in capturing most of his baggage. Antony was then besieging Phraaspa, the capital of Media Atropatene, whose king was a vassal of the Parthians, and he now found himself obliged to continue his operations without the equipment he had brought with him for the purpose. He was soon surrounded by the Parthian cavalry, who prevented the sending out of foraging parties, so that the loss of the supplies which he had expected from Armenia forced him to abandon the invasion and retreat as best he could. For a time it seemed likely that he would meet the fate of Crassus, but Antony rose to the occasion; marching with his men and sharing their hardships, he managed to retain their devotion and was able to reach Syria once more with a large part of his army (35 B.C.).

## § 2. THE NEW SITUATION

This failure destroyed much of Antony's prestige. He had expected to return as a triumphant conqueror, but instead he came back a defeated general who had saved himself by a masterly retreat. Much more important than this, however, was the fact that his army had suffered heavy losses, so that his first task was to fill the gaps in its ranks. The 20,000 soldiers promised him by Octavian were sorely needed, but he looked for them in vain. In place of the reinforcements Octavian sent his wife Octavia with some 2000 men and the ships which Antony had lent him for the war with Sextus Pompeius. The meaning of this was unmistakable: Octavian hoped to destroy Antony by cutting off his supply of recruits, for in the East Antony's army must slowly but surely melt away unless the Italian veterans, who were its solid nucleus, could be replaced as wounds or age disqualified them for service. It was war to the death between the two Triumvirs, and if Antony were to win he must force the issue without too much delay. This he thoroughly understood, but he was not ready to act at once. It was necessary for him to allow his soldiers some time to recuperate after the toil and hardship of the retreat and to restore as much as possible of his prestige. On the other side Octavian was anxious to delay the final breach as long as possible,[1] and so, though both men knew that they were at war, neither chose to make an open declaration of the fact for a time. Antony refused to receive Octavia and sent her back to her brother, but without divorcing her, and Octavian received her quietly.

Although Antony's position was difficult, it seemed by no means desperate ; he still had a powerful army thoroughly devoted to him, his prestige in the East was lowered but not wholly destroyed, and in Italy and Rome he retained a strong following. To re-establish himself in the eyes of the Eastern peoples of the empire, he must punish the Armenian king for the treachery which had ruined his invasion of Parthia. Accordingly, in the spring of 34 B.C., he marched into Armenia, pretending all the while that he wished the king's help in some measures which he was planning against the Parthians. By means of these pretences the king was finally induced to come to Antony's camp for a friendly conference, and Antony at once arrested him. The Armenians chose a new king and made some attempt at resistance, but a single engagement put an end to the war, and Antony was able to occupy the country, and to return to Egypt with a little easily won glory.

With Armenia apparently subdued, Antony had to choose between two alternatives : as a Roman general and proconsul he could invade the West and deal with Octavian, or he could adopt the policy which Cleopatra urged upon him, abandoning the West to his rival and attempting to create a powerful Eastern empire. Whichever course he took he ran a serious risk of failure, but he had also a chance of success. He attempted, however, to combine the two, so that, if he were defeated by Octavian, he could fall back upon the East and hold it against his rival.

In the absence of definite evidence we can only conjecture Cleopatra's aims and the extent of her influence. Fortunately, on these points it is possible to make so plausible a guess that it cannot be very far from the truth. The dynasty of which Cleopatra was the representative after an auspicious beginning had long been declining in power. The causes of this decline were easy to discern. The Ptolemies were a Greek family

[1] Delay would obviously weaken Antony's army, and besides Octavian was occupied at the time by a campaign in Illyricum (35–34 B.C.).

ruling in Egypt; and their power had always been based on the support of an army of Greek mercenaries. The Egyptians had no share in the government, their function being to pay taxes to the royal treasury and thus to furnish the necessary means to keep them in subjection. This system worked well as long as the Ptolemies ruled not only Egypt but Greek lands as well, where they could readily recruit their army of occupation, and in time of danger strengthen it as much as necessary. When Rome obtained the mastery of these lands it became impossible to find soldiers without her permission, so that their military strength steadily declined. To restore their greatness and render them independent of Rome the first essential was to regain a recruiting ground where they could find the materials for a strong Greek army, and this they could only secure as a gift from Rome, because she held the only territories available for the purpose. A less clever woman than Cleopatra could readily have seen the situation in its true light, and no Ptolemy could help wishing to remedy the weakness of his house. Cleopatra sought to restore the power of her family by using her own personal charm to induce first Cæsar and then Antony to restore to the Ptolemies some at least of their former possessions outside the valley of the Nile. Whether she ever dreamed of ruling the whole Roman and Greek world as the acknowledged consort of either cannot be determined with certainty, but her precarious position in Egypt drove her to exert all her influence to secure from each such support as would keep her on the throne, and she must have ardently desired to obtain from them enough Greek territory to free her from dependence upon the weaknesses or the temporary policy of Roman proconsuls. Antony's support had enabled her to hold her throne despite the smouldering discontent of her subjects, but if he returned to Italy, leaving her nothing more serious to rely upon than a marriage which in Roman eyes was no marriage at all, her position would be as precarious as ever. It can hardly be doubted that she tried earnestly to persuade him to give her some districts outside the valley of the Nile from which she could draw recruits, but until his return from Parthia he had done very little, perhaps because the territories she coveted must be taken from Rome, and he dreaded the resentment which such a cession would produce.

### § 3. THE DONATIONS OF ALEXANDRIA

Although Antony had not yielded far to her policy while he hoped to conquer Parthia, whatever may have been his infatuation with the queen herself, the defeated Antony was finally won over. He had failed in Parthia and he might fail against Octavian, so that Cleopatra could now appeal to his fears as well as his affection. She may have urged, and certainly he believed, that the revival of a Ptolemaic empire would secure a refuge where he could remain a powerful monarch even if he met with disaster in the West. A double aim forced him to adopt an ambiguous attitude, assuming regal authority in Egypt, while posing before the Romans as merely a proconsul and Triumvir. It was a difficult role to play, but Antony might have played it with success if he had not yielded too completely to the influence of Cleopatra. It was not his love for her that ruined him, but the fact that through ignorance of Roman sentiment she led him to commit * fatal errors in the acting of his part.

Cleopatra had already prevailed on him to make a public acknowledgment that he was the father of her three younger children, named Ptolemy, Cleopatra, and Alexander. It was only after his return from his Armenian campaign, however, that he took serious steps to revive a Ptolemaic empire. He then celebrated a splendid triumph in Alexandria, although hitherto a triumph had never been imagined except in Rome, and at the same time he bestowed extensive territories on Cleopatra and her children (34 B.C.). To her he gave the title of Queen of Kings, associating with her in the sovereignty of Egypt her eldest son Cæsarion, whom he recognized as * Cæsar's son, and to Egypt he added Cyprus and Coele-Syria. Ptolemy he declared king of Syria and Cilicia, Cleopatra queen of Cyrene, and Alexander king of Armenia, all these territories except Egypt and Armenia being taken from Rome. Antony was careful to refrain from assuming any new title himself and carried out these arrangements, known as the Donations of Alexandria, by virtue of his authority as proconsul and Triumvir. The Donations quite naturally were seized upon by Octavian as a means of turning public opinion in Italy against his rival, but at first with less success than might have been expected.

Antony himself announced the Donations to the senate by a letter in which he asked for their confirmation by the conscript fathers. We do not know how he justified his policy, but it would seem that he must have tried to represent it as in accordance with Roman interests. The most obvious way that suggests itself would be to urge the advantages of a strong buffer state between Rome and Parthia. Such a state would be forced to protect the Roman frontiers in self-defence, and it could be alleged with some plausibility that this was the cheapest method of defending them. The new Ptolemaic empire was, perhaps, no stronger than was necessary for this purpose, and the provinces which Rome gave up were of little real value to her. The most important of them was Syria, and it might be questioned whether Syria could much more than pay for the army which was required to protect it from Parthia. Whatever the nature of Antony's letter, the consuls, who were both his partisans, evidently did not believe that it would make a favourable impression, for they refused to make it public, so that for a time Octavian was unable to produce adequate evidence of his assertions, to which many gave little credence. Antony was thus able to retain the support of a large party in Italy, composed partly of those who regarded the reports of the Donations as false or exaggerated, and partly of men who like the consuls knew the truth, but either accepted Antony's arguments themselves or hoped that if he returned to Rome he could be persuaded to revoke or modify these obnoxious arrangements.

### § 4. THE WAR BETWEEN OCTAVIAN AND ANTONY

An open breach between the two rivals could not be long postponed, and probably neither had much desire for further delay. The Donations served to bring about a crisis, for in his efforts to utilize them Octavian became involved in a bitter quarrel with the consuls. After some preliminary negotiations with them Octavian surrounded the senate with his soldiers and delivered a speech in which he made many accusations against Antony and one of the consuls. No one dared to reply, but both consuls and a large number of the senators at once left Rome and joined Antony. Octavian was now master in Rome, for the leading members of the

Antonian party had fled, and the senate had thus been cleared of his opponents. Antony soon afterwards formally divorced Octavia, but this was little more than a gesture, for the fact that the two rivals were at war could no longer be concealed.

In Italy the position of Octavian was both difficult and anomalous. Since the Triumvirate had expired at the end of 33 B.C.,[1] he no longer held any office known to the Roman constitution. Nevertheless he was in control of the government, and the lack of a legal basis for his authority was of little practical importance. From the senate he easily secured a declaration of war against Cleopatra, and more and more he appeared as the champion of the West against the East. Throughout Italy the towns took an oath of allegiance to him as their leader, and, though the movement was doubtless organized and directed by his agents, it seems to have been in some degree voluntary and to have had a real public sentiment behind it. Nevertheless the new taxes which he was obliged to impose provoked some rioting and much discontent, but the opposition was put down without serious difficulty, and by the close of 32 Octavian had completed his preparations for the impending struggle.

It has often been said that Antony threw away his chance of victory by idleness and revelry, and that if he had invaded Italy at once he would have conquered his rival with ease. Such critics overlook the fact that when the war came Antony's forces in the East were scattered, and that time was necessary to concentrate his army and transport it to Greece. While he was waiting for his men Antony may have beguiled his enforced leisure in whatever ways appealed to him, but the mere record of what he did during 32 makes it probable that he acted as quickly as was possible under the circumstances. Since he could not invade Italy, he was compelled to let Octavian cross the Adriatic, so that the decisive campaign of the war was fought in Greece in and around the bay of Actium.

Although Antony must be acquitted of the charge of having wasted time in dissipation, yet it is certain that he committed

[1] When the Triumvirate expired is a matter of dispute. For an account of the controversy with references see Holmes, *The Architect of the Roman Empire*, I, pp. 231–45.

a serious blunder when he permitted Cleopatra to accompany him on his campaign. It had been impossible for him to play the part of king of Egypt without doing many things that offended the feelings of his Roman followers. They resented the compliance of their general with Eastern customs, and the way in which they were held aloof by the supple Greek courtiers and renegade Romans of Cleopatra's party. They had no love for the queen, and they were disgusted by her influence over Antony, which seemed to grow more and more complete. They had welcomed war because they hoped it would restore to them a Roman Antony, who would lead them back to Italy and reward them by an allotment of Italian land. On her side Cleopatra dared not trust Antony to his army and was resolutely determined to go with him, so that she might hold at bay the counsels and entreaties of his Roman officers. In the end she prevailed, thus playing directly into the hands of Octavian, for Antony's soldiers, stung by the taunt of their opponents that they were fighting for a Greek queen against their own country, were suspicious and uneasy, and though they still clung to their general their confidence in him was more or less shaken.

## § 5. ACTIUM

The battle of Actium, which made Octavian the master of the Roman world, will probably always remain more or less of a mystery. From the accounts which have come down to us it is clear that during the early empire the actual facts had become obscured, if they had ever been known, and their place had been supplied by legend. It is also clear that this legendary Actium was to a considerable extent the work of the victorious party, eager to glorify the conqueror by making the contrast between his self-restraint and patriotism and Antony's mad infatuation as great as possible. Such a tendency was natural and indeed inevitable, and after Antony's death there were few who felt any interest in defending him against the exaggerations and misrepresentations of his enemies. It is impossible, therefore, to determine with certainty what did really happen, and, although it is easy enough to show that some parts of the story as it has come down to us should be rejected without hesitation, the best reconstruction that can now be made must be more or less tentative and conjectural.[1]

The preliminary events in the decisive struggle are of little interest except for their general result. Antony and Octavian entrenched themselves on opposite sides of the bay of Actium; Octavian refused to risk a battle on land, since his army was weaker than that of his antagonist, but his fleet under Agrippa succeeded in blockading that of Antony in the bay. Antony's position became steadily more difficult, for Octavian could not be forced to risk a battle as long as he held the command of the sea and could obtain supplies in abundance by means of his fleet, while Antony was dependent on pillaging the country to feed his army, and this could not continue indefinitely. Moreover, in Antony's camp there were constant dissensions between Cleopatra and the Roman party, and some of the Romans, either discouraged or disgusted, began to desert to Octavian. Finally, Antony decided that some action was imperative to end a situation which threatened to result in his ruin if it were prolonged much further. A final struggle ensued between Cleopatra and the Romans over what action should be taken. Apparently the queen wished Antony to retreat to the East, abandoning the West to Octavian and using his army to defend Egypt and the new Ptolemaic empire. Before the army retreated, the fleet was to break through the blockade and sail to Egypt. It is possible that Cleopatra had no strong desire to see Octavian crushed, since a complete victory over him would take Antony to Rome, where redoubled pressure would be brought to bear to induce him to modify the Donations. She may well have doubted whether her influence would be sufficient to prevent his yielding to the pressure, and she may also have doubted whether he would dare resist it, however much he wished, since the demands of public opinion in Italy were likely to be backed by the sentiment of his own army. The last thing that Cleopatra desired was the defeat of Antony, but she may have thought that both his interests and hers would be best served by a defensive rather than an aggressive war. Against her were arrayed Antony's Roman officers; they were bitterly opposed

[1] As to the battle itself I have adopted the view of W. W. Tarn, *The Battle of Actium.*

to allowing the war to assume a defensive character, maintaining that the objective to be kept steadily in sight in any operations which might be undertaken was a triumphant return to Italy. Their plan was probably to have the fleet attack that of Octavian and make a desperate attempt to destroy it. If this attempt succeeded, then the tables would be turned upon Octavian, who would be forced to fight, since he would be unable to secure supplies by sea. If the fleet were defeated, the army was to retreat into the interior so as to draw Octavian away from the coast. It was on the action of the fleet that Cleopatra and the Romans were most immediately opposed, whether it should merely seek to escape to Egypt or should fight a serious battle, and Antony seems to have decided to adopt the Roman plan, but to fall back on that of Cleopatra if the battle went against him.

Preparations for the battle were at once begun, and here Antony's duality of purpose proved to be his undoing. By taking advantage of the wind he hoped to drive Octavian's fleet down the coast, and with the object of pursuing and destroying it in case of success he ordered that his warships should carry their sails into the battle. This was contrary to the usual practice, for the warships relied upon their oars when in action, and the sails were regarded as a useless encumbrance. In answer to the surprised questions of his captains Antony explained that the sails would be needed for pursuit, but the explanation failed to quiet the suspicion and uneasiness among the officers and men, for the dissensions which had raged around Antony were more or less well known, and the sails were suggestive of flight. This impression was strengthened when Antony had his treasure embarked on swift ships, which were to be stationed in the rear of the fighting line, and when Cleopatra went on board one of the Egyptian squadron, which was also to remain in the rear. Probably Antony's purpose went no further than to send the queen and his treasure to Egypt if he were defeated, but both would have been safe enough with his army, and such precautions very naturally gave the impression that the battle was a pretence and that his real intention was to escape; in other words, that he had yielded to his Roman officers only because he dared not refuse, that his acceptance of their plan was half-hearted at best, and that he meant to follow Cleopatra's advice if he could find the least excuse.

When at length the two fleets engaged on September 2, 31 B.C., the issue was already decided. The fighting had hardly begun when some of Antony's ships abandoned their places in the line and returned to the harbour. Faced by open mutiny in his fleet, Antony saw that victory was out of the question, so he hastily fell back upon his second plan. Cleopatra, either realizing the situation or receiving a signal from Antony, escaped with her squadron through a break in the line and made for Egypt, and Antony, quitting his flagship for a fast boat, followed her.[1] Their flight practically ended the battle, for most of Antony's ships which were not actually engaged surrendered to Octavian without making any further effort. The story of a long and obstinate struggle is in all probability a legend, arising from the fact that Octavian later burned some of the ships for which he had no use.

The battle of Actium, if the word battle may properly be used, cost Antony his fleet, but his army still confronted Octavian. In spite of the loss of the fleet, a retreat to the interior might even yet result in a battle in which a victory was possible. There was still some loyalty to Antony among his soldiers and they would probably have followed him in a strategic retreat if he had promptly returned to lead them. In fact this is what they seem to have expected him to do, since for seven days they rejected the overtures of Octavian. When, however, they were finally convinced that he had fled to Egypt, their loyalty broke down and they surrendered. It was not, therefore, Antony's flight in itself that ruined him, for no one could accuse him of cowardice, but it was his destination which was fatal. Cleopatra could imagine that Roman soldiers would fight for a Ptolemaic empire at the bidding of their general only because she was not herself a Roman. Individuals she could understand and influence, but the sentiments of the average Roman she did not understand, and so she was quite unable to foresee the probable conduct of a Roman army. Antony should have known his

[1] His flight with her in case of defeat may have been premeditated. If not, it was probably caused by the desertion of his fleet, which took him by surprise. In the first shock of so unexpected an event he might well believe that his army was equally untrustworthy and that flight to Egypt was his only chance.

own men, but there is evidence to show that he had been out of touch with them for some time past, being surrounded by the partisans and courtiers of Cleopatra, and he may have thought that they had not seen through the disguises by which he had striven to conceal his policy. Probably he realized only when it was too late that his flight to Egypt had torn away the disguises and made further deception impossible. By that act he made it clear to all that he was no longer a Roman general seeking to return to Italy, but an Oriental monarch waging war against Rome. If his soldiers continued to follow him they must resign themselves to a permanent exile in the East and give up their long-cherished hope of ending their lives as landed proprietors in their native country. Even if they had been willing to do this, Roman pride and Roman patriotism would have made further loyalty to Antony impossible, for no army recruited in Italy would consent to fight against Rome in the cause of any other state. It was inevitable, therefore, that when Antony could no longer pose as a Roman general his soldiers should cast him aside and submit to his rival.

## § 6. THE END OF THE WAR

Although Antony lost both his fleet and his army at Actium, he still had considerable forces in various parts of the East, and for a time he may have hoped to hold Egypt at least. Such dreams were soon dispelled. His Roman soldiers seized the first opportunity to imitate the example of his army after Actium, and neither the Greeks nor the Orientals were disposed to face the might of Rome for him or Cleopatra. Octavian had no need of further fighting: it was enough to advance and receive the submission of Antony's remaining followers. As the desertions multiplied Antony was left face to face with the inevitable. Cleopatra seeing clearly that he was doomed, made a desperate effort to save herself from perishing in the shipwreck of his fortunes. She sent him word that she had killed herself and he hastily followed her supposed example. In any case it was only a choice of the best moment for the act, unless he preferred to wait for the executioner, and Cleopatra's deception at the worst only shortened his life by a few days or weeks.

To estimate the real character or ability of Antony with any degree of confidence is impossible in view of the nature of our sources, which are all more or less hostile. Cicero in his Philippics denounces him in unmeasured terms, but that was to be expected under the circumstances; the orator was in no mood to be over-careful of the truth, since in his eyes Antony was the greatest menace to that Republic for whose sake he was risking his life. The struggle was too desperate for strict fact to seem of much importance. On every side Cicero saw blindness and timidity which threatened to ruin the Cause, and he realized that all was lost unless he could lash the nobles into energy and courage. He therefore painted Antony as a monster of iniquity, but it is absurd to place implicit faith in such a portrait. Later writers lacked Cicero's passion and excuse, but they accepted without question the official version of the victorious party, interpreting Antony's conduct in the worst sense. In the flight from Actium they saw, or perhaps chose to see, only a frantic impulse, even though their own narrative supplies clear proof to the contrary. Yet, making every allowance for misrepresentation and exaggeration, there must have been something in Antony to make the exaggeration and misrepresentation possible. We cannot readily imagine Cicero saying of Pompey what he says of Antony, and the conclusion seems irresistible that there was some foundation for his fierce denunciations. Antony was certainly a soldier of reckless courage and a general of more than average ability, who could win and retain in good fortune and in bad the devotion of his men. He seems to have been careless and dissolute, cruel on occasion, but capable of generous impulses. He was ready enough to proscribe his enemies in their absence, but when they could appeal to him in person he sometimes pardoned them. There can be little doubt that the stories of drunkenness and wild extravagance are much exaggerated, although he probably indulged in an occasional drinking bout like most of his soldiers, who, perhaps, liked him none the less on that account, and it is most unlikely that he exercised a strict economy in his expenditure. His need of money, however, seems to have been no more habitual than Octavian's, and the cause of their empty purses must be sought chiefly in the fact that they were obliged to lavish most of what they could obtain upon their armies. There is almost no evidence to show that Antony frittered away his opportunities in dissipation and revelry; where we can form any judgment of his activity he seems to have done as much as was possible in the circumstances. He showed on more than one occasion a shrewd political insight and no small degree of political dexterity. If it had not been for Cleopatra he might have defeated Octavian and become the successor to Cæsar. His connection with her ruined him, not because it offended the moral sentiment of Rome, but because her influence led him to make political blunders which in the end proved fatal. It is impossible to regret the result, for there is nothing in Antony's record to give us any reason to believe him half as capable of the task of restoring peace to the Roman world as Octavian proved himself to be.

After Antony's death Cleopatra still cherished the illusion that she might save herself and her throne by ingratiating herself with the conqueror. But Octavian was not a man to be easily ensnared. On his arrival in Egypt he treated the queen with outward courtesy, while keeping her under strict guard and making no promises for the future. Even if he had been captivated by her, he was far too cool and wary to commit the stupendous folly of allowing himself to be entangled. The war in which he had destroyed Antony had been nominally waged against her alone, and this in itself made it impossible to leave her on the throne. Moreover, since he had done everything in his power to lash the West into a fury against Antony because of her, he could not now permit the world to suspect that he in turn was smitten by her charms. Whatever else might happen, it was essential that he should show in the clearest fashion that he was immune from her influence. He might behave with courtesy toward the conquered, but she must grace his triumph in Rome notwithstanding. When Cleopatra realized this fact she saved herself from the humiliation, in spite of the vigilance of her guards and attendants, by committing suicide.[1] If she

[1] The story of the asp is very doubtful; Octavian seems to have given it some sanction, but other stories were told, and all we can be certain of is that she found some means of suicide. Of her children Cæsarion was put to death by Octavian, while those of whom Antony was the father were spared and brought up by Octavia. What finally became of the two boys is unknown, but the young Cleopatra married Juba II, king of Numidia and Mauretania.

could no longer hope to live and reign as a queen, she could at least die as one.

There is little need to attempt an estimate of her character. Beautiful she may have been despite the evidence of her portraits, great charm she certainly possessed. She employed all her attractions without scruple or hesitation to further her ambitions, and these ambitions were the natural and inevitable product of her birth and environment. The last ruler of a decaying dynasty, she fought a desperate battle with her wit and charm to revive the long-lost glories of her house. She failed at last because with all her cleverness she was a Greek princess and never had the opportunity to gain a real insight into the minds of ordinary Romans. Perhaps she would have been unable to understand them even with better facilities than it can be reasonably supposed that she enjoyed. The Roman was so different from the Orientalized Greek that it would have been a difficult matter even in the most favourable circumstances to bridge the gulf. Certainly she either failed to do so or deliberately chose to run all risks rather than abandon her project of a new Ptolemaic empire.

For two years after Actium Octavian remained in the East. Had he been Antony, the writers of the time would have had much to say about his idleness, but since he was the conqueror no such suggestions are to be found. He had in fact enough to occupy him, and he might have taken longer than he did without being open to any reasonable reproach. The fall of Antony and Cleopatra had left the entire eastern half of the empire in confusion, so that a general reorganization was imperative, and with the death of Cleopatra the disposition of Egypt became a pressing problem. Octavian determined that the Ptolemies should be set aside, and that their kingdom should henceforth be ruled from Rome. He did not make it an ordinary province, however, but recognized its exceptional position in the world by an exceptional arrangement: the government of the kingdom was to be vested in his hands alone, and he became in Eastern legal theory its king. Of course he carefully avoided any use of this title, but he did assume that he was the heir and successor of the late dynasty, and that all their rights and properties passed to him. To settle matters in Egypt alone must have required careful thought and study, and there were the other Eastern provinces to consider as well. Which of Antony's arrangements should stand and which be modified or cancelled, which of the petty princes whom he had set up or acknowledged should retain their thrones, and who should replace those whom it might seem expedient to dispossess, all these and many other matters must be somehow dealt with before Octavian could return to Italy. When this task was completed he had to face the far more difficult one of establishing some regular and permanent form of government for the Roman empire, a government that could be accepted by Roman sentiment but which at the same time should be strong enough and efficient enough to maintain peace and order throughout the Mediterranean world.

## CHAPTER XIX

# THE ROMAN WORLD IN THE LAST CENTURY OF THE REPUBLIC

### § 1. THE CITY OF ROME

THE expansion of Roman power was naturally accompanied by a growth of the city, and this growth was greatly stimulated by the agricultural crisis and the cheapness of food which resulted from the corn law. In addition to this, the rapid increase in wealth and the rising standards of living which accompanied it opened up new industries and new fields for business in ministering to the growing luxury of the higher classes. What the population of the city was at different periods of its history we can only conjecture, though it must have been between 800,000 and 1,000,000 in the time of Cicero.[1]

With its growth the outward aspect of the city was also changing. In the depressions between the hills, where the poorer classes lived, tenements and lodging houses several stories in height, precursors of the *insulæ* of the Empire, were becoming common, while the higher and more attractive regions were occupied by the residences of the rich, which grew constantly larger and more elaborate. The old building materials (wood, crude brick, and tufa) were replaced in edifices of the better sort by a cream-coloured limestone known as travertine, and about the time of the Gracchi concrete with outer facings of stone began to be employed. Some impressive public buildings were erected, such as the Tabularium, or public record office, and the new Capitoline temple, which must have done something to adorn and beautify the city. In spite of such improvements, however, to eyes accustomed to the splendour of the Eastern cities, and even of some in Italy, Rome must have presented a somewhat

[1] See Holmes, *The Roman Republic*, I, pp. 360–63.

squalid appearance with its ill-paved, crooked streets and narrow alleys; it was only under Augustus that in her outward appearance she became worthy of her imperial position. *

While the government made successful efforts by means of aqueducts to insure an adequate supply of good water to the people, many other public services which to-day are regarded as a matter of course were entirely neglected. The authorities made no effort to light the streets or to deal with the fires which were frequent and sometimes disastrous, especially in the poorer quarters. Neither was any attempt made to police the city, so that each man was left to protect himself and his property as best he could. Wealthy Romans were safe enough within their houses, guarded by their numerous slaves, freedmen, and clients, and they seldom went outside without an escort, partly to defend them and at night to light their way with torches, partly as a matter of pride and ostentation. The lack of a police force, therefore, was not so serious as might have been expected, for the rich were protected by their retainers and the poor were hardly worth the trouble of robbing. Nevertheless, there must have been enough violence and crime to cause much suffering and insecurity among that section of the lower class which was not entirely destitute. In some respects, however, the poor received more than ample consideration; the distribution of grain enabled them to live, and the festivals and games furnished gratuitous amusement.

## § 2. THE NOBILITY

The free inhabitants of the city fell into three distinct classes, the nobles, the knights, and the populace. The chief characteristics of these classes have been sufficiently explained in the preceding chapters, but a few further details in regard to each should be included in any survey of the period.

The nobility we have already seen as a proud and exclusive governing class, whose wealth consisted chiefly in large landed estates. As the more fortunate of the great office-holding families and many of the knights grew rich out of the spoils of conquest, ostentation and luxury replaced the earlier simplicity and frugality, and the standard of living among the wealthier class rose rapidly. To keep pace with the example set by the successful generals and provincial governors the poorer nobles were forced to contract debts, which sometimes resulted in the ruin and disappearance of their families. In many cases such debts led to a desperate struggle to secure the higher offices of the state, through the tenure of which there was a possibility of profit. Even from a poor province an honest governor might in a single year amass a considerable sum; Cicero, for example, in Cilicia made some £20,000, and the gains of the unscrupulous might be enormous. Successful generals still accumulated vast fortunes, as is evidenced by the wealth acquired by Sulla, Lucullus, Pompey, and Cæsar, and many less famous men profited largely by the continual fighting on the frontiers. Others who took no part in such activities as leading armies or governing provinces, whether from character and inclination or from lack of opportunity, found other means of accumulating money. Some became advocates, for, although fees were forbidden by law, grateful clients often left handsome legacies to those who had rendered them good service; others engaged in various business enterprises which were not legally closed to senators, or, evading the law, became secret partners in the enterprises of the knights. For example, Crassus invested largely in tenements in Rome and in mines in Spain, M. Junius Brutus loaned money at an extortionate rate of interest to cities in Cyprus, Cicero and Hortensius pleaded in the courts, and Cicero at least reaped a golden harvest in legacies as a result of his success.

The fortunes of the nobles, however gained, were in many cases hardly adequate to maintain their rank and station according to the prevalent standards. It was no longer sufficient to have a country estate worked for profit; fashion had come to require that a noble should spend part of his time in more or less elaborate villas in the Sabine hills or on the coast of Latium and Campania. In many of these villas, no doubt, profit was combined with luxury, but by no means all of them can have been paying properties; Cicero owned eight, for example, and their maintenance must have been a heavy drain upon his resources at times. In addition to his villas, a noble was expected to keep up an expensive residence in the city with a large number of slaves, clients, and freedmen, and to entertain his friends and retainers with a lavishness which sumptuary legislation proved powerless to check. Dinners consisted of many courses, including rare viands, and the guests were sometimes entertained by the dancing and music of slaves or hired performers. No doubt there were still many wealthy Romans who avoided extravagance and lived with comparative simplicity, and we need to be on our guard against hasty generalizations based on a few exceptional cases. It is probable that the majority of the nobles were still financially solvent, but those who were heavily encumbered with debt and ready to resort to any expedient to escape impending ruin were numerous enough to form a distinctive feature in the society of the day. The influence of Crassus was in no small degree due to his calculated liberality to senators and politicians of this class, and such men as Catiline and Curio are good representatives of it. If Roman governors too frequently plundered the provincials, they must in many cases have done so less from wickedness and greed than from grim necessity.

Another characteristic feature of the society of the later Republic is the increasingly prominent place taken by women. Under the new conditions the old Roman family was breaking down, and those forms of marriage by which the property of a wife passed completely under the control of her husband were more and more commonly replaced by others by which she herself or her family retained the control. Along with this weakening of the economic basis of the family went a rapid increase in the frequency of divorce. Public opinion ceased to be scandalized or even greatly interested if marriages were dissolved and new ones contracted to suit the pleasure, the convenience, or the political interests of the parties involved. The Roman matron of the old type, busy with the management of her household, was giving place to ladies who gathered around them a more or less distinguished circle of friends, and who often took a part in politics. As representatives of this class we may note Servilia, the mother of M. Junius Brutus, a woman of ready wit and extensive reading, in whose *salon* were to be found such men as Cæsar, and Fulvia, the wife first of Clodius, then of Curio, and finally of Antony.

In spite of much extravagance, frivolity, and immorality, the aristocracy was still far from being hopelessly decadent. As is true in all periods of history, picturesque vice bulks larger in the records than commonplace and uninteresting virtue. There must have been many men, like Cicero, who led upright and temperate lives in spite of occasional extravagance and consequent financial embarrassments. In some respects the changes in Roman society were distinctly for the better. The new standards of living brought with them not only senseless luxury and ostentatious profusion, but also a more cultivated taste, wider intellectual interests, and a real love for, and appreciation of, the best that the age could offer in the way of literature and art. If society was growing laxer in some respects, it was growing more humane and more refined in others. As the narrowness and rigidity of the past broke down, a new type of culture was dev loping among the governing class to fit it for its task of administering a world empire.

## § 3. THE KNIGHTS

Side by side with the nobility stood the knights, or business men and capitalists of the day, sharing in many ways the characteristics of the aristocracy but with special interests of their own. They no doubt imitated the social life of the nobles as far as their means permitted, and many obtained a footing in the most exclusive circles of society. Their political influence has already been sufficiently emphasized, but a few words further as to their business activities are called for. They were an indispensable adjunct of the government for many purposes, for it was through their syndicates that public works were constructed and a large part of the revenue of the state collected. These syndicates resembled more or less closely our modern stock companies, though there are many details of their organization which remain obscure. The state required a guaranty for the carrying out of the contract, so that some of the members of the syndicate were required to pledge their property for this purpose, while other members combined as partners to secure the contract from the censors. The necessary capital for the work was raised by the contributions of the partners and by a number of shareholders who invested smaller sums. There was a chairman (*magister*) for the syndicate, who directed its operations, and it would usually employ a considerable body of agents and workmen of all sorts. If the syndicate was engaged in building roads or in erecting public buildings, the rough work was no doubt performed by slaves, either bought by the syndicate or hired from their masters, but there must have been many freemen employed as agents and overseers of one kind or another.

The business enterprises in which these syndicates engaged were widely varied, but, since the Romans were reluctant to adopt the principle of limited liability except where the public interest rendered it necessary, all their operations had a more or less public character. They farmed the taxes in certain of the provinces, collected the port dues levied by Rome in Italy and in the provinces, constructed public works, and leased state properties, such as mines. Thus a considerable number of activities were open to them, of which they seem to have made full use. Not only did they operate under contracts from the Roman government, but they also undertook similar tasks for the client princes and for the provincial cities, so that their agents were to be found wherever the influence of Rome was strongly felt.

In addition to the syndicates there were individual knights and private partnerships engaged in trade, industry, money-lending, and banking throughout the Roman world and even beyond its limits, for Cæsar found Roman traders already established among the independent tribes of Gaul. The Roman government seems never to have followed the example of Carthage and sought to create commercial monopolies to the advantage of her citizens, but they could generally rely on some degree of favour from the provincial governors. In spite of this they had to meet the competition of all comers and enjoyed no exclusive privileges, so that if they obtained control of any form of business, it was due primarily to the fact that they alone possessed sufficient capital for the purpose.

The interests of the business men of Rome did not always coincide with those of the great landowners, as has been already sufficiently shown. In a general way they were more favourable to expansion and imperialism than the nobles, but they were by no means always and everywhere champions of such a policy. At times they might prefer the supervision of a client king to that of a Roman governor, so that they were far from being consistent advocates of a policy of conquest and annexation. Their support helped Pompey to secure the command against the pirates and to supersede

Lucullus in the East, but this was only when the pirates had become an intolerable nuisance to business and when Lucullus' failure was manifest. In his settlement of the East Pompey was friendly to them without subservience, and there is no reason to suppose that his annexation of Syria was due to their influence. In short, the business men of Rome were very like those of other countries and times and were far less concerned with general principles than with the immediate situation as it affected them.

## § 4. THE PLEBS

Below the knights were the plebs, the common people of the city. In the last days of the Republic there was a very large body of poor who depended chiefly on the corn dole for a living. The economic condition of the rabble had certainly grown worse rather than better after the establishment of the distribution of cheap grain by C. Gracchus, but it is impossible to say whether the abolition of all charge for it by Clodius was justified by any real necessity. The presence of this rabble, grown to the number of 320,000 by the time of Cæsar's dictatorship, should not blind us to the fact that there were in Rome many persons of small means who were more or less self-supporting. Cæsar restricted the number of the recipients of the free grain to 150,000 and sent some 80,000 to his colonies. As to what became of the rest we are not informed; employment may have been found for some upon his public works, and others may have received land outside his colonies, but it would seem that many were simply deprived of the grain and left to shift for themselves. This would suggest that a considerable number of those who had been taking advantage of the dole did not really need it, but could buy their bread in the market if necessary. Apart altogether from the rabble, in a city of the size of Rome there must have been many small business men and shopkeepers who were prosperous in a small way, and many workmen who were engaged in various industries. This class was probably composed largely of the descendants of freedmen, but, since the grandson of a freedman was considered in all respects on a level with any other citizen and no longer retained any taint because of his servile origin, in a generation or two the descendants of the slave and of the freeman became indistinguishable members of the populace.

That the racial character of the rabble was gradually affected by the large number of slaves who obtained manumission from their masters there can be no doubt, and the blood of all the peoples of the empire was to be found among the plebs in the city. It is impossible to say how far the lower class in Rome was of Italian stock in the last days of the Republic, for we have no means of determining how frequently the freedman married and left children. The drift of ruined farmers from the country to Rome never ceased, and the original stock was thus constantly reinforced. Neither have we any definite information as to the origin of the slaves who were set free and whose descendants were absorbed into the Roman plebs. Very probably they were mostly from Greece or Asia Minor, for it seems likely that the slaves drawn from the more barbarous races were largely employed on the country estates. In any case the Italian element appears to have remained dominant and to have more or less completely assimilated the foreign element, however numerous it may have been, and there is no reason to attribute any serious results to such racial changes as may have taken place. The behaviour of the rabble was very much what might be expected under the circumstances, and may be adequately explained by them without reference to its racial composition.

As has been pointed out, a portion of the city populace must have been fairly prosperous, or at least self-supporting; another portion was made up of the clients and retainers of the nobles and wealthy knights; below these two classes was what may properly be called the rabble, who relied chiefly upon the corn dole for support. Even this element, however, must have found some work, even if intermittent, for the state did not supply clothing or lodging to the poor, and they could not live upon the free grain alone. The rabble cannot, therefore, have been entirely idle, but its activity was doubtless limited, whether from choice or from necessity. That the assistance of the state was indispensable to them was the result primarily of the system of slavery, which left little opening for the poor freeman. Nearly all the household labour, and probably most of the industrial, was performed by slaves, while many of the shopkeepers were freedmen. Even when an unskilled free labourer could find work, the competition of the slave kept wages at a very low level, so that a bare living was the best that could be hoped for. Under such conditions a large proportion of the poor citizens must starve unless aided by the state, or unless the state could provide for them by allotments of land or colonization. Neither colonization nor allotment, however, proved feasible on an adequate scale, and hence the corn dole was the only available remedy for the unemployment problem. Unquestionably the remedy was one which aggravated the disease and perpetuated it, but the alternative of refusing public charity until such of the rabble as could not find work had been eliminated was practically impossible, whatever might be said for it in theory. A real cure must have begun with the abolition of slavery, or at least the suppression of the slave trade, but such heroic measures seem never to have occurred to Roman statesmen. Even Cæsar went no further than to impose some limitation on slave labour and made no attack upon slavery itself, so that the corn dole remained a necessary and permanent institution.

## § 5. THE SPREAD OF HELLENISM

Many of the changes which took place in the last century of the Republic were merely different aspects of one far-reaching movement, the spread of Hellenism. Slowly but surely Greek influences were permeating Roman life in every direction and in every class from the nobles to the dregs of the populace. In the palatial dwellings of the rich Greek slaves occupied a prominent place, while in the slums Greek freedmen were probably more numerous than those of any other race. How many of these Greeks were of genuine Hellenic descent it is impossible to say, but the majority were probably more or less thoroughly Hellenized natives of Asia Minor and other Eastern lands conquered by Alexander. In ancient times when prisoners taken in war and sometimes whole communities were sold as slaves, not only was the market crowded with human chattels whose value lay in their strength and endurance, but there was always available a considerable number of skilled artisans and educated men. The Romans soon discovered the superior qualities of the quick-witted and intelligent Greeks, and early began to employ slaves of exceptional training and capacity to keep their accounts and assist them in the transaction of their business. In time it became almost a matter of course that a wealthy Roman had as his secretary a Greek slave, while another might act as his business manager, and a third as the tutor of his children. Ultimately all three would usually receive their freedom, although they generally continued in close and confidential relations with their former master. The Romans of the upper class in the last days of the Republic had thus nearly all grown up surrounded from childhood by Greek influences, so that the tide of Hellenism became irresistible. The spoils of war filled Rome with Greek statues, paintings, and every sort of artistic work, and the taste for such things spread rapidly. The products of Greek genius were not only acquired by plunder, but they were extensively bought and imported. In due time Greek artists began to seek employment in Rome, where their work found a ready market, without interrupting the steady inflow from the East. Cicero had statues and paintings to decorate his villas purchased for him in Greece, and had a favourite bronze lamp which was made by his brother's order in Samos. The architecture of the city felt the change in taste, so that the new Capitoline temple, while retaining the old plan in the main, was decorated with high columns in the Greek style.

As soon as the Romans recognized the need of any education beyond that given in the family and in elementary schools of the simplest kind, they had recourse to Greek models. The first secondary schools, private as were all Roman schools under the Republic, were designed to give instruction in the Greek language and literature, and were naturally conducted chiefly by Greeks. Later Latin schools of the same sort developed, but they followed essentially the same lines, merely substituting the study of Latin writers for Greek, Ennius, for example, taking the place of Homer. The higher schools of rhetoric and philosophy remained largely in Greek hands; here the Romans became familiar with the Greek rules of composition and studied the great orators of Hellas as models.

Under the impact of these influences men of the educated class lost most of their faith in the old state religion, its place being taken by philosophy or scepticism. At the other end of the social scale the introduction and spread of new cults from the East is evidence that the Greek slaves and freedmen were making an impression on the masses. As early as 204 B.C. the worship of Cybele, the Great Mother, was brought from Asia Minor with the sanction of the senate, which later sought to restrict it narrowly. In the last century of the Republic the conscript fathers endeavoured vainly to suppress the cult of Isis, a Hellenized Egyptian goddess, and the struggle against her may be said to have ended in 42 B.C., when the Triumvirs constructed a temple in her honour.

Greek philosophy must early have made itself felt in Rome, if only through slaves and freedmen, but later some of the leaders of the Greek schools visited the city, and young Romans more and more commonly spent some time in Greece to complete their education under the most celebrated teachers of the day. Yet, although the Romans sat at the feet of their subjects, they were no mere passive learners of what the latter had to teach. To be accepted by the masters of the world, philosophy must be in some degree adapted to their temperament and to their fundamental ideas. The Romans were active rather than contemplative, with an ardent patriotism and a strong sense of obligation to the state, so that they were most attracted by the practical side of Greek thought and took little interest in speculation or science, except as these had a direct bearing upon conduct. The later Stoics, who relaxed somewhat the rigidity of the early school, conceding that the wise man might engage in public life, received an early welcome and enjoyed a lasting influence. Panætius of Rhodes, who lived for a time in Rome as the friend of Scipio Æmilianus, may be said to have founded Roman Stoicism by adapting Stoic ethics to Roman convictions. From him Cicero borrowed much, not only from his writings, but through his most important disciple, Posidonius, under whom the orator studied. The Gracchi had as a tutor the
* Stoic philosopher Blossius of Cumæ, but the best representative of Roman Stoicism under the Republic was, perhaps, Cato. The Epicurean school also enjoyed a considerable popularity among the higher classes for two opposite reasons. The doctrine that pleasure is the true end of life might easily be interpreted so as to furnish a justification for self-indulgence and luxury, and on the other hand the real doctrine of

Epicurus that the highest pleasure is to be found in contentment, the renunciation of ambition, and freedom from all fear, appealed to those who found no part for them to play in the fierce political struggles which marked the breakdown of the Republic. There were, of course, other philosophic schools which exercised a considerable influence on the Romans, especially the scepticism of the New Academy, but their chief importance lay in the modifications of the Stoic doctrines to which their criticisms led, and to the adoption of some of their ideas in eclectic systems, such as that of Cicero. If the Romans originated little or nothing in philosophy, they were in close and constant contact with contemporary Greek thought, and the finer minds among them were deeply impressed by it, although they always retained something of their essential Roman character.

## § 6. ITALY

The Romanization of Italy was very gradual and was not completed until the Republic was approaching its end. After her conquest Rome had organized the peoples of the peninsula into a confederacy, by which in legal theory a large number of separate and distinct communities were bound together in a league under her leadership. For once legal theory was an accurate expression of the facts, for in submitting to Rome the various Italic peoples in no wise gave up their individual peculiarities and differences. Although the Romans planted many colonies, which did much to familiarize the Italians with Latin speech and Roman customs, it is unlikely that the Romans were aiming consciously at any such results. Nevertheless, the results came in due time, and slowly but surely the Latin language displaced the other Italic dialects, the local laws and institutions were more and more modelled on the Roman, until at last the differences had become slight and unimportant. The Social War finally swept away all political distinctions and welded the population of Italy into a single nation. It was only after this war that the Latinization of Italy was completed, for Sulla's extensive and ruthless colonization of Samnium with his veterans destroyed the last important stronghold of the Oscan dialect, and Latin became henceforth the language of the whole peninsula.

The agricultural crisis affected the Italians as well as the Roman citizens, although they may have felt it somewhat less acutely because a large part of their territory lay beyond the reach of the cheap grain. Nevertheless, they must have paid their full share of the penalties of foreign conquest and received much less than their share of such profits as the empire brought with it. We know practically nothing of the conditions in their towns, but we can hardly doubt that many of them had to face the same problems and the same difficulties that confronted the statesmen of Rome. The ravages of the Social War must have fallen upon them more heavily than upon the Romans, and in the Civil War between Sulla and the democrats the majority of them took the losing side, so that some of their municipalities suffered severely at Sulla's hands.

At first sight, therefore, it might seem that only a gloomy picture can be drawn of the general condition of the peninsula in the last century of the Republic. Nevertheless, it is certain that over Italy as a whole there was a revival of prosperity. The small farmer had never entirely disappeared, and the legislation of the Gracchi did something to break up the great estates and to restore the land to peasant proprietors, many of whom no doubt prospered. The allotment of land to discharged veterans must also have had the same general result. It is true that the land so distributed did not all come from great estates, still Sulla, Pompey, Cæsar, and the Second Triumvirate in disposing of their armies must have broken up many of these estates.

To multiply small landowners, however, could have no permanent effect unless the economic conditions were such that they could make a living from their holdings. In many regions this presented no serious difficulty, for grain growing was still profitable in the neighbourhood of towns too far from the sea to import corn from abroad. Moreover, the agricultural crisis had turned attention to new forms of cultivation, and the old type of farming gave place to the production of olive oil and wine, and to the raising of fruit, vegetables, poultry, and stock. Fortunately we still possess the work of Varro on agriculture (*de re rustica*), from which much information can be drawn. He declares that no country in the world is better cultivated than Italy, and that fruit trees are so numerous that the whole land seems one vast orchard.[1] Although the book was written in 37 B.C., it professes to describe conditions before the Civil War, and there is no reason to doubt that his boasts had a very substantial foundation, even if some allowance is made for his patriotic enthusiasm. From him we gather that wheat was widely grown in Italy and even near Rome, for he notes the special method adopted there in harvesting it.[2] As to the extent to which the land was held in large estates we can draw no conclusion from his pages, because he wrote to show how men of his own class might profitably invest their money in farms of from 100 to 200 acres. It is assumed throughout that such farms would be cultivated by slaves under the direction of an overseer, who is himself a slave or a freedman. It seems probable that estates of this size were common and that much larger ones were the exception rather than the rule. While Varro takes for granted that the ordinary work of the farm will be done by slaves, he recognizes the need for some free labour on occasion, and he gives a standard form for leases. In the Latin of the time we find the word *colonus* losing its original sense and taking on the new meaning of *renter*. The largest estate of which we hear anything definite is that of Domitius Ahenobarbus, whose slaves, freedmen, and tenants (*coloni*) were so numerous that he manned seven ships with them to aid Massilia against Cæsar.[3] It seems clear, therefore, that the large estates were no longer wholly worked by slaves, but that the tenant farmer had not only made his appearance, but had become common enough to require a special name. Since it is no part of Varro's purpose to give advice to the small farmer, we can gather nothing from his work in regard to the numbers or condition of this class. It seems reasonably safe, however, to conclude that the peasant proprietor had his share in the agricultural prosperity which Varro pictures, the more so since some of the new forms of cultivation could be carried on with profit on a small scale; hence there was nothing in the economic situation which would make it impossible for many of the thousands who received allotments of land to make a success of their holdings.

[1] i, ch. 2.

[2] i, ch. 50.

[3] Cæsar, *b.c.* i, ch. 34. At the siege of Corfinium Domitius promised to give each of his soldiers four *jugera* of land out of his own estate (*b.c.* i, ch. 17). This would have required some 40,000 acres, since he had about 15,000 men

The extension of Roman power outside the peninsula, though it produced some disastrous economic, social, and political consequences, ultimately contributed in no small degree to the prosperity of Italy. In the end new provinces meant new markets, where the demand for Italian oil and wine constantly increased, and where the products of Italian artisans met with a ready sale, so that both agriculture and industry were stimulated. In the last century of the Republic there was an extensive export trade in articles of bronze from Capua and Etruria, and potteries were established in Arretium which were beginning to supply the western provinces with earthenware. In industry as in agriculture most of the workmen were probably slaves or freedmen, but much free labour must have found employment. Nevertheless, we may reasonably suppose that the army offered the most promising career to a large proportion of the poorer Italians, but it should be borne in mind that this was true only because service in the legions was the shortest path to the ownership of a small farm, so that, while the army constantly drew off the surplus free population of the countryside as recruits, it sent many of them back to it in a better economic position. It seems clear, therefore, that Italy as a whole was prosperous in spite of the temporary suffering caused by the wars, proscriptions, and confiscations of the last days of the Republic.

The total population of Italy must remain largely a matter of conjecture. Perhaps as fair an estimate as is possible in the circumstances is that the whole peninsula, including Cisalpine Gaul, at the time of the battle of Actium had about 14,000,000 inhabitants, of whom about 4,000,000 were slaves.[1] It would be interesting to know how far the racial character of the people had been modified by the influx of slaves, but on this matter we can do nothing better than guess. Since the slaves were mainly prisoners taken in war, the men must have greatly outnumbered the women, and the servile element was probably maintained rather by fresh accessions than by natural increase. Nevertheless, the free population in 30 B.C. must have included a considerable number of the descendants of freedmen, so that a foreign element was present, more or less mixed with the original Italian stock. It should be borne in mind in this connection that large numbers of the slaves

[1] Frank, *Roman Census Statistics*, pp. 340–41

employed in agriculture came from the barbarian peoples on the frontiers, and that many of these peoples did not differ greatly in origin from the Italians. The Gauls and Spaniards, at least, seem to have been the product of a mingling of much the same elements as occupied Italy before the rise of Rome, namely, Mediterranean, Alpine, and Nordic races in varying proportions. On the whole we may conclude, perhaps, that the foreign element was neither very large nor so different from the Italic type as to make its complete assimilation a matter of serious difficulty.

## § 7. THE ARMY AND FRONTIER DEFENCE

Of the organization of the Roman army enough has already been said, since after the reforms of Marius few changes were made. It remains only to consider briefly how the character of the army affected the problem of frontier defence. It is obvious that when Rome undertook to govern provinces she assumed the obligation of protecting them, and that unless she did so efficiently the *pax Romana*, of which she boasted, was a somewhat doubtful blessing. The method by which the legions were recruited, however, made it practically impossible for the Republic to discharge this duty in a really satisfactory fashion. A standing army on an adequate scale seems never to have been thought of and was certainly not maintained. When no serious danger threatened a province it was frequently left with a very small garrison, and even well-grounded apprehension of attack seldom brought prompt reinforcements. A single instance will suffice by way of illustration. When Cicero went to his province of Cilicia in 51 B.C. only two years had elapsed since the disaster of Carrhæ, and there was good reason to expect that the Parthians would follow up their victory by invading the Roman possessions in the East. Yet the only measure of precaution which the senate seems to have taken was to authorize Bibulus, the governor of Syria, to levy troops in his province if necessary. If any reinforcements had been sent their number seems to have been negligible, so that the force available in Syria, which must have been largely made up of the remnants of Crassus' beaten army, was quite incapable of meeting a formidable attack. The right to levy troops in the province proved to be a barren privilege, for Bibulus soon discovered that trustworthy recruits were not to be found. In Cilicia Cicero was supposed to have two legions, but he found them much depleted and disorganized. Had the Parthians come, they would have met with little resistance and could have overrun a large part of the East. The orator was appalled by the danger of the situation and sent an urgent message to Rome asking for large reinforcements.[1] The expected invasion fortunately did not take place, but Rome's Asiatic provinces owed their security to the apathy of the Parthians or their preoccupation with other matters rather than to her. When the fear of an invasion was greatest the senate did so far exert itself as to secure two legions, one from Pompey and one from Cæsar, a force which was obviously inadequate, and which could hardly have reached the East in time to be of much real use. At first one is likely to conclude that the conscript fathers were negligent of their duties and careless of what happened on the frontiers of the empire, but there are some factors to be considered before we can judge them fairly. It was easy for Cicero to point out the need of reinforcements, but to send them was a much more difficult matter. Large numbers of recruits could easily be found if a popular and trusted general were commissioned to raise an army. At the moment, however, the only such general available was Pompey, to whom the senate was unwilling to give such a commission, and who would probably have declined it if offered. It was useless to call for volunteers to serve under Cicero, who had no military experience or reputation, and probably Bibulus was little better for the purpose. Under the circumstances of the moment it was impossible to secure troops except by the method actually adopted, that is, by getting legions already raised from the commanders who had raised them.

It seems clear, therefore, that the introduction of volunteer armies did nothing to solve the problem of frontier defence in time of peace, although it did provide a means of dealing with a situation after it had become so acute as to require the appointment of one of the great generals of the day. Such an appointment inevitably interfered with the normal working of the constitution, and this fact made it practically

[1] *Fam.*, xv, 1.

impossible until its necessity was beyond dispute. It would very rarely happen that the general could be found among the magistrates for the year, and if he were there was little likelihood that he would draw the right province by lot. To create a great command, therefore, even if the general was at hand, the senate would have to resort to some unusual measures in the assignment of the provinces, and ordinarily it could only be done by a special law passed by the assembly. The senate was naturally reluctant to take either course, preferring to wait upon events rather than to anticipate them.

The soldiers who garrisoned the provinces in time of peace were probably mostly professionals. Even before Marius there seem to have been men ready to serve year after year for the regular pay and their share of the booty, but it seems hardly likely that such men were very numerous. What brought the recruits flocking to the standards of Sulla, Pompey, or Cæsar was the hope of exceptional rewards in the shape of booty, followed by an allotment of land when the war was over. Under the ordinary provincial governor there was little to be expected in the way of plunder, for any operations in which he engaged would probably be on a petty scale, grants of land were out of the question, and there was always the risk of disaster as a result of his inexperience or incompetence ; it may well be doubted whether such prospects would attract enough recruits to maintain adequate garrisons in all the provinces, so that the senate had to do the best it could with such forces as it had at its command. In theory conscription remained possible, but in view of its unpopularity the senate, whose political control had become weak and uncertain, must have been reluctant to resort to it. It is probable, therefore, that the numerical weakness of Cicero's legions was due chiefly to the small number of recruits who were attracted by the normal conditions of service, especially at a time when the armies of Cæsar and Pompey seemed to offer far greater rewards.

Another difficulty which must have hampered the senate in making adequate provision for frontier defence was the lack of money. While it is impossible to determine just what funds were available at any given time, it seems clear that the balance on hand was often low. It is true that large sums were occasionally paid into the treasury by victorious generals, but large expenditures were frequently called for. It must often have been necessary to practise a rigid economy to meet the expenses of the state, and to reduce the garrisons in peaceful provinces would be an obvious method. To reduce the amount devoted to the corn dole was to invite certain and immediate trouble, while the consequences of a reduction in the garrison stationed in Asia or Africa were uncertain and the chances were greatly against their being serious. It is not surprising, therefore, that the senate took risks abroad to escape difficulties at home.

Even with larger resources in both men and money the Republic would have found the defence of the frontiers a serious problem, since in the North they rested upon no natural geographical barriers. It was practically impossible to protect Macedonia from invasion without annexing the territory which lay between it and the Danube, or to maintain peace in Spain until the whole of the Iberian peninsula was thoroughly subdued. Neither task was seriously undertaken by the senate, and the result was almost constant border warfare, the success of which depended largely on the character of the governor in charge. Victories for which triumphs were celebrated in Rome brought little security to the provincials, for they were only too often followed by reverses; the turbulent tribes across the frontier renewed their attacks whenever an opportunity presented itself, sometimes carrying their raids far into the regions under the effective administration of Rome. The only real cure was to extend the empire until some natural barrier was reached which could be easily guarded, but such a policy of defensive imperialism seems never to have been seriously considered by the senate, partly perhaps because it lacked both armies and trustworthy generals.

At sea the government proved as inefficient as on land, for the coasts were more or less unsafe throughout the last century of the Republic. The Romans made no attempt to maintain a permanent fleet, but got one together as best they could when it was needed. For ships they were content to rely upon their allies, and each governor was expected to defend the coast as well as the land frontier, for which purpose he could require the towns to furnish ships, or money in place of them. Such a system of decentralized control was shown to be wholly inadequate by the steady increase of piracy. When finally the pirates had become an intolerable scourge, they could only be put down by the grant of sweeping powers to Pompey. He fulfilled his mission with complete success, but as soon as the seas were clear the senate reverted to the old system, and piracy revived. It was only under the Empire that real security was attained, and then only because the task of policing the seas was recognized as a duty of the central government and a permanent fleet created for the purpose. The reasons for the senate's reluctance to undertake the responsibility were probably substantially the same as in the case of the army: men, money, and trained officers were lacking, and without them mere ships would have been of very little use.

It may be admitted that the senate was often blind to danger until it had become acute, and that it did not always make the best use of the resources at its command, but is there any governing body of which this cannot be said? The worst disasters which befell Rome in consequence of her mismanagement of the frontier problem were due far less to the lack of preparedness than to the bungling of the men in charge: it was not an inadequate army but Mallius and Cæpio that left Italy exposed to an invasion of the Cimbri and Teutones. The method by which the provincial governors were chosen made it certain that important posts would often fall to men entirely unfitted for them. An additional legion or two in Cilicia would have made Cicero no more competent to face the Parthians, and it is not impossible that the senate had a suspicion of this fact. To safeguard the frontiers was more necessary than larger garrisons: it was essential that the governors in charge should be experienced and capable men, but under the Republic such men in the really important positions were a matter of accident. A new system of selecting the governors was imperative to secure any really serious improvement, and the introduction of such a system was impossible without a drastic change in the constitution of the Republic.

## § 8. THE ORGANIZATION OF THE PROVINCES

In spite of all the efforts of the senate to avoid expansion and to limit it when it could not be avoided, the empire grew steadily. By 146 B.C. the Republic had undertaken the government of six provinces, namely Sicily, Sardinia and Corsica, Hither Spain, Farther Spain, Macedonia, and Africa. Cisalpine Gaul was already conquered, but does not yet seem to have been regarded as a regular province, although, since it was finally recognized as one, it should, perhaps, be added to the list and counted as a seventh. The death of the king of Pergamum, combined with the exigencies of Gracchan politics, led to the annexation of Asia in 133 B.C.; Transalpine Gaul was organized not long after 120, and the depredations of the pirates forced Rome to occupy Cilicia about 103. These were the ten provinces for which Sulla provided governors when he remodelled the Republican constitution during his dictatorship. But the onward march of the empire could not be stopped. In the attempt to put down piracy Crete was annexed in 67, Pompey organized Bithynia-Pontus and annexed Syria after his victory over Mithridates, while Cæsar conquered the independent part of Gaul during his proconsulship.[1]

The inhabitants of these provinces were of many races and their degree of civilization varied greatly. In the East the population of the cities was Greek, or, at least, thoroughly Hellenized, but in the West there was no such dominant culture[2] until in the course of time the provincials were Romanized. In organizing and governing such an empire the narrowly practical bent of the Roman mind stood the conquerors in good stead. They had no love for theories, no concern for consistency, and seldom troubled themselves to look beyond the obvious needs of the moment, being content to deal with the immediate situation and to let the future take care of itself. If this tendency often led them to postpone preparations until some long-threatening danger had become acute, it gave to their administration an adaptability to circumstances and conditions without which they could hardly have held together so heterogeneous an agglomeration of peoples as their empire included. In general the Romans had no wish to meddle with their subjects, but were content

[1] I have omitted Illyricum, acquired before 146 B.C., Cyrene, bequeathed to Rome in 96, and Cyprus, annexed in 58, because they were not governed as separate provinces, but were joined with others.

[2] In Gaul and Spain the Celts might correspond in some degree to the Greeks in the East.

to let them do as they pleased so long as Roman interests were not injuriously affected. The result was that Roman rule was, on the whole, tolerable and that there were surprisingly few insurrections after it had been well established. Once thoroughly subdued, Rome's subjects seem to have found her government, with all its shortcomings and deficiencies, an improvement on their previous condition and to have realized that under her they had greater security and prosperity than before without too serious an abridgment of their freedom.

The fact that Rome was little concerned with anything beyond her own immediate interests led her to leave her subjects to govern themselves as far as possible, and hence to make as much use as circumstances would permit of the political institutions which she found among the people whom she conquered. A Roman governor was not expected to govern his province in the modern sense of the word; he was simply a representative of Rome charged with the duty of safeguarding her interests. His province was an aggregation of self-governing communities, called *civitates*, a term often translated *municipalities*. The people of each *civitas* enjoyed a large degree of local autonomy and were allowed to retain their traditional institutions, laws, customs, religion, and language. If they became Romanized, it was not because of any compulsion, but because in the course of time they came to recognize Roman ways as better than their own and voluntarily adopted them. No doubt the Roman carried everywhere the proud conviction of his own superiority, but he made little or no conscious effort to impose his civilization on his subjects. His attitude was probably the result of indifference rather than broad-minded tolerance, nevertheless the result was fortunate in that it left Roman civilization to spread by virtue of its real superiority unhampered by the antagonism which would inevitably have been aroused by violent and clumsy attempts to hasten the process.

The real nature of the *civitates*, which largely carried on the work of governing the inhabitants of the empire, varied from province to province and even within the provinces themselves. Where city states of the Greek type existed, Rome gladly used them to the utmost extent possible. There were many parts of the empire, however, where urban life had hardly more than begun, and where the people were still living in an earlier stage of social development. In regions like Gaul and Spain the old native tribes were of necessity accepted as the units of local administration. Confederations or leagues were in general broken up, and each community was treated as a separate and independent unit. Since the Romans always preferred the town to the tribe, they promoted the development of city life wherever and whenever possible, so that some of the *civitates* which had originally been tribal in character were gradually transformed into city states of the familiar sort. In consequence there was no hard and fast distinction between the two types of municipalities which were to be found throughout the empire.

In every province the rights and privileges as well as the obligations to Rome of the various municipalities were carefully defined by the provincial charter, known as the *lex provinciæ*, which was drawn up when the province was organized by a commission of ten senators sent to the province for this purpose. The provisions of these charters were thus deliberately framed to meet the local conditions, and no attempt was made to impose a rigid system. Even within a province there was no uniformity in the status of the *civitates*, for Rome was always ready to grant special privileges to some or to impose special restrictions upon others whenever the circumstances seemed to make such exceptions desirable. Some of the cities were entirely exempt from taxation and from the authority of the governor, being in theory independent republics bound to Rome by an offensive and defensive alliance, the obligations of which cannot in most cases have been very serious. Such cities usually owed their privileged position either to their past greatness, as in the case of Athens, or to their loyalty and services to Rome. Over the less favoured *civitates* the governor exercised a measure of control which was more or less strictly defined by the terms of the *lex provinciæ*, and which was considerably greater over some of the municipalities in the province than it was over others. In general the Roman policy seems to have been to leave to the different communities in each province as large a degree of freedom as appeared compatible with the security of Roman interests.

From all her provinces Rome exacted tribute, in levying and collecting which two methods were employed. In some provinces, such as Sicily and Asia, the tribute consisted of a definite percentage of the crop and the right to collect the tax was farmed. In most provinces, however, each of the separate *civitates* was assessed a fixed sum of money, which the local authorities were left to raise in any way they pleased. Where the tax was farmed the governor had the double duty of seeing that the farmers of the taxes were paid their due and of preventing them from extorting more from the provincials. Under the second system the governor merely received the money from the *civitates* and accounted for it to the Roman treasury. In no case did he have anything to say as to the amount of the tax, and his part in its collection was limited to the occasional application of pressure to recalcitrant individuals or communities.

Aside from his theoretically slight, but obviously necessary, part in the collection of the tribute, the governor's duties were numerous and important. He was bound to preserve the peace within his province and to protect its frontiers from attack. He acted as a judge, holding court regularly in different parts of his province to settle cases which might come before him on appeal from the local courts of the various *civitates*, or over which he exercised original jurisdiction. He might carry on diplomatic negotiations with client kings or independent tribes in the neighbourhood, and he might have to supervise the construction of roads or other public works. He was also expected to exercise some degree of control over the activities of the local governments, and his consent was often necessary before they were permitted to contract loans for any purpose. His functions were thus at once military, judicial, administrative, and sometimes diplomatic. It often happened that neither his previous experience nor his natural gifts fitted him to perform some of his varied tasks successfully, for he was merely a Roman politician who had been assigned his province by lot. Nevertheless, the conditions of Roman public life were such that most men who reached the point of governing a province had received some training in almost every field in which action was likely to be called for, so that they could fulfill their varied functions without much risk of absolute failure.

## § 9. THE ADMINISTRATION OF THE PROVINCES

If laws had been sufficient to ensure good government, the provinces would have had little reason to complain, for the provincial charters seem generally to have been wisely drawn, and a long series of statutes against extortion provided severe punishment for the governor who abused or exceeded his powers. Unfortunately, then as now, it was much easier to enact laws than to enforce them, and conditions under the Republic made the difficulty of enforcement unusually great. The slowness of communications made it obviously necessary to leave a great deal to the discretion of the man upon the spot and to permit him at times to violate the provisions of the provincial charter. It was necessary also to allow him to make requisitions on the *civitates* in order to protect the frontiers, if they were menaced by enemies without, and to take drastic measures in case of an emergency within. He was too far away to consult the senate before acting, and afterwards it was difficult to determine how far his action had been justified. It was inevitable, therefore, that a great deal of latitude should be left to the governor, and that the tendency should have been to judge his conduct very leniently as long as it admitted of excuse. Moreover, the character of the court before which a delinquent governor was tried was never satisfactory. Although the senate as a body seems to have desired good government in the provinces, the individual senators who served on the juries felt a natural reluctance to condemn a fellow senator. When C. Gracchus transferred the juries to the knights, whatever his intentions, there can be no doubt that he made matters worse, for the knights were directly interested in exploiting the provincials and were disposed to condemn any governor whose integrity restrained them. Under such conditions the governors could oppress with impunity the people confided to their care in many ways, and they often availed themselves of the opportunity in the last years of the Republic.

It is probable, however, that the provincials suffered more from the inherent defects of the system than from the rapacity and dishonesty of its representatives. At best the governor was an amateur sent to a province with whose real needs and conditions he was unacquainted and removed from his post at the end of a year or two. There was nothing in the nature of a permanent civil service, and for such help as he required he depended entirely upon his staff, which came from Rome and returned to the city with him. Everything depended, therefore, on the personal character of the man to whom the chances of the lot assigned the province, and incompetence might prove as disastrous as dishonesty. The decisions of his court, which he could practically control, might decide what interest the municipalities would have to pay upon their loans, and whether the agents of the tax-farmers could extort more than their due. It was possible for a governor, even if personally honest and well-intentioned, to lack the courage to enforce the law at the cost of incurring the resentment of powerful men at Rome, and to permit much of which he deeply disapproved through weakness and timidity. Moreover, a military blunder on the frontier might leave the province open to the raids of barbarian invaders and result in the fairest portions of it being ravaged and plundered, so that a courageous and upright man who had little experience in war might easily prove one of the worst of governors.

To determine how much the provinces had to endure from the deliberate maladministration of their rulers is very difficult. It has frequently been exaggerated by those who take Verres as a type and imagine that most governors were made in his image. We have no right to judge the average by the few whose misdeeds made a sensation in the courts, ignoring the fact that many were never prosecuted and that others, like Cicero, were certainly honest and humane. In spite of all allowances, however, it seems clear that the general tendency was downward. The fierce competition at Rome to secure the higher offices seems due in part at least to the increasing number of nobles who saw in a province the only way to escape from their financial embarrassments. Such men were certainly not likely to be scrupulous, although we have no reason to suppose that they often went to such lengths as Cicero accuses Verres of doing. It was possible to make a good deal of money in a province without being guilty of either pillage or oppression, and there must have been many governors like Cæsar, who seems to have been content with the legitimate profits of his proprætorship in Spain. Although the governor was not paid a salary, he was granted a sum of money for the expenses of administration, and at the close of his term he was neither required nor expected to return any unexpended balance to the treasury. If there was fighting on the frontier, the prisoners captured might be sold as slaves, and even on a small scale such warfare sometimes yielded a handsome profit. Of course, if a governor was unscrupulous, his opportunities were of the widest, and almost every act of his administration might be the occasion for a bribe or a corrupt bargain. Justice could be sold in his court, he could refuse his consent to any loans by the municipalities unless he received a share, he could give his sanction to the collection of extortionate interest by Roman money-lenders for a consideration, he could threaten to quarter troops in a town unless convinced by a gift that there was no danger of disorder ; in fact, the possibilities of gain were almost endless, and there is no reason to doubt that many governors took more or less advantage of these possibilities. Still, there were just as certainly many honest governors and many whose extortion was confined within comparatively narrow limits and did not cause any great damage to the province.

For much that they had to suffer the provincials had only themselves to thank, for some of the towns plunged recklessly into debt, borrowing at high rates of interest for extravagant public works and useless embassies. In other cases their financial difficulties were due neither to them nor to their governors, but to circumstances over which they had no control. In Asia Minor the Greek cities were plundered by Mithridates, and then heavily fined by Sulla. To pay what was required of them they were forced to borrow where they could and on any terms that were offered. In consequence Lucullus found them staggering under a burden of debt which was beyond their resources. In fact, the wealthy cities of the East were plundered again and again by Roman generals and proconsuls, until it might seem as though they must have been utterly and permanently ruined. This result did not follow, however, and the reason is not far to seek. The balance of trade was steadily against Rome and in favour of the East, since from the East came most of the articles of luxury for which the West was rapidly acquiring a taste. With the restoration of peace, therefore, the booty began to return to its source, and the prosperity of the Eastern cities began to revive. They paid Sulla heavily for having joined Mithridates, they paid Cæsar for having favoured Pompey, they were forced to pay for the army which Cassius led to Philippi, and they then paid Antony for having helped Cassius, yet they survived to flourish again when Augustus gave a lasting peace to the Roman world.

In spite of many and grave defects in its government of the provinces, the Republic may claim the merit of having laid the foundations for a better system. So far as laws went the Empire had little more to do than to enforce the legislation which it found upon the statute book. In the senatorial provinces under the Empire little more was actually done for many years, though in the imperial provinces a further improvement of the utmost importance was made by placing the choice of the governors in the hands of the emperor, who generally selected them with a view to their competence for the positions they were to hold. It is unjust to say that the Republic had entirely failed in its task, when we recall the large amount which it had actually achieved. It conquered and held together the entire Mediterranean world; it made a good beginning in the work of civilizing the more barbarous parts; it discovered the essential methods by which that world was to be governed for centuries; and it bequeathed to the Empire laws which secured justice for the provincials. On the other side it was unable to make its laws effective, it failed to furnish adequate protection to its subjects from border tribes and pirates, and its administration was often incompetent and corrupt. Whatever the abuses of the Republic's provincial government, it is clear that they were not directly responsible for its downfall. In reality, many of its shortcomings in this field were merely the inevitable results of the maladies from which it suffered nearer home. Indirectly the provinces did have their revenge, because they made necessary armies of a size and of a kind which the constitutional authorities could not control, with the inevitable result that the Republic gave place to a new form of government.

# CHAPTER XX

# ROMAN LITERATURE IN THE LAST CENTURY OF THE REPUBLIC

## * § 1. THE DEVELOPMENT OF LATIN POETRY

THAT Roman literature was an imitation of that of Greece is a well-known commonplace, but it was far from being a servile imitation. In this field, as in others, the Romans, while ready to learn, were no mere copyists, and, although they borrowed freely, they selected what suited their tastes, adapting and modifying what they borrowed, so that the result reflects unmistakably their national character and genius. The real foundation of Latin literature may be said to have been laid in the third century B.C. by Ennius, who took over the Greek forms of verse, discarding the earlier native metrical system. He composed an epic on Roman history, translated, more or less freely, a number of Greek tragedies and comedies, and wrote a few plays of purely Roman character. By his work Greek versification was successfully acclimatized in Rome.

The beginning once made, the development was rapid. In all the varied types of poetry which Ennius attempted he found successors, although his works continued to enjoy a great popularity to the end of the Republic. In the drama he was followed by his nephew, M. Pacuvius, who died at an advanced age about 130 B.C. He was considered by the Romans one of their two greatest tragic poets, the other being L. Accius, who died about 86 B.C. We possess only fragments of their plays and so can form no real judgment of their achievements. From the titles which have been preserved two things are clear. In the first place they adapted a large number of Greek tragedies for the Roman stage, and in the second they followed the example of Ennius in writing original plays on Roman themes, but the Greek adaptations seem to have been both more numerous and more popular. With these two poets Roman tragedy may be said to have come to an end, since we know of no important writer in this field after Accius. Tragedies continued to be written, it is true, but the theatre seems to have been largely content to reproduce those of Ennius, Pacuvius, and Accius, which were acted frequently until the period of the early Empire. The comparatively brief life of tragedy may have been due to the fact that in spite of all modifications it remained a somewhat exotic form of literature which flourished mainly under the patronage of the great noble families and died out with the decline of their influence, giving place to other forms of entertainment more congenial to the tastes of the less thoroughly Hellenized popular audiences.

The plays of Terence marked the highest point achieved in the adaptation of Greek comedies for the Roman stage. After his death in 159 B.C. other writers carried on the tradition, especially Turpilius, who died in 103, but a new type of comedy (the *fabula togata*) rapidly became popular, in which an attempt was made to portray Roman life and manners, although the plots were often borrowed from the Greeks. The first writer of such comedies was Titinius, who began writing soon after Terence, but the greatest masters in this field were T. Quinctius Atta and L. Afranius. The *fabula togata* seems to have flourished between the time of Terence and that of Sulla, since Atta died in 77 and Afranius was born about 150 B.C. Unfortunately none of these comedies has come down to us, and we can only conjecture their character from the titles and a few passages which have been preserved. Whatever its merits, this national comedy was destined to give way to another type with which we are even less well acquainted, namely, the Atellan farce.

These farces had their roots in Italian soil, originating among the Oscans. In the time of Sulla they were taken in hand by men of letters and were acted as after-pieces, following tragedies. They must have been short, therefore, and their authors seem to have contented themselves with the exhibition of a number of stock characters, such as an old man called Pappus, a fool called Maccus, and a lying braggart called Bucco. Since none of these farces has survived, any judgment as to their character must be based on scattered lines, some three hundred in number, and on the titles. Their style seems to have been somewhat rustic, with a good deal of homely vigour. For a generation or two they appear to have enjoyed great popularity, but about 50 B.C. they gave way to the mime, although some of them were revived under the Empire.

The mime, which replaced the Atellan farce as an afterpiece for tragedies, seems to have developed out of a dance in character under the influence of the Greek mime. The fact that the actors wore no masks and were barefooted gave opportunity for facial expression and agility of movement, and these features were more and more emphasized until the mime ultimately became a pantomime, in which form it had a long lease of life and enjoyed great popularity under the Empire. At first, however, it seems to have borne a close resemblance to the Atellan farce, except that it dealt with city rather than with country life. In the mime Roman comedy came to a somewhat dishonourable end. Its career shows three phases: in the first the new Greek comedy was transplanted to Rome with such adaptations as would make it intelligible to a Roman audience; then it became national in spirit and character, finding its subjects in contemporary Roman life; and finally it degenerated under the demands of the populace for broad and often coarse humour into the Atellan farce and the mime, after which it lost all pretence to a place as literature and became pantomime.

Aside from the drama the Romans were producing other types of poetry during the last century of the Republic. Although the epic of Ennius was not displaced in public favour until the time of Virgil, a number of others were produced. None of them, however, seems to have been of much importance, and they have left behind them only a few lines. It will suffice to mention that Accius in addition to his tragedies wrote an epic on Roman history, and that Hostius made the events of the Illyrian war of 125 the theme of another, while Cn. Matius translated the Iliad into Latin in the time of Sulla.

Didactic poetry was also cultivated, and for a time literary criticism took this form. Accius wrote a poem on the history of the drama, and his example was followed by Porcius Licinius and Volcatius Sedigitus, both of whom wrote poems on the Roman poets. Other subjects were treated, of course, ranging from cookery to science, but we have little more than the names of the early works in this field.

In another direction the Romans practically invented a new form of literature, namely, satire. The term was originally applied to a collection of poems on different subjects, and it was P. Lucilius who first gave the word its modern meaning. He was a native of Campania and served in Spain under Scipio Æmilianus, with whom he became intimate. Lucilius was debarred from public life, since he was an Italian and not a Roman citizen, but indirectly he took a part through his satires, of which he published some thirty books between 131 and 105 B.C. In them he ranged over a wide variety of subjects, for he poured into his poems all his experiences, feelings, and opinions. In one he describes a journey which he had made, in another a gladiatorial show, in others he accepts an invitation to dinner, gives his conception of virtue, portrays a miser, and denounces luxury and greed. His style was easy and unconventional, Horace thought it careless, but his naturalness, liveliness, and good sense atoned for his lack of polish in the eyes of his contemporaries. He used his opportunity to assail the political opponents of his friend Scipio, although he directed his attack rather at their personal characters than at their politics. After Scipio's death he continued to lash the follies of the times, the blunders of the government, the incompetence of the generals, and the vices of the rabble. He was outspoken and sincere, fearless and independent, standing for the right as he saw it and addressing himself to the average man of his day, and he had his reward in the long popularity which his poems enjoyed. Even in the time of the Flavian emperors there were still those who preferred him to all other poets, but his works are now known only by fragments, which are mostly short, the longest being a description of virtue in thirteen lines.

## § 2. ANTIQUITIES AND LAW

In law the Romans took a keen interest and early began to write on this subject, where naturally Greek influences were much less marked than in poetry. About 200 B.C. Sextus Ælius Pætus produced a treatise on the Twelve Tables and legal forms, which was later regarded as "the cradle of the law." The period of the Gracchi saw a remarkable development in this field, in which a single family bore the most conspicuous part. The two most important members of it were P. Mucius Scævola and his son Quintus. The father was consul in 133 and was elected *pontifex maximus* in 130 B.C. As a friend of Tiberius Gracchus and an enemy of Scipio he was attacked by Lucilius, but the attack seems to have done him little harm. As *pontifex maximus* he published a digest of the pontifical annals in eighty books, a work which yielded much material to historians. Q. Mucius Scævola held the consulship in 95, and like his father was *pontifex maximus*. He was murdered by the Marians in 82 B.C., when Sulla's victories compelled them to abandon Rome. He wrote a systematic treatise on law, and may be called the founder of its scientific study. His influence was also felt through his pupils Lucilius Balbus and Aquilius Gallus, who were the teachers of Sulpicius Rufus, the friend of Cicero.

Interest in law was closely associated with an interest in antiquities, as in the case of the first Scævola, though eventually antiquarian studies freed themselves from juristic trammels, and studies of grammar and literature, begun by the poets, came to be frequently combined with antiquarian research. The new combination is seen in L. Ælius Stilo, born about 150 B.C., who interested himself in the Latin language and literature, as well as in Roman antiquities, to all of which he applied the historical method. He inspired a considerable interest in these subjects, and Varro seems to have owed much to him, while Cicero was one of his pupils.

By far the greatest figure in antiquarian research was M. Terentius Varro. This celebrated scholar was born in the Sabine country in 116 B.C., and held the offices of tribune and ædile. He served against the pirates under Pompey, and perhaps also in the war against Mithridates. He opposed the First Triumvirate, on which he wrote a book called *The Three-Headed Monster*, but in spite of this he served on Cæsar's Land Commission to provide allotments for Pompey's veterans, and from this circumstance we may infer that his opposition was less bitter than the title of his book would suggest. In the Civil War he sided with Pompey, but after the defeat of his leader made his peace with Cæsar, who placed him in charge of the public library which he planned but did not live to establish. Under the Second Triumvirate Varro's name was included in the proscription, but he was saved by the devotion of his friends, and passed his last years in peace, dying at an advanced age in 27 B.C.

In the course of his long life it has been estimated that Varro published some 620 volumes on all manner of subjects. His works included 150 books of Menippean Satires, whose title was taken from the name of a Greek satirist, 41 books on antiquities, 15 books on civil law, 25 books on the Latin language, 9 books on education, which included a complete scheme, 3 books on agriculture, and treatises on literary history, mathematics, and astronomy. His 15 books of "Portraits" are the first illustrated work known and contained the portraits and lives of seven hundred eminent Greeks and Romans.[1] He also wrote on philosophy, both separately and in connection with various other subjects. Of his writings we possess that on agriculture practically entire, and six of the twenty-five books on the Latin language; of the rest only fragments survive.

From the historical point of view his most important work was that *On Human and Divine Antiquities*, whose loss we must deeply regret. Although much of its material has undoubtedly been incorporated in the works of the later historians, it cannot be doubted that a great deal which would now be of the highest interest has perished. He would seem to have been deficient in the critical faculty and no doubt made many blunders; still, his vast reading and extraordinary industry could hardly fail to bring together a large number of facts which would have served to illuminate many obscure problems.

In the Menippean Satires he does not seem to have followed the example of Lucilius, but to have reverted to the older type of satire. The 150 books were a mixture of prose and verse dealing with nearly every conceivable subject. The fragments

[1] Another writer of brief popular biographies was Cornelius Nepos, who was a contemporary of Varro and Cicero. He wrote a collection of lives of famous men (*de viris illustribus*), apparently in sixteen books, including both Romans and foreigners. Of these only a few survive.

from them which have come down to us aggregate about 600 lines, and in spite of their diversity two themes seem to have recurred with a good deal of regularity, namely, the futility of much Greek speculation, and the growth of luxury in contrast to the good old times. In one of them a Roman Rip Van Winkle awakes after a sleep of fifty years to find himself in a world which has completely changed. The satires doubtless contained much good sense and humour, but it is not likely that they had any great literary merit. Varro certainly can claim no high rank as an artist; it was as a collector of facts that he excelled, and as such he provided a wealth of material for later writers.

### § 3. HISTORY AND MEMOIRS

The earliest phase of Roman historical writing was the compilation of annals in Greek. Cato the Censor was the first to write a history in Latin and to enliven his narrative by the introduction of speeches. His example was followed by a number of writers, of whom only Cassius Hemina, Calpurnius Piso, and C. Fannius need be mentioned. None of them seems to have risen much above the level of the older annalists, contenting themselves with a meagre chronicle of events, although Fannius inserted some speeches. A new spirit soon made itself felt, however, and it probably was due in part to the influence of Polybius. This eminent historian was brought to Italy as a hostage after the Third Macedonian War and resided there for many years. He was taken into the house of L. Æmilius Paullus, where he became the tutor and friend of his host's son, Scipio Æmilianus. He was thus a member of the Scipionic circle, and became acquainted with many of the distinguished Romans of his day. Since his views of history must have been fairly well known, we may reasonably attribute to him some of the changes in method and outlook which we find in the historians of the Gracchan period. Hitherto the annalists had begun their accounts with the foundation of the city. Sempronius Asellio was the first to confine himself to his own times; having served as an officer under Scipio in Spain during the Numantine War, he makes this war the starting-point of his history, which he probably carried down to the death of M. Livius Drusus in

91 B.C. In another respect he departed from his predecessors, holding with Polybius that history should not confine itself to recording battles and events, but should seek to explain them by showing motives and causes. Another historian, L. Cælius Antipater, confined himself to the Second Punic War, which he investigated with considerable care, showing an exceptional impartiality and critical faculty by consulting Greek sources favourable to Carthage.

At the beginning of the first century B.C. a new group came upon the scene. Claudius Quadrigarius dropped the mythical period altogether and began with the sack of Rome by the Gauls. He seems to have anticipated Sallust, or perhaps followed Antipater, in mixing reflections with his narrative. Valerius Antias reverted to the earlier custom by starting with the foundation of the city. His history was disfigured by wild exaggerations and by partiality for the Valerii. In spite of these defects it was used by both Plutarch and Livy, although the latter finally became suspicious of the inflated statistics which it gave. Lastly we may note Cornelius Sisenna and Licinius Macer, who died within a year of each other in 67 and 66 B.C. Sisenna was chiefly concerned with the Social War and the civil wars between Sulla and his opponents. His style was marked by a fondness for archaic and unusual words, but Cicero speaks favourably of his learning. Macer seems to have marked a real development by exploring the early records with industry, if not always with sufficient care or caution. He deserves credit for making a serious attempt to base his work upon the study of the original sources. He wrote more or less from the standpoint of the popular party, to which he seems to have belonged, for during his tribuneship in 73 B.C. he tried to restore to the tribunes the powers of which Sulla had deprived them. Cicero characterizes his history as diffuse and sharply critizes some of the speeches in it, but the orator was probably prejudiced against him and may have exaggerated his defects.

The writings of all these historians are lost, except for scattered fragments, but they were extensively used by those who followed them. Enough is known, however, to enable us to trace the changes which they made. Certainly more attention was paid to style, and history grew somewhat more critical and decidedly more rhetorical as time went on. It became an accepted branch of literature, and the writers strove to make their work more entertaining than the bare enumeration of events after the fashion of the early annalists could hope to be. From a literary point of view perhaps the best was Valerius Antias, whose style was fluent and free from archaisms, but none of them seems to have attained any real distinction.

The bitter party strife which began with the Gracchi led naturally enough to the production of political pamphlets, mostly in the form of published orations, and to attempts on the part of various prominent men to justify and explain their acts by writing memoirs. Æmilius Scaurus, the leader of the senate at the time of the Jugurthine War, defended himself in three books of memoirs, and Rutilius Rufus, driven into exile by the knights in 93 B.C. for his rigid integrity, did the same in five books. Lutatius Catulus, who had been Marius' colleague in the consulship in 102, finding the public inclined to give all the credit for the defeat of the Cimbri at Vercellæ to Marius, sought to vindicate his claim to a share in the glory, although apparently with little success. Sulla, after he retired into private life, devoted much of his leisure to the writing of an autobiography, of which he completed the twenty-second book two days before his death. It is impossible to determine the value of any of these works, but it is likely that later writers were indebted to them for many details. There is no reason to suppose that any of the memoirs mentioned possessed any great literary value. Cicero held no high opinion of Roman historians previous to his own day, and his judgment was probably correct if we look rather to the form than to the substance. Unfortunately, a brilliant style is not always associated with diligence in the investigation of the facts or an uncompromising love of truth, and it is possible that some of the earlier historians, if their works had survived, would have been more reliable guides than the more famous ones who followed them.

## § 4. CÆSAR

Like so many of the prominent men of his generation, Cæsar tried his hand at various kinds of literature, but he achieved eminence and enduring fame only in the field of history. His other works have perished and their loss is probably not greatly to be deplored, yet they deserve at least passing mention if only to illustrate his versatility and wide interests. We know of a treatise on astronomy, one on grammar, and a collection of witty sayings. In the last years of his life he published an attack on Cato in two books, which was probably a political pamphlet intended to counteract the posthumous influence of the austere republican. He wrote poetry throughout his life; among his poems was an early tragedy on Œdipus, while shortly before his death he described in verse his journey to Spain to crush the sons of Pompey. There were also a number of love poems. Augustus suppressed his poetry, which seems to have possessed no great merit.

His historical work consists of his Commentaries on the Gallic and Civil Wars; these do not profess to be history at all, only materials for history, as the title, signifying notes or reports, indicates, but the achievement went so far beyond the professed aim that Cæsar remained the historian of his own wars. Moreover, it is certain that, while the professed aim may have been a real one, it was not the most important, and that the author was far less concerned about providing information for future historians than he was in vindicating himself in the eyes of his immediate contemporaries. The Commentaries are, in fact, political pamphlets in the guise of history, or perhaps it would be better to say history written to serve political ends. The seven books dealing with the Gallic wars were probably published in 51 B.C., when Cæsar and Pompey were still outwardly friends, but when a less astute man than Cæsar could easily foresee that they would soon become rivals. Furthermore, Cæsar's proconsulship in Gaul was drawing to its close, and he would soon return to Rome, where he might have to answer for his acts. If he could influence public opinion in his favour, it might give him a decided advantage and help to secure the second consulship on which he was counting. In spite of the fame and glory which he had won by his victories, he was well aware that he had many bitter enemies and some sharp critics in Rome. It seemed an opportune moment, therefore, to give the world an account of his achievements which would disarm criticism by furnishing a complete justification for his actions and impress the public with the greatness of his services. To avow such aims, or even to let them become apparent to the reader, would go far to defeat them, and with the instinct of true genius Cæsar confined himself to a clear and simple narrative of events, allowing the facts to speak for themselves. He writes in the third person with such calm and complete detachment that every reference to himself seems inevitable and almost reluctant. Although the style is simple and unadorned, it is dignified, elegant, terse, and vigorous. Rhetorical ornaments are almost entirely dispensed with, irrelevant or unnecessary details omitted, except for the occasional mention of the gallantry of soldiers or officers, and the broad outlines of the various campaigns are set forth with remarkable lucidity. The greatness of the writer stands out all the more impressively because he never obtrudes it upon the reader, but contents himself with showing what he did and why, leaving it to others to pass judgment on his conduct without a hint that he is conscious that there is any need of defending it. No one would suspect from his account of his dealings with the Usipetes and Tencteri that Cato had bitterly denounced him for treacherously violating his truce with these unhappy tribes. Cæsar merely states the facts, apparently with perfect candour, and leaves the reader to decide between him and his critics. In his Commentaries on the Civil War, which he did not live to finish, his attitude is the same. Here, too, we have a plain unvarnished narrative in which the events speak for themselves. In both works Cæsar assumes that the simple truth is a sufficient justification of his course, and that when the facts have been clearly set forth there is nothing more worth saying.

Certainly in Cæsar's hands the facts seem to constitute a complete justification according to the accepted standards of his time, but there have been grave doubts as to whether this impression is not due in some degree to dexterous manipulation. Was Cæsar as detached, impartial, and candid as he appears, or did he select and arrange the facts in accordance with a deliberate purpose ? No final solution of the problem is possible to-day, for we have too little outside evidence to determine how far, if at all, Cæsar may have tampered with the truth. He was far too astute to attempt falsehood in matters which were more or less well known and where exposure would be possible if not inevitable. Even here, however, by omitting some details and giving undue prominence to others much might be done to make events appear as Cæsar desired his readers to see them. Undoubtedly he wished to seem a lover of peace driven into war by his adversaries. Charged with having undertaken the conquest of Gaul without the sanction of the senate and with having drawn the sword against the constitution of his country to gratify his own ambition, he shows how the Gauls themselves forced him to conquer them, and how the bitter and unreasonable hatred of his enemies left him no alternative but to take arms in self-defence. Naturally enough some modern scholars have doubted the accuracy of such a picture, and have suspected that the real Cæsar bore a greater resemblance to the portrait painted by his opponents than to that which he has given of himself in his Commentaries. Proof is out of the question, but critical opinion is on the whole inclined to accept Cæsar's version as substantially trustworthy. Some reservations no doubt need to be made. No one can believe that he was reluctant to conquer Gaul, nor does he pretend that this was the case, yet, when every allowance is made for ambition on his part, the Gauls seem to have furnished provocation as well as opportunity. At the outbreak of the Civil War we may reasonably question the sincerity of some of his offers of compromise; still, Cicero's letters are unanswerable evidence that he could have avoided war only by submitting to political annihilation. At the worst we must conclude that, although Cæsar may have overstated his case, he has not created it by distorting the facts. Some slips and inaccuracies have, indeed, been detected in his two sets of Commentaries, but they are rather trivial and have little bearing on any large issue. They seem to be due to haste and carelessness, and to an over-confidence in his memory, rather than to deliberate purpose. The haste with which he wrote to serve an immediate purpose, together with the lack of opportunity for revision and correction, would explain and excuse such errors as he can definitely be shown to have committed.

In conclusion a word in regard to the continuations of his Commentaries may be of interest. His officer and friend Hirtius, who was consul in 43 and was killed in forcing Antony to raise the siege of Mutina, bridged the gap between the seventh book of the Commentaries on the Gallic Wars and the beginning of those on the Civil Wars by writing the eighth book of the former. The latter was continued by the Commentaries on the Alexandrian War, which have also been credited to Hirtius, although his authorship is far from certain. To these works must be added one on the African War, by an unknown participant of some literary ability, and one on the Spanish War by some ill-educated officer who served in it. All these works are valuable for the information they give us, if from no other standpoint, and enable us to reconstruct Cæsar's campaigns from the testimony of men who actually took part in them. It is possible, therefore, to form a more certain and accurate judgment of his generalship than of that of most other commanders of antiquity, and it need only be said that it has stood the test, winning the admiration of the best soldiers in all ages.

## § 5. SALLUST

Since Cæsar was essentially a military historian writing with a political purpose, Sallust must rank as the greatest historian of the Ciceronian age. Of his life we know little, but that little happens to be somewhat significant. C. Sallustius Crispus was born in 86 B.C. in the Sabine country. He entered politics in Rome and seems to have been a consistent democrat. He was tribune at the time of Clodius' murder and had a part in stirring up the disorders which followed that event. In 50 B.C. the censors expelled him from the senate on the charge of gross immorality, although the fact that he was a partisan of Cæsar may have contributed a good deal to their righteous indignation. However that may be, Cæsar replaced him among the conscript fathers in the following year, and in 48 he was given command of a legion in Illyricum. In 47 he was employed in suppressing a mutiny in Campania, and in 46, as prætor, he accompanied Cæsar to Africa. After the battle of Thapsus, when Cæsar punished Juba for aiding the Republicans by annexing his kingdom of Numidia as a province, he appointed Sallust as its first governor. In this capacity Sallust is said to have made himself rich by the practice of extortion ; certainly after Cæsar's death he abandoned public life and retired to a villa with beautiful gardens on the Quirinal, where he devoted his leisure to history until his death in 35 B.C. In his chosen field he produced three works, *The Conspiracy of Catiline*, *The Jugurthine War*, and a *History* in five books, covering the period from the death of Sulla in 78 to 67 B.C. The first two survive entire, but of the last we have only fragments. The most extensive of these fragments are four speeches and two letters, whose preservation we owe to the fact that they were studied separately as examples of rhetoric. A speech against Cicero, if authentic, which is doubtful, was a political pamphlet rather than a speech, and two letters to Cæsar attributed to him may, or may not, be genuine.

As a historian Sallust is a decided partisan, of Cæsar personally and of the democrats in general. This fact had much to do with his choice of subjects. His book on the conspiracy of Catiline was written chiefly to clear Cæsar of all complicity in the matter. The best way to accomplish this result appeared to be to write a history of the whole plot wherein Cæsar should be conspicuous by his absence. By adopting this method of vindicating his former leader Sallust is at once freed from any need of trying to defend Catiline and is quite prepared to accept Cicero's general view of the conspiracy. He is all the more inclined to paint it in the darkest colours because the leading conspirators belonged to the nobility, the degeneracy of the nobles being one of his favourite themes, and because their chief had been an adherent of Sulla, whom Sallust hated. Thus the historian was quite ready to accept without much hesitation or scepticism the worst that Cicero or anyone else could say about Catiline. Although the work adds little to our knowledge of the conspiracy, since it so largely repeats the Ciceronian version, still it is not without value. Sallust seems to have made no exhaustive investigation of the facts, but to have relied largely on Cicero, hearsay, and his own recollections. In one point at least he made a real advance in the writing of history, for he tries to paint vivid and lifelike portraits of his principal characters. From the purely literary point of view he is distinctly successful, but we can hardly help suspecting that he made more use of his imagination than of authentic sources in producing his portraits. In his narrative he assumes the attitude of a grave moralist and an impartial judge. He is fair to Cato in spite of his devotion to Cæsar, and praises

Cicero for suppressing the conspiracy, although in this the commendation could hardly be avoided and seems rather half-hearted.

Several reasons led Sallust to write upon the Jugurthine War, among which one was probably his personal knowledge of the country. The main attraction of the theme, however, seems to have been the opportunity to contrast the inefficiency and corruption of the nobles with the virtue and success of the democratic hero Marius. That this is the real purpose of the book is shown not only by the author's frank avowal but also by the carelessness with which military events are treated in what professes to be the history of a war. No attempt is made to explain the strategy of the generals, many of Marius' movements are obviously omitted and must be supplied by conjecture, and the only incidents in the campaigns of the hero of the work which are narrated with much detail are those wherein Sulla took part. The most probable explanation of this last fact is that Sallust drew the greater part of his information in regard to the closing years of the war from Sulla's memoirs. The main object of the author, to show how the arrogance of the nobility was resisted for the first time, is fully achieved, however, and all rumours and suspicions of the bribery of senators and generals which circulated in Rome at the time are carefully preserved and repeated. Some corruption there doubtless was, but Sallust is not concerned with sifting evidence, and the worse the reader thinks of the senate, the better from his point of view.

The most important work of Sallust was his *History*, which is unfortunately lost. Too little remains of it to show whether the author made any improvement on his methods as we see them in his two earlier monographs, and it is by these that we must judge him as a historian. He has certain qualities which appear to have been more or less new in Roman historical writing: he made a serious attempt to delineate character, and had a sense for the large movements of history. Taking Thucydides as his model, in spite of his strong party bias, he sought to deal fairly with the better leaders on the other side. In his style he cultivated a touch of the archaic, and carefully avoided the balanced style of Cicero, striving rather at epigrammatic terseness of expression. He unquestionably did much to develop Latin historical prose and to make history more vivid and entertaining.

## § 6. LUCRETIUS

The Ciceronian age saw two of the greatest poets that Rome ever produced, the elder of whom was T. Lucretius Carus. Of his life almost nothing is known. He appears to have been born about 99 and to have died in 55 B.C. We are told that he committed suicide in a fit of madness caused by a love-philtre, and that his works were published after his death by Cicero. His great poem "On the Nature of Things" concludes abruptly, so that the sudden death of the poet is highly probable. At any rate, Lucretius lived through stormy and troubled times, and this fact may have had much to do with his choice of a subject. He stood aloof from public life, became an ardent disciple of the Epicurean school of philosophy, and consecrated all his powers to the attempt to popularize its views. His poem is an exposition of the system of Epicurus, written with the fervour of an impassioned missionary and the genius of a poet of the first rank. The old Greek philosopher had in the common phrase made pleasure the supreme good, but pleasure to Epicurus meant not physical enjoyment but tranquillity of soul, the freedom of the mind from fear, ambition, anxiety, and passion. Such an ideal appealed powerfully to Lucretius, living as he did amid the turmoil and confusion of the dying Republic. Fear seemed to him the greatest evil which man had to overcome, above all the fear of death, and religion he regarded as the fertile source of superstitions and terrors. His aim was to deliver men from their needless anxieties about omens and prodigies, about the gods and lesser supernatural beings, and to teach them to confront the world with calmness, facing death without dread. In all this he followed his master, but he added an intensity and fervour of his own.

As the basis of his system Epicurus had adopted, with some modifications, the atomic theory of Democritus, which Lucretius takes over from him and explains in the first book of his poem. The universe is made up of an infinite number of atoms in an infinite space. In the second book he undertakes to show how the atoms falling through space come together and form the various substances of the world. In the third the soul is explained as material and as dying with the body, and a passionate attack is made upon religion and the fear of death. Since death ends all there is nothing to dread, and men should face the inevitable with equanimity. The fourth deals with the senses, whose reliability is emphatically maintained, with dreams, and with love, which is represented as a thing to be shunned or controlled. The fifth book describes the origin of the sun, moon, stars, and earth, and traces the beginning of life and the development of civilization. The sixth and last book is concerned with various natural phenomena such as thunder, lightning, and earthquakes, and the poem concludes with a description of the plague at Athens taken from Thucydides.

That a large part of the subject was not adapted to poetic treatment is obvious, and the warmest admirers of Lucretius are forced to admit that much of the poem, in spite of the dignity of the style and the genius of the poet, is more or less dull and prosaic. The high place assigned to Lucretius is based upon his finer passages, and few will question his greatness at his best. In his loftier flights the vividness and power of his imagination, combined with the splendour of his verse, have led many critics to rank him as the greatest of Roman poets.

### § 7. CATULLUS

C. Valerius Catullus, the other great poet of the Ciceronian period, was born in Verona about 84 B.C. His father was a man of means and a friend of Cæsar during his governorship of Cisalpine Gaul. Precisely when Catullus came to Rome is uncertain, but once there he secured admission to aristocratic society. About 61 B.C. he fell passionately in love with Clodia, the beautiful sister of Cicero's enemy, and this affair continued for some three years. To her, under the name of Lesbia, he addressed his finest lyrics, recording all his varying moods, devotion, ecstasy, doubt, jealousy, and bitterness, as he gradually realized her true character and faithlessness. He finally broke with her in 58, and, feeling the need of change of scene, he obtained a position on the staff of the governor of Bithynia in 57. He returned in the spring of 56 and died a year or two later at an early age.

Lucretius in his work stood apart from the fashions of the day, but Catullus eagerly accepted the prevailing literary tendencies. It was a time when Romans were devoted to the study and imitation of the Alexandrian poets. Like his friend Licinius Calvus, Catullus wrote wedding songs, epigrams, poems on mythological subjects ("Attis" and "Peleus and Thetis"), and translated a poem of Callimachus ("The Lock of Berenice"). These works reveal his genius, but they are overshadowed by his lyrics, which constitute his best title to immortality. In these the influence of his Alexandrian models is less marked than in his longer poems, for here he pours out his own feelings with a burning intensity unique in Latin literature. His metres may be borrowed from the Greeks, but he has made them his own, and through them he expresses with "passionate simplicity," directness, and force the emotions which dominated him. He had no concern with philosophy, being content to live and to record his experience of life. His interest in public affairs is casual and his attitude toward them is determined by his environment and personal feelings, rather than by any settled convictions. He hated Cæsar's quartermaster, Mamurra, who was his rival in an amorous intrigue, and he gives expression to his animosity in bitter and indecent epigrams directed at the offending officer and his master, until he becomes reconciled to Cæsar, perhaps through his father's influence. To discuss such a poet at any length is obviously a fruitless task. His work speaks for itself and must be read to be appreciated, for it cannot be adequately rendered in translation; his right to a place among the great lyric poets of the world, who have expressed in simple and melodious words the deep and abiding passions of mankind, is beyond dispute.

## § 8. CICERO

The life of Cicero has been sufficiently treated in what precedes, but some attempt must be made to estimate his place in Roman literature. He was not only the leading orator and one of the leading statesmen of his day, but he published a large number of works on a variety of subjects, chiefly oratory and philosophy, which have exercised a profound and enduring influence. Of his writings we possess a very little poetry, fifty-seven orations with fragments of twenty more, seven treatises on rhetoric, two on politics, eleven on philosophy, and about eight hundred letters. Most of his treatises were produced during two short intervals when he was forced to retire from active public life, the first during the ascendancy of the First Triumvirate, and the second during Cæsar's dictatorship.

In poetry Cicero accomplished nothing of serious importance, although he published a number of poems, some of them translations and some original. Of the latter the most important were a poem on Marius, perhaps a youthful work, a poem in three books on his consulship, and one on his own times, published after his exile and dealing with his misfortunes. He also translated two astronomical poems of Aratus, and passages from Homer and the Greek dramatists, with which he embellished his philosophical treatises. Of his original poems only a few fragments survive, so that we must judge him chiefly by his translations. In these he displays some talent, and the sneers provoked by a few unhappy lines in his poem on his consulship ought not to outweigh the merit which his translations undoubtedly possess. The fact remains, however, that he failed to obtain a place among Roman poets, a failure which he shares with Cæsar and many of his lesser contemporaries.

Cicero stands out first and foremost as an orator, and in his chosen field he is without a rival among Romans. Not only did he publish a large number of his speeches, but in several rhetorical treatises he set forth his theories of oratory and his ideal of what an orator should be. The art of public speaking had, of course, been practised at Rome from the earliest times, and Cicero had many illustrious predecessors. From the time of the Gracchi, if not before, there had been a series of great orators of whom Cicero has left us some account in his treatises. In his opinion Roman eloquence first rose to a level with that of Greece in C. Gracchus and the great orators who followed him. Of these the most eminent were M. Antonius (143–87 B.C.) and L. Licinius Crassus (140–91 B.C.), whom Cicero may have heard in his youth. Both were carefully trained in the precepts of Greek rhetoric, and Cicero ranked them as the greatest of his predecessors. When Cicero himself appeared upon the scene, he found himself pitted against formidable competitors, the chief of whom were Q. Hortensius Hortalus (114–50 B.C.) in the courts and Cæsar in the senate and assembly. Two rival schools had developed, of which the Asiatic, as it was called, was represented by Hortensius, while Cæsar belonged to the other, known as the Attic. The former was inclined to be florid and to employ an excess of ornamentation and embellishment, while the Atticists cultivated simplicity and restraint. Cicero takes an intermediate position between the two schools, seeking to avoid the excessive luxuriance of the one and the bareness and coldness of the other, although he leaned upon the whole to the Asiatic side. His success was early and decisive, for by his conduct of the case against Verres he won the first place at the bar from Hortensius and remained the foremost orator of Rome until his death. Nevertheless, there were many other distinguished speakers in his day, Cæsar among the foremost, so that Cicero was far from standing alone or of securing universal approbation, for many continued to prefer the Attic style.

In his orations Cicero may be said to have developed Latin prose to the highest point in one direction. The periodic sentence with its rounded majesty and sonorous rhythm was largely his achievement so far as we can determine. His style had its dangers, to which he sometimes fell a victim, especially the temptation to redundancy and verbosity, but he is generally careful to secure enough variety to prevent his long sentences from becoming monotonous, and at his best his prose has been a model for innumerable writers from his own day to the present. His rhetorical treatises claim at least a word, and may appropriately be considered in connection with his speeches. The most important were the *de oratore*, in which he discusses the studies necessary for an orator, the treatment of the subject, and the form and delivery of a speech, the *Brutus,* in which he traces the history of Roman eloquence, and the *orator*, in which he draws a portrait of the ideal orator, reaching the conclusion that he must be an ideal man. In these we find an exposition of the theories on which his own speeches were based, and of which they are admirable examples.

The main peculiarities of Cicero's prose style, whether in his orations, his treatises, or his more elaborate and carefully written letters, sprang from a fundamental conception. In his rhetorical works he commits himself to the proposition that prose should have a definite rhythm, but should not carry this so far as to become verse, a thing to be scrupulously avoided. The rhythm should be varied, but each sentence should have a sort of prose metre, which is most important in the closing words where it rounds out to a final cadence. To secure the effect at which he aimed Cicero is naturally led to employ the periodic sentence with carefully balanced parts. Of course in his composition he did not consciously scan his sentences, but worked with a keen instinct both for words and for their rhythmic arrangement. Those Roman writers who avoided the Ciceronian balance and long periods, such as Cæsar and Sallust, made no attempt to write rhythmic prose, perhaps studiously avoided it. In his own chosen style Cicero had no equal among Romans, although they were themselves divided on the merits of the style, not only in his own day but afterwards.

Cicero wrote two treatises on what we would call political science, namely the *Commonwealth* (*de re publica*) and the *Laws* (*de legibus*). Of the first, which was in six books, about a third survives. The other was intended as a sequel, but was never finished, and we have only fragments of it. The attitude of Cicero in these works is thoroughly conservative; his ideal state is the Roman Republic freed from some obvious abuses and corruptions. He admires the Roman constitution so heartily that he is prepared to defend it in almost all its parts. Apparently Sulla's reforms were largely satisfactory to him, and he saw little need of any further changes. It has been thought that he anticipated something more or less akin to the principate of Augustus, for he speaks of a *princeps* who is to be a guide or moderator of the commonwealth, but it seems probable from the brief fragments which survive on this point that he is merely drawing a picture of his ideal of a statesman, one whose advice would be listened to by all parties because he aimed solely at the public good. If Cicero thought of Pompey as a possible candidate for such a place, he was bitterly disappointed in him, and it is more likely that he had himself rather than another in mind. Whatever his views, they were without practical effect, and he seems to have shown little comprehension of the real problems of his day.

The philosophical writings of Cicero have an importance almost equal to that of his orations, because of their wide and lasting influence. It was after the death of his beloved daughter Tullia early in 45 B.C. that Cicero turned to philosophy for consolation in his grief, and he produced his works in this field with extreme rapidity. If we seek in them for original and profound thought we shall certainly be disappointed, but if we estimate them by their professed intention we shall find them worthy of high praise. Cicero makes no pretence to originality; his aim, as he himself puts it, was to make philosophy accessible to his fellow countrymen. He selects, adapts, and translates from various Greek thinkers, using his own judgment freely, but making no attempt to construct a system, even an eclectic one, and keeping practical considerations constantly in view. He accomplished his avowed purpose with extraordinary success, and furnished his contemporaries with a series of excellent manuals in which some of the leading ideas of the Greek philosophers were expressed in graceful, polished, and easily intelligible Latin. How great an achievement this was we can only appreciate if we recall the conditions when he undertook his work. At that time there were practically no books on philosophy in Latin except a few works by obscure adherents of the Epicurean school and the great poem of Lucretius. Cicero was breaking fresh ground, therefore, so he was forced to create almost the whole philosophic terminology in which he expresses himself and translates his Greek originals. The mere fact that he was able to manipulate the Latin language in such a fashion as to find simple and natural equivalents for the Greek technical terms is a striking testimony to his remarkable mastery of it; in this respect he far surpassed Lucretius, who suffered at times from the lack of an adequate vocabulary. Cicero's real achievement, and it was no mean one, was that he invented such a vocabulary and popularized many of the best ideas of Greek philosophy.

His most important philosophical treatises were those *On the Definition of Good and Evil* (*de finibus bonorum et malorum*), in five books, the *Tusculan Disputations*, also in five books, *On Duty* (*de officiis*), in three, the *Academics*, of which two books survive, *On the Nature of the Gods*, in three books, and *On Divination*, in two. It may be said in passing that all these works except the one on duty are in the form of dialogues. In modern times the best known are the two short dialogues *On Friendship* and *On Old Age.* The titles in all but two cases speak for themselves; in one of the surviving books of the *Academics* we have a brief sketch of the history of philosophy, the other is devoted to a discussion of the basis of knowledge and the question of whether certainty is possible, while the subject of the *Tusculan Disputations* is the essentials of happiness.

The position of Cicero in philosophy is in the main simple. On the speculative side he belonged to the New Academy and accepted the view of Carneades that certainty is impossible, so that probability is the only guide to truth. On the practical side he had a strong dislike for the Epicureans and was profoundly attracted by the lofty morality of the Stoics, although he would not follow them to extremes and criticizes some of their paradoxes. While willing to take a sceptical attitude in purely intellectual matters, he was opposed to this in ethics, where he felt the need of some definite and positive standards, and where the Stoic doctrine of the sovereignty of virtue appealed to him. He wrote too hastily to be always consistent and made little effort to fuse his ideas into a coherent system, but he accomplished what he set out to do, and his philosophic treatises not only influenced his contemporaries but succeeding ages as well.

In another field he won a somewhat unintentional, but highly distinguished, place. Although he seems to have had some thoughts of publishing a selection of his letters, this half-formed purpose was never carried out, and it was only after his death that they were given to the world. As we have them they are divided into four groups: sixteen books consist of letters to his friends (*ad familiares*), three books to his brother (*ad Quintum Fratrem*), sixteen books to Atticus (*ad Atticum*), and two books to Brutus (*ad Brutum*). In ancient times there were a number of others now lost; for instance, there were originally nine books to Brutus, and we hear of other books containing letters to his son, to Cæsar, to Pompey, and to Octavian. The letters to his friends were published soon after his death by his secretary, Tiro. We have good reason to believe that Cicero kept copies of many of these letters, and perhaps the whole collection was made up of these copies, although Tiro may have obtained some from the persons to whom they were sent. It is not unlikely that Tiro also published the letters to Q. Cicero, but he seems to have had nothing to do with the letters to Atticus, which were published later and far surpass the others in interest and value. *

The literary merit of Cicero's letters is very great and entitles him to a place among the first in this style of composition. In those to his friends he adapts himself to the character of his correspondent and to the nature of his subject with rare tact and versatility. The singular fascination of his letters to Atticus, however, lies in their utter frankness, and the completeness with which they reveal the soul of the writer. These he can have had no thought of publishing, and their supreme value is to be found precisely in this fact. From Atticus he appears to have had few, if any, secrets, and he constantly consults his friend on all matters of difficulty. The letters are in an easy conversational style with little or no attempt at literary finish, reflecting all his varied moods, his doubts, fears, hopes, and hesitations, giving the gossip of the hour and his real opinions of men and of events as they impressed him at the moment. In them we are able to look at Roman politics at several critical moments as it appeared to one living in the midst of it; whatever questions may arise as to Cicero's wisdom and consistency, no doubts can be felt as to his candour and sincerity. In addition to the light they throw upon the history of the last days of the Republic, they have the interest which springs from the vivid and convincing, because unconscious, picture of Cicero himself. Through them he is more intimately known to us than any other man of ancient times. With his own pen he has made us acquainted with all his faults and weaknesses, but he has equally betrayed his finer and better qualities. No other hand could have painted a portrait of such unquestionable accuracy, and it must be accounted to him as his truest glory that the Cicero of the letters to Atticus is a finer and a better man than the Cicero of Plutarch and the historians.

# APPENDICES

## 1

## THE CHIEF SOURCES FOR THE HISTORY OF THE LATER REPUBLIC

THE materials from which the history of the period from 146 to 30 B.C. must be reconstructed are surprisingly meagre, in view of the importance and interest of the period, and are not always of the most trustworthy character. In consequence many problems are left which do not admit of any certain solution owing to the vagueness or the contradictions among the few authorities at our disposal. A word or two in regard to the principal sources of such information as we can gather may be of interest to the reader.

In the last chapter of the text the surviving works of Cæsar and Sallust, as well as the continuations of Cæsar's Commentaries, have been sufficiently discussed. In regard to Cicero, however, some further comment is necessary. In his treatises he frequently uses illustrations taken from Roman history, and his speeches and letters obviously contain a large amount of historical material. It must be remembered, however, that in his speeches he is an advocate rather than a critic, and that we have no reason to believe that in his treatises he took much trouble to verify the accuracy of the incidents which he cites to illustrate some point. In his letters to Atticus he wrote his personal impressions of the events of the moment, but the undoubted frankness and sincerity of these letters does not alter the fact that he was far from being an impartial and unprejudiced observer. With all allowances made it remains true that his works are rich in invaluable information; they furnish us with most of our knowledge about several important episodes, and his chance references to earlier days enable us to check the vague or contradictory statements found in other works.

Unfortunately the books of Livy which dealt with this period are lost, but we have some knowledge of what his work contained derived from the *Epitomes* and from later writers whose works were based upon his history. The work of Livy was so long, being in 142 books, that abridgements of it were published not long after its appearance. Even these, however, were too bulky for a later age, and a synopsis of one of these abridgments was made, perhaps in the fourth century A.D. This synopsis, known as the *Epitomes*, has come down to us nearly complete. From this we can obtain a skeleton outline of Livy's treatment of the later Republic. We are able to amplify this outline at certain points from the writings of Granius Licinianus, who probably lived in the age of the Antonines. His history, which was brief, is preserved only in fragments; its framework was derived from Livy, though numerous antiquarian digressions are added. Much more important is the *Historia adversum Paganos* of Paulus Orosius, written at the beginning of the fifth century A.D. The author was a disciple of St. Augustine and undertook his *History* at his master's suggestion. The part of it which deals with the Republic was taken from Livy and furnishes us with our fullest information in regard to the contents of the lost books. In addition to Orosius and Licinianus there are clear traces of the Livian tradition in other writers, but since these writers used other works also it is not always possible to distinguish their sources.

The best connected account of the period in Latin is the *History* of Velleius Paterculus, written in the reign of Tiberius. As became an official of the empire, Velleius is strongly imperialistic. His summary of events is very brief, but he seems to have followed good authorities and gives us a few bits of information. For a continuous narrative of any fullness we are obliged to rely on the Greek historians Appian and Dio.

Appian, who lived in the time of the Antonines, wrote a *Roman History* which was chiefly concerned with the wars of the Romans. In treating these he grouped them by countries, Numidian wars, Spanish wars, etc. Most of the work has perished, but we have one book treating of the Mithridatic wars and five books on the *Civil Wars*. This last work is particularly important, for Appian considered that the civil wars began with the agitation of the Gracchi, and so begins with an account of them which is evidently drawn from an exceptionally reliable source. In general he is somewhat careless, but he supplies us with the only connected narrative, fuller than a mere outline, of the course of events from 133 to 68 B.C.

Dio Cassius, or more correctly, Cassius Dio Cocceianus, was a successful official under the dynasty of the Severi. His *History of Rome* was published in 80 books, but has not come down to us entire. For the period before 68 B.C. we have only a few scattered fragments; from that date, however, we have his account to supplement and check that of Appian. In this part of his work he seems to have relied mainly, though not exclusively, on Livy. As a historian Dio suffers from several defects, chief among them his imperfect knowledge of republican institutions. Neither was he a man of much critical capacity, and his value depends entirely on his sources, his merits being those of a good copyist. His work is thus uneven in quality, since he lacked any very sound basis for selecting his authorities, whom he sometimes misunderstood. Nevertheless, his *History* is of cardinal importance, preserving much that would otherwise be lost.

Aside from continuous histories, chiefly Appian and Dio, our main reliance is upon biographies of various persons who played a prominent part in the period. Most of these we owe to Plutarch, who was born about A.D. 46 and died in 120. Among his *Lives* are included biographies of Antony, M. Brutus, Cæsar, Cato, Cicero, Crassus, the Gracchi, Lucullus, Marius, Pompey, Sertorius, and Sulla. He was undoubtedly a man of wide and varied reading, who in composing his *Lives* consulted many books. In many cases the authorities whom he followed cannot be determined, but in a few we may reach a fairly safe conclusion as to some of them. It seems clear that he used the *History* of Sallust for the lives of Lucullus, Sertorius, Pompey, and Crassus, while for that of Sulla he consulted the dictator's own memoirs, and for that of Cicero he drew upon a biography of the orator written by Tiro. As to the value of Sallust as a source we are unable to pronounce a definite opinion, since his *History* may have been decidedly superior to his earlier monographs, but Tiro and Sulla ought to have furnished much reliable information, though whether either was impartial is another matter. The main weaknesses of Plutarch are two: as a biographer he was more interested in characteristic anecdotes than in important events, and as a moralist he was more concerned with edification than with truth. As a result he omits many important facts, is often careless in his chronology, and retails many stories which are of very uncertain authenticity. For serious historical purposes his *Lives* must be used with caution, but he supplies us with a good deal of information which seems to be reliable; at the worst his stories do something to illustrate the characters of the men about whom they were told and believed.

In addition to Plutarch we have Suetonius' life of Cæsar (*Divus Julius*) and that of Augustus (*Divus Augustus*), some parts of which deal with our period. The author, C. Suetonius Tranquillus, served as private secretary to the emperor Hadrian, a position which gave him access to many important documents in the Imperial archives. He seems to have made some use of his opportunity, although much less than modern historians feel that he should. In the main he seems to have drawn his material from the current histories, from earlier biographies, and from oral tradition and gossip. He read widely, if somewhat uncritically, and gathered his material from a variety of sources of very unequal reliability. His chief interest lay in personal anecdotes, which he diligently collected. As a biographer he has little gift for judging or depicting character, but usually contents himself with arranging his material so as to illustrate the good and bad sides of the emperors, without attempting to draw a unified portrait. His life of Cæsar is certainly one of his best, and he has recorded a number of facts concerning him which are not elsewhere preserved.

A work of far less importance, yet worthy of a passing mention, is the *de viris illustribus* commonly ascribed to Victor, but really by some unknown writer not earlier than the second century A.D. It contains brief sketches of a number of men who were prominent in the last days of the Republic, but the accounts are so brief that they are of little value. Another work adding a few bits of information to what we can gather from other and better sources is a collection of memorable sayings and deeds (*facta et dicta memorabilia*) compiled by Valerius Maximus in the reign of Tiberius.

There are scattered references to the events of the period in other places, such as the geographical works of Strabo and the *Natural History* of Pliny; there are also a few minor historical works, such as those of Florus and of Diodorus Siculus, but a discussion of them is hardly necessary.

Inscriptions, which are of such great importance for the period of the Empire, are not numerous for the time of the Republic. * Nevertheless, there are a few of interest and value.

In view of the fragmentary and dispersed character of our sources, aside from the main ones, a work bringing almost all the surviving material together in a single volume and arranging it chronologically is obviously one of very great utility. Such a work was published in 1903 by A. H. J. Greenidge and A. M. Clay under the title *Sources for Roman History B.C.* 133–70. The paucity of our material will be at once evident from the small size of the volume, which contains only 229 pages aside from the index. The collection is not exhaustive, yet it is so nearly complete that the few omissions do not detract materially from its value. Of more consequence is the fact that some of the extracts read apart from their context, as is inevitable in any work of this kind, are open to misconstruction, but the reader who consults it will at least find a very full set of references on every event during the period which it covers.

Another work giving in limited compass a collection of important source material on the economic development of Rome has recently appeared in the first volume of *An Economic Survey of Ancient Rome* under the editorship of Tenney Frank. This volume, the only one so far published, is written by the editor and deals with Rome and Italy during the period of the Republic. The work gives the source material, both literary and inscriptional, in the original followed by a translation. This is of especial value as our knowledge of the economic life of the period is derived from sources even more scattered and less easily accessible than is the case with its political history.

2

## THE POLITICAL MACHINE IN ANCIENT ROME

THE existence of a political machine behind the Roman senate has been so generally ignored that it seems desirable to indicate briefly some of the grounds on which I have based my conclusions in regard to it and to give some additional details as to its organization. It must be admitted that direct evidence on the subject is not to be found in the ancient historians, but this fact admits of easy explanation. Roman literature was to a very large extent written by, or for, the wealthy leisured class, and, as a consequence, mainly from the side of the senatorial machine. It is quite unlikely that such writers would think it either desirable or necessary to explain the means by which the senate controlled the government, since political machines never voluntarily reveal their methods to the world. Senators and the adherents of their party would naturally represent the ascendancy of the senate as due to its merits rather than to a manipulation of the system of group voting. The democratic opposition perhaps spoke out frankly, but we know little or nothing of what they may have said. Our knowledge comes chiefly from authors who wrote under the Empire and who had no personal experience of the real working of the Republic; not understanding such hints as they found in the earlier writers, they ignored them and tended strongly to idealize the past. The few historical writers of the later Republic whose works have come down to us are almost all partisans of the senate, like Cicero, or, when democrats in politics, like Cæsar and Sallust, wrote on special subjects where a full and explicit treatment of the political methods of the times was uncalled for. We must expect, therefore, that the evidence for a senatorial machine will be indirect. Even if indirect evidence were wholly lacking, the system of group voting offered such obvious opportunities for manipulation that it seems incredible that the Roman politicians should have failed to see and take advantage of them. If we once examine *how* such manipulation was possible we shall readily discover at least some indications that it actually took place.

In the text it has been pointed out that groups of clients and freedmen *could* be used to control the vote of the rural tribes and hence of the assembly. As to clients there is little to be said and their importance must remain largely hypothetical; this is natural, because when they became clients they were already registered in a tribe, and their new relationship would not affect their registration. With the freedmen it was different, and the question of where they should be registered was a matter of dispute at least from the censorship of Appius Claudius in 312 to that of Ti. Sempronius Gracchus, the father of the two tribunes, in 169 B.C. In 312 Appius Claudius admitted the freedmen to all the existing tribes, but in 304 they were restricted to the four city tribes. At this time the nobility was still in process of formation, and the aims and purposes behind both measures are obscure. As the nobility took shape and grew self-conscious and exclusive the restriction was quietly ignored, and by 220 Flaminius, a censor belonging to the popular party who in 232 had carried an agrarian law in spite of aristocratic opposition, found it desirable, from his point of view, to eject the freedmen from the rural tribes and put them in the city tribes again. During the Second Punic War they seem to have reappeared in the rural tribes, for a somewhat confused struggle broke out again, which only ended when in 169 Gracchus and his colleague, C. Claudius Pulcher, made a new settlement. Their censorship began with a violent quarrel with the knights, and at its close they were thanked by the senate for their work, so that we are justified in thinking that they acted in the interests of the nobles. As to the freedmen, they left the older ones where they were while the others were to vote in a single city tribe, chosen on each occasion by lot.[1] After this we hear little about the matter, and then only when some democratic leader proposes, with what seems a complete change of front, to enrol the freedmen in all the tribes.

The conclusion to be drawn from these facts seems clear. Up to 169 it was to the advantage of the nobles to have their freedmen registered in the rural tribes, and after that date they wished this only for the older freedmen. The most probable explanation seems to be that by 169 the knights had begun creating freedmen on such a scale that the nobles now thought some restriction would be to their advantage. We may venture to doubt whether the settlement of the question by the censors in 169 was actually observed very strictly in practice, since none of the preceding settlements had been. The nobles may have been content to evade the restrictions to some extent themselves, while enforcing them more or less rigidly against the knights. This would explain the change

[1] For further details see my article *In Defense of the Corn-Dole*, pp. 17–18.

in the attitude of the democrats, since legislation would under such conditions benefit their equestrian allies.

The long controversy over the registration of the freedmen is difficult to explain unless it had a real political importance, and the question must have turned primarily on those who resided in Rome. In registering them two methods might be followed; they might be put in the tribe where they actually resided, or they might be put in the same tribe as their former master. If the first method was adopted all those who lived in the city and so counted politically would be dumped into the city tribes. The censors who desired this result apparently found it necessary to go further and to put all freedmen without distinction into the city tribes, since otherwise the former master, or the freedmen themselves, could declare that they lived in the country, as many doubtless did, and to investigate each case would require too much time. The same difficulty would not arise in the case of freemen, since, when they came of age, they were registered in the tribe of their father, and the policy of the censors who favoured the nobility amounted to treating the former master as the father of the emancipated slave in so far as his registration was concerned.

As the agricultural crisis developed it is very likely that the importance of the freedmen diminished and that of the clients increased. Rome now contained many poor freemen who were still registered in the rural tribes, and to draw such men into a condition of dependence was obviously to the political advantage of the nobles and of the rich knights as well. Perhaps they had come to be less expensive than freedmen, and in any case their registration could not readily be tampered with. Possibly the nobles accepted the arrangement of 169 partly because they were now seeking their retainers chiefly among the poor country folk in the city.

Unfortunately we do not know the exact boundaries of the rural tribes, but the approximate location of many of them is known and will repay a brief examination. There were perhaps 18 of the tribes which were situated, in whole or in part, within ten miles of Rome. The remaining 13 were outside, some of them far outside, that limit. From these latter tribes very few of the small farmers were likely to come to Rome to vote except on rare occasions, and they could, therefore, be packed by retainers of the nobles without much difficulty. It was only necessary to secure control of 5 more tribes to have control of the tribal assembly. The raising of grain had long ceased to be profitable in the vicinity of Rome, and this must have greatly reduced the number of small farmers in the tribes near the city.[1] That the small farmer had disappeared

[1] See Frank, *Econ. Hist. of Rome*, pp. 55–68.

from all of them is, however, unlikely. Rome must have offered a market for fresh vegetables, poultry, eggs, etc., which could be produced on a small scale, and it seems probable that a considerable number of poor but independent, as well as moderately prosperous, country folk were to be found close enough to the city to be able to attend the assembly with some degree of regularity. It is, therefore, possible that there was a genuine rural element in some of the nearer tribes, yet the course of events makes it clear that this element was not particularly strong. The things which the peasant proprietor could still produce at a profit could also be produced on a large estate, and probably such estates were numerous in the district surrounding the city, so that some of the nearer tribes may have been as easy to pack as those at a greater distance. If we assume that in eight of these eighteen tribes the small landowners were so few that these tribes could be controlled by the retainers of the nobles, the senatorial machine would dispose of 21 votes in the assembly, against 14 which might go to the opposition.

An attempt to reconstruct a rural tribe as it actually voted in the assembly may make the situation clearer. Several classes of citizens would be present in varying numbers according to the tribe. The chief classes of voters may be grouped as follows :

1. Wealthy landowners residing in Rome but registered in the tribe. They were probably for the most part nobles.
2. Wealthy landowners residing in the country but present at the meeting. As their interests would in the main be identical with those of the nobles they would probably vote in the same way.
3. Business men (knights and others) residing in Rome but owning an estate, large or small, within the tribe and so registered in it.
4. Small landowners and rural labourers residing in the country who had come to Rome to vote.
5. Retainers of the nobles or knights residing in Rome but registered in the tribe.
6. Members of the city populace who had retained their registration in the tribe in spite of the fact that they or their ancestors had moved to Rome and who had not become dependents of the nobles or knights.

It is evident that the number of voters in the first three classes would not be very large and that the wealthy class was powerful chiefly through their bands of retainers (class 5). The number of voters in class 4 would vary greatly, but would ordinarily be great enough to be important only in some of the rural tribes near Rome. Moreover, the number of voters in class 6 tended constantly to grow, as did those in class 5. The situation in the last century of the Republic can be deduced with reasonable certainty from the course of events. The nobles had no longer a firm control of the rural tribes and the city populace had gained greatly in influence, but the knights with their retainers held the balance of power.

It is difficult to form an equally clear idea of the assembly of centuries. All the citizens registered in each tribe, urban or rural, were divided into five classes according to their property, and each class into two centuries. The five classes may roughly be described as the rich, the wealthy, the upper middle class, the lower middle class, and the poor. In the rural tribes the total amount of a man's property was considered and not merely the value of his land in one particular tribe. Thus a rich business man residing in Rome who owned a small estate in the country would be put in one of the centuries of the first class of the tribe in which his estate was situated. In the four urban tribes the centuries of the first and second class would be dominated by the knights, but, if enough of the knights chose, they could by investing a small amount of money in land secure the control of the centuries of these classes in some of the rural tribes as well. The centuries of the third and fourth class would certainly include small landowners in the rural tribes and the less wealthy business men in the city tribes. It may be doubted whether many business men of these classes could afford country estates even on a very modest scale, but there would certainly be some countrymen who had moved to Rome and had met with sufficient success to be registered in these classes in their original tribes. As to the fifth class there is much uncertainty. Theoretically at least the members of this class were required to possess a property qualification sufficient to exclude the poorest citizens, and this exclusion was accompanied by exemption from military service. If the qualification was enforced in practice the bulk of the city rabble and of the rural proletariat would have been restricted to the five extra centuries, but, if the urban rabble had practically no power in the centuriate assembly, it is difficult to understand the importance of the ædileship as a stepping-stone to the higher offices,[1] so that it seems safe to conclude that the property qualification for the fifth class was not strictly observed. After the military reforms of Marius it is possible that, since the exemption from military service had become meaningless, the qualification was ignored in practice, although there is no reason to think that it was ever legally abolished. It is, however, probable that it had been very laxly

[1] Of course, splendid shows and games might win popularity with the third and fourth classes, but our sources distinctly suggest that the mob was worth courting.

enforced for a long time before his reforms. Just as the censors made no inquiry into the actual residence of the poorer citizens, they may have made no attempt to assess the value of their property and have left them registered in the class where they found them. Censorial carelessness on both points was no doubt partly due to lack of time and the pressure of other business, but it should be noted that such carelessness at first and for long worked to the advantage of the nobles. If the censors were careless, the result would be that when a farmer lost his farm and moved to Rome he not only remained a member of the tribe where his farm was situated, but also retained his place in the class in which he had been registered on the basis of its value. Even if the censors made some attempt to enforce the property qualification, the nobles and knights might get their retainers registered in the fifth class by various evasions, such as giving them nominal possession of some property for the purpose. At any rate, it seems clear that in some way many of the urban rabble and many of the retainers of the rich did actually vote in the tribal centuries of the fifth class.

To sum up, it seems that in the rural tribes the centuries of the first four classes were composed of both landowners and business men and that many of the fifth were largely filled with the retainers of the rich and the urban rabble. The comparative strength of these elements must have varied considerably in the different tribes. In the time of the Gracchi most of the 18 equestrian centuries may have been dominated by the nobles, though the knights probably controlled some of them.[1] The nobles and the knights must also have dominated the 140 centuries of the first and second class. The 140 centuries of the third and fourth class are doubtful, but must on the whole have been controlled by the middle class of the city and country, though their political leanings remain uncertain. If the nobles and knights were united the middle class would have little importance; since 187 centuries constituted a majority, only 29 were needed in addition to the equestrian centuries and those of the first and second class. Probably the knights and nobles through their retainers controlled more than this number of the 70 centuries of the fifth class, so that together they were masters of the *comitia centuriata*. If they quarrelled, or were divided among themselves, the votes of the independent centuries would decide the issue. In general the senatorial machine could always count on a very considerable number of centuries, but a combination of the knights with the opposition could outvote

[1] The senators as well as the young nobles voted in these centuries until the time of C. Gracchus at least, but in Cicero's day the senators were excluded (Willems, *Le sénat.*, I, pp. 195–96) and all, or nearly all, the 18 centuries were controlled by the young knights (Cicero, *de pet. cons.*, ch. 8).

them, so that here as in the tribal assembly the knights, if sufficiently united, held the balance of power.

It is probably owing to the system of group voting that bribery became so prominent a factor in Roman politics in the last period of the Republic. Neither knights nor nobles were always united, and there were certain at all times to be a number of centuries and tribes where the various elements were so evenly balanced that the result was doubtful. As the knights grew in power and the grip of the senatorial machine weakened the importance of these doubtful centuries or tribes became steadily greater and the issue of an election or the fate of a bill might depend upon their votes. Under such circumstances no efforts would be spared to carry them and bribery inevitably flourished. This fact should not be taken as proving any widespread degeneracy of the Roman people nor even of the Roman rabble, since it would be a sufficient explanation to assume that the number and importance of the doubtful groups were steadily increasing.

After the extension of citizenship to the Latin and Italian allies the influence of the out-voters (those who resided outside the city) must have been very much greater. There were undoubtedly many of the new citizens who were able to attend the assembly if they chose and there is evidence that, on certain occasions at least, efforts were made to induce them to come to Rome.[1] Some of them in all probability were unwilling or unable to remain in the city for any considerable length of time, and one motive for the organized rioting in the last days of the Republic was almost certainly to delay a vote in the assembly till the patience of the out-voters was exhausted and many of them had gone home.

The existence of a number of doubtful groups (centuries or tribes) will serve to explain some curious results of the elections. Not only were the tribunes often at odds among themselves, but consuls violently opposed to each other were occasionally elected. Since both consuls were elected at the same meeting of the centuriate assembly it seems strange at first glance that men of different parties should be successful. Thus Marius in 102 was joined with the aristocrat Catulus; Cicero received Antonius, an ally of Catiline, as his colleague; and Cæsar was hampered by Bibulus. In 102 the result was perhaps due to military considerations; the knights had great faith in Marius, but many of them may also have had confidence in Catulus. At the election in 64 the personal popularity of Cicero and the presence of a number of Italian voters who were proud of his successful career may have won some doubtful centuries from Catiline, yet some of these same voters may have been willing to allow the gold of Crassus to persuade them to

[1] Cicero, *de pet. cons.*, ch. 8.

vote for Antonius. The same thing would apply to the election in 60 which returned Cæsar and Bibulus. This last case is the clearest. Money was spent freely to secure the return of Lucceius with Cæsar, while the nobles spent with equal freedom to elect Bibulus. Now many voters may have had enough enthusiasm for Cæsar to insist on voting for him, but some of them who cared little for Lucceius may have been ready to accept a bribe to vote for Bibulus. The number of such persons may have been small, but they may have been numerous enough to turn the scale in a good many very evenly divided centuries. In other words, the presence of a comparatively few citizens in the doubtful centuries who would not vote against Cæsar or Cicero but who could be persuaded by money or other forms of influence to vote for Antonius and Bibulus might decide the issue.

In conclusion it seems to me that historians in dealing with the political history of the Republic have generally failed to remember the complex organization of the assembly, and how it must have worked in actual practice. To forget these points inevitably results in seeing many events in a misleading light. Above all, it has led to the false conception that the city rabble was dominant in politics. Such a position it never held in reality. Its support was valuable because it controlled some tribes and centuries, but by itself it was helpless. Neither could bribery accomplish more than to secure a few tribes and centuries. Money and the mob could not win victories by themselves, but, when the nobles and knights were divided, they might turn the scale to one side or the other.

## 3

# THE SOURCES FOR THE CAREER OF TIBERIUS GRACCHUS

THE character and reliability of the sources from which we derive our knowledge of the career of Tiberius Gracchus have been a subject of much controversy. A detailed examination of all the views put forward is hardly necessary, but a word or two seems called for to justify, or at least explain, the treatment in the text. I have in the main accepted the views of Carcopino, which in many points agree with those of Cardinali.[1] On some points where they differ I have been content to keep an open mind.

The essential question is that of the relations between Plutarch and Appian—the two writers who give us our most detailed accounts of Tiberius, and their relative credibility. There seems no doubt that Appian has borrowed his account from a single source and that Plutarch has used several. Whether the source of Appian was or was not among those of Plutarch it is unnecessary to decide; Carcopino, who takes the negative view in opposition to Cardinali, appears to me to have proved that, if Plutarch used Appian's source at all, he has added much that is inconsistent with it. It seems to me that Carcopino has also advanced convincing reasons for believing that Appian's source was more trustworthy than some of those consulted by Plutarch. I have, therefore, based my account of Tiberius on Appian and have rejected all elements in Plutarch which either directly or by implication are in conflict with Appian.

The chief points of difference may be summarized as follows:

1. Appian represents the veto of Octavius as a surprise to Tiberius, while according to Plutarch the two had been in conflict for some time. The subsequent conduct of Tiberius seems to be that of a man met by an unexpected obstacle rather than that of a man facing a difficulty which he had foreseen.

2. Plutarch tells us that Tiberius publicly offered to buy with his

[1] Carcopino, *Autour des Gracques*; G. Cardinali, *Studi Graccani.* Numerous
* further references will be found in these two works.

private funds, although his fortune was not great, the public lands held by Octavius. We know, however, that Tiberius was rich, and it is difficult to believe that he would make such an offer publicly. Appian says nothing about it.

3. Plutarch affirms that in his anger at the opposition to his bill Tiberius made it more severe by striking out the provisions it had originally contained granting compensation to the possessors. Appian makes no mention of any change in the bill. *

4. According to Plutarch, Tiberius issued an edict closing the courts and the treasury and forbidding the magistrates to transact any public business till his bill had been voted on. Appian makes no mention of such an edict. Carcopino has, I think, clearly shown that Plutarch's story is absurd, since the tribunes possessed no such sweeping powers. *

5. According to Plutarch, Octavius after his deposition was driven from the assembly with violence; Appian represents him as leaving quietly.

6. Appian says nothing of the Pergamene treasure or of any new programme put forward by Tiberius.

On the first five points I have followed Appian without hesitation, but on the last I do not think that his silence is decisive. He expressly tells us that he intends to mention only the most important events, in this probably simply following his source, so that he, or the writer from whom he borrowed, might well omit the appropriation of a treasure which the Romans did not get for four years and proposals which were never carried. The Pergamene treasure is mentioned not only by Plutarch but also by Livy (Ep. lviii) and by the author of *de viris illustribus* (ch. 64). This testimony, of course, adds nothing to that of Plutarch if all three writers were copying the same source, except to show that Plutarch's statement was not a mere blunder, and that he has correctly reproduced the common authority. It has not, however, been proved that they did all use the same source without comparison with other works, and it seems probable that the statement occurred in more than one of the earlier histories. Dio also (fr. 83) confirms Plutarch as to the proposals of Tiberius to limit military service and to admit knights to the juries.

My main reason, however, for accepting the new programme is its inherent probability. Carcopino argues that Tiberius would seek to limit his quarrel with the nobles to a single issue rather than broaden it by raising new questions. With all respect it seems to me that the exact reverse would be true. As soon as Tiberius made up his mind to stand for re-election he would naturally seek to justify his candidacy and to divide the ranks of his enemies by bringing forward new proposals of reform. Among these proposals we should expect to find bids for the support of all classes except the nobles, and the measures which he is represented as advocating are of this character. I have, therefore, accepted all those attributed to him except one. This one, the proposal to extend Roman citizenship to all Italians, is mentioned only by Velleius Paterculus (ii, ch. 2). It seems to me incredible that so sweeping a reform should have been ignored by all other writers, and I have set it aside as a blunder, or at least a gross exaggeration, of Velleius or his source.

In regard to the Pergamene treasure Carcopino holds (pp. 34–40) that the proposal of Tiberius must be rejected on chronological grounds, contending that the death of Attalus III did not occur until after that of Tiberius himself. To me his argument seems wholly unconvincing because of his failure to distinguish between the fate of the royal treasure and the fate of the cities of the kingdom. According to Plutarch Tiberius actually proposed, if he did not carry, a bill appropriating the treasure, but he merely announced his intention of dealing with the cities later. Now the most important evidence produced by Carcopino consists of two Greek inscriptions.[1] The first contains a decree of the city of Pergamum dated the 19th of Eumeneios, a month whose place in the Pergamene calendar is uncertain but which Carcopino makes extend from July 24 to August 23. In this the municipal authorities are still in doubt whether Rome will accept the legacy of the late king. The second contains a decree of the Roman senate, ratifying the will, and, from the fragment of the date which survives, the decree must have been passed in the latter half of the year. These inscriptions seem to me to have no real bearing on the point in question. We have not the slightest reason to suppose that Tiberius ever carried any law regarding the cities of Asia, and the municipal authorities of Pergamum might, therefore, know all about his appropriation of the treasure and still remain in doubt as to whether the provisions of the will relating to the kingdom itself would be ratified, while after the death of Tiberius the senate might at any time proceed to act upon the territorial clauses of the will. If Carcopino's chronological argument be accepted, we should have to assume some confusion in the source, or sources, used by Plutarch, Livy, and the author of *de viris illustribus*. I do not see, however, that the omission of any proposal for appropriating the Pergamene treasure would materially affect our judgment of Tiberius.

[1] Dittenberger, *O.G.I.S.*, 338 and 435.

*

## 4

## THE REGISTRATION OF THE ITALIANS

The question of how the Italian and Latin allies should be registered was not only a bitterly contested one in Roman politics, but it has occasioned considerable perplexity to modern scholars. There was a party which desired to restrict them to a limited number of tribes, while another party demanded their distribution among all the thirty-five. Appian (*b.c.* i, ch. 49) states that the restrictionists proposed to put them in ten new tribes, but Velleius Paterculus (ii, ch. 20) says that they were to be enrolled in eight tribes and seems obviously to mean eight of the old ones. Attempts have been made to reconcile the two with each other and with a phrase from Sisenna, a contemporary writer, which refers vaguely to two new tribes.[1] It seems to me that a reconciliation is hardly necessary and that both Appian and Velleius may be correct. Appian mentions the new tribes in connection with the *lex Julia* of 90 B.C., while Velleius is referring to some arrangement in force in the consulship of Cinna in 87. In the course of those three years much had happened, and it is quite possible that what was intended in 90 had been modified later.

When the *lex Julia* was passed the restrictionists favoured the plan of creating ten new tribes for the new citizens. Since the law was intended to check the spread of the revolt, it may have been silent on this point, although it may have contained a clause providing for the organization of the new tribes. Moreover, in 90 censors were appointed, and there can be no doubt that their appointment was a direct consequence of the law, since there had been censors in 92 and since one of the new censors was L. Julius Cæsar, the author of the law. From Appian we gather that the Italians welcomed the grant of citizenship, but that later they resented the restriction imposed. Perhaps they first learned of the

[1] See Heitland, *The Roman Republic,* II, pp. 447–49, and Holmes, *The Roman Republic,* I, p. 356. I think Velleius clearly means eight of the old tribes and that Holmes is wrong in thinking that this makes him contradict himself. Velleius says the motive for restricting them to eight tribes was to prevent their having greater power than the old citizens. They would outnumber the old citizens in eight tribes but could not control the assembly.

restriction when the censors began their work in 89, and it may have been because of the opposition and resentment of the Italians that the censors failed to complete the census. At any rate, Cicero (*pro Archia*, ch. 5, 11) explicitly says that no return was made of any part of the people. It is possible that the newly enfranchised communities were assigned as communities to ten new tribes, but it seems much more probable that the new tribes were not organized at all, so that in 88 the question was still an open one and the new citizens had not yet been registered anywhere. Sulpicius Rufus now proposed to abandon the restrictionist policy and carried a law providing for the enrolment of the Italians in all the thirty-five tribes. When Sulla occupied Rome the law of Sulpicius was cancelled and the whole question was unsettled again. Before his departure for the East Sulla and his colleague, Q. Pompeius Rufus, passed a number of laws which to some extent remodelled the Roman constitution and concerning which we are practically dependent on Appian for such information as we have. It is true that Appian makes no mention of any law in regard to the Italians, but nevertheless it is possible that Sulla seized the opportunity to attempt a settlement along restrictionist lines. At any rate, the language of Velleius implies that when Sulla left for the East there was a settlement in force by which the Italians were to be registered in eight of the old tribes. It is possible that between the retirement of the censors in 89 and the Sulpician law in 88 another law was passed which recovered its validity when the Sulpician law was cancelled, but it seems more probable that the settlement described by Velleius was due to Sulla. In either case it is evident that the restrictionists had changed their policy to the extent of abandoning the new tribes and putting the Italians in a limited number of the old.

There were several ways in which the new arrangement might be carried out. The quickest and easiest would be to allow the new citizens to vote in eight tribes determined by lot on each occasion, the eight namely whose votes were to be announced last. To this there was the objection that, since the Italians would have no fixed place in any of the tribes, they could not be registered in the centuries which were formed within the tribes. According to Appian (ch. 59) Sulla enacted that in the assembly the voting was to be by centuries, and, if we take this statement at its face value, membership in a tribe would have little meaning except to secure a place in one of the tribal centuries.[1] It is possible that Appian

[1] I do not think that Appian means that Sulla abolished the existing organization of the centuries and restored the old Servian organization. To have attempted this would have required a new division into centuries of the old citizens before the assembly would be able to act at all.

meant that the vote in elections was to be by centuries and that laws were still to be voted on by tribes; in this case the new citizens would have no voice in the choice of magistrates,[1] but would have some influence in legislation. Sulla may, however, have adopted another plan, putting the new citizens into the nearest of the rural tribes, or authorizing their future registration in these tribes by some means. In this case Etruria might have been incorporated in the Sabatina, Stellatina, and Clustumina; Umbria might have been added to the Velina; the Marsi might have joined the Aniensis; Samnium might have been divided between the Quirina and the Teretina; and the southern allies might have found a place in the Falerna. Our knowledge of the exact boundaries of the Roman tribes is defective, but some such arrangement would appear possible, and in a scheme of this sort the new citizens would take their proper place in the centuries of these tribes as soon as their property had been assessed.[2]

It is easy to understand why any form of restricted registration should arouse the suspicion and resentment of the new citizens. So far as we know, the Italian unrest first made itself felt in connection with the agrarian legislation, which threatened to deprive them of the public land in their possession. Without political rights they were obviously in a position to be plundered with impunity by Roman demagogues and politicians, and it was only by obtaining the franchise that they could defend their rights and interests. It was of course true that very few of them would be able to go to Rome to vote, but this fact did not impair the value of the vote, since a comparatively small number, if widely distributed among the voting groups in the assembly, might hold the balance of power. The very fact that a powerful party in Rome was bent upon restricting their registration might be taken as evidence of a desire to revoke the concessions which had been extorted by force of arms, so that, if they allowed their votes to be made practically worthless, it might well appear to them that the revolt had failed to achieve its purpose. After a long and bloody struggle they were in no mood to accept any arrangement which would leave them at the mercy of the old citizens.

The motives of the party which sought to restrict the new citizens may also be conjectured. A majority of the senate and a portion of the rabble seem to have favoured this policy, while

[1] Unless some of the wealthiest were enrolled in the eighteen centuries of knights, and the rest in the five extra-tribal centuries.

[2] Of course, the eight tribes might have been selected in some other way than by geographical location, although this seems the most natural. If otherwise selected the chances of manipulation in the interest of the senate would be increased if anything.

apparently the knights as a class supported the claims of the Italians. Since the knights had bitterly opposed Drusus, we have here an abrupt change in their attitude. The attitude of both the senate and the knights is at once intelligible if we assume that the restrictions were so contrived that the result would be advantageous to the aristocratic machine. This would obviously be the case if the eight tribes in which it was proposed to register the Italians were all or most of them tribes which the knights had hitherto been able to control through their retainers. To any such arrangement the knights would of course object, and they might naturally prefer the bill of Sulpicius, which distributed the new citizen through all the tribes but at the same time allowed the registration of freedmen in them all. Since the centuries were based upon the tribes the restriction of the Italians to eight out of the thirty-five tribes would automatically restrict them to eighty out of the 373 centuries, and if Sulla made the century the sole group used for voting in the assembly the tribal restriction had a centuriate restriction as its aim. At the moment the new citizens were probably not included in the centuries at all, but Sulla may have made some provision for the assessment of their property and their registration in the centuries in the future. Normally this would have been part of the regular work of the censors, but it is conceivable that some special arrangement was made by which the matter could be dealt with at once.

Our information for this period is too imperfect to admit of any positive conclusions, and all I have intended to do in this brief discussion is to point out some possible reasons for the importance which the question of the registration of the Italians evidently had for the Romans of that day.

## 5

# THE ARMIES OF POMPEY AND CRASSUS IN 70 B.C.

APPIAN (*b.c.* i, ch. 121) expressly says that Pompey and Crassus did not dismiss their armies until their public reconciliation, and from Plutarch (*Crassus*, ch. 12, and *Pompey*, ch. 23) it would seem that this reconciliation took place towards the close of 70 B.C. Plutarch, however, says nothing about the retention of the armies after the two became consuls, and from his account we should naturally infer that they were disbanded after the triumphs. Certainly neither Appian nor Plutarch is free from mistakes, but it seems to me that the positive statement of one outweighs the silence of the other. Moreover, in this particular case it is clear that the account which Plutarch gives of the events of 70 B.C. is careless and inaccurate. He affirms that Pompey supported the candidacy of Crassus because he was anxious to do Crassus a favour (*Crassus*, ch. 12, and *Pompey*, ch. 22), and that Crassus was not only the richest but the greatest man and most powerful orator of the time (*Pompey*, ch. 22), neither of which statements can possibly be accepted. In the life of Crassus we are told that Pompey became a candidate for the consulship after his triumph, but Velleius (ii, ch. 30) expressly tells us that Pompey celebrated his triumph the day before he entered on his consulship. Plutarch also contradicts himself. In his life of Crassus he says that owing to the quarrels between the two consuls their consulship was without political events, yet in his *Pompey* he mentions the restoration of the powers of the tribunes and the jury law. In his *Crassus* (ch. 11) he says that Crassus had written to the senate that Pompey must be summoned home from Spain and Lucullus from Thrace to help conquer Spartacus; in his *Pompey* (ch. 21) he makes Pompey arrive by chance when the servile war was at its height. We might reconcile the two passages by assuming that the senate had paid no attention to Crassus' letter, but for the fact that Appian (ch. 120) mentions the arrival of Lucullus (whom he confuses with his brother then engaged in the war with Mithridates) soon after the arrival of Pompey. Two chance arrivals at the critical moment seem too many, and we can hardly avoid the conclusion that the senate acted on the suggestion of Crassus. It is evident from these contradictions and inaccuracies that Plutarch was careless in his treatment of the events of 70 B.C. This is not surprising, for his interest in both Pompey and Crassus is centred on other portions of their careers. This being the case, it seems to me that his silence as to the retention of the armies cannot justify us in setting aside the positive and definite statement of Appian.

Holmes raises an objection of another sort by asking how the money was found for paying and feeding the men, saying that it is not "easy to believe that the senate was bullied into finding the money against its own interest from a depleted treasury."[1] To me this point does not seem well taken. If the presence of the armies had frightened the senate into conceding the consulship to Crassus and Pompey, I cannot believe that it would have dared to let these same armies starve. How great the burden on the treasury was it is impossible to determine, for it is surely unnecessary to assume that the entire armies of the two generals shared in their triumphs. If any provision in the way of lands was made for the soldiers, we should naturally suppose that they would be disbanded gradually, and this might also be the case if no lands were assigned. All Appian can reasonably be taken to mean is that both Pompey and Crassus kept armies up to the time of their public reconciliation, and that these armies were large enough to cause fears of a civil war.

However, if the view that the armies were dismissed after the celebration of the triumphs be accepted, we may suppose that the sanction of the senate to the bill restoring the powers of the tribunes was extorted by the consuls immediately after they took office, or perhaps before. The sanction once given, there would be no actual necessity for retaining the armies, and the other events of the year might follow without military pressure. It has been maintained that Sulla imposed no restriction on the legislative initiative of the consuls and prætors, and on this theory the armies could have been dispensed with as soon as Pompey and Crassus had taken office. It does not seem to me that the acceptance of either of these views would make any material difference, since it was certainly the presence of the armies that made possible the overthrow of Sulla's constitution; the precise moment at which they were no longer required to secure this result is a matter of detail.

[1] *The Roman Republic*, I, p. 391.

## 6

## THE DATE OF THE VATINIAN LAW

In my former work, *The Founding of the Roman Empire*, I advanced the view of the date and purpose of the Vatinian law to which I have adhered in this volume. My reasons were given in some detail in that book and in an article on *The Chronology of Cæsar's Consulship* in which I discussed several other theories, among them that of Gelzer. A year later Gelzer published an article[1] in which he criticized my conclusions and gave further developments to his theory, advancing some new arguments. Since his view as to the date of the law has met with some favour, it seems desirable to examine briefly the evidence on this point.

Gelzer holds that the Vatinian law was passed not earlier than the latter part of May (p. 122). He bases his conclusion chiefly on two grounds, namely, the " historiographic tradition " and the failure of Cicero to mention it in his letters to Atticus written between April 13 and the first days of May (*Att.* ii, 4–17). As to the first, Gelzer invokes (p. 114) the testimony of the ancient historians, and shows that they all place Cæsar's two agrarian laws before the acquisition of the Gauls. This is true, and, if we confine our comparison of our sources to these two points, their unanimity seems impressive. If, however, we extend our comparison to include a few other events, the result will be somewhat different. The use of symbols will make for clearness and brevity. Let A represent the agrarian laws ; G Cæsar's acquisition of the Gauls ; M the marriage of Julia and Pompey ; and V the affair of Vettius. Our authorities are four, namely, Plutarch, Appian, Dio, and Suetonius. Plutarch gives an account of Cæsar's consulship in three of his lives, namely, those of Cato, Pompey, and Cæsar. He does not mention the affair of Vettius in any of them, and in the two last he does not distinguish between the two agrarian laws, but does between their introduction and their passage. Let us represent their introduction by A′ and their passage by A″. The order of events in our sources stands as follows :

[1] *Die Lex Vatinia de Imperio Cæsaris.*

| | |
|---|---|
| Plutarch—*Cato* . . . . | M, A, G. |
| ,, *Pompey* and *Cæsar* . | A′, M, A″, G. |
| Appian . . . . . . | A, V, G, M. |
| Dio . . . . . . | A, G, M, V. |
| Suetonius . . . . . | A, V, M, G. |

Leaving Plutarch out of account for the moment, it is certain from Cicero's letters that the affair of Vettius followed the marriage, so that Appian and Suetonius have both placed V wrongly in relation to M. According to Gelzer, Dio and Appian have both placed G and M in the wrong order. Plutarch, moreover, in his *Cato*, where Gelzer thinks his chronology is most exact, is wrong as to A and M, since he makes the marriage *precede* the introduction of the first agrarian law.

On the face of it we should have to conclude that these four writers either did not know the sequence of events or paid little attention to it. In my article I adopted the second alternative and tried to show that all of them followed a logical and natural order with little regard to strict chronology. They all begin with Cæsar's agrarian legislation because Cæsar began his consulship by proposing the first agrarian law. After a bitter struggle this was passed, probably early in April, and at the end of that month the second agrarian law, dealing with the Campanian land, was published and must have been enacted sometime in May. The agrarian legislation was thus spread out over a considerable time, and it was more or less inevitable that any account of Cæsar's consulship should begin with it. Moreover, it would be very natural that writers not particularly interested in chronology, having once introduced the subject, should finish their discussion of it before turning to another topic. This Appian, Dio, and Suetonius have done, and they have violated the chronological order in so doing, for the marriage occurred after the publication of the second agrarian law but before its passage. This is exactly what we should expect, since no writer would be likely to interrupt his account of the agrarian legislation by mentioning the marriage unless he had some motive for such a course. Plutarch (*Pompey* and *Cæsar*) does so break into his narrative, but his reason for so doing is clear. In his *Pompey* he describes the opposition to the agrarian laws (the two laws are not distinguished), and says that Cæsar brought Pompey before the people, and Pompey declared that in case of resistance to the laws he would meet force with force. Plutarch continues that Pompey's friends tried to apologize for this speech, saying that the words were uttered on the spur of the moment. But, Plutarch adds, his subsequent acts showed that he was wholly under Cæsar's influence, for he married Cæsar's daughter Julia. In his *Cæsar*, Plutarch mentions the marriage in the same connection and gives much the same reason. In his *Cato* he says that Cæsar when a candidate for the consulship attached himself to Pompey and after the election gave his daughter Julia to Pompey in marriage. Evidently Plutarch has mentioned the marriage to illustrate how completely Pompey was under Cæsar's influence (*Pompey*, ch. 47); how Cæsar attached Pompey to himself (*Cato*, ch. 31); how Cæsar sought to use Pompey's support to a still greater extent than he had so far done (*Cæsar*, ch. 14). It seems obvious that no conclusion can be drawn from Plutarch as to the actual sequence of events on this point; in so far as he is chronologically right it is by accident and not design. The fact that all four of our authorities finish their account of the agrarian laws before they mention the assignment of the Gauls to Cæsar seems to me to furnish no reliable basis for determining the date of the Vatinian law.

Gelzer's theory, however, puts the marriage before the Vatinian law, and he declares (p. 119) that in the "historiographic tradition" this is the case. A glance at the comparative table will show that in this assertion the testimony of Appian and Dio is entirely ignored, and that only Plutarch and Suetonius support the order upon which Gelzer insists. From what has just been said it seems to me that Plutarch's evidence is of no value on this point, but it remains to consider Suetonius. His arrangement of events is obviously logical and not strictly chronological. He begins (ch. 20) with the first agrarian law and the struggle over it till Bibulus shuts himself up in his house, and continues with the second agrarian law and other laws of Cæsar, saying that he passed them either without opposition or by intimidating his opponents. Then follow Cæsar's various acts of intimidation culminating in the affair of Vettius. After this (ch. 21) Suetonius says that about the same time (*sub idem tempus*) Cæsar married Calpurnia, the daughter of Piso, who was to be his successor as consul, and married Julia to Pompey. The marriage was at the beginning of May, and the affair of Vettius in July or August, so that the somewhat elastic phrase *sub idem tempus* seems sufficiently justified. Now (ch. 22) comes the vital passage; Suetonius continues that backed by his father-in-law (Piso) and by his son-in-law (Pompey) Cæsar selected the Gauls out of all the provinces as the most likely to furnish him wealth and an opportunity for triumphs. Then he adds, by way of parenthesis or correction, "*Et initio quidem Galliam Cisalpinam Illyrico adiecto lege Vatinia accepit; mox per senatum Comatam quoque, veritis patribus ne, si ipsi negassent, populus et hanc daret.*" Evidently at the beginning Suetonius is thinking of Transalpine Gaul, where Cæsar won a vast fortune and his military glory, and which Pompey after the marriage took an active part in securing for him. Then he modifies his first statement by distinguishing the different ways in which Cæsar got the two Gauls, noting that he received the Cisalpine province before the other. How long before ? Suetonius does not say, but Gelzer reasons from the use of the term son-in-law that it must have been *after* the marriage. This seems to me much too literal ; the use of the term son-in-law is natural, for Suetonius has just spoken of the marriage, and the Transalpine province was the really important one for Cæsar's future career. The correction of the first sweeping statement affords no serious reason to suppose that Suetonius thought that the Vatinian law was passed after the marriage rather than before it. Is there anything in this passage to show that Suetonius was scrupulously exact in his use of words ? If he was, it might be argued that Cæsar did not marry Calpurnia till after the consular elections, which were put off till October, and that the Vatinian law was only passed after this marriage.

It seems to me that there is no reason to conclude that either Suetonius or Plutarch thought that the Vatinian law was passed after the marriage, but there is reason to believe that Appian and Dio, in putting it before the marriage did really think this the true order of events, since they both tell us that Cæsar arranged the marriage because he was afraid of what might happen during his long absence. Of course, Appian and Dio may have been mistaken, but the weight of the " historiographic tradition," such as it is, would appear to be against Gelzer.

That the Vatinian law followed the marriage of Julia and Pompey is an assumption which Gelzer's second argument for his date makes essential to his theory. This argument is from the silence of Cicero's letters between April 13 and the beginning of May in regard to the Vatinian law, and it is in the last of these that he mentions the marriage of Julia, of which he has just heard. Gelzer reasons that if the Vatinian law had been passed before May, Cicero could not have failed to make some allusion to it in these letters. I am willing to grant that, if it had been passed between April 13 and May 3 or 4, Atticus would certainly have informed Cicero, and the orator would probably have made *some* comment on the matter, but if it had been passed before Cicero left Rome, that is before April 12, he might not allude to it at all, since Atticus presumably knew his views on the subject. If it was passed before the marriage, therefore, it is highly probable that it was passed before April 12. It is not, however, by any means certain that Cicero did not refer to the Vatinian law in his letters. On April 15 (*Att.* ii, 6) he speaks of Vatinius as though he had done something remarkable, and in the next letter Cicero expects that

Vatinius will be given a lucrative mission. To have carried the Vatinian law would certainly have made him notorious and have given him a claim to some reward. I am inclined to think that probably Cicero *is* referring to the law in these letters, in much the same fashion in which he refers to the first agrarian law, which had certainly been passed. Gelzer contends that the reference may be to something else that Vatinius had done or to some other law or laws which he had passed, and I am ready to retreat so far from my original position as to admit that this is quite possible. But until it is proved that the reference cannot be to the Vatinian law concerning Cæsar's provinces, I do not see that the argument from silence is of any force. Such an argument is in all cases somewhat weak, and it is surely without value unless the silence is proved beyond doubt. Even if the silence were established, I do not think the argument would have much weight, for Cicero in his letters fixes his attention on the present and only alludes to past events incidentally, so that a failure to refer to the Vatinian law would, in my judgment, mean very little.

My chief reason for thinking that the Vatinian law was passed before April 13 is that in a letter to Atticus (ii, 16) written on May 1 or 2 Cicero represents Pompey as meeting all objections to the Campanian land law by saying " I will hold you down by Cæsar's army " (*Oppressos vos tenebo exercitu Cæsaris*). From this I assumed that at the time Cæsar had an army which he secured under the terms of the Vatinian law. Gelzer, however, contends that the expression " Cæsar's army " is intended figuratively and means merely Cæsar's partisans. To prove this he has collected a number of instances where the word *exercitus* is, as he claims, so used. I am perfectly willing to admit that Cicero did sometimes use military terms in a metaphorical sense, but it seems to me that we should construe words literally if there is nothing in the context which suggests that they were not so meant. In a number of the instances cited by Gelzer I am firmly persuaded that Cicero did mean what he said, and that the context shows this. In particular Gelzer notes (p. 116) the similarity in the language used by Cicero in his speech against the agrarian bill of Rullus and in his letter to Atticus, but the very point of Cicero's argument in the speech is that the bill will give the ten commissioners the power to raise an army with which they can oppress the Republic, and an army in the most literal sense. Nor can I believe that when in his speeches after his recall from exile Cicero mentions the threat of Cæsar's army as the means by which Clodius was able to banish him there is anything figurative in his language. In the *pro Sestio* (ch. 18) he says, " Moreover, Cæsar himself was at the gates, he held the *imperium*, his army was in Italy and in that army he had given a command to the brother of that very tribune of the people who was my enemy." Here I am wholly unable to accept Gelzer's view (p. 118) that Cicero means by the army in Italy the three legions which were spending the winter around Aquileia. I think it clear from these speeches[1] that in the first months of 58 Cæsar had an organized body of troops near Rome, which Cicero calls Cæsar's army, and I believe that the reasonable conclusion is that Cæsar had such a body of troops when Cicero first used this expression.

Even if the words " Cæsar's army " in the letter to Atticus are taken figuratively, and if the possible allusions to the Vatinian law in these early letters are construed as references to something else, my main contention would still remain untouched, for that contention is simply that it was by means of an army near Rome that Cæsar was able to overawe the opposition. Cicero confesses that at the beginning of his consulship Cæsar was popular,[2] and he may well have relied at first on mob violence to carry his measures. Unless, however, Cicero was wholly deceived, the Triumvirs became very unpopular later in the year, and I believe that their control then was based on the fear of Cæsar's army. Just when Cæsar got the army seems to me a somewhat minor question, and I fixed the date simply on the basis of the evidence as I construed it. Gelzer holds (p. 117) that it was impossible for Cæsar to have an army near Rome during his consulship, and that he did not become proconsul of Gaul till he left the city *paludatus* because a consul could not take over his province during his year of office except with the authorization of the senate. This may be true of a consular province conferred by the senate, but Cæsar held Cisalpine Gaul by the Vatinian law, and what he could do was determined by the provisions of that law. Gelzer himself admits that it is conceivable that the law authorized Cæsar to go to his province while consul, as Crassus did in 55 under the *lex Trebonia.* Is it not equally conceivable that the *lex Vatinia* was so framed that Cæsar could begin recruiting soldiers for service in his legions at once ?[3] In point of fact I believe that the law did permit this. Gelzer's view is that the three legions assigned him by the law were the three which in his Commentaries (i, 10) he

[1] *Post red. in sen.*, ch. 13, 32 (in ch. 12, 32 the word *exercitus* is used figuratively of the Catilinarian conspirators) ; *pro domo*, ch. 3, 5 ; *de harusp. resp.*, ch. 22, 47 ; *pro Sest.*, ch. 17, 40 ; ch. 18, 41 ; ch. 19, 43 ; ch. 23, 52.

[2] *Att.*, ii, 21.

[3] If it gave him a larger army than was stationed in the province and authorized him to go there at any time, he would have to recruit the extra troops so as to have them ready. According to Dio (xxxix, ch. 39) both Pompey and Crassus began levying troops in 55 while still consuls.

says were wintering around Aquileia when he went to the Transalpine province in March, 58. With this I agree, but Gelzer goes further and maintains that these legions had been under the command of Afranius, who preceded Cæsar as proconsul. There is no evidence, so far as I am aware, to connect these legions with Cæsar before 58, but there is also none to connect them with Afranius or to show that they existed at all before the winter of 59–58. My own opinion is that two of them were raised by Cæsar in 59, and that they were sent north only in that winter, perhaps arriving at Aquileia after the beginning of 58. To me the supposition that they had been under the command of Afranius during 59 seems highly improbable. In 60 the senate was so much frightened by the news of fighting among the tribes of Gaul and of raids on the Transalpine province that it decreed both the Gallic provinces to the consuls for the year.[1] These consuls were Metellus Celer and Afranius, and the former received Transalpine and the latter Cisalpine Gaul.[2] It is surely unlikely that the senate gave Metellus only one legion with which to meet the danger, while assigning three to Afranius in a province where there appears to have been no disturbance whatever.[3] Yet Cæsar found only one legion in Transalpine Gaul when he arrived there, and three in winter quarters around Aquileia. From this fact I infer that two of the three legions had been recruited by Cæsar during his consulship, and that he kept them near Rome till late in 59, when he sent them North to spend the rest of the winter in the Cisalpine province. I also assume that he still kept a considerable force near Rome,[4] which may have been later embodied in the additional legion which he raised in Italy after he had gone to Gaul.

Gelzer urges rather emphatically that my view is contradicted by Cæsar himself. In my article (p. 516) I said that the Vatinian law made Cæsar "proconsul of Gaul while he was still consul; and, as proconsul, he could enlist soldiers for service in his provinces and keep them near Rome until he was ready to leave the city. Later, as proconsul of the Spains, Pompey did precisely this same thing." Gelzer's comment (p. 119) is as follows, "Den schlagenden Gegenbeweis gibt Cæsar selbst (*b.c.* I, 85, 8): *in se*

[1] *Att.*, i, 19. Written in March, 60. [2] *Att.*, i, 20. Written in May, 60.

[3] The senate in its alarm ordered that troops should be recruited, and I think that they would have been used to strengthen the army in Transalpine Gaul if the panic had not subsided rather quickly. I can see no reason for strengthening the garrison in the Cisalpine province.

[4] He may have sent his whole force north, and later raised new troops when he saw that Clodius would need support. Perhaps the part of his army which remained near Rome was recruited from Pompey's veterans and was never really intended for service in Gaul. Of course, the legions at Aquileia were an additional force which could be called back if necessary.

*novi generis imperia constitui, ut idem ad portas urbanis præsideat rebus et duas bellicosissimas provincias absens tot annos obtineat.* Wie hätte er 49 so sprechen können, wenn ihm selbst 59 die Lex Vatinia offenkundig dieses Recht eingeräumt hätte?" I meant that as proconsul Pompey could and did recruit troops for service in Spain and keep some of them under his command in Italy until he was ready to go to his province. What Cæsar complains of is that Pompey stayed in Italy for so many years, five in fact, governing the Spains by legates and overawing the city by his troops. Cæsar himself had lingered near Rome with an armed force, as I believe, for between two and three months after he laid down the consulship, but he certainly never dreamed of staying in Italy for the entire period of his proconsulship as Pompey did. Surely the difference between two or three months and five years was quite sufficient to justify Cæsar's language, and a proconsul who never went to his province at all, but governed it from Italy throughout his term of office, even if that term had been only a single year, was an innovation in Roman politics to which Cæsar could reasonably object as a violation of all precedent.

I assigned the date of February 28 for the passage of the Vatinian law to account for the fact that Cæsar's proconsulship would end on March 1, 54. Gelzer, however, advances the theory that the law specified that Cæsar should hold Cisalpine Gaul till the fifth Kalends of March. If passed after March 1, 59, the fifth Kalends would be March 1, 54. Our sources agree in saying that the province was given for five years, but if Cæsar stayed in Rome throughout his term as consul this would be the case, since we know that the two months of 54 would make it impossible for a successor to take over the province before January 1, 53. My chief objection to this theory is that I can see no reason why, if the Vatinian law was intended to make his proconsulship end January 1, 53, it should have said the fifth Kalends of March instead of the sixth Kalends of January. This objection is not decisive, because there may have been technical reasons or precedents of which we know nothing for using one phrase rather than the other. If Gelzer's view is accepted, I should then maintain that the Vatinian Law was passed sometime in March rather than on February 28. Gelzer also holds that the *lex Pompeia-Licinia* in 55 was framed in the same way as *lex Vatinia*, and that it prolonged Cæsar's proconsulship till the fifth Kalends of March after its passage, which would make the second quinquennium end March 1, 50. For this date I can see no evidence at all; if I were to fix a specific date for the termination of Cæsar's proconsulship, I should prefer that suggested by Adcock, namely, the Ides of November.[1]

[1] F. E. Adcock, *The Legal Term of Cæsar's Governorship in Gaul.*

7

## THE LEGAL ISSUE BETWEEN CÆSAR AND THE SENATE *

I HAVE discussed elsewhere most of the theories as to the date at which Cæsar's proconsulship in Gaul legally terminated,[1] and I have no desire to enter into the general question in this place, but it seems necessary to indicate briefly the nature of the difficulties which hampered the senate in the appointment of a successor. Since these difficulties differed according to the date assumed for the end of Cæsar's term, they must be discussed from several different standpoints.

The date generally accepted by English scholars is that proposed by Mommsen; according to his theory the Pompeian-Licinian law extended Cæsar's term for five years from the time when it expired under the Vatinian law, which would carry it to March 1, 49. If his term did end on this date, the senate could not send a successor to take over his provinces before the beginning of 48, because it was necessary for proconsuls and proprætors to possess the *imperium* in their provinces as soon as they laid down their office in Rome. This made it impossible to assign the Gauls to any of the magistrates for 50, since during the first two months of 49 Cæsar was still legally in charge. The first magistrates who could be appointed were, therefore, those for 49, and they could not leave Rome to go to their provinces until the beginning of 48. The new system of provincial administration was intended to remedy this situation by making it possible to send out governors in the course of the year. Under Pompey's law the senate could assign provinces to the ex-consuls and ex-prætors whenever it pleased, because they were to receive the *imperium* by a special vote of the assembly,[2] which could be passed at one time as well as another.

[1] See *The Founding of the Roman Empire*, pp. 275–89.

[2] The consuls and prætors after their election by the *comitia centuriata* were invested with the *imperium* by a formal law passed by the *comitia curiata*; this law was not subject to the veto. Pompey applied this procedure to the provincial governors, although he probably substituted the *comitia centuriata* for the *comitia curiata*.

In opposition to Mommsen's theory a number of scholars have maintained that Cæsar's proconsulship ended some time in 50, but they are not agreed as to the day, ranging from March 1 to the end of December. For our present purpose these differences are of little importance, since the legal obstacles were the same. By the Sempronian law the consular provinces had to be designated by the senate before the election of the consuls who were to hold them, and the tribunes were deprived of the right to veto this designation. It has been generally held that the Pompeian-Licinian law contained a clause forbidding any discussion by the senate of a successor to Cæsar before March 1, 50.[1] This clause made it impossible to assign the Gauls as consular provinces to any consuls before those elected in 50. These consuls, however, would serve in Rome during 49, and could not go to their provinces before the beginning of 48. Cæsar, therefore, could not be superseded by a consul until more than a year after his term expired. If the Gauls were made prætorian provinces, they could be assigned to the prætors for 50, who could take possession at the beginning of 49, but the tribunes had the right to veto the assignment of the prætorian provinces, so that Cæsar could prevent the appointment of a successor of prætorian rank as long as there was a single tribune devoted to his interests. Pompey's new law was primarily intended to repeal the Sempronian law, and so to permit the assignment of the Gauls as consular provinces in 50 or 49. On this supposition the fact that by the repeal of the Sempronian law the tribunes regained the right to veto the assignment of the consular provinces was either overlooked, or Pompey counted on being able to treat such a use of the veto as an act of rebellion on Cæsar's part. Cæsar's dexterity in availing himself of Curio's services destroyed the plausibility of such an argument, and Pompey found himself unable to deal with the veto except by invoking the last decree of the senate. This decree he could only extort from the conscript fathers by bringing such obvious pressure to bear upon them that it was robbed of all moral value.

Cæsar's right to stand for the consulship *in absentia* was also involved in the controversy. This right was conferred by the law of the Ten Tribunes. It could be argued that the privilege had been repealed by a later law of Pompey requiring all candidates to make a personal canvass. To this law, after it had been enacted, Pompey added a clause exempting Cæsar.[2] The legality of the addition was open to question, but Pompey himself apparently based his opposition to Cæsar's candidacy on other grounds.

[1] The existence of such a clause has recently been very seriously questioned. See F. A. Adcock, *The Legal Term of Cæsar's Governorship in Gaul.*

[2] Suetonius, *Div. Jul.*, ch. 28.

Laqueur maintains[1] that the law of the Ten Tribunes authorized Cæsar to stand for the consulship not only *in absentia* but while proconsul of Gaul, and that this provision could be interpreted in two ways. If under Sulla's law he could not become a candidate till 49, the plebiscite might be construed as a permission to stand in 50 before his term in Gaul expired, or as extending his term there until after the elections in 49. According to this theory Pompey took the view that Cæsar's privilege lapsed when he failed to take advantage of it in 50, while Cæsar contended for the other interpretation ; Laqueur holds that this was the *Rechtsfrage* between the two. Cæsar seems to have argued that the plebiscite had somehow extended his *imperium*, and Cicero seems to admit it,[2] but speculation as to the wording of a law whose text is lost can obviously lead to no certain result. It is quite possible that Pompey did not challenge Cæsar's right to become a candidate *in absentia* in 49, and that his whole purpose was to render the privilege worthless by superseding Cæsar as proconsul before the elections in that year. On his side Cæsar could point out that the people could not have meant to grant him a favour which was without value, that the obvious purpose of the plebiscite was to permit his election as consul without his leaving his province, and so by implication that it prolonged his *imperium*. So far as I can see there was no single *Rechtsfrage* in the controversy. Pompey was trying to secure the legal appointment of successors to take over Cæsar's provinces as soon as possible, while Cæsar was employing the tribunician veto to prevent such an appointment until he was ready to leave. The question at issue was simply whether Pompey could find some way of overriding the veto which would not make him appear as the aggressor in the inevitable war and so alienate the public opinion of Italy.

In the text I have endeavoured to give an account of the political duel between Pompey and Cæsar which will be true in the main whatever theory may be adopted as to the date when Cæsar's proconsulship expired, because it seems to me that the problem does not admit of any certain solution. Perhaps, however, I ought not to leave the matter without a brief statement of my own personal views. It seems to me that the balance of probability is in favour of the assumption that Cæsar's term ended sometime in 50. Within that year three dates appear about equally probable. If the Pompeian-Licinian law went into effect immediately on its passage the date would be sometime in May, since the Trebonian law had been announced, if it had not actually been passed, by

[1] R. Laqueur, *Die Rechtsfrage zwischen Cäsar und dem Senat.*

[2] Cæsar, *b.c.* i, ch. 9 ; *Att.*, vii, 7.

April 27,[1] and it is highly probable that the Pompeian-Licinian followed it very shortly.[2] If, on the other hand, the laws specified when they were to go into effect, any date might have been fixed, and Cæsar's command may have terminated on March 1, 50, as Gelzer maintains, or on November 13, 50, as Adcock suggests. I join Adcock in doubting the existence of any clause in the Pompeian-Licinian law forbidding the discussion of a successor to Cæsar before March 1, 50, and I am inclined to believe that Cæsar originally intended to become a candidate in that year and to hold the consulship in 49.[3] Whether he was legally eligible to be consul in 49 does not seem to me to matter, since he needed a special privilege to be elected in his absence in any case, and the privilege could cover both points as well as one. It seems to me possible that the law of the Ten Tribunes was ambiguously worded on purpose to enable him to stand in 50 or in 49 as he might prefer. If he had any intention of standing in 50, he abandoned it on account of the situation in Gaul. The great revolt of 52 and the necessity of constant campaigning throughout 51 may have convinced him that it would be desirable to put off his departure for another year. It seems to me that the letter of Cælius Rufus to Cicero written in October, 51, shows clearly that Cælius at least considered Cæsar's candidacy in 50 a possibility.[4] It may be that there was no ambiguity anywhere, but that some of Cæsar's friends were proposing that he be allowed to stand before the legal time, and that Cælius means that Cæsar will not insist upon this point. At any rate, in the latter part of 50 Cæsar was planning to be a candidate in 49 and was claiming that his term in Gaul had been extended by the plebiscite until after the elections in that year, while Pompey was determined to deprive him of his provinces and his army before the elections.

The abandonment of the theory that there was a clause in the Pompeian-Licinian law prohibiting discussion of a successor to Cæsar before March 1, 50, raises a difficulty unless we assume that under the law of Sulla Cæsar could hold the consulship for the second time in 49. If he was not eligible until 48, there was no necessity for repealing the Sempronian law, since the senate could assign the Gauls as consular provinces to the consuls for 50, who

[1] *Att.*, iv, 9.

[2] Dio, xxxix, ch. 33–36. From this we would infer that both laws were passed on the same day, but that seems very improbable. That Cæsar's *imperium* might last for a month or more longer than Pompey's would be practically unimportant, since under the old system neither could be superseded till the beginning of the next year.

[3] It is generally held that under the law of Sulla he was not legally eligible to hold the consulship a second time until 48, but the evidence for this view does not seem to me conclusive.

[4] *Fam.*, viii, 8.

could take possession of them at the beginning of 49. In this case the problem of why Pompey introduced the new system of provincial administration obviously presents itself. Cæsar alleges that it was directed against him,[1] but he could do this with some plausibility, whatever its real purpose may have been, because his enemies attempted to use it to his disadvantage. It is possible that the reasons publicly given for the new system were actually the real reasons, and that it was not aimed at Cæsar.[2] Pompey, however, either because of pledges given at Luca, or because he was not yet ready for a final break with Cæsar, procured the passage of the law of the Ten Tribunes. If that law was ambiguous, as Laqueur thinks, the ambiguity may have been intentional, so that Pompey could later interpret it to suit himself. If there was no ambiguity in the law, then it might be assumed that Pompey's apparent blundering in repealing it and afterward adding a clause restoring its validity was intentional, and that his aim was to furnish a pretext for refusing to let Cæsar profit by the concession. On this supposition Pompey realized too late that the repeal of the Sempronian law had become a blunder when it was followed by the plebiscite, since Cæsar could now use the veto of his tribunes to retain his command until he came to Rome to take office as consul. Having involved himself in a difficulty, Pompey tried to extricate himself as best he could, and his method was as clumsy as most of his political manœuvres.

I may say in conclusion that I have modified my earlier views in only two really important particulars. As a result of Adcock's article I have come to regard the clause in the Pompeian-Licinian law forbidding discussion as very doubtful, and I feel less certain than formerly that Cæsar could not legally hold the consulship until 48.

[1] *b.c.* i, ch. 85.

[2] In urging Pompey to set up the new system the senators may have seen that Cæsar might be able to retain his provinces somewhat longer by the use of the veto, but have thought that this was not very important. In fact, delay in superseding him only became dangerous when he received the privilege of election *in absentia*, a concession which his enemies may not have expected.

8

## * THE MISSION OF ROSCIUS AND L. CÆSAR

WE learn from Cæsar[1] that the prætor Roscius and L. Cæsar, a distant relative, whose father was one of Cæsar's officers, came to Ariminum bearing a personal message from Pompey to the effect that Pompey was anxious to clear himself in Cæsar's eyes and that Cæsar "should not construe as an insult to him what he [Pompey] had done in the interest of the commonwealth. He had always put the interests of the state above his private friendships. Cæsar also ought to put aside, for the sake of the commonwealth, both his party spirit and his anger, and not cherish such bitter wrath at his enemies as to injure the commonwealth in the hope of injuring them." Cæsar was not much impressed by the message, but he sent the envoys back to Pompey with definite terms of peace, an ultimatum, in fact. We know from Cicero's letters that L. Cæsar communicated these proposals to Pompey at Teanum on January 23, and that Pompey had a reply drawn up, which was discussed by the consuls and a number of senators, Cicero among them, at Capua on the 25th.[2] Whether the envoys returned to Cæsar from Teanum or from Capua is not certain, although the latter seems the more probable. There are a number of points in regard to their mission which are obscure and concerning which opinion is divided.

In the first place, were they sent from Rome before or after Cæsar's occupation of Ariminum was known? Holmes[3] and others maintain that they left after the news had arrived and were sent in consequence of it. It is also held that they were charged not only with a private message from Pompey, but also with an official message from the senate informing Cæsar of the decree which required him to give up his provinces on a certain day or be declared a public enemy. Cæsar, however, says nothing of a message from the senate, and if they bore any such communication it seems to me obvious that they must have received it before the

[1] *b.c.*, i, chs. 8–11. [2] *Att.*, vii, 13b; 14; 15.

[3] Holmes, *The Roman Republic*, III, pp. 3–4; 358–61; 375–77.

seizure of Ariminum was known, since the occupation of that town made Cæsar legally a rebel, and to warn him that he would be declared a traitor in the future when he was one already seems to me too absurd even for a panic-stricken senate. Moreover, if the senate had sent them to make an official communication to Cæsar, it seems difficult to explain the surprise felt by Cicero at the choice of L. Cæsar as an envoy, since it would have been obvious that he was sent to deliver a reply to the senate because he had been the bearer of a message from the senate, and Cicero could hardly have written to Atticus,[1] "I saw L. Cæsar at Minturnæ on the morning of January 23 with the most absurd commission. He isn't a man, but an untied broom, so that it seems to me that Cæsar is making fun of us when he gave so important a commission to such a fellow. Perhaps, however, he did not give it, but Lucius has seized upon something said in conversation and is turning it to account." If Cicero knew why the "untied broom" had been selected such language is rather curious. It seems to me probable, therefore, that the two envoys were not the bearers of any official communication, but only of a private message from Pompey.

The question remains, however, of whether Pompey sent them before or after he heard of the occupation of Ariminum. This event took place on the morning of January 12, and Holmes has drawn up a time-table by which he shows that it would have been physically possible for the news to have reached Rome before they left. The time-table requires, however, a number of assumptions: *if* Cæsar did not prevent couriers from leaving Ariminum when he occupied that city, *if* they travelled with great speed, *if* Pompey decided on his message very promptly, *if* the envoys set out without delay and travelled very rapidly, *if* Cæsar took only one day to prepare his ultimatum, and *if* the envoys encountered no delays on their return, they could have reached Minturnæ on the morning of the 23rd when Cicero met L. Cæsar there. It seems to me that there are so many assumptions involved that no conclusion can be drawn from the time-table, and that the question must be decided on the basis of the character of the message of which the envoys were the bearers. Unless Cæsar has misrepresented this message it seems more likely to have been sent before Pompey knew of the occupation of Ariminum. It was surely absurd to ask Cæsar not to take personal offence at Pompey's recent conduct if Cæsar had actually begun a war because of it: on the other hand such a message is much less absurd if sent while Pompey believed that Cæsar would make no immediate move. I am therefore inclined to think that the envoys were sent before Pompey heard that Cæsar had crossed the Rubicon. The point is

[1] *Att.*, vii, 13b.

not of great importance, since the significance of the message is much the same whenever it was sent. If Pompey did know at the time that Ariminum had been occupied, he would hardly have despatched the envoys unless he had believed that Cæsar would not make a serious advance before spring, and that negotiations were still possible with him ; this idea may have been abandoned only when the news arrived of the occupation of other places.

# ADDITIONAL NOTES

In these notes the following abbreviations are used:

| | |
|---|---|
| *A.J.A.* . . | American Journal of Archæology. |
| *A.J.P.* . . | American Journal of Philology. |
| Bruns, *Fontes* | Fontes Iuris Romani Antiqui, 7th edition (1909). |
| *C.A.H.* . . | Cambridge Ancient History. |
| *C.P.* . . . | Classical Philology. |
| *C.Q.* . . . | Classical Quarterly. |
| *C.R.* . . . | Classical Review. |
| *I.G.R.R.* . . | Inscriptiones Græcæ ad Res Romanas Pertinentes. |
| *J.R.S.* . . | Journal of Roman Studies. |
| *O.G.I.S.* . . | Dittenberger, Orientis Græci Inscriptiones Selectæ. |
| Riccobono, *F.I.R.A.* . | Fontes Iuris Romani AnteIustiniani, 2nd edition (1940). |
| *T.A.P.A.* . . | Transactions of the American Philological Association. |
| Warmington, *R.O.L.* . | Remains of Old Latin, Vol. 4 (Loeb Classical Library). |

(p. 3.) On the equites see H. Hill, *The Roman Middle Class* (1952).

(p. 7, n. 1.) A list of the legions of 200–168 B.C. will be found in A. Afzelius, *Die römische Kriegsmacht* (1946), p. 47.

(p. 8.) T. Frank (*Econ. Survey*, i, pp. 158 ff.) argues that for the period 200–150 B.C. most of the provincial grain was needed for the army and that in consequence little of it was thrown on the open market at Rome. With the decrease of fighting after 146, however, it would tend to compete with the cereal production of Italy.

(p. 16.) At any rate by Cicero's day, if not before (from *c.* 133 ?), *nobilitas* connoted men or their descendants who had held the consulship, not merely *any* curule magistracy. Cicero's remarks (*Pro Murena*, 15) about Murena, whose ancestors had been prætors, seem decisive. (See M. Gelzer, *Die Nobilitat der romischen Republik*, p. 26; cf. R. Syme, *Rom. Revolut.*, p. 10; A. Afzelius, *Classica et Med.*, 1938, pp. 40 ff., and H. H. Scullard, *Roman Politics*, p. 10 f.)

(p. 19.) A central point of F. B. Marsh's view of the method by which the nobility controlled the Assemblies is that they needed to concentrate on winning the support only of those members of the rural tribes that happened to be present in Rome on any given occasion: " although the urban populace might greatly outnumber the country folk, they were politically negligible . . ." (p. 19) because they were practically confined to the four urban tribes *vis-à-vis* the thirty-one rural tribes. But this basic assumption that the *plebs urbana* was confined to the urban tribes at this period has been shown to be highly improbable by H. Last in a review of this book (*A.J.P.*, lviii, 1937, pp. 467 ff.). Here and there Marsh does recognize the presence of urban members in rural tribes, e.g. " later many of these dependents (i.e. of the great families) who moved to the city kept their registration in the rural tribes " (p. 22); and again, class 6 of his analysis of a rural tribe as it actually voted (p. 373): " members of the city populace who had retained their registration in the tribe in spite of the fact that they or their ancestors had moved to Rome and who had not become dependents of the nobles or knights "; and " the number of voters in class 6 tended constantly to grow " (pp. 373–4). The important point is when did this element become large enough to exercise real political power? Marsh implies that it was small enough to be indecisive, whereas Last has shown that the urban rabble, having a strong representation in the rural tribes, became by Gracchan times a formidable menace to the country voters (as the source of Appian, *Bell. Civ.*, i, believed). See further H. Last (*op. cit.*), who also points out that, this being so, Marsh's view (p. 372) that the group-vote enabled the nobility to concentrate on gaining a bare majority of the tribes " loses much of its plausibility if the effective strength of *all* the tribes lay in the more or less homogeneous mass of the urban plebs." It may be observed further that the Roman nobles may have found it not less easy to gain (by whatever means) the support of those members of rural tribes who resided in Rome than that of " visiting " members of rural tribes. It is not clear whether Marsh modified his views on this point in any way in the light of Last's review: they are also set out in Marsh's *Modern Problems in the Ancient World*, part ii, ch. 2, which was published posthumously in 1943, but of which the preface, written by the author, was dated 1st January, 1937, i.e. before the publication of the review.

(p. 21, n. 1.) On the *leges Ælia et Fufia* (*c.* 150 B.C.), see S. Weinstock, *J.R.S.*, 1937, pp. 215 ff.

(p. 33.) The intimate friend of Scipio Æmilianus, C. Lælius, raised the question of the public land sometime between his tribunate in 151 and his consulship in 140, perhaps in this latter year, but dropped it when he met with strong opposition: hence, according to Plutarch (*Ti. Gr.*, 8, 3) he gained the name "Sapiens," a *cognomen* which in fact more probably rested on the wider basis of his achievements in general. Soon afterwards two measures were passed which slightly lessened the political control of the aristocracy: in 139 a tribune, A. Gabinius, the grandson of a slave (Livy, *Oxyrrh.*, *Per.*, 1. 193), brought in a measure which established secret ballot at elections, thus giving clients greater freedom to vote as they wished (Cic., *de legibus*, iii, 16, 35); and in 137 another tribune, L. Cassius Longinus, sponsored another measure which extended the secret ballot to the judicial assemblies of the People (Cic., *loc. cit*).

(p. 33.) On the First Servile War, for which the chief source is Diodorus, xxxiv, 1–12 (deriving from Poseidonius), see further H. Last, *C.A.H.*, ix, pp. 11–16; J. Carcopino, *Hist. Rom.*, pp. 176–9 (p. 177, n. 35, on chronology). On the grievances of the slaves, including the disregard of their customary rights, see W. L. Westermann, *C.P.*, 1945, pp. 1 ff. The organization of the slave leader Eunus, who styled himself "Antiochus, King of the Slaves" on the coins which he issued (cf. E. S. G. Robinson, *Numismatic Chron.*, 1920, p. 175), was good. The early Roman setbacks were only made good when the fall of Numantia in Spain in 133 permitted the use of seasoned troops in Sicily. P. Rupilius, the consul of 132, who finally suppressed the rising, settled the province and with the help of a decemviral senatorial commission issued a new charter for Sicily (the lex Rupilia: see Cic., *In Verr.*, ii, 13, 32; 15, 37; 16, 39; 24, 59). It may be noted that Rupilius was a *novus homo.* The construction of a military road from Capua to Rhegium (a continuation of the Via Appia from Capua down the west coast) by P. Popillius, colleague of Rupilius in the consulship of 132, was probably connected with the slave-war: see the inscription of Popillius, who had served as prætor in Sicily in 135, in Dessau, *Inscr. Lat. Sel.*, n. 23.

(p. 33.) There were two aspects of the economic problem: the re-establishment of the small peasant farmer throughout Italy and the reduction of the pauper unemployed proletariate in the towns. The latter aspect has been stressed by D. Kontchalowski (*Revue Historique*, 1926, pp. 161 ff.) and H. Last (*C.A.H.*, ix, p. 9 f.).

(p. 34.) The extent of the support that Ti. Gracchus received from senatorial circles must remain uncertain, but there was a group of nobles who were hostile to the coterie around Æmilianus. Cicero in the *De Republica* (i, 19; the dramatic date of the dialogue is 129 B.C.) names Appius Claudius Pulcher, *princeps senatus* and father-in-law of Tiberius (the Claudian *gens* produced many conservative demagogues), Q. Cæcilius Metellus Macedonicus, the conqueror of Andriscus (in 138 he defended L. Aurelius Cotta against Æmilianus), P. Licinius Crassus Mucianus, jurist, scholar, and Pontifex Maximus (probably after Nasica, *c.* 132–1) who married Clodia, sister of App. Claudius, and became the father-in-law of Gaius Gracchus ; and his brother P. Mucius Scævola, a leading jurist and consul in 133, who succeeded his brother as Pontifex Maximus when the latter died in 130. This was obviously a powerful group and with its backing (or less probably, as J. Carcopino believes, as its tool) Tiberius could not easily be disregarded. For further discussion, see F. Münzer, *Römische Adelsparteien*, pp. 245 ff., and J. Carcopino, *Hist. Rom.*, pp. 171 ff., who believe that this group began about 138 to shake the influence of Æmilianus and the dominant oligarchy. At any rate the political situation appeared favourable for Tiberius when he entered upon his tribunate in December 134 : of the two consuls, Æmilianus was in Spain and C. Fulvius Flaccus in Sicily, while of the consuls designate, L. Calpurnius Piso was to go to Spain, while his colleague P. Mucius Scævola, Tiberius' supporter, would be at home.

Other more intimate influences on Tiberius were his mother and tutors. His mother Cornelia, daughter of Scipio Africanus Maior, had married Gracchus (*c.* 175 : so Carcopino) and was a woman of great culture and distinction. After her husband's death (*c.* 154) she was left to educate her family (she remained a widow, having refused the hand of a reigning monarch, Ptolemy of Egypt). She employed the services of a rhetorician, Diophanes, a political exile from Mitylene, who taught Tiberius to become a great orator. Tiberius also was influenced by the democratic ideas of the Stoic Blossius of Cumæ (see D. R. Dudley, *J.R.S.*, 1941, pp. 94 ff., who suggests that Blossius was not, as is often thought, a teacher employed by Cornelia and that his democratic ideas derived less from his Stoicism than from the connexion of his family with the democratic party at Capua).

(p. 35.) In all probability the fertile *ager Campanus*, from which the State drew good revenue, was excepted from redistribution under Tiberius' bill (Cic., *de leg. agr.*, i, 7, 21 ; ii, 29, 81 ; Bruns, *Fontes*[7], 11, 1. 6, Lex Agraria). The view (based on Plutarch's reference, *Ti. Gr.*, 9, 2, to τιμή, which may represent a misunderstanding of what Appian records in *Bell. Civ.*, i, 11, 5) that some compensation was granted for the land surrendered or for improvements on it, is improbable. The "compensation" which the "possessors" received according to Appian was ownership of land retained (quoted above at the bottom of p. 38). On ownership, see also additional note to p. 379.

(p. 37.) For a somewhat more appreciative estimate of Tiberius, see, e.g., H. Last, *C.A.H.*, ix, ch. i.

(p. 39.) By translating Appian's phrase *ἐς τὴν ἐπιοῦσαν ἀγοράν* (*Bell. Civ.*, i, 12) as "to the next meeting," i.e. the next comitial day, instead of as "till the following day," R. M. Geer (*T.A.P.A.*, 1939, p. 30 f.) attempts to date the passage of the law. On the assumption that Appian and Plutarch can be taken literally, he compares the intervals between the three Assembly meetings and the Roman calendar and suggests that they occurred on January 29th and February 18th and 19th (less probably April 4th, 24th, 25th), i.e. the meetings at which (1) Octavius vetoes and Tiberius adjourns, (2) Octavius again vetoes and Tiberius again adjourns, and (3) Tiberius proposes the deposing of Octavius.

(p. 39.) On the constitutional implications of the deposing of Octavius, see further H. Last, *C.A.H.*, ix, pp. 25–9.

(p. 44.) Tiberius' additional programme (Plut., *Ti. Gr.*, 16, 1; Dio Cassius, frg. 83, 7 goes even further; see also below, p. 379 f.) is rejected by some as being a retrojection of his brother Gaius' proposals. The chief argument against it is the silence of Appian, but it may be noted that, however obscure the details, Appian does state (*B.C.*, i, 14) that since the country people could not come to Rome because of the harvest Gracchus "had recourse to the People in the city." Thus whether or not he appealed to equestrian interests, he almost certainly must have brought forward some fresh measures to win popular support in Rome.

(p. 46.) On the social unrest in Asia Minor, on Aristonicus' proposal to found a Utopian City of the Sun, and on the war itself, see H. Last, *C.A.H.*, ix, pp. 102 ff., E. V. Hansen, *The Attalids of Pergamon* (1947), pp. 142 ff., and D. Magie, *Roman Rule in Asia Minor* (1950), ch. vi. The revolt at first was met only by local resistance which was encouraged by Nasica and his fellow-commissioners, who secured the co-operation of Mithridates V of Pontus, Nicomedes II of Bithynia and Ariarathes V of Cappadocia. Roman troops arrived under the consul Crassus in 131, but met with little success. The revolt was really broken by Perperna (*cos.* 130), while his successor M'. Aquilius merely stamped out the embers.

(p. 47, n. 1.) On the basis of his interpretation of Appian's phrase ἐναλλασσομένους κατ' ἔτος (*B.C.*, i, 9, 37), J. Carcopino has drawn up an elaborate rota of the commissioners' activities. Even if he is correct in his belief that one commissioner took the lead each year, this need not be interpreted as a legally defined position (cf. H. Last, *C.A.H.*, ix, p. 30 n.), nor should it perhaps be rigidly applied. F. B. Marsh believes that when Pulcher died in the latter half of 130 " there was probably a relaxation in the activity of the commission " (p. 47); but even in this extreme case (for the second triumvir, Crassus, was in Asia), it need not be supposed that the third, Gaius Gracchus (nor the newcomers, Flaccus and Carbo), were unable to take any action.

(p. 47.) The opposition of the Italians to the working of the land commission in 129 would in itself be sufficient to discredit the view of J. Göhler (*Röm und Italien*, 1939) that Tiberius had carried his agrarian bill in 133 largely in the interests of the Italians. There is no evidence that they shared in the allotments distributed under the bill. The Italians, who had been allowed to become *possessores* in the past, had no more ground for complaint than Roman citizens had, but this grievance was not their only source of discontent.

(p. 48.) The interpretation, given in the text, of Appian's phrase ἠξίουν τὰς δίκας οὐκ ἐπὶ τῶν διαιρούντων (*B.C.*, i, 19, 2), i.e. that the commissioners were deprived of their judicial powers and in consequence their work of distribution ceased, is hard to accept for three reasons (cf. H. Last, *C.A.H.*, ix, pp. 42 ff.): (*a*) only a law passed by the People could effect this, while Appian refers only to senatorial action, (*b*) the rise in the census figures of 126 (see above, p. 48, n. 3), however these figures may be interpreted (cf. A. H. M. Jones, *Ancient Economic History*, 1947, pp. 3 ff.), almost certainly implies the continued activity of the commissioners, and (*c*) this continued activity after Scipio's death is asserted by Dio Cassius (frg. 84, 2: " they plundered almost the whole of Italy "), by Livy (*Epit.*, lix: defuncto eo acrius seditiones triumvirales exarserunt), and by Appian (*B.C.*, i, 21, 1). The alternative explanation, therefore, advanced by E. G. Hardy (*Six Roman Laws*, p. 39) and accepted by H. Last, has much to commend it: see above p. 48, n. 1.

(p. 51, n. 1.) The cause of the death of Æmilianus (whether natural, suicide, or murder, the alleged murderers including Fulvius Flaccus, Papirius Carbo, Gaius Gracchus, and even his wife Sempronia and her mother Cornelia) is investigated by J. Carcopino, *Autour des Gracques*, pp. 83 ff.

(p. 52, n.) On the settlement of Asia, see A. H. M. Jones, *Cities of East. Roman Prov.* (1937), pp. 58 ff., and D. Magie, *Roman Rule in Asia Minor* (1950), pp. 154 ff. Gaius Gracchus delivered a speech against a Lex Aufeia (see Aulus Gellius, xi, 10, for a fragment) which it is often believed had something to do with the cession of Phrygia to Mithridates of Pontus whose bribes were more effective than those of Nicomedes of Bithynia; Aquillius' acceptance of bribes from Mithridates may have formed one of the charges at his subsequent trial (as Appian, *Mithr.*, 12, 57). D. Magie (*op. cit.*, p. 1043, n. 27; 1049, n. 41), however, believes that such connexions do not in fact exist. H. Hill (*C.R.*, 1948, p. 112 f.) has suggested that the word Aufeia is a corruption of Aquillia and that the measure will have been Aquillius' settlement of Asia. After the death of Mithridates in 120 B.C. Phrygia was either added to or brought under the control of the Roman province of Asia: for the relevant *senatus consultum*, see a fragmentary inscription, dated 116, in Dittenberger, *O.G.I.S.*, n. 436.

(p. 52.) It was probably before Flaccus' proposal that in 126 a tribune, M. Iunius Pennus, issued an edict which ordered foreigners to leave Rome: details are uncertain, but it must have been directed chiefly against Italians who were thronging to Rome to press their claims (Carcopino's view, that Pennus' action followed Flaccus' proposal, is less probable). It should be noted that Flaccus wisely proposed to grant the right of appeal to the Roman People to those Italians who did not wish for Roman citizenship (Valerius Maximus, ix, 5, 1).

(p. 53.) It is perhaps unnecessary to postulate any formal agreement between Gaius and the knights in order to explain his election (cf. H. Last, *A.J.P.*, 1937, p. 471).

(p. 54, n.) Despite the difficulties which F. B. Marsh finds in H. Last's account, many may still feel that it is legitimate to seek some guidance to the chronological development of Gaius' programme in the discrepancies which are to be found in the statements of the ancient sources.

(p. 59.) It should be noted that a measure of Gaius made the bribery of senatorial jurors a criminal offence: this preliminary attempt to deal with the jury question clearly must have been carried before Gaius took the extreme step of transferring the courts to the knights, and it is important that the new equestrian courts, when established, were thus free from the provision of this measure (Cic., *Pro Cluent.*, 151; 154). See also p. 175, n. 2.

There survives an inscription giving the text of a judiciary law, which is almost certainly a lex Acilia (Cic., *In Verr.*, 1, 17, 51). An internal reference (line

22) to the lex Rubria (the Gracchan measure for founding the colony at Carthage, carried in 122 and repealed in 121) and a reference in an inscription from Astypalæa to a lex Rubria Acilia (*I.G.R.R.*, iv, 1028, l. 12) make it almost certain that the date was 122. Thus this law is to be identified with that for which Gaius was responsible and which must therefore have been carried by a friendly tribune Acilius. The older view, more recently revived by J. Carcopino, that the inscription was the lex Servilia repetundarum, is highly improbable. The passages of the lex Acilia, which lay down the positive qualifications of the non-senators to whom the courts were now transferred (lines 12; 16), are unfortunately corrupt, but they probably prescribed the property-qualification for the new jurors, thus referring to the equestrian order in a wide sense without necessarily naming them "equites." For the lex Acilia, see Bruns, *Fontes*[7], 10; Riccobono, *F.I.R.A.*, 1, 84; E. G. Hardy, *Six Roman Laws* (translation); E. H. Warmington, *R.O.L.*, iv, pp. 316 ff.; for a discussion of it, see H. Last, *C.A.H.*, ix, pp. 892 ff. On procedure see M. I. Henderson, *J.R.S.*, 1951, pp. 71 ff; and A. N. Sherwin-White, *ibid.*, 1952, pp. 43 ff.

(p. 62.) Plutarch (*C. Gr.*, 9, 2) records that the colonists were drawn from the more prosperous (*οἱ χαριεστάτοι*) and therefore, to the extent that this statement is true, the colonies will have provided an outlet for a somewhat different class than did the allotments, although doubtless many of the really poor must in fact have shared in the settlements. The law which authorized the founding of a colony at Carthage was proposed by a tribune Rubrius, almost certainly in 122 after Drusus' legislation (so Plutarch); here also, since some at any rate of the allotments were to be 200 *iugera*, the scheme would include men with some moderate capital; there were to be 6000 allotments available at Junonia, the name of the new colony which was to be settled on land outside the area which the Romans had solemnly cursed in 146.

(p. 65.) The counter-proposals of Drusus included one to forbid the scourging of Latins even on military service. If, as is probable, Gaius had at first only suggested giving the franchise to the Latins (and not to all the Italians), this was a smart move since it would satisfy those Latins who wanted citizenship chiefly for the protection it afforded and at the same time it would avoid offending those Romans who did not wish to share their citizenship more widely. It was perhaps only after this that Gaius proposed to deal with Latins and Italians together. It may be noted that Drusus' colonial bill imposed no property qualifications and thus would appeal more to the poor than did that of Gaius. Drusus also proposed to free all who had received land since 133 from the payment of rent. These measures were passed and, with the exception of the colonial bill, may have been implemented, although this is not certain. Drusus avoided the mistake made by Tiberius Gracchus: he did not sit on any commission appointed to carry out his laws (it is uncertain when such action was made illegal by the leges Licinia and Æbutia; Cicero, *de leg. agr.*, ii, 21, calls these laws "veteres tribuniciæ," but they are not certainly pre-Gracchan).

(p. 70, n. 1.) On the S.C. ultimum, see further Ch. Wirszubski, *Libertas as a Political Idea at Rome* (1950), pp. 55 ff.

(p. 71.) According to Appian (*B.C.*, i, 27) three agrarian laws were passed soon after the time of Gaius. The first, probably in 121, allowed the sale of allotments, hitherto inalienable. Appian states that the rich began to get control of the allotments; this may mean that the rich began to profit by speculative buying and selling of such land, because the large landowners cannot legally have obtained the alienated allotments since the legal limit of 500 *iugera* apparently remained in force. The second law, recorded by Appian, of 119 (*a*) abolished the land commission, (*b*) granted perpetual tenancy to *possessores* of public land and (*c*) re-imposed rent on such land. Appian attributes this law, probably wrongly, to a tribune Sp. Thorius (the MSS. give Borios). The third law, probably of 111, abolished all rent; probably Thorius was the author (Cic., *Brut.*, 36, 136). This law is almost certainly to be identified with the lex agraria which survives on one side of the tablet which also contains the lex iudiciaria; besides abolishing rent, this law enacted that all public land dealt with by the Gracchan commission should become the private property of its occupants, gave to all colonies and municipia security of tenure in *ager publicus* which had been granted to them, abolished the system of *possessio*, and dealt with land in Africa and at Corinth. For this law, see Bruns, *Fontes*[7], 11; Riccobono, *F.I.R.A.*, i, p. 102; E. G. Hardy, *Six Roman Laws*, pp. 35 ff.; E. H. Warmington, *R.O.L.*, iv, pp. 370 ff.

Another agrarian law is the lex Mamilia Roscia Peducæa Alliena Fabia (Bruns, *op. cit.*, p. 15; Riccobono, *op. cit.*, p. 138). It has been attributed to a tribune of 109, Mamilius Limetanus, and his colleagues (by E. Fabricius, *Sitz. Ber. Akad. Wiss. Heidelberg*, 1924–5, and others), but more probably it is to be connected with

Julius Cæsar's activities (in 55, or less probably in 59) and provided allotments in colonies (see M. Cary, *J.R.S.*, 1929, pp. 113 ff.).

For a suggestion that the lex Thoria mentioned by Cicero belongs to the period *after* 111 B.C. and relieved *pasture*-land from *vectigal*, see E. F. d'Arms, *A.J.P.*, 1935, pp. 232 ff.

(p. 71.) Roman intervention in southern Gaul had resulted from an appeal from Massilia in 125 against raids of the Salluvii, who were defeated by the Gracchan M. Fulvius Flaccus, consul of 125, and by his successor Calvinus, consul of 124; a protective settlement of Roman veterans was established at Aquæ Sextiæ. This Roman intervention provoked the subsequent attack of the Allobroges and Arverni, who were defeated by Cn. Domitius Ahenobarbus (*cos.* 122) and Q. Fabius Maximus (*cos.* 121), the latter receiving the *cognomen* Allobrogicus while the former stopped behind to complete the settlement which resulted in the formation of the new province of Gallia Transalpina. Roman policy in 125, in which some would see the expansionist views of the Gracchan group, was probably dictated only by military considerations by the Senate. The founding of Narbo Martius was perhaps more in line with the Gracchan tradition, and senatorial opposition may have derived in part from the problems of defence which were involved, in part from a desire not to promote the interests of the knights. For an altar which depicted the founding of the colony, see *C. A. H., Plates*, IV, p. 86. For the coins (serrate *denarii*) which were struck in connexion with the foundation, see E. A. Sydenham, *Roman Republican Coinage* (1952), pp. 64; 222. For the Gallic wars, see C. Jullian, *Histoire de la Gaule*, iii, pp. 1 ff.; M. Clerc, *Massalia*, ii, pp. 36 ff. The main road through Gallia Narbonensis to Spain was named the Via Domitia. A milestone of this road has recently been found and gives the earliest known Roman inscription from Gaul: "Cn. Domitius Ahenobarbus Cn. f. imperator" (see *Gallia*, 1949; *A.J.A.*, 1951, p. 371; *Compt. rend.*, 1951, pp. 161 ff.).

Sardinia, which was restless, was pacified by M. Cæcilius Metellus (*cos.* 115) by 111. The Balearic Islands, which formed a base for pirates who could interfere with Rome's maritime communications with Spain, were reduced by Q. Metellus (123–121), who received the *cognomen* Balearicus. He settled two colonies of Roman citizens in the islands at Palma and Pollentia; here again, as in southern Gaul, military and commercial motives may have combined.

(p. 72.) Aemilius Scaurus brought his *gens* into prominence once more: he became consul and *princeps senatus* in 115 and censor in 109. He had acquired a large fortune and is said to have hesitated between a commercial and political career; he will not therefore have been blind to the interests of the knights. He married Metella, daughter of L. Cæcilius Metellus Delmeticus (she later became the wife of Sulla); this marriage brought him into political friendship with the Metelli, who were one of the dominating forces in Roman politics at this time. Eight members of this family became consuls between 123 and 109 and four gained the censorship. They played a considerable part in stabilizing the Balkan frontier of Italy: L. Metellus, consul in 119, defeated the Dalmatians and was called Delmaticus; Aemilius Scaurus as consul advanced up the Save and defeated the Taurisci; C. Metellus Caprarius dealt with the Scordisci in 113–112. This group has been compared with a Whig oligarchy: see J. Carcopino, *Hist. Rom.*, ii, p. 268.

(p. 72.) For the suggestion that Cirta should be identified with El Kef rather than with Constantine, see R. Charlier, *L'Antiquité Class.*, 1950, pp. 289 ff.

(p. 73.) Cf. K. von Fritz, " Sallust and the Attitude of the Roman Nobility at the Time of the Wars against Jugurtha" (*T.A.P.A.*, 1943, pp. 134 ff.).

(p. 77.) As tribune Marius, despite senatorial opposition, forced through a ballot law which was designed to check intimidation of voters; he also opposed some scheme for extending the corn dole (Plut. *Mar.*, 4). On his early political career, see A. Passerini, " Caio Mario come uomo politico," *Athenæum*, 1934, pp. 10 ff., who tries to disentangle the pro-Marian and anti-Marian threads in Plutarch's narrative.

(p. 78.) But see additional note for p. 16.

(p. 79.) E. Gabba (*Athenæum*, 1949, pp. 173 ff.) has examined the *dilectus* of 107 B.C. and believes, as F. B. Marsh (above, p. 86), that the volunteers were probably mainly rural proletariat, and that, owing to the successive reductions of the minimum financial qualification for the fifth *classis*, the " proletarianization " of the citizen army had already gone a long way before 107. See also above, p. 85. Gabba has continued his study of the army from Marius to Augustus: see *Athenæum*, 1951, pp. 171–273.

(p. 80.) For further detail and discussion of the military and chronological problems of Marius' campaigns, see M. Holroyd, *J.R.S.*, 1928, pp. 1 ff., and H. Last, *C.A.H.*, ix, pp. 113 ff.

(p. 81, n. 1.) The whole question of the jury courts during this period has been examined in a valuable paper, "The History of the Extortion Court at Rome, 123–70 B.C." (*Papers of the Brit. School at Rome*, xiv, 1938), by J. P. V. D. Balsdon. He points out that Cicero's well-known remark that the equites sat on the jury "annos prope quinquaginta continuos" (*In Verr.*, 1, 38) is not incompatible with the existence of mixed senatorial and equestrian juries; while Cicero's statement (*Pro Cornelio*, 79), "cum primum senatores cum equitibus Romanis lege Plotia iudicarent," may mean "as soon as the lex Plotia established mixed juries" and therefore does not exclude the existence of mixed juries before 89 B.C. (the date of lex Plotia). Thus the way is open to accept what is probably the Livian tradition about Cæpio's measure in 106, namely that he established mixed juries, in preference to the tradition in Tacitus (*Annals*, xii, 60, 4) that the juries of the *quæstio repetundarum* were transferred again to the senators. In view of the strength of the popular party in 106, this measure of Cæpio's may be considered a striking success for the senate, which could hardly have hoped to regain *complete* control of the court. The view of E. G. Hardy (*J.P.*, 1913, pp. 99 ff.) that Cæpio's bill was not actually carried has not found much support.

(p. 82.) Cæpio's final trial (perhaps in 103) may have been in a new court established by Saturninus' law *de maiestate* (cf. additional note to p. 90).

(p. 84.) On the part played by Sulla in the Cimbric war, see E. Sadée, *Rhein. Museum*, 1939, pp. 43 ff. On the strategy of the German attack, see F. Miltner, *Klio*, 1940, pp. 289 ff., and for 101 B.C. E. Sadée, *Klio*, 1940, pp. 225 ff.

(p. 89, n. 1.) Glaucia's judiciary law (*a*) introduced the system of *comperendinatio* (i.e. the division of a trial into two parts; under this procedure Cicero prosecuted, e.g. Verres); (*b*) allowed the prosecution of accessories to a crime; and (*c*) almost certainly repealed Cæpio's law and transferred the juries back to the equites alone (this, and not (*a*) and (*b*) alone, would explain Cicero's strong statement, in *Brut.*, 224, that Glaucia "equestrem ordinem beneficio legis devinxerat"). The date of the law is probably 104 or 101: see J. P. V. D. Balsdon (*op. cit.* in additional note to p. 81), who argues against Mommsen's date (111; this is bound up with the Naples tablet, which contains the judiciary and agrarian laws: see additional notes to pp. 59 and 71 above); and also against the theory of J. Carcopino, who identifies Glaucia's law with that contained in the Naples inscription which on this view is dated in 108.

There has recently been published (*Epigraphica*, ix) a fragment of a bronze tablet, found at Tarentum and bearing the text of a Roman law, probably a *lex de pecuniis repetundis*. Part of the second half coincides in phraseology with the lex Bantia (on which see additional note to p. 90), and deals with the obligation of magistrates to take an oath in respect to the law. For the suggestion that it is part of the law of Servilius Glaucia and that this should be dated in 100, see A. Piganiol, *Comptes rendus de l'Acad. des Inscr.*, 1951, pp. 58 ff.

(p. 89, n. 2.) According to our only source (the treatise *Ad Herennium*, 1, 12, 21) Saturninus' proposal was to sell corn at " semissibus et trientibus," i.e. at five-sixths of an *as* (? for a *modius*) or one-eighth of the Gracchan price. But H. Last (*loc. cit.*, on p. 89, n. 2) thinks it by no means impossible that " senis " should be read for " semissibus," i.e. the Gracchan arrangement and price will have been re-introduced (for its earlier abrogation or modification, see above, p. 69, n. 1). If this is accepted, Saturninus' demagogy will have been more moderate.

(p. 90, n. 1.) The existing charge of *perduellio* was not a very satisfactory basis on which to try men accused of military incompetence or neglect, such as C. Popillius Lænas, who made a humiliating treaty with the Tigurini in 106 : cf. H. Last, *C.A.H.*, ix, pp. 159 ff. It is probable that the *Lex Appuleia de maiestate* established a new standing court for treason trials ; it is likely, although there are considerable difficulties in accepting the view, that part of this law is preserved in the *Lex Latina Bantiæ reperta* (as H. Stuart Jones, *J.R.S.*, xvi, 1926, p. 171). This inscription, found at Bantia on the borders of Apulia, contains two documents, one in Oscan dealing with local affairs, the other in Latin forming part of a Roman law. The latter refers to a " iudicium publicum," but only the *sanctio* at the end survives. See Bruns, *Fontes*[7], 9 ; Riccobono, *F.I.R.A.*, 1, p. 82 ; Warmington, *R.O.L.*, iv, p. 294.

(p. 91.) Unless they formed a *lex satura*, Saturninus' agrarian and colonial bills should be separated : at any rate Appian (*B.C.*, i, 29) records that it was to the agrarian law, by which Gallic land once held by the Cimbri was to be distributed, that the clause demanding a compulsory oath was attached. In general, the agrarian and colonial work of Saturninus and Marius may have been considerable : it is now apparent that a commission was established for this purpose and that the father of Julius Cæsar was a member of it. Two inscriptions refer to him; one contains the letters "dic" (which probably forms part of the phrase "xvir agr. dand. adtri. iudic."), while the other states "colonos Cerce (inam deduxit)," Cercina being an island off Africa. Another Cæsar, C. Iulius Cæsar Strabo, may also have been a member of the commission: his *elogium* refers to him as "(xvir agr. dand.) adtri. iu(d)." For these inscriptions, see *Inscr. Italiæ*, xiii, 3, n. 6 and 7; cf. also T. Frank, *A.J.P.*, 1937, pp. 90 ff. and T. R. S. Broughton, *A.J.A.*, 1948, pp. 323 ff.

On Marius' settlements in Africa, see Broughton, *The Romanization of Africa Proconsularis*, pp. 31 ff. The *cognomen* Marianum appears in the titles of the African towns of Thibaris and Uchi Maius. A recently found inscription (see *Comptes rendus*, 1950, pp. 332 ff.) shows that Thuburnica (near Ghardimarou) claimed Marius as the "conditor coloniæ." Thus the area of his settlements in Africa is shown to be more extensive than it was once thought to be.

Another measure of Saturninus may have been a law for mobilizing resources for a drive against the pirates of the eastern Mediterranean. Part of this measure is preserved in the so-called "Pirate Law" found at Delphi (see Riccobono, *F.I.R.A.*, 1, pp. 121 ff.). The date of this law is probably 101–100 (cf. H. Stuart Jones, *J.R.S.*, 1926, pp. 155 ff.). J. Carcopino (*Mélanges Glotz*, i, pp. 119 ff.) has suggested that the real purpose was to create an extra-ordinary command in Asia for Marius. But even if such a far-reaching plan has not been proved, the measure might still form part of Saturninus' legislation: it would be popular with the equites (cf. A. Passerini, *Athenæum*, 1934, pp. 134 ff.).

This measure will have been the sequel to the campaign of M. Antonius, a prætor who was sent out with proconsular imperium in 102 to deal with the pirates off the coasts of Pamphylia and western Cilicia (cf. above, p. 106). On Antonius' command, which he held until 100, see T. R. S. Broughton, *T.A.P.A.*, 1946, pp. 35 ff. Antonius' legate, Lucilius Hirrus, has left a record in elegiac verse of his exploit in getting the Roman fleet carried over the Isthmus of Corinth: see *C.I.L.*i.$^2$, 2, 2662, and cf. S. Dow, *Harvard Stud. Class. Phil.*, 1951, pp. 81 ff.

(p. 93.) For the view, based largely on Cicero, *de leg.*, ii, 6, that only the laws of Saturninus' second tribunate in 100 and not those of his first in 103 were abrogated, see E. Gabba, *Athenæum*, 1951, pp. 12 ff.

(p. 93.) Under the lex Licinia-Mucia not only were the citizenship rolls carefully scrutinized, but most of the Latins and

Italians who happened to be in Rome were actually expelled from the city. This orderly but tactless measure of the two consuls naturally exacerbated the feelings of the allies towards Rome.

(p. 94.) On Rutilius Rufus, who had served as legate to Q. Mucius Scævola in Asia, and on the date of Scævola's governorship, see J. P. V. D. Balsdon (*C.R.*, li (1937), pp. 8 ff.) who argues for 98–97 B.C.; D. Magie, however (*Roman Rule in Asia Minor*, p. 1064), supports the later date, 94–93.

(p. 94, n. 1.) Velleius (ii, 13,2) records that Drusus wished to restore the courts to the senate, Appian (*B.C.*, i, 35), that he wanted to add 300 equites to the senate and to entrust the courts to this enlarged senate, while the Epitome of Livy (lxxi) says that he carried a law establishing mixed juries. One of his objects will have been to remove the anomaly of the Gracchan law against judicial corruption by making equestrian as well as senatorial jurors liable to prosecution for receiving bribes. See additional note to p. 59 and above, p. 175, n. 2.

(p. 96.) For the decemviral agrarian commission, see *C.I.L.*, x, 44, and C. Cichorius, *Röm. Studien*, pp. 116 ff.

(p. 97, n. 1.) On the so-called oath of Philippus (Diod., xxxvii, 11), see H. J. Rose, *Harvard Theol. Rev.*, 1937, pp. 165 ff. Note the phrase: "If I become a citizen by the law of Drusus I will regard Rome as my native land."

(p. 98.) On the aims of the allies, see A. N. Sherwin-White, *The Roman Citizenship* (1939), pp. 126 ff.: they wanted "not enfranchisement in the modern sense, but the attainment of social and political equality, that is, equality of treatment and opportunity in the new world won for Rome with the assistance of the allies themselves": it was this desire to be free from oppression that made the right of appeal (*ius provocationis*) a possible alternative to enfranchisement (cf. Lex Acilia, 78). On the influence of party struggles in Rome upon the Social War, see A. Bernardi, *Nuova Rivista Storica*, 1944–5, pp. 60 ff.

(p. 98.) The precise nature of the Italian organization (see esp. Diod., xxxvii, 2; Strabo, v, 241) is an interesting but baffling problem, especially the extent to which the constitution was modelled on that of Rome and the extent to which the system was representative. See R. Gardner, *C.A.H.*, ix, pp. 186 ff., for this and for an attempted reconstruction of the course of the war. The literary sources, which are more numerous than satisfactory, can be supplemented by the war coinage which the Italians issued (see E. A. Sydenham, *Roman Rep. Coinage*, pp. 89 ff.); the inscribed sling-bullets, which survive from Asculum, are of interest (*C.I.L.*, i², 848–84; ix, 6086).

(p. 98, n. 2.) The lex Julia (Appian, *B.C.*, i, 49; Cic., *Pro Balb.*, 21; Vell., ii, 16; Gellius, iv, 4, 3) granted citizenship to allied communities as *populi* (probably to rebels who laid down arms as well as to the loyal: cf. A. N. Sherwin-White, *The Roman Citizenship*, p. 130 f.) and at the same time empowered generals to make individual grants of citizenship (cf. Dessau, *I.L.S.*, 8888, an inscription which records how Cn. Pompeius Strabo, the consul of 89 who captured Asculum (and the father of Pompeius Magnus), enfranchised thirty Spanish horsemen for their services during the siege in accordance with the Julian law). Strabo carried a supplementary measure (lex Pompeia) to deal with Cisalpine Gaul: citizenship granted to Latin colonies was confirmed, while Latin rights were granted to the Transpadanes. On Strabo's career and his influence on his son Pompey, see M. Gelzer, *Vom römischen Staat* (1942), ii, pp. 56 ff.

(p. 99, n. 1.) The usual view of the lex Plautia-Papiria has been that it dealt with individuals, but A. N. Sherwin-White (*op. cit.*, pp. 132 ff.) believes that it supplemented the lex Julia by dealing with *ascripti* who happened not to be resident in their adoptive *patria* when the lex Julia was passed but who were domiciled in Italy (e.g. in Rome itself).

(p. 100, n. 2.) By the lex Plautia "mixed" juries were established for trials of *maiestas* and perhaps also for *repetundæ* (Cic., *Pro Cornelio*, *ap.* Ascon., p. 79).

(p. 102, n. 1.) See also H. Last, *C.A.H.*, ix, pp. 207 ff.

(p. 104.) Marius' adventures and sufferings during his exile may have been exaggerated, but his earlier establishment of a colony at Cercina (cf. note to p. 91) and his settlements in Africa suggest that he sought refuge among his veterans in the former after the governor of Africa may have considered his presence on the mainland as disturbing and provocative. An inscription from Minturnæ (Johnson, *Excavations at Minturnæ*, ii, p. 63) refers to a slave of a C. Marius: perhaps the exile of 88 had a villa in the neighbourhood. Cf. A. Passerini, *Athenæum*, 1934, pp. 368 ff.

(p. 105.) The distribution of the new citizens in all the tribes may have been carried out in 87–86 (the repeal of Sulla's legislation of 88 in 87 might have been taken to imply the restoration of Sulpicius' law about them), but it may not have been achieved until 84, since Livy (*Epit.*, lxxxiv) says that they then gained the *ius suffragii*, i.e. their votes became effective.

Not all the rebels had been enfranchised in 89.

Appian (*B.C.*, i, 53) says that "the whole of Italy came into the Roman state except, for the time being, the Lucanians and Samnites." They will probably have received citizenship from the Senate in the struggle between Cinna and Octavius (cf. J. L. Strachan-Davidson on App., i, 53, 2, and 66, 5); Licinianus (27) says "dediticiis omnibus a senatu civitas data," and Livy (*Epit.*, lxxx) "Italicis populis a senatu civitas data." The Lucanians and Samnites probably received citizenship from Cinna at the same time when the senate had failed to reach terms with them.

H. Rudolph has advanced the view (*Stadt und Staat im römischen Italien* (1935)) that the settlement of 89 involved the crushing of all local independence: the jurisdiction of local magistrates was abolished and the Italians were subject to the city courts of Rome, until later Julius Cæsar established a system of devolved jurisdiction through *duoviri iure dicundo* and others. This view has been rejected by A. N. Sherwin-White (*The Roman Citizenship*, pp. 136 ff.) and others.

(p. 107.) Further detail on the social, economic and political conditions of Pontus will be found in M. Rostovtzeff, *C.A.H.*, ix, ch. v. On the Greek cities there, see A. H. M. Jones, *Cities of East. Roman Prov.* (1937), ch. vi. On Pontus and the Mithridatic wars, see the full and documented account by D. Magie, *Roman Rule in Asia Minor*, esp. chs. viii, ix, xiv and xv.

(p. 111.) On the battle of Chæronea, see N. G. L. Hammond, *Klio*, 1938, pp. 186 ff. Plutarch's account (*Sulla*, 16–19) derives ultimately from Sulla's Memoirs, while Plutarch himself had a local interest since he was a native of Chæronea.

(p. 114.) On Sulla's settlement of Asia, see A. H. M. Jones, *Cities of East. Roman Prov.*, pp. 62 ff.; Broughton, *Econ. Survey*, iv, pp. 516 ff.; Magie, *Roman Rule in Asia Minor*, pp. 232 ff., 1111 ff. The status of the whole province differed radically from its position under the settlement of 129 B.C.: it was now conquered territory. Even the free cities, which had been Rome's allies, had, by receiving the enemy, lost their former rights and independence. Any privileges they now received were granted by the grace of Sulla and Rome: thus even those cities, which were treated with generosity and were allowed to recover their freedom and autonomy, must have felt that their relationship towards Rome had undergone a change. While those cities which had sided with the enemy lost their independence, those that had remained faithful to Rome or managed to justify their conduct (e.g. Cos, which had been forced to surrender to Mithridates, but had saved the Romans on the island from Mithridates' massacre) recovered their independence. Stratonicea and Tabæ, for instance, became free and allies of Rome: their autonomy was confirmed by *senatusconsulta* of *c.* 81 B.C. (Stratonicea, *O.G.I.S.*, 441. Tabæ, *ibid.*, 442, *I.G.R.R.*, i, 63, *Mon. Asiæ Min. Ant.*, vi, 162. Termessus became an ally somewhat later, after 72 B.C.: see Dessau, *I.L.S.*, 38 = Bruns, *Fontes*[7], no. 14.) There survives part of a letter of Sulla to Cos, written about 81 B.C. (see *Riv. di Filologia*, 1938, pp. 253 ff.), which records his grant (confirmed by a *senatusconsultum*) of the continuance of certain privileges and exemptions to the Asianic guild of Artists of Dionysus. As dictator Sulla allowed a representative of the guild permission to erect a marble stele to commemorate this benefaction.

It may well be that besides cities, certain individuals received the mark of Rome's favour through the grant of the title of "Friend of Rome." This practice was becoming more common in the first century (cf. *O.G.I.S.*, 438) and is exemplified in an interesting document, a senatorial decree of 78 B.C., which rewarded in this manner three Greek ships' captains who had rendered Rome valued service at the outbreak of the "Italian War" (i.e. probably the Social War, less probably, Sulla's war in Italy in 83–82 B.C. See *C.I.L.*, i[2], 588 = *I.G.R.R.*, i, no. 118 = Bruns, *Fontes*[7], no. 41; translation in N. Lewis and M. Reinhold, *Roman Civilization*, i (1951), pp. 267 ff.).

The burden that Sulla imposed on the province was immense. Beside billeting his army on towns as a private penalty during the winter 85–84 (the hosts had to give each soldier 16 drachmæ daily: this alone, apart from food and clothing, may have cost some 20,000 talents: see Broughton, *Econ. Survey*, iv, p. 517), Sulla demanded 20,000 talents, which probably represents the estimated cost of the war together with five years' arrears of taxes. The province may have been divided into 44 regions for the local raising of the tax, but it is improbable, though not quite certain, that the farming of taxes was temporarily abolished by Sulla (on this point, see T. Rice Holmes, *Roman Republic*, i, p. 395).

(p. 116.) "Sulla cum Italicis populis, ne timeretur ab his velut erepturus civitatem et suffragii ius nuper datum, fœdus percussit" (Livy, *Epit.*, lxxxvi). By this arrangement Sulla finally settled the franchise question of the allies.

(p. 118, n. 1.) Appian (*B.C.*, i, 95) gives 40 senators and 1600 knights as the number actually proscribed.

(p. 123.) The procedure which resulted in Sulla's dictatorship was that, since both consuls of 82 (young Marius and Carbo) were dead, the Senate chose the Princeps Senatus, L. Valerius Flaccus, as *interrex*, and he instead of nominating *consules suffecti* introduced a bill in the Comitia for Sulla's appointment. Before this Sulla's past acts as consul and proconsul had been confirmed by the senate (App., *B.C.*, i, 97, 2); the lex Valeria, while granting him indemnity for future official actions (and possibly supplementing that already accorded to him for past actions), probably did not authorize the proscriptions (as Plut., *Sulla*, 33, 1, may suggest) which were covered by a lex Cornelia (Cic., ii, *In Verr.*, i, 123). On this cf. H. Last, *C.A.H.*, ix, p. 284.

(p. 126.) The reason suggested for the hesitation to spread the new citizens throughout all the tribes is weakened in proportion as it is thought that the real strength of *all* the tribes rested in the urban plebs (cf. above note to p. 19).

(p. 128.) A fragment of the Lex de XX Quæstoribus survives; this, the eighth section, deals chiefly with the minor officers (*viatores* and *præcones*) attached to quæstors. See Bruns, *Fontes*[7], 12; Riccobono, *F.I.R.A.*, p. 131; Warmington, *R.O.L.*, iv, p. 302.

The automatic filling of the senate by ex-quæstors deprived the censors of one of their most important functions, the *lectio senatus*. Sulla was obviously suspicious of the censorship, but apparently did not go as far as to abolish it outright. Nothing is known about the *census* proper, but the fact that in 80 and after a five-year interval in 75 some contracts (*censoriæ locationes*) were handled by the consuls points to the deliberate exclusion of censors from this duty (*Cic.*, ii, *In Verr.*, i, 130; iii, 18). On Sulla's attitude to the censorship, see H. Last, *C.A.H.*, ix, pp. 286 ff., 299 ff.

(p. 128, n. 1.) The tradition that the new senators were drawn from the "ordo equester" (App., *B.C.*, i, 100, 5; Livy, *Epit.*, lxxxix) is to be preferred to that of Sallust ("ex gregariis militibus": *Catil.*, 37, 6) and Dionysius ("from ordinary men": v, 77, 5). See also R. Syme, *Papers of Brit. School at Rome*, 1938, pp. 22 ff.

(p. 129, n. 1.) Cf. R. Syme, *op. cit.*, p. 10.

(p. 132.) The first standing *quæstio* had been established in 149; the early history of the others is uncertain in detail. Sulla, however, clearly re-organized and amplified the whole system and from his time there were seven *quæstiones perpetuæ*, viz.: *de repetundis, de sicariis et veneficiis, de maiestate, de falsis, de ambitu, de peculatu,* and *de iniuriis.* Shortly before or after this a lex

Plautia added a *quæstio de vi publica* to the *iudicia publica.* Six of these courts were presided over by prætors (2 of the 8 prætors were needed for civil jurisdiction), the others by ex-ædiles (*iudices quæstionum*).

(p. 133.) It was the view of Mommsen that Sulla carried a law which forbade consuls and prætors to leave Italy during their year of office. H. Last (*C.A.H.*, ix, pp. 294 ff.) supposes that the growing custom, whereby magistrates normally exercised their *imperium* at home and promagistrates in the provinces, was hardening into rule, but that Sulla did not by law debar magistrates from military duties during their term of office. J. P. V. D. Balsdon (*J.R.S.*, 1939, pp. 58 ff.) goes further and argues that there was not even any conventional (let alone legal) restraint on a consul leaving Rome before the end of his consular office. It is thus, at very least, probable that Sulla did not hamper the senate's freedom of decision by any rigid legislation.

Sulla did, however, define more rigidly offences which were punishable under the *lex maiestatis*: it became treason for a provincial governor, without express authorization from the senate and Roman People, to make war beyond the frontiers of his province, to leave his province, and so forth (cf. Cic., *In Pis.*, 50).

(p. 136.) On the meaning of Sulla's *cognomen* Felix, see J. P. V. D. Balsdon, *J.R.S.*, 1951, pp. 1 ff.

(p. 139.) For a new fragment of Sallust's History, see *Catalogue of Greek and Latin Papyri in John Rylands Library*, iii (1938), ed. C. H. Roberts. It may refer to Sertorius' adventures in 81 or Lepidus' flight or (see E. Lepore, *Athenæum,* 1950, pp. 280 ff.) the operations of M. Antonius against the pirates in 74.

(p. 140.) From his headquarters at Metellinum (modern Medellin), Cæcilius Metellus struck out in different directions: north to Castra Cæcilia (near Carceres, where traces of his camp survive) and Cæcilius Vicus (Baños), west to Cæciliana (near Lisbon), and south-west to Lacobriga (near Cape St. Vincent). See A. Schulten, *Sertorius,* pp. 66 ff. The sources for the Sertorian War are usefully collected by A. Schulten, *Fontes Hispaniæ Antiquæ*, iv, *Las Guerras de* 154–72 *a. de J.C.* (1937), pp. 160 ff.

(p. 141.) Lepidus' attitude to the restoration of the tribunate is ambiguous: according to the speech which Sallust put into the mouth of Marcius Philippus, who later persuaded the senate to pass the "last decree," Lepidus demanded its restoration, while Licinianus says he opposed this. Lepidus probably changed his policy, but it is uncertain which attitude was his first. On this and other problems connected with Lepidus (e.g. whether he marched on Rome twice), see Rice Holmes, *Roman Republic*, i, pp. 363 ff.

(p. 142.) In 76 Metellus defeated Sertorius' general Hirtuleius at Italica: it was this victory that enabled him to join Pompey in the north for the winter.

(p. 143, n. 1.) Both the date (76/5, 75, or 74) and the terms of Sertorius' negotiations with Mithridates are uncertain. According to Plutarch (*Sertorius*, 23) Sertorius recognized the king's claim to Bithynia and Cappadocia, but not to Asia, while Appian (*Mithr.*, 68) includes Asia, thus making a traitor of Sertorius. This harsh judgement is accepted by H. Berve (*Hermes*, 1929, pp. 202 ff.), but this must remain uncertain. Mommsen regarded Sertorius as one of Rome's greatest sons. Berve's generally unfavourable estimate of Sertorius has been criticized by M. Gelzer (*Philolog. Wochenschr.*, 1932, pp. 1129 ff.) and W. Schvr (*Sallust als Historiker*, pp. 223 ff.).

(p. 144.) The law which allowed tribunes once again to stand for other offices was passed in 75. Thereafter, however, tribunes continued to agitate for full restoration of tribunician powers, e.g. L. Quinctius in 74 and the annalist C. Licinius Macer in 73 (cf. Macer's speech in Sallust).

(p. 144.) Though the Livian tradition and Appian record that Nicomedes bequeathed his kingdom to Rome, the Scholia Gronoviana (ed. Stangl, p. 316) says that he died intestate and this perhaps records Sallust's view. Thus some caution is necessary, since the former tradition might represent an official Roman explanation and not necessarily the whole truth. Such doubts, however, are rejected by D. Magie (*Roman Rule in Asia Minor*, p. 1201) on the basis of Cicero's reference in 63 to Bithynia as a *hereditas* (*de leg. agr.*, ii, 40). The fact that the senate had never ratified the Peace of Dardanus, which Mithridates had made with Sulla, must have helped to increase the king's suspicions of Roman intentions.

(p. 145.) The two chief authorities for the war of Spartacus are Appian and Plutarch. For a discussion of some of the difficulties in their accounts, see Rice Holmes, *Roman Republic*, i, pp. 386 ff.

(p. 148.) On Pompey's first consulship and his commands in 67 and 66, see M. Gelzer, *Abhand. Preuss. Akad.*, 1943.

(p. 149.) The senatorial juries were discredited by the Verres scandal which came to a head in the late summer of 70: on 5th August there commenced the prosecution of Verres, who had grossly misgoverned Sicily, 73–71. The trial gave point to the need for reform. For a description of its political setting, see L. R. Taylor, *Party Politics in the Age of Cæsar* (1949), ch. v. It is hardly necessary to add that Cicero's Verrine orations are one of our most valuable sources of knowledge of Roman provincial government. The lex Aurelia, transferring the *iudicia publicia* from a purely senatorial panel, came after 5th August.

At some time between 73 and 69 (probably in 73 or 70) a lex Plautia de reditu Lepidanorum, allowing the return of Lepidus' exiled supporters to Rome, was passed; Julius Cæsar supported it (Sueton., *Iul.*, 5). For the date, see H. Last, *C.A.H.*, ix, p. 896.

(p. 150.) On Lucullus, see further J. M. Cobban, *Senate and Provinces, 78–49 B.C.* (1935), pp. 99 ff., and forh is campaign against Mithridates, see D. Magie, *Roman Rule in Asia Minor*, ch. xiv.

(p. 153.) On the campaigns of Servilius Isauricus, see H. A. Ormerod, *J.R.S.*, 1922, pp. 35 ff. (and for some alternative interpretations, Sir Wm. Ramsay, *J.H.S.*, 1928, pp. 46, and *Klio*, 1929, pp. 381 ff.); and D. Magie, *Roman Rule in Asia Minor*, pp. 287 ff.

(p. 154.) Gabinius also carried a measure, formulated by his colleague C. Cornelius, which forbade the lending of money to provincials in Rome. Cornelius himself carried three laws: (*a*) that prætors should administer justice only in accordance with their own edicts, i.e. the rules they had laid down when entering office; (*b*) a severe law against electoral bribery; and (*c*) that *privilegia* (the grant to individuals of dispensation from the law) should be granted by the senate only if 200 members were present (Cornelius failed to rob the senate completely of this right). Cf. W. McDonald, *C.Q.*, 1929, pp. 196 ff. Cornelius' subsequent trial was doubtless the outcome of his attack on senatorial prerogatives which angered the Optimates; he was defended by Cicero (see Asconius' commentary, *In Cornelianam*). On the career of Gabinius, see E. V. Sanford, *T.A.P.A.*, 1939, pp. 64 ff.

(p. 154.) The constitutional nature of Pompey's authority, whether his *imperium* was *maius* or *æquum*, has been a matter for doubt. Most recent historians have accepted the view of Velleius Paterculus (ii, 31) that it was *æquum*, but W. R. Loader (*C.R.*, 1940, pp. 134 ff.) has revived Mommsen's belief that it was equal to that of proconsular provincial governors but *maius* than that of proprætorian governors. Mommsen's view has, however, again recently been rejected by H. Last in a consideration of Imperium Maius (*J.R.S.*, 1947, pp. 160 ff.).

(p. 155.) For further detail of Pompey's remarkable achievement against the pirates, see P. Groebe, *Klio*, 1910, pp. 374 ff., and H. A. Ormerod, *Liverpool Annals of Arch., etc.*, 1923, pp. 46 ff. On his organization of the province of Cilicia and the settlement of ex-pirates in many depopulated cities, see A. H. M. Jones, *Cities of East. Roman Prov.* (1937), pp. 202 ff.

(p. 155.) It scarcely needs emphasizing that Cicero's speech *De imperio Cn. Pompeii* in support of the lex Manilia is a document of the greatest importance. Already in 68 the senate had assigned the provinces of Asia and Cilicia to other governors, thus reducing Lucullus' command to Bithynia and Pontus. In 67 he was deprived of these last two provinces which, by a bill carried by Gabinius, were transferred to the command of Acilius Glabrio. The latter's inefficiency paved the way for his supersession by Pompey under the lex Manilia.

(p. 157.) In 65 Pompey systematically reduced the Albanians in the Caucasus and marched to within three days of the Caspian. It is uncertain whether his object was to develop a trans-Caspian trade-route (cf. Pliny, *N.H.*, vi, 52), to find a possible water frontier for the empire in the East, or perhaps more probably merely to win military glory in the eyes of the Roman people.

Thereafter in 64 Pompey followed his lieutenants to Syria, where there was disorder. In Palestine civil war had broken out between the two sons of Alexander Jannæus: Hyrcanus, supported by the Nabatæan Arab Aretas, was besieging Aristobulus in Jerusalem. In 63 Pompey went to Damascus, where he decided in favour of Hyrcanus (thus reversing the decision of his lieutenant Gabinius), but he was prevented from undertaking an expedition to Petra by further trouble in Jerusalem which he captured after a three-months' siege: Hyrcanus was left as High Priest.

Pompey's settlement of the East was conceived on broad lines (Plutarch, *Pomp.*, 38; Appian, *Mithr.*, 114–15; Dio Cassius, xxxvii, 7*a*). Thereafter the coast-line of Asia was guarded by a continuous line of Roman provinces: Bithynia et Pontus, Asia, Cilicia, and Syria, with outposts at Crete and (later, in 58) Cyprus. The eastern frontiers of these provinces were covered by a large number of client kingdoms, which included Galatia (under Deiotarus, who received eastern Pontus), E. Galatia (under Brogitarus), Paphlagonia (under Attalus and Pylæmenes), Cappadocia (under Ariobarzanes), Armenia Minor (perhaps granted by Pompey to Deiotarus), Commagene (under Antiochus I), an area of Eastern Cilicia at the head of the Gulf of Issus (under

Tarcondimotus), and in the north Bosporus (the treacherous Pharnaces was granted his father Mithridates' Russian domains); east of the Euphrates an Arab sheikh Abgar received Osrhoene, while Tigranes retained Gordyene (around Nisibis); east of Syria were Sampsiceramus of Emesa and Ptolemy of Chalcis, while the Nabatæans regained Damascus. Beyond this loomed the Parthian Empire with which Pompey had some diplomatic, though not very friendly, contacts: thus Rome's strategic frontier in the East lay along the Euphrates and Syrian desert.

One of the chief features of Pompey's settlement was the number of cities he founded or restored, thus following the policy of Alexander and the Hellenistic kings. These foundations must have formed a bond which helped to direct the sentiments of these areas away from Parthia and towards the Hellenistic world and Rome. Pompey's motives may, however, have been less cultural and civilizing than administrative: see A. H. M. Jones, *The Greek City* (1940), pp. 56 ff., who points out that while Pompey met no radical difficulties in Syria and Cilicia, he had a harder problem in Bithynia and Pontus, where amateur Roman governors would find it difficult to try to work a complicated centralized bureaucratic machine: administration must largely devolve on local authorities, which had therefore to be created. Cf. A. H. M. Jones, *Cities of East. Roman Prov.*, pp. 157 ff., 202 ff., 258 ff., and W. G. Fletcher, "The Pontic Cities of Pompey," *T.A.P.A.*, 1939, pp. 17 ff. See also D. Magie, *Roman Rule in Asia Minor*, ch. xv.

(p. 158.) The career of Crassus is discussed in three articles by A. Garzetti (*Athenæum*, 1941, 1942, 1944–5). The view expressed above, that Crassus during Pompey's absence was seeking to build up definite military power, may seem to some to go too far. Crassus undoubtedly sought to consolidate his political position, to gain a corner in land which Pompey would need for his veterans, and perhaps to get some control of the resources of Egypt, but this is not to say that he consciously from the beginning envisaged the need to threaten a military clash to avoid being proscribed when Pompey returned.

(p. 160.) On Cæsar's early career, see L. R. Taylor, *C.P.*, 1941, pp. 113 ff.; H. Strasburger, *Cæsars Eintritt in die Geschichte* (1938). His father, Gaius, was prætor and governed Asia in the 'nineties, dying in 84: for his career and *elogium*, see T. Frank, *A.J.P.*, 1937, pp. 90 ff., and T. R. S. Broughton, *A.J.A.*, 1948, pp. 323 ff.

(p. 163.) The opposition to the Egyptian scheme was led by Q. Catulus and ably supported by Cicero who in a speech De Rege Alexandrino argued that Egypt had not been bequeathed to Rome (of the speech only a few fragments survive).

(p. 165.) Some fragments of Cicero's electioneering speech In Toga Candida are preserved in Asconius' Commentary (ed. A. C. Clark, *O.C.T.*). Cicero not only denounced his rivals, but hinted at Catiline's secret backers.

(p. 166.) On Cicero's speeches In Legem Agrariam, see E. G. Hardy, *Some Problems of Roman History*, pp. 68 ff. On Rullus' legislation, see also A. Afzelius, *Classica et Med.*, 1940, pp. 214 ff., and L. Agnes, *Riv. di Filologia*, 1943, pp. 35 ff.

(p. 167.) In 63 Cæsar won a double political success by his election to a prætorship for 62 and his election as Pontifex Maximus in which he defeated the Optimate leader Catulus: on this, see L. R. Taylor, *C.P.*, 1942, pp. 421 ff. and cf. *ibid.*, 1941, pp. 113 ff., and *A.J.P.*, 1942, pp. 385 ff. On the Optimate clique around Catulus, see L. R. Taylor, *Party Politics in the Age of Cæsar*, p. 119. Cæsar also prosecuted under the obsolete procedure for *perduellio* an elderly senator, C. Rabirius, on the charge of having taken some part in the murder of Saturninus in 100. Cæsar was thwarted by Cicero (who defended Rabirius: see *Pro C. Rabirio*), but his original intention is not clear: it was perhaps less an attack on the *senatus consultum ultimum* (as Cicero represented it) than a criticism of its possible misuse and an attempt by Cæsar to keep in the public eye. Cf. E. G. Hardy, *Some Problems of Roman History*, pp. 102 ff.

(p. 167, n. 1.) For the suggestion that it was news of Mithridates' death that led Crassus to abandon his support of Catiline for the consulship of 62, see E. T. Salmon, *A.J.P.*, 1935, pp. 309 ff.

(p. 167, n. 2.) Sallust falsely antedates Catiline's revolutionary programme to 64 (*Cat.*, xiv, 4 ff.).

(p. 169.) H. Last has recently drawn attention to the fact that in Sallust's account (*Cat.*, l, 1–3) the reason why Cicero convened the senate for 5th December was a threat to release the prisoners by force: he discusses the significance of this for Cicero's later action (see *J.R.S.*, 1943, pp. 95 ff.).

(p. 181.) It may be noted that Cæsar received Illyricum, which either formed part of Cisapline Gaul at this time or else was added to Cæsar's command (Sueton., *Iul.*, 22, 1: Illyrico adiecto). On Vatinius' career, see L. G. Pocock, *A Commentary on Cicero In Vatinium*, pp. 29 ff.

(p. 182, n. 1.) (Cf. Appendix 6.) L. R. Taylor, writing "On the Chronology of Cæsar's First Consulship" (*A.J.P.*, 1951, pp. 254 ff.), supports Gelzer against Marsh in placing the lex Vatinia *after* the agrarian law. While believing that Gelzer is right on the order of the laws and on the date of the lex Vatinia, she would place the first agrarian law earlier, namely its proposal *c.* 1st January and its passing on 28th January. Thus Cæsar depended for the success of the lex Vatinia upon the popularity he gained from both his agrarian laws.

(p. 185.) It is not clear whether the senate assigned Transalpine Gaul to Cæsar for a period of five years or in the first instance for one year only: Velleius, who does not distinguish between the lex Vatinia and the later *senatus consultum*, says (ii, 44, 5), "tum Cæsari decretæ in quinquennium Galliæ."

(p. 186.) On the Vettius affair, see additional note to p. 387.

(p. 187.) Cyprus was ruled by a brother of Ptolemy Auletes, the king of Egypt; unlike Auletes, he had not bribed Cæsar. Cyprus was now declared Roman, the pretext being that it had helped the pirates. Cato entered the island without opposition and the reigning Ptolemy committed suicide. It was incorporated into the province of Cilicia.

(p. 188.) Cicero regarded Clodius' acquittal as a fatal blow to his own moderate settlement and his hopes for a *concordia ordinum* (see *ad Att.*, i, 16, esp. 6 ff.; 18).

(p. 188.) On this, see S. Weinstock, "Clodius and the lex Aelia Fufia," *J.R.S.*, 1937, pp. 215 ff.

(p. 188.) Already early in 59, when defending his former colleague in the consulship, C. Antonius, against a charge of misgovernment in Macedonia, Cicero had made some unwise references to the triumvirs. Cæsar, however, had tried to win him over or to save him by offering him some official position (e.g. on his own staff in Gaul or on the land-commission: *ad Att.*, ii, 18, 3; 19, 4 f.), but Cicero had declined and thus had to face the consequences.

(p. 192, n. 1.) The precise nature of Cicero's motion on the Campanian land law is uncertain: it is unlikely that he proposed its cancellation, more probably its suspension until funds were more plentiful (cf. M. Cary, *C.Q.*, 1923, pp. 103 ff.). Cicero attacked both Clodius and Vatinius in his speeches Pro Sestio and In Vatinium, though he was more guarded in what he said about Vatinius' master, Cæsar. At the same time Cæsar was more openly threatened by L. Domitius Ahenobarbus, who declared that if he were elected consul for 55 he would introduce a bill to deprive Cæsar of his provinces (it is not clear whether before or after the end of his legal period).

(p. 204.) On Cæsar's two expeditions to Britain, see R. G. Collingwood, *Roman Britain and the English Settlements* (The Oxford History of England), ch. iii. C. E. Stevens has argued (*Antiquity*, 1947) that Cæsar's motives were mainly political, Cassivellaunus' *oppidum* was probably at Wheathampstead (see R. E. M. Wheeler, *Antiquity*, 1933, pp. 21 ff.).

(p. 213.) At Pompey's request Cicero dropped his motion on the Campanian land (see p. 192). In his mortification he wrote a letter to Pompey, which no longer survives but which is probably to be identified with his " palinode " mentioned in a letter to Atticus (iv, 5, 1). The view that the palinode was Cicero's speech *De Provinciis Consularibus* is improbable: see the edition of that speech by H. E. Butler and M. Cary (1924), pp. 106 ff. In this speech, delivered later in the year, Cicero by praising Cæsar's exploits in Gaul made some amends for his earlier attack on Cæsar's domestic legislation, but this apology was not the " recantation." After this Cicero virtually dropped out of active politics until after Cæsar's death.

(p. 213, n. 2.) See further additional note to p. 395.

(p. 216.) It was in 54 that Julia, Pompey's wife, died. Cæsar offered (in 53 ?) to renew the marriage alliance by divorcing his wife Calpurnia and marrying Pompey's daughter, while Pompey was to marry Octavia, the granddaughter of Cæsar's sister; Pompey declined (Sueton., *Iul.*, 27, 1). When in 53 Pompey married Cornelia, the widow of young P. Crassus, Cæsar was not embittered.

Cicero's public activities in 54 can have given him little pleasure. Under pressure from Cæsar he was forced to defend Vatinius, who was being prosecuted under a law carried by Crassus in 55 which dealt with bribery and the misuse of clubs (*sodalicia*) for political purposes. Pompey insisted that Cicero should also defend Gabinius, whom he had bitterly attacked two years before in his speech on the consular provinces. Gabinius had been acquitted on a charge of *maiestas* for having led his army beyond the frontiers of his province of Syria when he restored Ptolemy to the throne of Egypt in return for a large bribe; he then had to face a charge *de repetundis* and was condemned despite Cicero's support. Cicero also defended, apparently with greater success, C. Rabirius Postumus, who had acted as Ptolemy's finance minister. It was in 54 also that Cicero began his *De Re Publica*, which cannot have been unaffected by contemporary events (see p. 360).

(p. 218.) Although Cato had seconded the proposal in the senate for

Pompey's sole consulship, Pompey was not yet fully reconciled with the Optimates, many of whom wished to save Milo whom Pompey was determined should be convicted (Asconius, p. 34 Clark, lines 15 ff.). Pompey had still to make a final choice between Cæsar and the Optimates: when Cato was defeated at the consular elections for 51, Pompey, no less than Cæsar, rejoiced.

(p. 219, n. 2.) See additional note to p. 395.

(p. 231.) The political allegiance of Labienus has been discussed by R. Syme who believes that he was an old partisan of Pompey to whose support old loyalties recalled him: *J.R.S.*, 1938, pp. 113 ff.

(p. 233.) On Pompey's early decision to evacuate Italy and on his relation with the Optimates, cf. K. von Fritz, *T.A.P.A.*, 1942, pp. 145 ff.

(p. 236.) The prætor was Lepidus, the future triumvir, for whom Cæsar revived the old office of Prefect of the City.

(p. 242.) L. E. Lord has argued (*J.R.S.*, 1938, pp. 18 ff.) that Cæsar left Alexandria about May 1st, 47, and thus did not dally there when he was needed elsewhere.

(p. 243.) On Cato, see L. R. Taylor, *Party Politics in the Age of Cæsar* (1949), ch. viii; M. Gelzer, *Vom römischen Staat*, ii, pp. 99 ff. ( = *Die Antike*, 1934, pp. 59 ff.); A. Afzelius, *Classica et Med.*, 1941, pp. 100–203. On the portrait of Cato, found recently at Volubilis, see F. Poulsen, *Acta Archæologica*, 1947, pp. 117 ff.

(p. 245.) Cæsar received some advice on methods of reconstruction and reform in two documents, *Epistulæ ad Cæsarem senem de republica*, if these are in fact contemporary. They are attributed to Sallust (cf. above, p. 353). Often believed to be *suasoriæ* written under the Empire, their Sallustian authorship has been asserted by E. Meyer (*Cæsars Monarchie*², pp. 563 ff.), G. Carlsson (*Eine Denkschrift an Cæsar über den Staat* (1936)), L. R. Taylor (*Party Politics in the Age of Cæsar* (1949), pp. 154 ff., 185 f, 232 ff.), and others; the two last-named writers date the second letter, the earlier of the two, to 51 rather than to 50 or 49. Others have been more sceptical, e.g. H. Last (*C.Q.*, 1923, pp. 87 ff., 151 ff., *Mélanges offerts a J. Marouzeau* (1948), pp. 357 ff.), F. E. Adcock, *J.R.S.*, 1950, p. 139, E. Fraenkel, *J.R.S.*, 1951, pp. 192 ff. If they could be accepted as contemporary documents, their interest would be considerable.

(p. 246.) The scale of Cæsar's colonial plans was large. Some 20,000 veterans from his Gallic campaigns alone needed settlement: some were settled in southern Gaul (at Arelate and Narbo Martius), more in Italy itself (for these the way may have been paved by the lex Mamilia in 55: cf. additional note to p. 71). The needs of the urban proletariate, as well as those of the veterans, were met by colonies which offered commercial and industrial opportunities. Colonies founded or planned by Cæsar, include settlements at Corinth, Sinope, Carthage, Clupea, Cirta, Carthago Nova, Tarraco and Hispalis. The surviving portion of the Charter of the colony of Genetiva Iulia at Urso in Spain (see E. G. Hardy, *Three Spanish Charters*, pp. 23 ff.) shows the character of these settlements: the clause which specified the right of freedmen to hold the office of local senator (*decurio*) reveals Cæsar's generous policy towards this class. For the evidence afforded by coinage on colonial foundations, see M. Grant, *From Imperium to Auctoritas* (1946). On Cæsar's colonization, see now the important work by F. Vittinghoff, *Romische Kolonisation und Bürgerrechtspolitik unter Cæsar und Augustus* (1952), esp. pp. 49–95.

(p. 246, n. 1.) The so-called lex Julia Municipalis, an inscription on a bronze tablet found at Heraclea in south Italy (see E. G. Hardy, *Six Roman Laws*, pp. 149 ff., for translation and commentary; text in, e.g., Bruns, *Fontes*[7], 18) has been shown by A. v. Premerstein (*Zeitschr. der Savigny-Stiftung, Röm. Abt.*, 1922, pp. 45 ff.) to comprise the drafts of four measures prepared by Cæsar and enacted by Antony in June 44. One measure provides for greater care in the carrying out of municipal censuses; another prescribes uniform measures for the municipal *cursus honorum* and for admission to municipal councils. It has been argued by H. Rudolph (*Stadt und Staat im römischen Italien*, 1935) that Cæsar carried through a comprehensive reform of all the municipal constitutions and assigned jurisdiction to the local courts (Mommsen had placed the beginning of this function after the Social War), all the Italians, on this view, having come for judicial purposes directly under the courts in Rome during the period between the Social War and Cæsar. For criticisms of Rudolph's view, see H. Stuart Jones, *J.R.S.*, 1936, pp. 269 ff.; M. Cary, *ibid.*, 1937, pp. 48 ff.; and A. N. Sherwin-White, *The Roman Citizenship* (1939), pp. 136 ff.; see also above, p. 419.

(p. 247.) On Cæsar's extension of Roman citizenship and Latin rights in provincial areas, see A. N. Sherwin-White, *op. cit.*, pp. 170 ff. For the extent of Cæsar's grants of Latin rights in Spain (extensive in Hispania Ulterior, limited in Citerior), see M. I. Henderson, *J.R.S.*, 1942, pp. 1 ff.

(p. 247.) The view that Cæsar planned a survey of the whole empire for census purposes rests on the sole authority of a fifth-century writer, Iulius Honorius (*Geogr. Lat. min*, 21) and must remain doubtful.

(p. 248.) Although many of the older nobility in the senate were bitterly hostile to Cæsar, he had after all raised the number of senators from about 600 to 900 and the new members would be his adherents. Many of these new men who became senators and even reached high office came from parts of Italy enfranchised during the Social War but had failed to win office : Cæsar's policy therefore helped to unite Rome and Italy. For the new senators, see R. Syme, *Papers of Brit. School at Rome*, 1938, pp. 1 ff., and *Rom. Revolut.* (1939), ch. vi. For an analysis of Cæsar's party and following, senators, knights and centurions, business men and provincials, kings and dynasts, see R. Syme, *op. cit.*, ch. v. During the last months of Cæsar's life the senate decreed that an oath of allegiance should be taken in Cæsar's name (see Suet., *Div. Iul.*, 84, 2 ; Appian, *B.C.*, ii, esp. 145). A von Premerstein (*Vom Werden und Wesen des Prinzipats*, 1937, pp. 32 ff.) believes that the oath was general and not confined to senators ; if this is so, Cæsar became the patron of the whole state.

(p. 249.) The belief that Cæsar aimed at monarchy on Hellenistic lines has been advanced by Ed. Meyer (*Kl. Schr.*, i, pp. 423 ff., *Cæsars Monarchie*[3] (1922), pp. 508 ff.), J. Carcopino (*Points de vue sur l'impérialisme romaine* (1934), pp. 89 ff., *Histoire romaine*, ii, *César* (1936)) and others. Such a theory must presuppose hereditary succession and divine worship : but evidence is lacking that Cæsar intended that Octavian, his adopted son, should become a crown prince and succeed to his autocracy, and while the evidence for Cæsar's religious policy is more complex it has appeared to many to fall short of establishing belief in Cæsar's desire for a cult and worship of himself (despite the difficulties of such passages as Cicero, *Phil.*, ii, 110). Meyer's view, which sought to contrast Cæsar's monarchic rule with both the Principate of Augustus and the " Principate of Pompey " (i.e. Pompey, not Cæsar, was the true predecessor of Augustus) has been criticized at length by F. E. Adcock (*C.A.H.*, ix, pp. 718 ff.), who believes that Cæsar never finally resolved to end the republic. Cf. also H. Last (*J.R.S.*, 1944, p. 119) and R. Syme (*Rom. Revolut.*, pp. 53 ff.), who writes : " This [i.e. Cæsar as Hellenistic monarch] is only a Cæsar of myth or rational construction, a lay-figure set up to point a contrast with Pompeius or Augustus—as though Augustus did not assume a more than human name and found a monarchy, complete with court and hereditary succession ; as though Pompeius, the conqueror of the East and of every continent, did not exploit for his own vanity the resemblance to Alexander in warlike fame and even in bodily form. Cæsar was a truer Roman than either of them."

(p. 250.) Augustus, however, succeeded in creating a *de facto* monarchy without asserting divine rights.

(p. 251.) If *nobilitas* depended strictly upon the consulship or consular ancestors, many of Cæsar's new prætors would not attain to the inner circle of the nobility (cf. additional note to p. 16).

(p. 259.) On the growth of the Cato legend, see L. R. Taylor, *Party Politics in the Age of Cæsar*, ch. viii; R. Syme, *Rom. Revolut.*, pp. 317 ff., 506 ff.; W. V. Alexander, *Trans. Royal Soc. of Canada*, 35 (1941), sec. ii, pp. 15 ff., 40 (1946), pp. 59 ff.

(p. 261.) On the period covered by chs. xvii and xviii (44–31 B.C.), see further T. Rice Holmes, *The Architect of the Roman Empire*, i (1928); M. P. Charlesworth and W. W. Tarn, *C.A.H.*, x, chs. i–iii (1934); M. A. Levi, *Ottaviano Capoparte* (1933); R. Syme, *Rom. Revolut.*, chs. vii–xxi; H. Frisch, *Cicero's Fight for the Republic* (1946).

(p. 279.) Exciting stories about the proscriptions are told by Appian (*B.C.*, iv., 11–30). The so-called Laudatio Turiæ (Dessau, *I.L.S.*, 8393) commemorates the devotion of a wife to her husband (whether proscribed now or exiled earlier as a partisan of Pompey) and exposes the cruelty of Lepidus. See the recent edition by M. Durry (*Éloge d'une matrone romaine*, 1950) and for a new fragment of the inscription, see *A.J.A.*, 1950, pp. 223 ff.

(p. 280.) J. Carcopino in a recent work (*Les Secrets de la correspondance de Cicero*, 1947; Engl. trans. entitled *Cicero: The Secrets of his Correspondence*, 1951), which is stimulating but misleading (especially for the more general reader for whom presumably the English translation is primarily designed), attempts to undermine the historical value of Cicero's letters. His main contention is that the letters were published not under the later Julio-Claudians but at the instigation of Octavian in the years following his break with Antony (*c.* 34). A selection of the letters was chosen for purposes of political propaganda: they exposed the villanies of Cicero, the Republicans, the Pompeians and Antony, while throwing a favourable light on Cæsar and Octavian. If this theory were accepted, involving as it does falsification by omission if not by alteration in the correspondence, the value of the letters as historical evidence would of course be very different from its usual assessment. But in fact Carcopino's ingenious but perverse views have not met with acceptance (cf. the reviews). The matter cannot be discussed further here except to note that the theory involves the assumption that the impression of Cicero's character which a reader of his letters would receive is so vile as to be self-damnatory. But despite many weaknesses in Cicero's character this is not the impression that generations of readers have received, and the doubt remains whether they all have been wrong and Carcopino alone has seen the truth (cf. above, p. 363).

(p. 287.) The general rejoicings may have been reflected in Virgil's Fourth Eclogue, which foretells the birth of a child who will inaugurate a Golden Age. The identification of the child has been the subject of endless debate : the most reasonable solution is perhaps that of W. W. Tarn (*J.R.S.*, 1932, pp. 135 ff.), who believes that Virgil had in mind a son that might be born to Antony and Octavia.

(p. 291.) The ancient sources are contradictory on the question of the renewal of the triumvirate : see Rice Holmes, *The Architect of the Roman Empire*, i, pp. 231 ff. ; M. A. Levi, *Ottaviano*, ii, pp. 71 ff. ; M. P. Charlesworth, *C.A.H.*, x, pp. 59 and (for bibliography) 902.

(p. 292.) It was probably for services rendered in the campaign that culminated at Naulochus that one of Octavian's admirals, a certain Seleucus of Rhosus in Syria, was rewarded with a grant of Roman citizenship and other privileges (cf. M. A. Levi, *Riv. di Filologia*, 1938, pp. 113 ff.) Letters and an edict of Octavian to Rhosus, between 41 and 30 B.C., record this : see V. Ehrenberg and A. H. M. Jones, *Documents illustrating the Reigns of Augustus and Tiberius*, no. 301. Seleucus was granted immunity from taxation and liturgies in his city of Rhosus (for similar grants, though without that of Roman citizenship, to three other ships' captains in 78, see above, additional note to p. 114). The growth of a class of such specially privileged men in a city would naturally tend to annoy their fellow-citizens (cf. the complaint of Mitylene to Julius Cæsar on this matter and his reply : *I.G.R.R.*, iv, 33*b*, and *Rev. Ét. Gr.*, 1929, p. 426) ; Augustus in 7–6 B.C. made an attempt to control the privileges of this class of people (see the Cyrene edicts : Ehrenberg and Jones, *ibid.*, no. 311, iii and cf. F. De Visscher, *Les Édits d'Auguste*, ch. iv, and H. Last, *J.R.S.*, 1945, pp. 94 ff.).

(p. 294.) On his return to Rome, Octavian received many honours (on his supporters, see R. Syme, *Rom. Revolut.*, pp. 234 ff.). He celebrated an *ovatio* (November 13th) ; he was granted sacrosanctity like that of the tribunes (so Dio Cassius, 49, 15, 5, *contra* Appian, *B.C.*, v, 132 and Orosius, vi, 18, 34 : on this, see now H. Last, *Rendiconti, Ist. Lomb. d. Sc. e Lett.*, 1951, pp. 95 ff.) ; a golden statue was set up in the Forum, commemorating that he had restored order by land and sea (on the formula "terra marique," see A. Momigliano, *J.R.S.*, 1942, esp. p. 63). At the same time he proclaimed security and peace for Italy (in this year Varro's work on agriculture appeared and Virgil was composing the Georgics). In 36 also Octavian dedicated a temple to Apollo on the Palatine, and during the next few years he and his friends beautified and improved the city with other buildings. By these means and by reviving pride in old Roman religious institutions, Octavian attempted to stimulate national consciousness in Rome and Italy, and incidentally foreshadowed a policy which he was to develop more fully later as Augustus.

(p. 295.) On P. Ventidius (his *cognomen* Bassus is not well attested), see R. Syme, *Rom. Revolut.* (see index). His career had been spectacular. This army contractor from Picenum had as a child been captured by Pompeius Strabo at Asculum and had been led in a Roman triumph. Later he attached himself to Cæsar and Antony whom he served well and was rewarded with the consulship (43). In the East he defeated the Parthians in three battles, at the Cilician Gates, at Mount Amanus (39) and at Gindarus (38): Q. Labienus, the renegade son of T. Labienus, who was serving with the Parthians, was killed. When Antony arrived to receive the capitulation of Samasata, Ventidius returned to Rome, where he rode in a second triumphal procession, this time as triumphator not captive. C. Sosius, another *novus homo*, succeeded Ventidius as governor of Syria and pacified Judæa, which had welcomed the Parthians, after a successful siege of Jerusalem (37): Herod the Great was installed as king. Before starting on his Parthian campaign Antony re-organized some other client-kingdoms: Amyntas was established in Galatia, Archelaus in Cappadocia, and Polemo in a reconstituted Pontus.

(p. 298.) The story that Antony seized Artavasdes by treachery may derive from the hostile propaganda of Octavian (cf. W. W. Tarn, *C.A.H.*, x, p. 78).

(p. 298.) On Antony's following of Roman senators—provincial governors, generals, admirals and diplomats—in 33 B.C., see R. Syme, *Rom. Revolut.*, pp. 266 ff.

(p. 298, n. 1.) Octavian's successful campaigns in Illyricum were doubly important: they strengthened the vulnerable north-east frontier of Italy and at the same time allowed Octavian to win a military reputation (Agrippa and Statilius Taurus were there to help unostentatiously, but Octavian himself displayed great personal courage). On the campaigns, see E. Swoboda, *Octavian und Illyricum* (cf. R. Syme, *J.R.S.*, 1933, p. 66); M. P. Charlesworth, *C.A.H.*, x, pp. 83 ff. and (for bibliography) 903.

(p. 300.) W. W. Tarn has developed the view (*J.R.S.*, 1932, pp. 135 ff.; *C.A.H.*, x, ch. iii) that Cleopatra aimed at world rule in line with a nameless Greek oracle that she would throw down Rome and then raise it up again, inaugurating a Golden Age of peace and universal brotherhood in which East and West, Asia and Europe, would be reconciled. R. Syme, however, believes (*Rom. Revolut.*, p. 274 f.) that it is not certain that her ambitions went beyond the desire to secure and augment her Ptolemaic kingdom under Rome's protection: " The propaganda of Octavianus magnified Cleopatra beyond all measure and decency. . . . The policy and ambitions of Antonius or of Cleopatra were not the true cause of the War of Actium; they were a pretext in the strife for power, the magnificent lie upon which was built the supremacy of Cæsar's heir and the resurgent nation of Italy " (*op. cit.*, p. 275).

(p. 300.) On the question whether Julius Cæsar was in fact the father of Cæsarion certainty can hardly be attained: for a brief discussion, see M. Cary on Suetonius, *Div. Iul.*, 52, 1. J. Carcopino has argued against Cæsar's paternity on chronological grounds (*Annales de l'École des Hautes Études de Gand*, i, 1937; cf. *Points de vue sur l'imperialisme romain*, pp. 141 ff.). This view has been questioned by K. W. Meiklejohn (*J.R.S.*, 1934, pp. 194 ff.), who emphasizes the importance of Cæsarion's name to Antony in the last two years before Actium and (*contra* W. W. Tarn) the failure of Antony's attempt to use Alexander Helios.

(p. 302.) The official version of the oath of allegiance (the *coniuratio*) is given in the Res Gestæ of Augustus (25): " iuravit in mea verba tota Italia sponte sua et me belli quo vici ad Actium ducem depoposcit." On this, see R. Syme (*Rom. Revolut.*, pp. 284 ff.), who points out that it attached the whole people to the *clientela* of a party leader: " the oath was personal in character . . . of the Roman State, of Senate and People, no word . . . the last of the monarchic faction-leaders based his rule on personal allegiance " (p. 288). Cf. A. v. Premerstein, *Vom Werden und Wesen des Prinzipats*, pp. 26 ff. On Octavian's supporters, see Syme, *op. cit.*, p. 292 f., and E. Groag, *Laureæ Aquincenses*, ii, 1941, pp. 30 ff.

(p. 304, n. 1.) The view of J. Kromayer, that Antony hoped to escape from the blockade rather than to fight a full-scale action, has been rejected by W. W. Tarn (*J.R.S.*, 1931, pp. 173 ff.). To this Kromayer (*Hermes*, 1933, pp. 361 ff.) and G. W. Richardson (*J.R.S.*, 1937, pp. 153 ff.) have replied, while Tarn has defended his position (*J.R.S.*, 1938, pp. 165 ff.). After Actium, Octavian founded Nicopolis, where he concentrated many Acarnanians and Epirots. On the religious results of Actium, see J. Gagé, *Mélanges d'arch. . . . d'École française de Rome*, 1936, pp. 37 ff. The services of Selencus of Rhosus, who served as his admiral, are recorded in a letter of Octavian (see additional note to p. 292). For an edict of Octavian (probably 31 B.C.), granting privileges to veterans see Ehrenberg and Jones, *Documents . . . of Augustus and Tiberius*, n. 302.

(p. 309, n. 1.) For the view that Octavian countenanced Cleopatra's death, see W. W. Tarn (*C.A.H.*, x, p. 110), who also follows W. Spiegelberg's view that she used the asp because it was the divine minister of the Sun-god and deified its victim.

(p. 313.) During the period of the *principes*, from Sulla to Cæsar, much systematic building and planning was undertaken in the centre of the city. The Tabularium, completed by Catulus in 78, linked the Forum and Capitol as an architectural unit (for the Sullan Forum, which included a restoration of the Curia and probably a rebuilding of the Rostra, see E. B. Van Deeman, *J.R.S.*, 1922, pp. 1 ff.). Pompey was responsible for a group of buildings centred upon his theatre and portico, while Julius Cæsar's new Forum (a colonnaded area with *tabernæ* behind: it included a new Curia, new Rostra, a temple to Venus Genetrix and an equestrian statue of the dictator) was finished only by Augustus (e.g. the Basilica Iulia and the Sæpta). Augustus' own great building schemes started long before his final victory and settlement: from 36 B.C. he was already striving to foster national pride and consciousness. For the buildings for which he, his friends and lieutenants were responsible in this early period, see M. P. Charlesworth, *C.A.H.*, x, pp. 88–9. For the buildings of central Rome during this period as a whole, see G. Lugli, *Roma antica: Il centro monumentale* (1946).

(p. 322.) But see also additional note to p. 34.

(p. 323.) The process was perhaps completed only under Augustus. Cf. R. Syme (*Rom. Revolut.*, p. 287), who writes: "A conscious and united Italy cannot have arisen, total and immediate, from the plebiscite of the year 32: that act was but the beginning of the work that Augustus the Princeps was later to consummate."

(p. 340.) On Roman drama, farces and mimes, see W. Beare, *The Roman Stage* (1950).

(p. 349.) For the alternate view that the books were published separately (and for the earlier literature), see K. Barwick, *Cæsar's Commentarii und das Corpus Cæsarianum* (*Philologus*, Sb. xxxi, 2, 1938).

(p. 351.) On Hirtius, see O. Seel, *Hirtius* (*Klio*, Beiheft, 1935). For his epitaph, see *Année Epigraphique*, 1940, pp. 41 ff.

(p. 352.) Reference may be made to the forthcoming *Bibliography of Sallust* by A. D. Leeman. A good deal has been written on Sallust in recent years since the appearance of W. Schur, *Sallust als Historiker* (1934) and K. Latte, *Sallust* (1935). Cf. M. L. W. Laistner, *The Greater Roman Historians* (1947), ch. iii.

(p. 353.) Cf. additional note to p. 244.

(p. 353.) See H. Last, " Sallust and Cæsar in the ' Bellum Catilinæ ' " (*Mélanges . . . à J. Marouzeau* (1948), pp. 355 ff.).

(p. 363.) Cf. additional note to p. 280.

(p. 368.) Some of the more important inscriptions are to be found in C. G. Bruns, *Fontes Iuris Romani Antiqui* (7th ed. 1909); E. G. Hardy, *Roman Laws and Charters* (1912); Riccobono, *Fontes Iuris Romani Ante Isutiniani*, I (1941); E. H. Warmington, *Remains of Old Latin* IV, *Archaic Inscriptions*. Coins form an important source of knowledge for this period of history, especially for the later part of it. For these, see H. A. Grueber, *Coins of the Roman Republic in the British Museum* (1910); H. Mattingly, *Roman Coins* (1928); E. A. Sydenham, *Roman Republican Coinage* (1952); and for the period 49–30 B.C., M. Grant, *From Imperium to Auctoritas. A Historical Study of the Æs Coinage of the Roman Empire*, 49 B.C.–A.D. 14 (1946).

(p. 371.) In 169 freedmen already registered were left alone; their status naturally depends on what had happened to them before this, i.e. on the interpretation of two difficult passages of Livy: xl, 51, 9 and xlv, 15, 1–2. The most likely explanation is that either in 189 or more probably in 179 two classes of freedmen were allowed to be registered in the rural tribes (i.e. were not to be confined to the urban tribes), viz. (*a*) those who possessed land valued above 30,000 sesterces, and (*b*) those who had a son and possessed property in a rural tribe. In 174 this privilege was apparently withdrawn for the future from men of the type of class (*b*), i.e. it had applied only to those registered in 179. Thus those who retained the privilege in 169 and thereafter would be, apart from a few beneficiaries under the 179 dispensation, class (*a*) alone; the rest would be confined to a single urban tribe. See A. H. McDonald, *Cambr. Historical Journal*, 1939, pp. 134 and 138.

(p. 378, n. 1.) Cf. R. M. Geer, " Plutarch and Appian on Tiberius Gracchus," *Classical Studies in Honor of E. K. Rand* (1938), pp. 105 ff., who rejects Carcopino's view and tries to show that Plutarch's chief source was the same authority as Appian's sole source and that Plutarch has preserved much that Appian has omitted as well as adding material from other sources, i.e. that much of the material not in Appian but preserved by Plutarch is reasonable in itself.

(p. 379, n. 3.) The fact that land (up to 500 or 1000 *iugera*) retained by possessors did not become their full property (*ager privatus*) until 111 B.C. (although they paid no rent on it between 133 and 118) suggests that this limitation may have been imposed by Tiberius in the redrafting of his bill which Plutarch records. Cf. H. Last, *C.A.H.*, ix, p. 25.

(p. 379, n. 4.) On the probability that Tiberius did by a *iustitium* or threats of veto temporarily bring public business to a standstill, see R. M. Geer, *op. cit.*, pp. 107 ff.

(p. 380, n. 1.) Doubts have been raised about the date of the latter inscription (*O.G.I.S.*, 435) which contains a decree of the Senate enacted at a meeting presided over by an unknown prætor, C. Popillius. It is dated to the later part of a year, but the year itself is uncertain. It is usually assigned to late 133 before news of Aristonicus' revolt reached Rome, but D. Magie (*Roman Rule in Asia Minor*, p. 1033, n. 1) has argued that its purpose was not necessarily the ratification of Attalus' will and that it belonged to a time when the revolt had been crushed ; he suggests reasons for its attribution to 129. With its date is linked the problem of that of another Senatus Consultum, the SC de Agro Pergameno, found at Adramyttium, which refers to a dispute between Pergamum and the *publicani* (*I.G.R.R.*, iv, 262). This used to be dated after the legislation of Gaius Gracchus, about 110 B.C., on the evidence provided by possible identifications of the Romans given as members of the *consilium*, but the discovery of fragments of another copy at Smyrna (see A. Passerini, *Athenæum*, 1937, pp. 252 ff.) suggests that 129 is a more likely date (the two consuls mentioned, whose names end in -nius and -ullius, would then be Sempronius and Aquillius). If this date is accepted, the Popillius decree (*O.G.I.S.*, 435) should be put earlier and may be retained in its usually accepted year of 133. Magie (*op. cit.*, p. 1055, n. 25) has attempted to date the Adramyttium decree to the end of the century, but his views have been rejected by T. R. S. Broughton (*The Magistrates of the Roman Republic*, i, p. 496 f.) who points out that, since Aristonicus' revolt had been broken by Perperna, Aquillius on arrival in Asia would be ready to start re-organizing the pacified area and that this was just the time when disputes about exact boundaries would be likely to arise.

(p. 381.) On the other hand, Appian (*B.C.*, i, 49, 4) seems to imply that the proposal to enrol the citizens in ten new tribes was effected, while Velleius' view that they were limited to eight of the existing tribes appears to refer to the period when they were originally granted citizenship rather than a later modification.

(p. 387.) See additional note to p. 182.

(p. 387.) The Vettius affair, to which reference is made here and on pp. 388–9, remains obscure, the chief source being Cicero, *Ad Att.*, ii, 24. L. Vettius, when charged with implication in a plot to murder Pompey, turned King's evidence and himself tried to implicate members of the aristocracy ; he was imprisoned and died there. He is not likely to have been employed by Cæsar, though possibly he was by Vatinius (as Cicero later alleged), but more probably he was a free-lance. The incident is usually dated between August and October 18 of the year 59, but L. R. Taylor (*Historia*, i, 1950, pp. 45 ff.) has argued that it is earlier, in mid-July, and that Vettius was acting for Cæsar, who wished to bring Curio into bad repute and so check his campaign to secure the election, for 58, of magistrates hostile to Cæsar.

(p. 395.) Three recent papers have dealt with the " *legis dies*," the terminal date of Cæsar's command. J. P. V. D. Balsdon (*J.R.S.*, 1939, pp. 57 ff. and 167 ff.) argues that no such day was laid down by law. C. E. Stevens (*A.J.P.*, 1938, pp. 169 ff.) suggests that the day lay between July and October, 50. G. R. Elton (*J.R.S.*, 1946, pp. 18 ff.) has subjected both these views, together with those of F. B. Marsh and F. E. Adcock, to a thorough examination and has reached the conclusion that Mommsen and Hardy were right in their belief that the command was to end on 28th February, 49 B.C. Cæsar claimed that his personal honour was at stake : " sibi semper primam fuisse dignitatem vitaque potiorem " (*B.C.*, i, 9, 2). On his *dignitas*, see R. Syme, *Rom. Revolut.*, p. 48.

(p. 400.) This mission has recently been discussed by K. von Fritz (*T.A.P.A.*, 1941, pp. 125 ff.), who argues that Cæsar's offers were designed merely to win over public opinion and to sow confusion in the ranks of his opponents. In addition to the chronology of the negotiations, which is discussed above, there is also the vexed question of their content. Cæsar's insistence on a personal interview with Pompey, when he replied to Pompey's first letter, is important in its potential implications. The terms of Pompey's reply (which Roscius and L. Cæsar carried from Capua on January 25th) are uncertain in one crucial matter: according to Cæsar's version (*B.C.*, i, 10, 3–4) Pompey insisted that for the moment he should be allowed to continue levying troops, while according to Cicero (*Ad fam.*, xvi, 12, 3) Pompey's reply was to accept most of Cæsar's terms but Cicero has omitted the levy clause. Cæsar obviously could not allow the levying to continue, but whatever the truth behind the two versions may be, Cæsar rejected the proposals. After the fall of Corfinium, Cæsar sent Numerius Magius to Pompey with some fresh proposals, to which Pompey made some answer, but Cæsar has not disclosed the terms (*Ad Att.*, ix, 13A ; Cæs., *B.C.*, i, 24, 5 ; 26, 2). Still later attempts by Cæsar to arrange an interview at Brundisium failed.

# SELECT BIBLIOGRAPHY

(In view of the fact that a full bibliography will be found in the Cambridge Ancient History, Vol. IX, I have included in this list only such books and articles as are referred to in the notes, with such others as I thought most likely to be of interest to the general reader.)

## A. GENERAL

(1) *Histories.*


G. Bloch and J. Carcopino, *Histoire romaine.* Vol. II, *La Republique romaine de* 133 *à* 44 *av. J.–C.* (Paris, 1935.)

M. Cary, *A History of Rome.* (London, 1935.)

S. A. Cook, F. E. Adcock, and M. P. Charlesworth, *The Cambridge Ancient History.* Vol. IX, *The Roman Republic* 133–44 B.C. (Cambridge, 1932.) Vol. X, *The Augustan Empire*, 44 B.C.–A.D. 70. (1934.)

G. Ferrero, *The Greatness and Decline of Rome*, English translation in 5 vols. (London, 1907–9.)

A. H. J. Greenidge, *A History of Rome from the Tribunate of Tiberius Gracchus to the End of the Jugurthine War*, 133–104 B.C. (London, 1904.)

W. E. Heitland, *The Roman Republic*, 3 vols. (Cambridge, 1909.)

T. Rice Holmes, *The Roman Republic and the Founder of the Empire*, 3 vols. (Oxford, 1923.)

T. Rice Holmes, *The Architect of the Roman Empire*, Vol. I. (Oxford, 1928.)

F. B. Marsh, *The Founding of the Roman Empire*, 2nd ed. (Oxford, 1927.)

Th. Mommsen, *The History of Rome*, English translation in 5 vols. (London, 1894–5.)

A. Piganiol, *Histoire de Rome*, 2nd ed. (Paris, 1946.)

R. Syme, *The Roman Revolution.* (Oxford, 1939.)

(2) *Economic Histories.*

T. Frank, *An Economic History of Rome*, 2nd ed. (Baltimore, 1927.)

T. Frank, *An Economic Survey of Ancient Rome.* Vol. I, *Rome and Italy of the Republic.* (Baltimore, 1933.)

P. Louis, *Ancient Rome at Work*, English translation. (New York, 1927.)

M. Rostovtzeff, *The Social and Economic History of the Roman Empire.* (Chap. I.) (Oxford, 1926.)

M. Rostovtzeff, *The Social and Economic History of the Hellenistic World*, 3 vols. (Oxford, 1941.)

(3) *Government and Administration.*

F. F. Abbott and A. C. Johnson, *Municipal Administration in the Roman Empire.* (Princeton, 1926.)

G. W. Botsford, *The Roman Assemblies from their Origin to the End of the Republic.* (New York, 1909.)

T. R. S. Broughton, *The Magistrates of the Roman Republic*, 2 vols. (New York, Vol. I, 1951.)

J. M. Cobban, *Senate and Provinces*, 78–49 B.C. (Cambridge, 1935.)

A. H. J. Greenidge, *Roman Public Life.* (London, 1911.)

A. H. M. Jones, *Cities of the Eastern Roman Provinces.* (Oxford, 1937.)

J. S. Reid, *The Municipalities of the Roman Empire.* (Cambridge, 1913.)

A. N. Sherwin-White, *The Roman Citizenship.* (Oxford, 1939.)

G. H. Stevenson, *Roman Provincial Administration.* (Oxford, 1939.)

T. M. Taylor, *Constitutional and Political History of Rome from the Earliest Times to the Reign of Domitian*, 5th ed. (London, 1923.)

P. Willems, *Le droit public romain*, 7th ed. (Paris, 1910.)

P. Willems, *Le sénat de la république romaine, sa composition et ses attributions*, 2 vols. (Louvain, 1883–5.)

(4) *Sources.*

C. G. Bruns, *Fontes Iuris Romani Antiqui*, 7th ed. (Tübingen, 1909.)

W. Dittenberger, *Orientis Græci Inscriptiones Selectæ*, 2 vols. (Leipzig, 1903–5.)

E. W. Fischer, *Römische Zeittafeln bis auf Augustus' Tod*, 2nd ed. (1858.)

A. H. J. Greenidge and A. M. Clay, *Sources for Roman History*, B.C. 133–70. (Oxford, 1903.)

E. G. Hardy, *Roman Laws and Charters*. (Oxford, 1912.)

N. Lewis and M. Reinhold, *Roman Civilization*. Vol. I, *The Republic*. (Columbia, 1951.)

S. Riccobono, *Fontes Iuris Romani AnteIustiniani*, Vol. I. (Florence, 1941.)

E. H. Warmington, *Remains of Old Latin*. Vol. IV, *Archaic Inscriptions*. (Cambridge, Mass., 1940.)

## B. SPECIAL

F. E. Adcock, *The Legal Term of Cæsar's Governorship in Gaul*. (The Classical Quarterly, XXVI, 1932, pp. 14–26.)

J. G. C. Anderson, *Pompey's Campaigns against Mithridates*. (Journal of Roman Studies, XII, 1922, pp. 99–105.)

E. F. d'Arms, *The Date and Nature of the Lex Thoria*. (American Journal of Philology, 1935, pp. 232–45.)

J. P. V. D. Balsdon, *The History of the Extortion Court at Rome, 123–70* B.C. (Papers of the British School at Rome, 1938, pp. 98–114.)

J. P. V. D. Balsdon, *Consular Provinces under the Late Republic*. (Journal of Roman Studies, 1939, pp. 57–73 and 167–83.)

J. P. V. D. Balsdon, *Sulla Felix*. (Journal of Roman Studies, 1951, pp. 1–10.)

J. Carcopino, *Autour des Gracques : Études critiques*. (Paris, 1928.)

J. Carcopino, *Sylla : ou la monarchie manquée*. (Paris, 1931.)

G. Cardinali, *Studi Graccani*. (Genoa, 1912.)

M. Cary, *The Land Legislation of Julius Cæsar's First Consulship*. (Journal of Philology, XXXV, 1920, pp. 174–90.)

M. Cary, *Notes on the Legislation of Julius Cæsar*. (Journal of Roman Studies, XIX, 1929, pp. 113–19.)

M. E. Deutsch, *Antony's Funeral Speech*. (University of California Publications in Classical Philology, IX, 1928, pp. 127–48.)

D. R. Dudley, *Blossius of Cumæ.* (Journal of Roman Studies, 1941, pp. 94–9.)

G. R. Elton, *The Terminal Date of Cæsar's Gallic Proconsulate.* (Journal of Roman Studies, 1946, pp. 18–42.)

T. Frank, *The Public Finances of Rome,* 200–157 B.C. (American Journal of Philology, LIII, 1932, pp. 1–20.)

T. Frank, *Roman Census Statistics from* 225 to 28 B.C. (Classical Philology, XIX, 1924, pp. 329–41.)

T. Frank, *Roman Imperialism,* 2nd ed. (New York, 1925.)

K. von Fritz, *Sallust and the Attitude of the Roman Nobility at the Time of the Wars against Jugurtha.* (Trans. Amer. Phil. Soc., 1943, pp. 132–68.)

K. von Fritz, *Pompey's Attitude before and after the Outbreak of the Civil War.* (Trans. Amer. Phil. Soc., 1942, pp. 145–80.)

K. von Fritz, *The Mission of L. Cæsar and L. Roscius.* (Trans. Amer. Phil. Soc., 1941, pp. 125–56.)

E. Garzetti, *M. Licinio Crasso.* (Athenæum, 1941, pp. 1–37 ; 1942, pp. 12–40 ; 1944–5, pp. 1–62.)

R. M. Geer, *Notes on the Land Law of Tiberius Gracchus.* (Trans. Amer. Phil. Soc., 1939, pp. 30–6.)

M. Gelzer, *Die Lex Vatinia de Imperio Cæsaris.* (Hermes, LXIII, 1928, pp. 113–37.)

A. H. J. Greenidge, *The Legal Procedure of Cicero's Time.* (Oxford, 1901.)

E. G. Hardy, *The Catilinarian Conspiracy in its Context : A Re-study of the Evidence.* (Oxford, 1924.)

E. G. Hardy, *Some Problems in Roman History. Ten Essays bearing on the administrative and legislative work of Julius Cæsar.* (Oxford, 1924.)

H. Hill, *Sulla's New Senators in* 81 B.C. (The Classical Quarterly, XXVI, 1932, pp. 170–7.)

T. Rice Holmes, *Ancient Britain and the Invasions of Julius Cæsar.* (Oxford, 1907.)

T. Rice Holmes, *Cæsar's Conquest of Gaul,* 2nd ed. (Oxford, 1911.)

M. Holroyd, *The Jugurthine War : was Marius or Metellus the real victor ?* (Journal of Roman Studies, XVIII, 1928, pp. 1–20.)

H. Stuart Jones, *A Companion to Roman History.* (Oxford, 1912.)

J. W. KUBITSCHEK, *Imperium Romanorum tributim Discriptum.* (Leipzig, 1889.)

R. LAQUEUR, *Die Rechtsfrage zwischen Cäsar und dem Senat.* (Neue Jahrbücher für klassisches Altertum, XLVII, 1921, pp. 239–50.)

L. E. LORD, *The Date of Julius Cæsar's Departure from Alexandria.* (Journal of Roman Studies, 1938, pp. 19–40.)

D. MAGIE, *Roman Rule in Asia Minor,* 2 vols. (Princeton, 1950.)

F. B. MARSH, *The Chronology of Cæsar's Consulship.* (The Classical Journal, XXII, 1927, pp. 504–24.)

F. B. MARSH, *In Defence of the Corn-Dole.* (The Classical Journal, XXII, 1926, pp. 10–25.)

F. B. MARSH, *The Policy of Clodius from* 58 *to* 56 B.C. (The Classical Quarterly, XXI, 1927, pp. 30–6.)

E. T. MERRILL, *On Cæs.* B.C. I, 2, 6 *Ante Certam Diem.* (Classical Philology, VII, 1912, pp. 248–50.)

ED. MEYER, *Cæsars Monarchie und das Principat des Pompejus,* 2nd ed. (Berlin, 1919.)

C. OMAN, *Seven Roman Statesmen of the Later Republic.* (New York and London, 1902.)

H. A. ORMEROD, *Piracy in the Ancient World.* (Liverpool, 1924.)

A. PASSERINI, *Caio Mario come uomo politico.* (Athenæum, 1934, pp. 10–44 ; 109–43 ; 257–97 ; 340–80.)

M. REINHOLD, *The Perusine War.* (The Classical Weekly, XXVI, 1933, pp. 180–2.)

G. W. RICHARDSON, *Actium.* (Journal of Roman Studies, 1937, pp. 153–64.)

P. A. SEYMOUR, *The Policy of Livius Drusus the Younger.* (The English Historical Review, XXIX, 1914, pp. 417–25.)

C. E. STEVENS, *The Terminal Date of Cæsar's Command.* (American Journal of Philology, 1938, pp. 169–208.)

W. W. TARN, *The Battle of Actium.* (Journal of Roman Studies, XXI, 1931, pp. 173–99.)

W. W. TARN, *Alexander Helios and the Golden Age.* (Journal of Roman Studies, 1932, pp. 135–60.)

L. R. TAYLOR, *Party Politics in the Age of Cæsar.* (Berkeley, 1949.)

L. R. TAYLOR, *The Date and the meaning of the Vettius Affair.* (Historia, 1950, pp. 45–51.)

L. R. TAYLOR, *On the Chronology of Cæsar's First Consulship.* (American Journal of Philology, 1951, pp. 254–68.)

L. R. TAYLOR, *The Divinity of the Roman Emperor.* (Chap. III.) (Middletown, Conn., U.S.A., 1931.)

C. WIRSZUBSKI, *Libertas as a Political Idea at Rome.* (Cambridge, 1950.)

## C. BIOGRAPHIES

J. B. FIRTH, *Augustus Cæsar and the Organization of the Empire of Rome.* (London, 1903.)

W. WARDE FOWLER, *Julius Cæsar and the Foundation of the Roman Imperial System.* (New York and London, 1904.)

M. GELZER, *Cäsar der Politiker und Staatsmann*, 2nd ed. (Stuttgart and Berlin, 1941.)

M. GELZER, *Pompeius.* (Munich, 1949.)

M. HADAS, *Sextus Pompey.* (New York, 1930.)

H. J. HASKELL, *This Was Cicero.* (London, 1942.)

M. A. LEVI, *Ottaviano Capoparte*, 2 vols. (Florence, 1933.)

T. PETERSSON, *Cicero.* (Berkeley, 1920.)

TH. REINACH, *Mithridate Eupator, roi de Pont.* (Paris, 1890.)

M. REINHOLD, *Marcus Agrippa : a Biography.* (Geneva, N.Y., 1933.)

A. SCHULTEN, *Sertorius.* (Leipzig, 1926.)

E. S. SHUCKBURGH, *Augustus : the Life and Times of the Founder of the Roman Empire.* (London, 1908.)

E. G. SIHLER, *Cicero of Arpinum.* (New Haven, 1914.)

J. L. STRACHAN-DAVIDSON, *Cicero and the Fall of the Roman Republic.* (New York and London, 1898.)

A. WEIGALL, *The Life and Times of Marc Antony.* (London, 1931.)

## D. ROMAN LITERATURE

(1) *General.*

H. D. BROADHEAD, *Latin Prose Rhythm.* (Cambridge, 1928.)

M. S. DIMSDALE, *A History of Latin Literature.* (London, 1915.)

J. WIGHT DUFF, *A Literary History of Rome from the Origins to the Close of the Golden Age.* (London, 1927.)

M. L. W. Laistner, *The Greater Roman Historians.* (Berkeley, 1947.)

H. J. Rose, *A Handbook of Latin Literature*, 2nd ed. (London, 1950.)

(2) *Catullus.*

T. Frank, *Catullus and Horace : Two Poets in their Environment.* (New York and Oxford, 1928.)

K. P. Harrington, *Catullus and his Influence.* (Boston and London, 1924.)

E. A. Havelock, *The Lyric Genius of Catullus.* (Oxford, 1939.)

(3) *Cicero.*

J. C. Rolfe, *Cicero and his Influence.* (Boston and London, 1923.)

(4) *Lucretius.*

C. Bailey, *Lucretius*, 3 vols. (Oxford, 1947.)

C. H. Herford, *The Poetry of Lucretius.* (Manchester, 1918.)

J. Masson, *Lucretius, Epicurean and Poet*, 2 vols. (London, 1907–9.)

E. E. Sikes, *Lucretius.* (Cambridge, 1936.)

# INDEX

Printed in Great Britain
by Butler & Tanner Ltd.,
Frome and London